Effective Instruction for Special Education

Second Edition

Effective Instruction for Special Education

Second Edition

Margo A. Mastropieri
Thomas E. Scruggs

pro·ed

8700 Shoal Creek Boulevard
Austin, Texas 78757-6897

pro·ed

© 1987, 1994 by PRO-ED, Inc.
8700 Shoal Creek Boulevard
Austin, Texas 78757-6897

Library of Congress Cataloging-in-Publication Data

Mastropieri, Margo A., 1951–
    Effective instruction for special education / Margo A.
Mastropieri, Thomas E. Scruggs.
      p.   cm.
    Includes bibliographical references and index.
    ISBN 0-89079-572-X
     1. Handicapped—Education—United States.   2. Teaching.
   3. Teachers of handicapped children—Training of—United States.
   4. Special education—United States.   I. Scruggs, Thomas E., 1948–
. II. Title.
LC4031.M35   1994
371.9'0973—dc20   93-41947
                                                 CIP

This book is designed in Century Schoolbook and Gill Sans.

Production Manager: Alan Grimes
Production Coordinator: Adrienne Booth
Art Director: Lori Kopp
Reprints Buyer: Alicia Woods
Editor: Tracy Sergo
Editorial Assistant: Claudette Landry

Printed in the United States of America

2   3   4   5   6   7   8   9   10   98   97   96   95

To our parents,
Francis and Dorothy Mastropieri
and
Edward B. and Janet H. Scruggs,
with love.

Contents

List of Tables and Figures

TABLES

FIGURES

Foreword

IN MY COMMENTS IN THE FIRST EDITION OF THIS TEXT, I EXPRESSED MY enormous admiration for the authors and their accomplishments. After using their text in my own classes and after previewing this second edition, I find myself reaching for additional superlatives.

It is rare to find authors of a methods text who have such extraordinary classroom experience. Margo Mastropieri was a full-time special education classroom teacher prior to completing her Ph.D. in 1983 and for more than a dozen years has taught methods courses and supervised student teachers in special education at three different universities. Tom Scruggs was not only a full-time special education teacher up until 1979 but, after finishing his Ph.D. in 1982, returned to teach a special education class on an Arizona Indian reservation for a year. He has since been equally involved in teacher education.

It is perhaps even more rare to find authors of a special education methods text who have done such extensive research on classroom teaching of children and adolescents who are learning disabled, mentally retarded, and behaviorally disordered. At the time of this writing, they have published nearly 150 papers in special education and related journals dealing with research or practice in teaching exceptional children. They are recognized as *the* experts in the development of mnemonic strategies for use in instructional situations in the classroom.

This combination of teaching and research experience has produced a truly remarkable book. On the one hand, it is a text that is a "handbook" in the very best sense of the word. It is not only designed as a text for preservice education but undoubtedly will be the book that both new and experienced teachers will want to have "in hand" as they go through the school day working with children with various disabilities. Herein are *practical* approaches to teaching, right down to specific examples of what to say and when to say it, when dealing with children who are, by definition, difficult to teach. The authors even have provided sections on potential problems (i.e., what can go wrong when applying certain techniques). On the other hand, this text has substance. It is based on the very best of what researchers have learned in both regular and special education about effective instruction, much of it from Mastropieri's and Scruggs' own research as cited in nearly every chapter—indeed a testimony to the breadth of their expertise. Rather than interrupt the narrative to describe these studies, they have chosen merely to reference this research at the end of each chapter, so that those with a further interest can explore the scientific foundations of these practical suggestions. In this second edition, they also have provided at the end of each chapter suggestions for curricular materials, computer software, and related technology to assist practitioners in implementing the methods or techniques discussed in that chapter. They also have added a great deal of information regarding cultural diversity issues in the classroom.

We continue to be preoccupied in special education with controversies over how to identify, diagnose, or determine the characteristics of children who are learning disabled, mentally retarded, or behaviorally disordered. We traditionally begin our teacher training with a sequence of courses on characteristics of special children and other related issues. Most teachers, however, seem less concerned with these questions than we professors often are. What classroom teachers want are answers to the question, "What do we do at 9 o'clock on Monday morning?" It seems to me that we should begin the training of special education teachers with a book like this.

Steven R. Forness, Ed.D.

❖ ❖ ❖

Preface

THIS BOOK IS INTENDED TO PROVIDE PRACTICAL INFORMATION RELEVANT to the instruction of students with mild disabilities, whether in self-contained, resource, or regular classroom settings. It is meant to be useful to preservice or in-service special educators or regular educators concerned with the instruction of mainstreamed students. We have tried to base the information included in this book on the most recent research available on effective teaching methods in special education; however, we also have tried to present research-based information through the perspective of practitioners in special education.

Although several high-quality books on teaching methods exist, we have attempted to write a book that would address directly the actual practice of teaching and include step-by-step examples of effective teaching methods. To accomplish this, we first have described general principles of classroom organization, instruction, evaluation, and management, followed by more specific details associated with instruction in certain academic areas. We have included throughout examples of possible sequences of objectives and excerpts of possible teacher dialogue relevant to particular objectives. We do not intend to suggest by this that sequence of objectives should be invariant or that teachers necessarily should deliver lessons from prepared scripts. We have provided such examples as models of possible sequences only, although we feel that employing instruction that closely resembles such models is likely to result in higher levels of achievement. A list of the tables and figures containing these examples is given on pages ix–xiii.

The reader also will notice that we have referred infrequently to specific categories of exceptionality—including such labels as *learning disabilities, emotional disturbance or behavioral disorders,* or *mild mental retardation.* We do not mean to deny the value of such assignation for purposes of research, organization, advocacy, or external funding; however, the practices we suggest are likely to be effective with all such types of students, though some sections of the book can be emphasized more for classes involving specific categorical areas. For a methods class in learning disabilities, for example, instructors may wish to emphasize chapters dealing with basic skills instruction. For a methods class in behavior disorders, instructors may wish to emphasize sections dealing with the collection of behavioral data, behavior management, and social skills instruction. For a class in mental retardation, instructors may wish to emphasize sections dealing with life skills and vocational education. We feel, however, that *all* chapters have relevance to all of these areas of exceptionality. For example, research has indicated that many students classified as "learning disabled" exhibit relative deficits in social functioning. Likewise, students with behavior problems often exhibit academic deficiencies that must be corrected before mainstreaming efforts can succeed. Similarly, students with mental retardation often exhibit deficiencies in academic and social functioning. We feel, therefore, that the special education teacher needs skills in all areas of teaching, although the relative emphasis may vary from student to student.

Although we have tried to provide as practical an orientation as is possible in a textbook, we would like to add our belief that supervised practice with children in instructional settings implementing these procedures is invaluable in developing effective teaching practices. In our own experiences with earlier versions of this book, we combined instructional classroom presentations with supervised practica in implementing these strategies with students at the Purdue Achievement Center. During these practicum teaching sessions, specific teaching behaviors were observed directly by supervisors. Practicum students found videotape feedback of their teaching sessions particularly helpful in self-evaluation. We feel that didactic instruction in effective teaching practices coupled with supervised experience can optimize both preservice and in-service teacher preparation.

We have tried to be sparing in the use of textual citations, in response to comments we frequently have heard that highly referenced material can disrupt the flow of a textbook and inhibit comprehension. For those who are interested in supporting information (and we hope that many will be), we have included major supporting references at the end of each chapter. Instructors may wish to assign some of these primary and secondary sources as supplementary materials for students at the master's level.

We have made numerous changes in this second edition, in addition to our general updating of references. First, although we stressed the role of *meaning* in the first edition, we felt we needed to provide additional emphasis and examples of how meaning and active thinking can be used to enhance learning. We have maintained our task-analytic approach to instruction, including the use of tables of specification. However, in specifying subtasks or subroutines in need of remediation, teachers need to be careful that they have not deprived these tasks of meaning, and we have altered some of our text and examples to reflect this caution. Second, we have expanded our discussion of the application of mnemonic and other techniques for enhancing content area learning, which reflects the growing research support in these areas. Third, we have added discussions of multicultural issues and considerations where they appear relevant. Finally, we have listed some relevant curricular materials and software at the end of appropriate chapters, and a list of publishers at the end of the book. We do not mean by this to imply an unqualified endorsement of these materials; however, we felt that beginning teachers typically are unfamiliar with many curricular materials and software, and we decided to provide them with a starting place in their search for appropriate classroom materials. When these materials are used, we hope teachers will monitor their effectiveness with particular students in particular teaching situations.

In our first edition, we thanked Mary Ellen Heiner; Debra Peck; Steve Forness; Roy Halleran; and Lisa, Francis, and Dorothy Mastropieri—in addition to all the "special" students who provided us with opportunities to teach and learn. For this second edition, we also would like to thank Alan Grimes, Jim Patton, and Don Hammill of PRO-ED, Inc., for their support and assistance; Jeff Bakken and Ana Canavero for their assistance in editing our revisions; and numerous Purdue University students who provided us with helpful feedback on our previous edition. A renewed thanks also goes to Steve Forness for his foreword to this edition.

West Lafayette, Indiana
July, 1993

❖ ❖ ❖

CHAPTER 1

Teacher Effectiveness

THIS BOOK IS CONCERNED WITH EFFECTIVE TEACHING. EFFECTIVE TEACH-ing refers to those variables produced by teachers that result in high levels of student achievement. Research over the past 25 years has demonstrated that the type of behavior teachers exhibit can have a significant impact on student learning. In fact, the type of skills teachers exhibit can make the difference between student success and failure. This book is intended to describe the most critical of these teaching skills.

This chapter presents an overview of the history of research into effective teaching, followed by a discussion of the most important teacher-effectiveness variables. This chapter also includes a description of these variables, along with a model for delivery of instruction.

HISTORICAL OVERVIEW

Research has not always addressed the issue of teacher effectiveness. Many years ago researchers examined the influence of variables such as teacher personality, intelligence level, and style of dress in determining teacher effectiveness. These variables, however, were not examined with respect to student achievement but, rather, on whether teachers were liked by students and other school personnel. Later researchers began to examine the superiority of one teaching method over another. For example, many researchers in the early 1950s were interested in knowing whether methods such as "phonic" or "look–say" were better for teaching reading. This research presumed that one method would be found to be clearly superior and that different methods could not be incorporated into the same instructional sequence. Around the same time, some researchers examined the quality of student–teacher interactions. Although these early efforts represented an attempt to examine teacher behaviors, they failed to define various types of interactions precisely, and they did not closely relate these interactions to curriculum and student achievement.

In the "Sputnik" era, many Americans feared that the United States was losing its technological advantage. Simultaneously, efforts to improve education in mathematics and the sciences focused on developing new curricula, such as objectives and materials for teaching what was referred to as the "new math." This type of research and development effort failed to take into account the role of teachers, focusing entirely on content and curriculum. Because of this, little knowledge was gained on effective teacher behaviors.

In the 1960s, researchers examined social variables such as racial integration. Although this research was of political and economic importance, it minimized the important role of the teacher in student learning. Researchers focused their attention on the role of schools in their various social and economic dimensions but said little concerning the fact that some classrooms within these schools succeeded while other classrooms failed.

In the early 1970s, researchers again began to focus on the role of teachers in promoting student learning. This time, however, they focused on behaviors exhibited by teachers that were linked to student achievement gains. This research was important because it finally began to address the issue of what teachers could do to maximize student learning. Although the initial findings were limited, they were positive enough to result in federal funding of several research centers that focused on determining more specifically the role of the teacher in student learning. More recently, the roles of variables such as meaningfulness, concreteness, and active thinking have been investigated. These variables also have been found to be associated positively with student learning.

It is important to know that several myths about teaching have been dispelled. Studies have demonstrated conclusively that teachers do make a difference in student learning and that teachers who learn and practice certain teaching skills are more effective than teachers who do not. The elitist notion that anyone can teach also has been refuted, with teaching now defined more strictly than just a "presence in a classroom." It is now known that teachers can manipulate their behavior to make critical differences in student learning. This fact is as true for special education as it is for "regular" education.

For example, teacher-directed instruction was found to be highly related to achievement of students with mild disabilities (learning disabilities, mild mental retardation, and behavior disorders) (Englert, 1983, 1984; Sindelar, Smith, Harriman, Hale, & Wilson, 1986). Teacher-directed instruction was defined as teachers asking questions during presentations and monitoring responses at all times, including during flash card drills and group recitation. When instruction was effective, it was directly related to instructional objectives, and the special education students were engaged in relevant activities. For example, Haynes and Jenkins (1986) observed reading instruction in several special education resource programs and concluded that the amount of reading instruction that occurred was remarkably low. Similarly, Leinhardt, Zigmond, and Cooley (1981) reported that many self-contained special education learning disabilities teachers spent an average of only 16 minutes a day instructing students in reading. Studies such as these support the notion that special educators can increase the amount of time spent on academic tasks and can improve instruction by (a) actively engaging students on task during instruction; (b) presenting information in clear, concise ways; (c) asking students questions relevant to the instructional objectives; (d) keeping students actively involved in relevant instructional activities; and (e) monitoring students' performance.

TEACHER-EFFECTIVENESS VARIABLES

The first and most important teacher-effectiveness variable is time-on-task. This variable can be broken further into allocated and engaged time. Another important variable is the amount of content covered. This critical variable interacts with both time and pacing of instruction. The third variable of importance, referred to as delivery of instruction, includes methods teachers can use to present new facts, concepts, or procedures. Next, questioning and feedback refer to the ways in which teachers can respond to and interact with students. Following this, guided and independent practice activities are briefly discussed. Formative evaluation refers to the ways in which teachers can evaluate the effectiveness of their instruction by examining student progress and performance. Figure 1.1 provides an overview of these variables. Finally, multicultural issues in effective teaching are considered.

Time-on-Task

Time-on-task can be defined as the amount of time students spend on a particular task. However, the term is usually further subdivided into allocated time and engaged time. Researchers asked teachers to specify the amounts of time taken for each academic subject during each day. At the same time they observed the teachers' classrooms to determine how much time the students actually spent engaged in instructional activities. They found that, although the amount of allocated (scheduled) time for instruction was similar for all teachers, the amount of time students were actually engaged in relevant activities varied considerably from teacher to teacher and was consistently less than the amount of allocated time for all teachers. In a study of special education resource rooms, Haynes and Jenkins (1986) reported that only 44% of the allocated time, on average, was spent actively engaged in relevant instruction. It also was found that engaged time-on-task was directly related to higher levels of student achievement.

What are students doing when they are actively engaged (involved) in instruction? Engaged time-on-task activities are those that involve active participation of students in areas that are directly relevant to instructional objectives. These activities include eye contact with the teacher, active attend-

Variable	Description
Time-on-task (engaged)	Time students are *actually working* on specific tasks (not simply scheduled or allocated time).
Content covered	Amount of information presented to students in a given time period.
Scope and sequence	Total amount of content to be covered and order of presentation.
Objectives	Description of behavioral outcomes of instruction.
Pacing	Rate at which objectives are met.
Providing information	Teacher delivery of content.
Questioning	Prompting of overt student responses relevant to instructional objectives.
Feedback	Teacher consequation of student responses.
Guided and independent practice	Provision of opportunities for students to practice learned information in supervised and unsupervised conditions.
Formative evaluation	Continuous assessment of learner progress toward pre-specified goals and objectives.

FIGURE 1.1. General teacher-effectiveness variables.

ing to teacher presentation, direct responding to teacher questions, and active engagement with relevant instructional materials. The findings of engaged time-on-task research have been consistently clear: the more actively students participate in the instructional process, the more they will achieve. These findings are particularly important for special education, because virtually all students referred for special education services exhibit academic deficiencies and, therefore, have the greatest need for effective, time-efficient instruction. Later, this book presents specific teaching procedures for maximizing time-on-task (see Chapter 4).

Activities referred to as active engagement have been summarized briefly, but what types of classroom activities are not considered engaged and are not related to student achievement? These inefficient activities are those that do not demand active student participation and that are not directly relevant to instructional objectives. These activities include such transitional management tasks as sharpening a pencil, passing out and handing in papers, making general announcements, and taking bathroom breaks. In addition, verbal off-task behaviors include any teacher or student conversation not directly relevant to instructional objectives. Finally, inefficient classroom management includes time spent on disciplinary actions such as reprimanding or lecturing students for classroom misbehavior. All of the above off-task activities may be necessary at some point during the

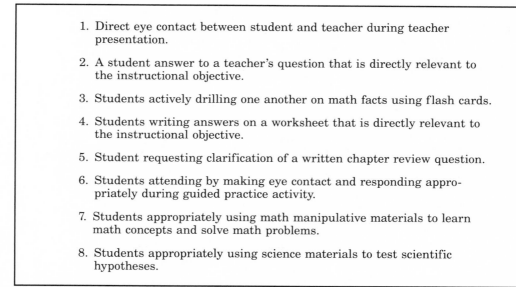

1. Direct eye contact between student and teacher during teacher presentation.

2. A student answer to a teacher's question that is directly relevant to the instructional objective.

3. Students actively drilling one another on math facts using flash cards.

4. Students writing answers on a worksheet that is directly relevant to the instructional objective.

5. Student requesting clarification of a written chapter review question.

6. Students attending by making eye contact and responding appropriately during guided practice activity.

7. Students appropriately using math manipulative materials to learn math concepts and solve math problems.

8. Students appropriately using science materials to test scientific hypotheses.

FIGURE I.2. Engaged on-task behavior.

school day. It is hard to imagine a classroom in which time is never spent sharpening pencils or reminding students of class rules. However, the most effective teachers have learned how to minimize these activities so that the time spent actively engaged in instruction is maximized. Ideally, if a teacher allocates 60 minutes to reading instruction, this time should include 60 minutes of active engagement in reading instruction. Passing out papers and making announcements may be necessary activities, but they should not be included as part of the engaged instructional time. Additionally, research has demonstrated that the least effective teachers spend excessive amounts of time attempting to manage classroom behaviors. Figure 1.2 presents additional information on these on-task behaviors. Behavior-management techniques are described in more detail in Chapter 4.

The first thing teachers can do is determine allocated versus engaged time rates in their classrooms. This can be done by writing down the time periods designated for specific academic subjects. Another person can be enlisted to observe directly the amount of time actually spent on those academic activities, using observation procedures described in Chapter 3 (see the Procedures for Collecting Formative Data section). Teachers should aim for 100% engaged time during their allocated times so that time spent off task during these periods is minimized. The teacher should analyze the time that was spent off task and make decisions to decrease those activities that detracted from the engaged time activities. The following sections describe some examples of off-task activities and corresponding strategies to minimize them. Additional off-task behaviors are given in Figure 1.3. Figure 1.4 provides an example of a teacher evaluating and modifying engagement rates to increase achievement.

ACTIVITIES	BEHAVIOR	EXAMPLE
	Teacher Off-Task	
During Instruction	Unnecessary digression	Talk about personal experiences.
	Description of academic information not directly relevant to instructional objectives	Discussion about different kinds of cars during the solving of miles-per-hour word problems.
	Classroom management	Lecturing inappropriate behavior during spelling class.
During Seatwork	Unnecessary wait time	Teacher has misplaced worksheets.
	Unnecessary interruptions	Teacher disrupts entire class to reprimand one student.
	Inappropriate assignments	Students provided with a worksheet that is not relevant to instructional objective or at the correct level of difficulty.
During Transitions	Unnecessary wait time	Teacher is late returning from break.
	Mismanagement	Directions for student behavior not clearly specified.
	Student Off-Task	
During Instruction	Unnecessary digression	Student comments about a recent television program.
	Lack of attention	Student looks out window during instruction.
	Inappropriate social behavior	Student pokes neighbor.
During Seatwork	Unnecessary disruptions	Student requests to go to restroom or nurse's office.
	Lack of sustained engagement with task	Student spends time looking for eraser in desk.
	Inappropriate social behavior	Student writes and passes notes to neighbors.
During Transitions	Procrastination	Student lingers in hallway after bell has rung.
	Inappropriate social behavior	Student unnecessarily pushes peers.

FIGURE 1.3. Off-task behavior during different instructional activities.

Ms. M evaluated her formative data from the previous several weeks of instruction and felt that the rate of recent progress was inadequate to fulfill long-term objectives for many of her students. From examination of her scheduling records, she determined that she could not schedule additional instructional time during her already crowded day. As a consequence, she solicited the help of the consulting teacher from the district office to help her evaluate her level of engaged time-on-task.

The consulting teacher, Ms. C, came to her classroom on three consecutive days for three different classroom activities. During each visit, Ms. C used an interval recording procedure (see Chapter 3) to record the engaged on-task behaviors of three students that Ms. M had designated as representative of her class. Ms. C further divided the observational times into beginning, middle, and end of the instructional periods. Ms. C found that the overall engagement rate was 74%. Furthermore, it was found that engagement rates during the middle of lessons were very high (near 100%); however, rates of engagement were lower during early parts of lessons (76%) and lowest (52%) at the end of lessons. Ms. M then instituted a program to enhance engaged time-on-task at the beginning and end of class. This included strict limits for transition, a different seating arrangement in which two of the more distractible students were separated, and a token system for rewarding prompt and accurate completion of independent practice activities. In addition, Ms. M modified her instructional procedures to include higher levels of questioning during the beginning of lessons and higher levels of observation and contact with students during independent practice activities. Several weeks later, a reevaluation demonstrated that on-task engagement had risen to 94% and academic progress had greatly increased. In addition, Ms. M's own record keeping indicated that classroom disruption had greatly decreased.

FIGURE I.4. Scenario for evaluating time-on-task.

Transitional activities

Research has indicated that transitions constitute a major source of off-task activities. Transition refers to students moving from one class, group, or subject to another. During this time, behaviors such as sharpening a pencil, using the rest room, obtaining drinks from the water fountain, and socializing inappropriately may occur. These activities are problematic if they interfere with engaged time. Since some transition activities are necessary, teachers can plan for these activities to occur during prespecified times throughout the day, rather than during a supposed engaged-time activity. In addition, teachers can establish an expectation that students move from one activity to another quickly, quietly, and efficiently. Teachers also can enforce these behaviors positively by awarding points, tokens, or stickers (see Chapter 4) for prompt transitions, or the teacher can simply inform the students that time lost in transition will be made up during free time. More specific examples of transition behaviors are given in Figure 1.5.

Transitional Time	Procedures	Possible Off-Task Behavior
Before school	Sharpen pencils. Obtain drinks from water fountain. Use restroom. Organize class materials. Be seated prior to bell.	Socializing before transitional activities are completed. "Hanging out" too long in the playground. Standing in the hallways.
Between academic periods	Put away last period's materials. Hand in completed assignment. Get out appropriate text materials. Be prepared with pencil, paper, and notebook. Move to appropriate seat. Be seated prior to bell.	Not putting away materials. Unnecessary talking. Unnecessary moving around in classroom. Not sitting in the appropriate place.
Classroom to outdoor activity	Stay seated until bell rings. Put away all work materials after the bell rings. Hand in completed assignments. Use restroom. Obtain drinks from water fountain. Sharpen pencils. Obtain coats. Line up by the door.	Getting ready before bell rings. Leaving work on desk. Leaving classroom furniture in a disorganized state. Pencils, papers, etc., left out that will have to be put away later.
Outdoor to classroom activity	Prior to final bell: Obtain drinks. Use restroom. Sharpen pencils. Obtain appropriate materials (e.g., texts, paper, pencils). Sit in appropriate place.	Tardy to class. Coat not hung up. Inappropriate socializing. Playing with ball, etc., inside the classroom.

FIGURE I.5. Decreasing transitional time.

Inappropriate verbalizations

Another major source of off-task behavior is inappropriate verbal behavior used by students or teachers that is not directly related to instructional objectives. Such inappropriate verbalizations include describing personal experiences, digressing to inappropriate subjects, and questioning students on information that is irrelevant to the particular content area objectives. Teachers can monitor this behavior simply by tape-recording their lessons. In relistening to the recording, teachers can evaluate the appropriateness of classroom verbalizations. Given such feedback, teachers can more easily remind themselves or their students when they are getting verbally off-task. This is another area in which teacher expectations play an important role. If teachers clearly communicate the expectation that discussion remain directly relevant to the lesson, students will be more likely to exhibit appropriate verbalizations.

Inappropriate social behavior

Any inappropriate social behavior constitutes a major threat to effective instruction. When students exhibit behaviors such as teasing, arguing, fighting, or any other type of disruptive behavior, it not only detracts from engaged time-on-task but also turns the classroom away from an atmosphere that is conducive to learning. Teachers should not be overly punitive; neither should they waste classroom time with lengthy lectures on classroom behavior. Disruptive behavior should be dealt with effectively and efficiently so that time lost in behavior management is minimized. Again, the expectation of a serious classroom environment can be especially helpful. More specific details on classroom management are provided in Chapter 4.

One of the most important variables uncovered by researchers on teacher effectiveness is engaged time-on-task. Some strategies for maximizing time-on-task are given in Figure 1.6. In the preceding section, general strategies were offered for maximizing engaged time-on-task. The chapters that follow describe more content-specific strategies for maximizing students' time engagement rates. The next section describes an area closely related to time-on-task, the area of content covered during instruction.

Content Covered

In part, the content covered during instruction is determined by the length of the school day, the length of the school year, and the amount of time the student is placed in special services. However, these variables reflect only opportunities to cover content. Research has shown that student achievement increases directly with the amount of content covered during the school year. In order to maximize opportunities to cover content, teachers need to attend carefully to scope and curriculum sequences of all curricular materials, to prioritize objectives within content areas, and to pace instruction so that the amount of content covered throughout the year can be maximized. These areas are described in detail in the following sections. Specific strategies for increasing the amount of content covered are given in Figure 1.7.

1. Verbally praise students who exhibit on-task behavior. It is particularly important to praise students who are less often on-task. This is part of a general "catch them being good" strategy.

2. Provide rewards (tokens, free time, privileges) for rapid, accurate completion of academic tasks.

3. Frequently question students regarding their knowledge of the content being covered. Students' minds are more likely to wander when they do not understand the content being covered.

4. If possible, schedule conceptually more difficult material (e.g., math or reading) earlier in the day, more routine tasks (e.g., handwriting practice) toward the end of the day.

5. Set an egg timer to ring at random intervals. If all students are on-task when the timer rings, reward the class as a whole (for example, with an additional minute of recess).

6. Select materials that make learning as concrete, meaningful, and interesting as possible. Heightening task interest generally increases engagement.

FIGURE 1.6. Strategies for maximizing engaged time-on-task.

Curriculum

A critical consideration in effective teaching is the choice of a curricular material or curriculum adaptation that most easily will facilitate learning. Curriculum considerations will be discussed throughout this text and vary from subject to subject. However, some general considerations can be mentioned. Curricula are most likely to meet the learning needs of students with mild disabilities if they are directly relevant to learning objectives, if they are carefully sequenced and include step-by-step presentations, if they provide sufficient redundancy in content covered, and if they contain relevant activities for evaluation of student progress. Additionally, it is important that curricular materials make learning as concrete and as meaningful as possible. Information that is concrete and meaningful is much easier to learn than information that is abstract and unrelated to students' experiences. When selecting instructional materials, be certain that they are meaningful and relevant for all students, including students from different cultural backgrounds and of different gender. To the extent that curricular materials do not contain all these elements, special education teachers must make adaptations so that these variables are included.

Scope and sequence

Scope and sequence refers to the amount of content that will be covered and the order in which it will be presented. All academic areas of instruction should be presented with respect to a scope and sequence. In

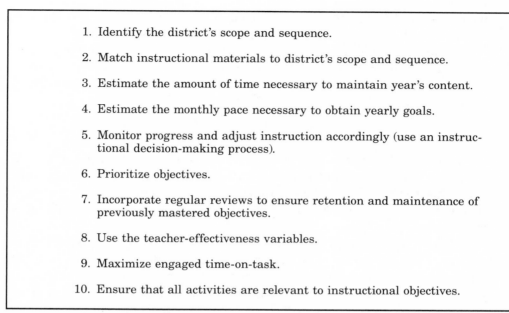

1. Identify the district's scope and sequence.

2. Match instructional materials to district's scope and sequence.

3. Estimate the amount of time necessary to maintain year's content.

4. Estimate the monthly pace necessary to obtain yearly goals.

5. Monitor progress and adjust instruction accordingly (use an instructional decision-making process).

6. Prioritize objectives.

7. Incorporate regular reviews to ensure retention and maintenance of previously mastered objectives.

8. Use the teacher-effectiveness variables.

9. Maximize engaged time-on-task.

10. Ensure that all activities are relevant to instructional objectives.

FIGURE 1.7. Strategies for maximizing content coverage.

this way, teachers can set goals for the amount of content to be covered in a year and monitor progress toward meeting these goals throughout the school year. In special education, scope and sequence may parallel those used in the mainstream settings. Since a major goal of special education is to integrate students into the mainstream, it may be necessary to design a scope and sequence in which some content is covered at a faster rate than in mainstream settings so that students can meet the ultimate objective of catching up.

Additionally, special education teachers may want to determine which components of the regular education scope and sequences are critical for passing school district and state competency tests. In special education settings, it also is important to prioritize objectives, so that unnecessary objectives can be deleted and more important objectives emphasized. More time can be allocated to the most important components.

Objectives

All instruction is based on objectives. An objective describes the behavioral outcome of instruction. In other words, it specifies what a student will be able to do at the end of the instructional period. Objectives describe the behavior, the content and conditions under which a student's performance will be assessed, and the criteria for acceptable performance. For example, statements such as "The student will orally read 100 Dolch sight words from a list in 1 minute with 90% accuracy" or "The student will list in writing six precipitating causes of the Civil War in order of importance with 100% accuracy" are behavioral objectives.

Since the amount of content covered consists of behavioral objectives, it is important to maximize the number of objectives covered during a school year. Objectives will be discussed more thoroughly in Chapter 2.

Pacing

Pacing refers to the rate at which objectives are met within a particular scope and sequence of instruction. Given relevant and carefully specified objectives within a well-planned scope and sequence, the pacing of instruction will ensure that a sufficient amount of appropriate instruction is delivered.

Pacing refers not only to the rate at which information is presented during a lesson but also to the rate at which information is presented during the school year. Pacing of instruction during the school year also can reflect time-on-task variables such as the amount of time spent actively engaged in mastering the specific objectives. If teachers pace instruction well, students can cover enough content to meet important instructional goals necessary for successful mainstreaming.

Scope and sequence, objectives, and pacing are all means by which the amount of content covered can be maximized. Scope and sequence and objectives can ensure that time is spent on relevant and critical content, while optimal pacing can ensure that content covered is maximized.

Delivery of Information

Delivery of information is critical to effective teaching. Like other aspects of education, delivery of instruction has several components, each of which is necessary for teaching effectiveness. Three of these components, described in more detail in the following sections, are providing information, questioning, and offering feedback. Additional strategies for delivery are provided in Figure 1.8.

Most instruction begins with teacher-delivered presentations. In order for these presentations to be effective, several elements of teacher behavior must be included. The acronym SCREAM can facilitate learning the elements of effective delivery of instruction (S = structure, C = clarity, R = redundancy, E = enthusiasm, A = appropriate rate, M = maximize engagement). First, teacher presentations must provide *structure*. Lessons are structured when teachers obtain students' attention and provide an overview of the lesson, including a description of lesson objectives; when they provide outlines of lesson materials and indicate transitional points in the lesson; when they emphasize critical components of the lesson; and when they summarize and review as the lesson proceeds.

1. Initially prepare scripts of teacher language to ensure that all words are necessary, clear, direct, and *relevant* to the objective. After some practice, scripts may be unnecessary.

2. Prepare many illustrations or examples of the information to be covered. All examples should include all the critical attributes.

3. Prepare noninstances of the information.

4. Compare the relevant and critical attributes with the irrelevant ones.

5. Prepare an abundance of teacher questions that require active participation on the part of all of the students.

6. Use questioning techniques that require all students to think through (covertly) the response (e.g., "Everyone, think about . . .") and then require *overt* responding (e.g., "Now, everyone write his/her answer").

7. Provide immediate corrective feedback (e.g., "What is the answer you all should have written, Cyndi? That's right, the answer is . . .").

8. Ensure that all students know what the correct response should be.

9. Monitor and adjust instruction based upon student performance.
   a. If students answer correctly:
      (1) proceed more rapidly,
      (2) proceed to independent practice,
      (3) introduce the next objective, or
      (4) test for mastery.
   b. If students answer incorrectly or do not answer:
      (1) repeat previously made questions and statements,
      (2) reintroduce previous content,
      (3) insert more illustrations using different instances and noninstances,
      (4) lead students through another example,
      (5) retest for mastery, or
      (6) verify students have necessary preskills.

10. Attempt to involve all of the students all of the time or most of the students most of the time.

11. *All* information and questions need to be directly relevant to instructional objectives.

FIGURE I.8. Strategies for effective delivery of information.

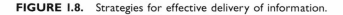

Second, teacher presentations must provide *clarity*. Clarity involves speaking clearly and directly to the point of the objectives, avoiding unclear or vague terminology, and providing relevant, concrete examples. All verbalizations must be directly pertinent to the lesson objective. Furthermore, clear presentations address only one objective at a time.

Third, teacher presentations must provide *redundancy*. Repetition of key elements of a lesson, particularly important concepts and rules, is related to higher levels of achievement. Redundancy is particularly important during lecture formats.

Fourth, teacher presentations must be *enthusiastic*. Enthusiasm helps maintain student attention and provides a positive attitude toward learning. Although enthusiasm is consistently related to affective outcomes, such as attitude toward school, it also is related to school achievement at the higher grade levels.

Fifth, information must be presented at an *appropriate rate*. Although the speed of delivery depends on the nature of the content and the students' level of prior knowledge, the type of basic skills instruction typically provided in special education is delivered most effectively at a rapid pace. This helps maintain student attention and the momentum of the lesson and interacts easily with enthusiasm variables.

Finally, in special education settings, teachers must maximize engagement by providing for *active participation* by students. This must be encouraged throughout the presentation and is described below. By providing structure, clarity, redundancy, enthusiasm, and an appropriate pace and by maximizing engagement, teachers can ensure that information has been provided effectively and efficiently.

Questioning

Delivering information is only one component of instruction. In order to provide immediate practice and evaluation of student learning, some type of questioning must take place. Most teachers' questions should elicit thinking and correct answers, and all questions should elicit some type of substantive response. A general rule of thumb to maximize learning is to elicit at least 80% correct responding. If most students respond incorrectly to teacher questioning, or if many questions yield no response at all, then teachers should modify their instruction. For the type of basic skills instruction that frequently occurs in special education settings, high rates of correct responding to rapid teacher questioning are desirable. For higher level content or when students are asked to generalize, apply, or make decisions based on their learning, teachers will need to ask questions that require slower, more thoughtful responses and for which more than a single answer may be correct.

Also, for basic skills instruction, questions that seem most appropriate are delivered on a low cognitive level (e.g., "What is the *i* before *e* rule?"). Low cognitive level refers to questioning that requires direct, literal responses to recently presented information. Again, for evaluation or application objectives, higher level questioning may be appropriate (e.g., "How could you use the *i* before *e* rule to spell the word 'receive'?").

For activities intended to promote inferential reasoning, higher level questioning is appropriate. Questions such as "Why does it make sense that moss generally grows on the north side of trees?" and "Why do anteaters have long front claws?" are examples of questions designed to promote active thinking and reasoning. These types of questions are delivered at a slower rate, so that students have time to think and consider the question carefully. If answers are not immediately found, additional coaching and questioning can help activate students' relevant prior knowledge about the topic (e.g., moss, trees, and the sun, or what anteaters eat).

Sometimes students fail to respond to a question because they do not understand it. For this reason, clarity of questioning is of particular importance. Regardless of the level of the question, it should be phrased in such a way that the meaning of the question and the type of expected response are clear.

Finally, teachers should question students equally. They should employ procedures of questioning that guarantee that both the most assertive and the most reticent students, males and females, and students from different cultural backgrounds will be questioned equally. Outside observers or audiotape recordings can help ensure that all students are receiving equal attention. Sometimes it may be helpful to require choral responding, in which all students answer at the same time on a signal from the teacher. This procedure allows many more students to practice responding, although teachers must be sure that students are not simply copying peer responses. Whether students should be allowed to call out answers depends on the classroom. Generally, if students are motivated and enthusiastic, allowing students to call out answers will not relate to achievement. However, if students are generally reticent and slow to volunteer answers, it can be helpful to encourage open responding.

It can be seen, then, that the type of questions teachers ask, as well as the ways in which they ask them, are of critical importance to student achievement. Questioning procedures will be described in more detail in Chapters 5 through 8.

Feedback

The teacher must monitor and react to a student response. Just as there are better and worse ways of asking questions, there are better and worse ways of providing feedback to students' correct responses. First, teacher feedback should be overt, so that all students in the class will know whether the response was correct. Overt feedback may take the form of repeating the correct response, making more elaborations on the response, or simply acknowledging the correct answer with a smile or head nod. However, researchers have found that such overt responding should be limited during rapid-paced drill activities. Although it is important for teachers to be positive toward correct responses, effusive or overelaborate

Response	Feedback
Correct	Overt acknowledgment ("That is correct.")
	Not overly elaborate; appropriate to response.
	Should be more limited during rapid-paced drill activities.
Partially correct	Acknowledge correct aspect of response.
	Provide prompt or rephrase question.
	Provide answer or call on another student if necessary.
	Repeat question later in the lesson.
Incorrect	State simply that the response is incorrect.
	Do not prod or probe students who obviously do not know the answer.
	State correct response or call on another student.
	Do not criticize the student unless incorrect response is due to inattention, lack of effort, or refusal to follow directions; be judicious with criticism.
Lack of overt response	Question further to determine source of nonresponding.
	Elicit an overt response, even if "don't know" is most appropriate.
	When response is overt—correct or incorrect—respond as described above.

FIGURE 1.9. Feedback to student responses.

praise is unnecessary and, in some cases, may have an embarrassing or inhibiting effect, particularly at the secondary level. Nevertheless, teacher feedback for correct responses should be prompt, direct, and positive. Additional information on positive feedback is provided in Figure 1.9, and additional information on the use of verbal praise is given in Figure 1.10 (summarized from Brophy [1981]).

Feedback to partially correct responses should first acknowledge the correct aspect of the response. Teachers should then provide prompts to elicit the complete response or rephrase the question. If this fails, teachers can provide the answer or call on another student. If a student gives the correct answer, the teacher should ask the same question later in the lesson to determine whether the students have mastered the content.

Feedback to incorrect responses in most cases should consist simply of a statement that the response was incorrect. Although clueing, coaching, prompting, and reminding may be helpful in eliciting a correct response, continuous prodding of students for answers they obviously do not know is counterproductive. Instead, teachers should either call on another student or state the correct response. It is rarely helpful to criticize a student for an incorrect response; however, in certain cases in which lack of a correct response reflects inattention, refusal to follow directions, or an obvious

1. Praise should be used to reinforce specific student behaviors. It should not be given in a random or unsystematic fashion. Students should know that it is a specific behavior of theirs that is being praised.

2. Praise should specify exactly what the student has done to merit praise (e.g., "Billy, you did a good job of getting in your seat quickly and opening your book to the correct page"). If students know *exactly* what behaviors were praiseworthy, they will be more likely to repeat them than if the praise is ambiguous (e.g., "Good work, Billy").

3. Praise should sound genuine and believable. Refrain from monotonous or routine-sounding praise, and vary language used to praise.

4. Praise should describe specific performance criteria (e.g., "You got over 90% correct") and relate the achievement to the student's previous performance (e.g., "This is your best work yet!").

5. Praise should be delivered for noteworthy effort. If a task was easy for the student to accomplish, the praise may be devalued or interpreted as a sign that modest efforts are encouraged.

6. Praise should demonstrate the relationship between hard work and achievement (e.g., "Aren't you glad you worked so hard on that project?") rather than luck or low level of task difficulty (e.g., "You're lucky you got that right," or "See, it was easy to do").

7. Praise should promote a sense of personal satisfaction in achievement (e.g., "You should be proud of yourself that you have completed such a difficult assignment so well").

FIGURE 1.10. Use of effective praise.

lack of preparation, some form of negative feedback may help to reinforce the attitude that appropriate levels of effort are expected. If such feedback is necessary, it is important that it be used in the context of a generally positive classroom environment.

Lack of overt responses can lead to uncertainty in the classroom atmosphere. If a response is not delivered promptly, teachers should question further to determine whether the answer is unknown, the question is unclear, or the student did not hear the question. In this context, a prompt "don't know" response may be the most appropriate. It is important to note that a response must be rendered overtly before feedback can be provided. Feedback delivered in the absence of a response presumes a knowledge of the student's intention, which may or may not be accurate.

Responding to unsolicited questions and comments that are relevant to the subject is important, especially at the higher grade levels. If a comment is not completely relevant, the teacher should restate it in such a way that the student's comment is accepted and its relevance to the lesson is made explicit. The teacher can either directly answer the student's questions or redirect them to the class. Such an approach indicates to students that their contributions are valued.

Feedback for student responses is critical for teacher effectiveness. Presentation, questioning, and feedback are three components necessary for truly effective teaching.

Guided and Independent Practice Activities

Practice activities should not be used as a vehicle for consuming time; neither should they be viewed as the dominant component of instruction. Students in general, and special education students in particular, do not learn new content efficiently through workbook-type activities. However, practice activities can function as important supplements to instruction, serve to reinforce previous learning, and provide opportunities for independent work.

Teachers should be careful to select practice activities that directly reflect instructional objectives. In addition, such activities must be on an appropriate level of difficulty. Since practice activities are undertaken independently and feedback is often not immediate, it is important that such seatwork be completed with approximately 100% success rate. It also is important that students understand directions and formats. Teachers should carefully specify exactly what students are expected to do and provide practice and feedback on examples. Finally, since many students easily tire of worksheet activities, the teacher should be careful to select materials that are motivating and interesting and to provide positive feedback for work that is completed quickly, accurately, and neatly. Some strategies for maximizing the effectiveness of practice activities are provided in Figure 1.11. Further discussion of different types of practice activities and their uses appears in the Guided Practice and Independent Practice subsections of this chapter and in Chapters 5 through 8.

Many software programs are available that can be used for practice activities. Advantages of computer software are that they may be motivating for students and that they can provide immediate feedback for student responses. A disadvantage is that they might not reflect exactly the class instructional objectives. More information on software programs is provided throughout this text.

Formative Evaluation

Anyone who has been to school is familiar with end-of-year achievement tests. Such tests are *summative* because they provide a summary statement of the year's learning. Unlike summative evaluation, *formative* evaluation techniques gather information on a regular basis throughout the

Rules for Both Guided and Independent Practice

1. All activities must be directly relevant to the instructional objective.

    Example A: If the instructional objective covers long division, then all practice activities must require students to practice long division.

    Example B: If the objective requires the learning of the causes of the Civil War, then all activities must require students to learn (by identifying, locating, writing, or reflecting on) those causes.

2. All activities must allow students many opportunities to practice responding with the correct answers.

3. Students must be provided with corrective feedback.

Guided Practice

1. Guided practice activities allow teachers to interact with students and to provide students with immediate corrective feedback.

    Example A: Everyone got that answer correct!

    Example B: The correct answer is . . . .
    Remember the steps are . . . .

2. During guided practice activities teachers can actively involve all of the students in responding.

    Example A: When I say go, everyone write the answer on his or her paper.

    Example B: Everyone who wrote this . . . , hold up his or her paper.

    Example C: When I say go, everyone who thinks he or she has the answer put his or her hand up.

    Example D: Everyone who has the answer put his or her thumbs up.

    Example E: When I say go, turn to your neighbor on your left. Left-side partners, say the answer as quickly and as accurately as you can. Right-side partners, listen and provide corrective feedback. Ready? Go.

    Example F: Everyone write the solution to the problem on the blackboard. Ready? Go.

3. Guided practice activities allow teachers to monitor and to verify whether or not students have "caught on" to the new instructional objective. Teachers can provide additional information if necessary.

4. When students respond at a high level of accuracy (e.g., 85 to 95%) they are ready to try some relevant independent practice.

(continues)

FIGURE I.II. Strategies for maximizing the effectiveness of guided and independent practice activities.

Independent Practice

1. Independent practice activities allow students to become firm at responding accurately.

2. Independent practice activities can be used to build accurate and more rapid responding.

3. Independent practice activities can be used to facilitate overlearning.

4. Independent practice activities can include review of previously mastered content.

5. Independent practice activities can be used to facilitate application, generalization, and maintenance of skills.

FIGURE I.II.   continued

year. For example, daily or weekly quizzes (or probes) can provide teachers with valuable information on student progress and performance. Such information can assist teachers in making optimal instructional decisions for the design and delivery of their lessons.

In many cases, student performance can be placed on a chart or graphic display so that rate of progress can be determined. In other cases, permanent products such as handwriting samples and tape recordings of reading performances or science reports can be saved systematically in a portfolio to provide later feedback with current performance levels. Research has shown that such formative evaluation techniques are helpful in raising levels of student achievement. Ideally, formative evaluation should be based directly on instructional materials and the curriculum being used. The integration of assessment techniques with curriculum has been referred to as curriculum-based assessment.

Formative evaluation is helpful because it allows teachers to alter their instructional procedures based on student performance. When instruction is planned initially, it should follow a scope and sequence of objectives to be mastered throughout the year. Formative evaluation techniques can reveal to teachers whether those objectives are being met at an appropriate rate. If this rate (pace) is insufficient, the content covered throughout the year will be inadequate. If formative evaluation techniques reveal an insufficient rate of progress, the teacher will need to decide what modifications to make to improve the rate of learning. Generally, these decisions will reflect one of the critical variables discussed in this chapter. The most obvious example is to increase the amount of engaged time spent on that task (objective). Another might be to increase the pace at which content is covered during lessons. A third might be to improve the structure, clarity,

Behavior	Possible Formative Evaluation Procedures
Math facts	Daily rate of correct versus error responses per minute plotted on graph paper.
Handwriting	Handwriting samples collected regularly and evaluated with respect to a specified standard for comparison.
Inappropriate behavior	Number of disciplinary referrals per week for prespecified behaviors.
Oral reading expression	Tape-recorded oral reading samples compared with a recorded standard of reading expression.
Out of seat	Daily number of out-of-seat occurrences plotted on graph paper.
Decoding CVC words	Oral reading rate of correctly and incorrectly read "nonsense" CVC words plotted on graph paper.
State history facts	Cumulative number of facts correctly stated on criterion-referenced tests measured against number of facts needed to pass school competency test.
Spelling	Number of words spelled correctly on weekly and monthly (cumulative) spelling tests.

FIGURE 1.12. Some formative evaluation techniques.

and facility with which information is delivered. It also might be possible to alter the rate and type of teacher questioning and feedback. Additionally, variation in seatwork and practice activities might be called for. Through careful monitoring and manipulation of these variables, teachers can better ensure accurate mastery of intended objectives. Examples of formative evaluation techniques are provided in Figure 1.12, and examples of strategies for making decisions based on formative data are provided in Figure 1.13.

Multicultural Issues

Finally, use of effective instruction variables will result in successful learning if the instruction is sensitive to the needs of culturally and linguistically diverse students. Surveys of students and meetings with family and community members can help identify particular cultural needs and interests, which can then be incorporated into the class curriculum. Generally, all students should feel that their particular cultural background is valued and supported and is an important component of the classroom.

Some specific recommendations for teaching multicultural and linguistically diverse students, summarized from the work of Franklin (1992) and Cummins (1989), are given in Figure 1.14. (See also New Zealand Depart-

If student progress and performance is good, then:

1. Maintain instruction

2. Possibly increase pace of instruction

If student progress and performance is inadequate, then:

1. Verify student has necessary preskills

2. Verify instructional objective is at the correct level of learning for:
   a. acquisition
   b. fluency
   c. application
   d. generalization

3. Alter teacher-effectiveness variables:
   a. increase time-on-task
   b. increase or alter teacher presentation
   c. increase or alter guided practice activities
   d. increase or alter independent practice activities
   e. check to ensure appropriateness of formative evaluation procedure

FIGURE 1.13. Strategies for effective instructional decision-making based on student progress and performance.

ment of Education [1988], cited in Cummins [1989].) As can be seen in Figure 1.14, most of these variables are important considerations for any classroom. Although earlier teacher effectiveness research de-emphasized such "non-alterable" variables as teacher personality, it has become clear that establishing and maintaining a warm, positive, accepting classroom environment is an important prerequisite to the other teacher effectiveness variables. For example, maximizing time-on-task or content coverage is of little use in a hostile or confrontational classroom atmosphere. On the other hand, teachers who create warm, supportive, caring classroom environments are more likely to receive the active cooperation of students.

Students from culturally diverse backgrounds may identify less strongly with the school and classroom environment, so it is essential that teachers do all they can to make all students feel welcome and important. This is particularly important for students in special education, most of whom may have experienced failures in school and who may be less likely to invest themselves in classroom learning.

Baker et al. (1982) listed eight components of a warm and accepting classroom atmosphere: collecting personal information, using positive body language, using a personal approach to student interaction, giving honest praise, spending time each day with the student, expressing affection, reduc-

1. Create and maintain a positive, accepting, supportive classroom environment.

2. Vary the format of classroom instruction and increase classroom energy.

3. Increase verbal interaction and promote open-ended, divergent thinking.

4. Use resources, materials, and activities that are realistic to learners' cultural environment.

5. Maximize person-to-person interaction.

6. Use cooperative group activities when appropriate, and encourage positive student interactions.

7. Use bilingual or multilingual signs in school and classrooms.

8. Display pictures representing different cultures in school.

9. Use books and other printed material in different languages when appropriate.

10. Employ paraprofessionals who can tutor students in their primary language.

11. Encourage parental involvement in class and school activities.

12. Encourage students to use their primary language in class and school activities.

13. Encourage meaningful use of English, rather than precise grammar.

14. Integrate language use across content areas, rather than teaching language as an isolated subject.

15. Emphasize higher level cognitive skills.

16. Consider local circumstances and individual needs when adapting methods and materials.

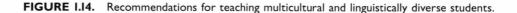

FIGURE 1.14. Recommendations for teaching multicultural and linguistically diverse students.

ing grading pressure, and giving students time to answer questions. By creating a positive, personal atmosphere, increasing contacts with family and community members, and including culturally relevant and meaningful instructional materials, teachers can effectively accommodate cultural and linguistic diversity in their classrooms. Additional information concerning multicultural issues is provided in subsequent chapters.

A MODEL FOR DELIVERY OF INSTRUCTION

This section describes how teachers should deliver classroom instruction. A general model of teacher-led instruction of a daily lesson is described. This model includes the following teacher functions: (a) daily review, (b) presentation, (c) guided practice, (d) independent practice, (e) weekly and monthly reviews, and (f) formative evaluation. An example of a lesson that incorporates most of these components is included in Figure 1.15.

Daily Review

Each lesson should begin with a daily review. During this time, teachers have an opportunity to monitor and adjust instruction based on student performance and to provide corrective feedback to students. Additionally, this time allows the students an opportunity for overlearning facts, rules, procedures, and concepts.

There are many effective components to daily review. First, it is important to ask questions about information previously covered in order to determine whether the information needs to be retaught. This type of questioning should parallel information gained at the end of daily lessons described in the previous section as formative evaluation. For example, if students are found to respond accurately at the end of a lesson but do not respond accurately at the beginning of the next lesson, the problem reflects retention of information and initial learning. Using this information, teachers can make decisions about the optimal level of difficulty for students and monitor and adjust their instruction accordingly. The question of previously learned materials (overlearning), for example, can be beneficial for retention.

Another important component concerns handling of previously assigned homework. There are several methods by which homework can be reviewed. It may be helpful to quiz students at the beginning of class on material from the previous homework assignment. It also may be helpful for students to check each other's homework papers. In special education settings, however, students must be taught the specific procedures for checking homework. The students also can review homework in small group settings. It should be noted that the homework assignments must be relevant to the instructional objectives in order to be beneficial. Additionally, homework is a type of independent activity, which is discussed later in Chapters 5 through 8.

Finally, students should generate summaries of material from homework assignments and previously learned content. Students can either prepare questions and ask them to the class or provide written summaries of the previous lesson (assuming that students have adequate prerequisite writing skills). Above all, students must be encouraged to ask questions about previously covered material that they may not understand.

Time	Component	Materials	Examples
9:00	*Daily review.*	Overhead projector	"Last week we started talking about different kinds of words. Who remembers what kinds of words we talked about?" [Student response.] "Correct. One kind of word was a *noun*. [Write on board.] Tell us what a noun is, Jimmy, . . ."
9:08	*Presentation of material to be learned.*	Overhead projector	"Today we're going to learn about another kind of word. This word is called an *adjective*. [Write on board.] Everybody say adjective with me. Ready? [Signal.] Adjective. Adjective. Good."
			". . . I think you're beginning to get the idea of what an adjective is. Now watch what I write this time. [Write.] 'A sour apple.' Everybody, which word is the adjective? [Signal.] Good, *sour* is the adjective. Sue, what was the rule we said that tells you why *sour* is an adjective?"
9:20	*Guided practice.*	Worksheets	"Now, everybody take a worksheet and we can practice finding adjectives together. Read the first sentence, Fred. [Fred reads.] So, in that sentence, everybody circle the adjective, and we'll see who can get it right."
9:30	*Independent practice.*	Worksheets	"Does anyone have a question about how to find adjectives? Tell us again what we're going to do, Julie. [Julie responds.] O.K., everybody go back to your desks quietly and finish your worksheet."
9:40	*Formative evaluation.*	Test	"Everybody stop, make sure your name is on the worksheet, and pass it in. I'm going to pass out a 2-minute timing so you can show how much you've learned about adjectives. Don't turn the paper over until I tell you. Now, when I say 'go,' turn over the paper and circle as many adjectives as you can in 2 minutes. Bill, what are you going to do? [Responds.] Correct. Now, is everybody ready?"

FIGURE 1.15. Model for sample 45-minute lesson on identifying adjectives.

Presentation of Material to be Learned

Research has shown that the most effective teachers spend more time on the presentation of new content. However, time is not the only variable of importance in the effectiveness of presentations. For presentations to be clear and effective, teachers must obtain the students' attention and

1. clarify goals and main points to be covered;

2. include step-by-step presentation of new material;

3. provide modeling and demonstrations of new procedures;

4. monitor student understanding and adjust as necessary;

5. provide corrective feedback; and

6. consider the needs of culturally and linguistically diverse students.

Each of these considerations is now described.

When presenting new information, it is important that teachers begin by obtaining all students' attention and by clearly stating the overall goals and specific objectives of the lesson. At this point, teachers should provide an overview of the main points to be covered in the lesson. In some cases it may be helpful to write these main points on the blackboard or overhead projector. As the main points are covered, teachers should focus on one specific point at a time. This is critical in promoting a clear understanding of the presentation. It is also important to keep all verbalizations relevant to the specific objectives that will be covered. Although providing examples is helpful, such examples need to be clearly relevant to the presentation. Finally, it is essential that the language used in the presentation be clear and direct. (Language such as "sort of" and "pretty much" should be avoided.) In special education settings it can be critical that the level of vocabulary used is appropriate for the students' comprehension level.

Step-by-step presentations are also critical to clear presentations. Teachers should subdivide material into component steps that can be easily understood by students. The material should be well organized and presented in such a fashion that one step is mastered before the next step is presented. When possible, any directions should be clear and explicit. The subdivision of a larger task into smaller and more easily understood tasks is referred to as task analysis. This is discussed in Chapter 2 (see the Designing Instruction section).

Modeling and demonstrations are necessary to promote understanding of new content. When appropriate, teachers should directly perform the skill or process that is being taught. This modeling should include explicit and overemphasized demonstration. When examples are presented, they should be concrete and directly relevant to the content being taught. Concrete examples are particularly important in special education settings where students may not catch on easily to novel concepts or discriminations. In such instances it is critical for teachers to provide a variety of relevant examples and nonexamples so that students will be able to discriminate the examples from the nonexamples (e.g., This is an instance. Is this an instance?).

Monitoring and adjusting instruction is a necessary component of clear presentations. It is not always possible to predict what will be easily understood by a group of students. In addition, it is generally difficult to infer whether students have understood what was presented. Consequently, teachers should elicit active responses from students throughout the presentation stage. This is usually done by asking direct questions that are relevant to the presentation objectives. Teachers also can require students to summarize the information presented. Teachers should attempt to involve all of the students all of the time or most of the students most of the time. Simple questioning that requires all students to respond chorally or by hand raising can provide teachers with immediate feedback on student understanding. Another technique for increasing students' active participation that simultaneously provides teachers with the level of students' understanding is requiring students to pair off with one another and verbally summarize information to each other. Further specific examples for increasing students' active participation during guided practice are provided in Figure 1.11. All of these procedures can provide a teacher with an immediate assessment of a student's level of understanding and can assist the teacher in making decisions like whether to proceed to a new step or to review the last step.

Finally, corrective feedback is a critical component. During presentation and guided practice, teachers should frequently question students to monitor their understanding of the content being taught. However, the corrective feedback students are given on their responses plays an important role in the amount students learn. Corrective feedback can be oral or written, but during teacher presentation and guided practice it typically is oral. Often the type of feedback depends on the type of response.

If responses are prompt and accurate, teachers should either provide a short acknowledgment (e.g., "That's correct.") or simply proceed to the next question. Effusive praise for a correct response often embarrasses the student and disrupts the momentum of the lesson. In some cases in special education settings, however, praise may be helpful for reticent students.

If a response is correct but indicates some uncertainty on the part of a student, the learning may be incomplete. Feedback for this type of response should be overt (e.g., "Correct."). It also may be helpful to restate the entire correct response and the steps used to arrive at the response (e.g., "That's correct because . . ."). If responses are hesitant, the same questions should be asked again later.

Responses can be incorrect either because of carelessness or because of lack of knowledge. If incorrect responses are due to carelessness, teachers should simply correct the problem and move on. If students consistently make careless responses, teachers should encourage and reinforce more careful attending to responding. If incorrect responses are due to lack of knowledge, teachers can either prompt students for correct answers or reteach the content. Prompting is employed when the student appears to be on the right track, and it involves restating some component of the objective or asking a simpler question. Such prompting must be brief and direct and should not disturb the pace or momentum of the lesson. If students cannot respond immediately to a prompt, the information should be retaught. Endless "pumping" of a student who clearly does not know the correct response is not productive and may contribute to a negative classroom environment.

Guided Practice

Immediately following teacher presentation, students are asked to practice learned information. Such practice is designed to develop consistent and accurate responding under the direct observation of the teacher. Guided practice usually takes the form of teacher-led, small-group questions and answers or immediate teacher monitoring of written student responses. All of the examples described for facilitating students' active participation can be incorporated into guided practice activities. Initially, practice takes place with high levels of teacher involvement. During this time, responses need to be as overt (observable) as possible, so that teachers can easily monitor students' behavior.

In addition, it is important for questions to be delivered at a high frequency and to be directly relevant to the content. Responses to these questions are evaluated for understanding of the content. When necessary, teachers provide additional explanations, modeling, or demonstrations of relevant skills.

Finally, teachers must ensure that all students have participated and have received feedback. Guided practice activities are intended to lead to independent performance. Therefore, guided practice should continue until all students are responding at a high rate of accuracy (usually above 80%).

Independent Practice

Independent practice usually follows guided practice and typically takes the form of some type of independent seatwork. It is important to remember that students must have achieved a high level of accuracy in guided practice before they can move to independent practice. Independent practice provides students with opportunities to integrate what they have learned with previous content, to develop fluency in the execution of new skills and to apply and generalize newly acquired information. In independent practice activities, students' work is initially slower and more hesitant than in guided practice activities, but it should be as accurate as guided practice. As students develop fluency (accuracy plus rate of responding), responses become more confident and more automatic. The advantage of fluid, automatic responses is that they allow students to concentrate on learning new skills or applying learned skills to new situations. For example, students who are automatic at reading decoding skills can concentrate on comprehension, while students who are fluent at math facts can concentrate on solving complex computation problems.

Sometimes seatwork activities are employed simply to consume time. This is unfortunate, because students who are managed effectively can benefit greatly from seatwork activities. In order for students to benefit, however, the material should be directly relevant to the lesson objectives. It also is important that students have exhibited sufficient accuracy during guided practice to ensure their successful functioning in independent activities. Finally, it is helpful for seatwork to follow guided practice activities directly and for teachers to guide students through the first few problems or examples.

Teachers can manage effectively the level of engagement during seatwork by establishing general procedural guidelines for seatwork activities so that students know what they are expected to do, how to obtain extra help, and what to do upon completion of the assignment. In special education settings, teachers are often engaged in other activities such as delivering small-group instruction, while some students are completing seatwork assignments. In such cases teachers can arrange seating so that they can observe the entire classroom at a glance. However, if teachers are not engaged in instruction, they should circulate among students to provide feedback, answer questions, and monitor student engagement.

Several alternatives can replace or supplement the typical paper–pencil worksheet type of independent seatwork activity. First, independent seatwork can be replaced by additional teacher-led practice. This can be accomplished by a teacher or a paraprofessional (aide, volunteer, or parent). Such teacher-led practice may be beneficial in special education settings where students may be in need of more direct feedback and in which smaller class sizes allow the opportunity for group responses.

Another alternative to independent practice is the use of peers in tutoring or cooperative learning situations. In peer tutoring, one student is selected to monitor the performance of another student. If "tutors" are not on a higher academic level than their respective "tutees," it must be determined that tutors can recognize or identify inappropriate responses. Flash cards are helpful when tutors are unaware of correct responses. Tutoring dyads (pairs) of similar abilities can easily exchange roles to ensure that both members of the pair are receiving practice experience and feedback. If, on the other hand, tutors are selected because their academic skills are higher than those of the tutees, care must be taken to ensure that tutors also receive opportunities for practice and feedback. The fact that tutors are sometimes seen to gain from the tutoring process does not mean that they will always gain or that what they gain will be directly relevant to their instructional objectives. Teachers must try to ensure that all students benefit from peer-led instruction.

A closely related activity, cooperative learning, involves small groups of students who cooperate on the completion of seatwork activities. These groups are comprised of students of different abilities who work together in competition with other cooperative groups in their classroom. Groups that work most efficiently are given rewards for their performance.

Other types of independent practice activities can incorporate the use of computers and other audiovisual aids. Many of these devices provide immediate feedback to student responses. For the practice to be relevant, however, the computer software programs must match instructional objectives.

Weekly and Monthly Reviews

As mentioned earlier, daily review is critical in order for teachers to monitor and adjust instruction. Additionally, in special education it is necessary to use cumulative reviews on weekly and monthly bases. These reviews provide information on how well students retain important content. Retention is critical, especially when succeeding content builds upon facts and concepts covered previously. Teachers need to incorporate student performance on these daily, weekly, and monthly reviews into their formative evaluation plans. If reviews are done properly, teachers are better able to monitor and adjust instruction to include more thorough periodic reviews and reteaching.

Formative Evaluation

Formative evaluation is a continuous monitoring system that can be used to assess students' performance and progress. Additionally, the information obtained from formative evaluation can be used to adjust instructional procedures if necessary. Recently, it has been shown that 1- and 2-minute samples of students' work are sufficient to document performance. Chapter 3 provides more information on specific formative evaluation procedures.

EFFECTIVE SPECIAL EDUCATION: USING THE "PASS" VARIABLES

Special education teachers can be effective if they always remember to employ the "PASS" variables in their teaching. First, special education teachers should "Prioritize" their objectives, emphasizing the most important objectives and de-emphasizing or eliminating less critical objectives. Second, special education teachers should "Adapt" their instruction to the needs of the learner. These adaptations could include more time-on-task, more concrete materials, specific learning and memory strategies, specialized apparatus or learning materials, or modification of the physical environment. The adaptations should reflect the interaction of the curriculum and the individual student. Third, special education teachers should remember to "SCREAM" when presenting information to students. These variables (structure, clarity, redundancy, enthusiasm, appropriate pace, and maximized engagement) are critical to special education teaching effectiveness. Finally, special education teachers should be certain to "Systematically evaluate" progress toward specific educational objectives and be prepared to reprioritize, readapt, etc., when needed to ensure that all students experience success.

SUMMARY

This chapter provided an overview of the practices that are most highly related to effective teaching in special education. First, critical variables related to achievement were described. These included time on task, content covered, delivery of information, guided and independent practice activities, and formative evaluation. These variables are important to consider when designing instruction. Second, a model for delivery of daily lessons is described. This model includes daily review, presentation of material, guided practice, independent practice, weekly and monthly reviews, and formative evaluation. These components include teacher-effectiveness variables and provide a general framework for delivery of daily lessons. In the chapters that follow, more information is provided on the use of these variables for specific content in special education.

RELEVANT RESEARCH

Much of the research on teacher effectiveness is summarized in Wittrock's (1986) edited work on research on teaching. Chapters of the Wittrock book that deal directly with the variables described in Chapter 1 are authored by Brophy and Good (1986), Rosenshine and Stevens (1986), Doyle (1986), Walberg (1986), and Biddle and Anderson (1986). Some of the most important original research in this area was conducted by Anderson, Evertson, and Brophy (1979); Anderson, Evertson, and Emmer (1980); Berliner and Rosenshine (1977); Brophy (1979); Good and Grouws (1979); Robbins (1986); Rosenshine (1983); and Stallings and Krasavage (1986). Mastropieri (1989) described an application of teacher effectiveness research in a special education teacher preparation program, and Scruggs and Mastropieri (in press-b) described the importance of field-based experiences. Much of the research cited above involved "average" students, although the research involving lower achieving students, younger students, and students of lower socioeconomic status is more relevant to special education. Research replicating these findings on special education populations is reported by Englert (1983, 1984); Haynes and Jenkins (1986); Leinhardt, Zigmond, and Cooley (1981); Sindelar et al. (1986); and Wilson and Wesson (1986). Pace of introduction of new information was studied by Gleason,

(continues)

(Relevant Research continued)

Carnine, and Vala (1991). The positive effects of teacher enthusiasm in special education settings are documented by Brigham, Scruggs, and Mastropieri (1992). The positive effects of higher order questioning are described by Scruggs, Mastropieri, Sullivan, and Hesser (1993); Scruggs, Mastropieri, and Sullivan (in press); and Sullivan (1993). Issues of teaching multicultural and linguistically diverse students are described in Issue 2, Volume 56 (Obiakor, Patton, & Ford, 1989) and Issue 2, Volume 59 (Figueroa, Fradd, & Correa, 1992) of *Exceptional Children.* Particularly useful are articles by Cummins (1989) and Franklin (1992). Additional research in multicultural special education settings has provided specific support for: teacher enthusiasm (Brigham, Scruggs, & Mastropieri, 1992); cooperative group learning (Brigham, Bakken, Scruggs, & Mastropieri, 1992); and use of relevant, meaningful materials (Scruggs, Mastropieri, Bakken, & Brigham, 1993). Support for the facilitative effects of a positive classroom atmosphere for special education students is given by Mastropieri, Scruggs, and Bohs (1994). Finally, much of the literature on special education teacher effectiveness is summarized in Issue 6, Volume 52 of *Exceptional Children* (Algozzine & Meheady, 1986), particularly in articles by Bickel and Bickel (1986); Morsink, Soar, Soar, and Thomas (1986); and Reid (1986).

❖ ❖ ❖

CHAPTER 2

Instructional Design

THE PREVIOUS CHAPTER DESCRIBED VARIABLES RELATED TO TEACHER effectiveness. This chapter describes the design of instruction. In order for effective teaching to occur, teachers must design their lessons carefully and systematically. In special education, federal law (Individuals with Disabilities Education Act [IDEA], Public Law 101–476) requires that all instruction be based on prespecified goals and objectives (U.S. Department of Education, 1992). Individual goals and objectives for each student are specified on Individualized Education Programs (IEPs), which must be reviewed at least annually. An example of a portion of an IEP is provided in Appendix A.

Instruction for students is designed on the basis of goals and objectives from the IEP. This is accomplished by prioritizing objectives from the scope and sequence and by developing and implementing instructional guidelines. To develop such guidelines, provisions must be made within individual lesson plans for all the teacher-effectiveness variables discussed in the last chapter. These include time-on-task, content covered, delivering information, questioning, feedback, practice activities, and formative evaluation.

When developing instructional objectives, it is important to attend not only to the level of the content presented but also to the level of the knowledge that is expected from the learner. For example, anyone who has taken tests realizes that multiple-choice questions are easier to answer than short-answer or fill-in-the-blank questions. This is partly because identifying correct answers is easier than producing correct answers. Therefore, objectives and their corresponding lessons need to specify the level of learning that is expected. In addition, the performance criteria must be specified. Prior to the lesson, teachers should know not only that a specific objective will be met but also that students will respond with a given level of accuracy (e.g., 80%) on a specified evaluation measure.

It is essential, therefore, that teachers develop goals and objectives, performance criteria for meeting those objectives, and lesson plans that specify how teacher-effectiveness variables will be used. The remainder of this chapter is devoted to a more complete discussion of these issues.

THE INDIVIDUALIZED EDUCATION PROGRAM

The Individualized Education Program, or IEP, includes a list of goals and objectives for a specific student. These goals and objectives should reflect the overall goal of returning the student into the mainstream or a less restrictive environment (for example, the regular classroom). In addition to the overall objectives, an IEP contains statements regarding current levels of academic and social performance, persons responsible for the implementation of specific objectives, and settings in which instruction will be delivered. Finally, the IEP is signed by members of the multidisciplinary team (parents, teachers, and other relevant school personnel, including social workers and school nurses).

Types of Objectives

The fundamental component of the IEP is the instructional objective. IEP objectives can be divided into general and specific or long- and short-term objectives. Long-term objectives typically refer to the skills the student needs to reenter the regular classroom or a less restrictive environment. These objectives include such general statements as "Student will improve reading performance to the appropriate grade equivalent level, as measured by achievement tests." This overall objective describes the global skills the student needs to acquire in order to function at an average level in that mainstreamed classroom. However, it does not specify the precise skills the student needs to master in order to read at the appropriate grade level. These skills are specified in the short-term objectives, which describe the prerequisite steps students must take in order to meet the long-term objective. In the reading example, a short-term objective may include a statement such as "Student will read word samples from passages with 100% accuracy." In another example, the long-term objective for social behavior might be "Student will exhibit appropriate verbal behavior according to school rules at all times." The corresponding short-term objectives might be "Student will identify 50 examples and nonexamples of appropriate verbal responses to teacher questions" and "In a role-playing situation the student will respond appropriately to teacher criticism and questions for 20 examples."

Common Elements of Objectives

As can be seen by the above examples and those in Figure 2.1, all objectives have certain common elements. This is true whether objectives are short- or long-term and whether they deal with reading, math, or social skills. These common components include: (a) the behavior to be exhibited,

Area	Student Behavior	Conditions	Performance Criteria
Reading	Oral reading	100-word passage from appropriate reading level	In 1 minute with 100% accuracy
Handwriting	Copying	Lowercase letters A–K	With 100% accuracy
Spelling	Oral spelling	50 Dolch words	With 90% accuracy
Arithmetic	Computation	50 single-digit addition problems	In 1 minute with 90% accuracy
Language	Identification	20 instances of *on* and *in* from pictures	With 90% accuracy
Social Behavior	Ignoring	Teasing of others	9 times out of 10

FIGURE 2.1. Sample behavioral objectives.

(b) the conditions (circumstances) under which the behavior is to be exhibited, and (c) the performance criteria. Often an objective will take the following form: "Given 20 division problems, including 2-digit divisors and 3-digit dividends, the student will compute answers and remainders at a criterion of 90% accuracy in less than 5 minutes." In this example note that the computation of the answers to the division problems specifies the behavior to be evaluated. The behavior is an observable, measurable performance of the student. By this definition, behaviors include oral reading, walking, talking, and permanent products such as handwriting samples. Covert operations such as thinking are not considered behaviors because they are not directly observable; however, these covert operations often are necessary for the execution of the behavior. In the final analysis, teachers can directly evaluate only observable behaviors.

The second critical component of an objective is the specified conditions under which the behavior will occur. In the example on long division, the objective specifies that the student has been provided with 20 division problems of a certain type. These problems constitute the circumstances under which the behavior will be performed. Circumstances also may include paper, pencil, a desk, a quiet environment, and teacher directions; however, space considerations may preclude the inclusion of such implicit conditions. Care must be taken, however, to ensure that all of the necessary conditions are specified and that there is general agreement regarding implicit conditions.

The final component of an objective is the performance criteria to be exhibited. When stating the performance criteria, it is necessary to include accuracy and perhaps fluency criteria. In the division example, an accuracy criterion of 90% is specified, as is a rate of four problems per minute. Such criteria should be based on overall performance goals expected of all students at their respective age and grade levels. One way of establishing such criteria is to determine performance levels of regular education students who have been identified by their teachers as competent at that skill. For example, if special education teachers were uncertain about the performance criteria for the division objective, they could ask regular educators at that grade level to identify several students competent in long division whose rate and accuracy on those 20 division problems could provide a basis for performance criteria. In addition to the mainstreaming criteria, teachers also need to ensure that the performance criteria for one objective lead to easy mastery of the next objective. Research has shown that students who have thoroughly mastered one objective can learn the next objective more easily when the scope and sequence follows an established hierarchy of skill development. However, it also must be remembered that spending too much time on one objective can interfere with the amount of content covered throughout the school year.

In summary, IEPs describe individual student goals and objectives. Objectives must include the behaviors to be assessed, conditions for assessing the behavior, and performance criteria. Objectives not only are a critical component of IEP assessment but also provide the basis for instructional design. The remainder of this chapter discusses means for incorporating instructional objectives into the design of instruction and matching instruction with expected levels of learning.

LEVELS OF LEARNING

Identification and Production

As stated earlier, academic or social behavior can occur in identification or production formats. Identification refers to student performances such as matching, multiple choice, true/false, pointing, and selecting. Identification is usually important in the very early stages of learning that require the mastery of basic discriminations. For example, in the initial stages of reading instruction, students must be able to identify certain letters. At the higher grade levels, identification of novel concepts is often a necessary first step toward developing understanding of those concepts. Identification also is important when the amount of content being taught is large and when objective tests of the multiple-choice type represent the only practical means for assessing the learning of a large number of students. Some tasks, furthermore, may require learning only at the identification level, for example, identification of different traffic lights.

In many cases, however, students ultimately must be required to produce appropriate responses. For example, although it may be a necessary prerequisite for students to identify appropriate playground interactions, they must ultimately be able to produce appropriate playground interactions in order to function successfully in the mainstream. Production refers

Area	Student Identification	Student Production
Reading	Points to vowels.	Orally reads vowels.
	Chooses which of four sentences represents main idea of passage.	Reads passage and states 'main idea.'
Handwriting	Identifies correct cursive formation of capital S.	Writes cursive capital S.
Spelling	Given four choices, identifies correct spelling of "lamb."	Orally spells "lamb" correctly.
Arithmetic	Identifies regrouping problem.	Computes problem with regrouping.
Language	Identifies correct noun/verb agreement.	Orally produces sentences with correct noun/verb agreement.
Social Behavior	Points out students who are sharing a classroom toy.	Shares classroom toys.

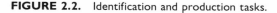

FIGURE 2.2.   Identification and production tasks.

to a student's observable rendition of task-relevant behavior. Such production tasks include oral reading, writing, speaking, computing, and performing. Figure 2.2 provides some additional examples of identification and production tasks.

Acquisition and Fluency

Just as identification and production reflect the type of behavior specified, acquisition and fluency reflect the performance criteria of those behaviors. Basically, acquisition refers to an accuracy criteria. Teaching on an acquisition level is oriented toward higher levels of accuracy without regard for the rate of performance. For example, in teaching regrouping in simple addition, the initial emphasis may be on the acquisition of the relevant rule as assessed by accurate performance. Also, teaching any basic discrimination such as *b* versus *d* may initially require an accuracy criterion during the acquisition of this discrimination. For such levels of initial learning, rate of performance is not as important as correct performance.

Once novel concepts or facts have been acquired, the next stage of instruction usually involves some type of *fluency* training. It may not be sufficient for students to decode a reading passage as accurately as their regular classroom counterparts—if it takes them twice as long to do so. Once accurate responding has been established, it is generally necessary to establish fluency as assessed by accuracy plus rate criteria. The student who is fluent at reading, then, not only reads at the same level of accuracy

Behavior	Accuracy Criteria (% correct)	Fluency Rate Criteria
Reading CVC+e words	90	40 correct per min
Answering comprehension questions	90	5 correct per min
Orally answering "+8" facts	100	50 correct per min
Printing capital letters	100	20 correct per min
Spelling *ou* words	100	10 correct per min
Writing sentences	100	6 correct in 30 min
Saying "thank you"	90*	10 times when appropriate during a day

*appropriate times

FIGURE 2.3. Accuracy and fluency criteria.

as other competent students but also at a similar rate. In most of the basic skill areas that are covered in special education classes, the attainment of both accuracy and fluency levels is critical. Figure 2.3 provides some examples of accuracy and fluency criteria.

Application and Generalization

Application and generalization follow acquisition and fluency. *Application* refers to students exhibiting a critical skill in an appropriate context that is directly relevant to the area of instruction. For example, it is of little use for students to be able to multiply 3-digit numbers accurately *and* fluently if they cannot use these skills to solve word problems. Once basic skills have been mastered, it is important that students be taught to apply them in intended contexts. For another example, social skills training often is conducted in the context of role playing in which students are required to produce appropriate social responses in contrived settings. In order for this learning to be of real importance, however, students need to apply those appropriate social behaviors in their classroom. Application refers not only to the behavior that is exhibited but also to the conditions under which it is to be exhibited (i.e., the applied context).

Generalization as used here is similar to application but refers to a broader and more global domain of conditions, which are generally outside the immediate control of the special education teacher. For example, assume that students have been taught to take turns in a role-play playground setting and have attained accuracy and fluency levels of performance. In this instance, application would refer to exhibiting turn-taking skills on the playground. Generalization would refer to the demonstration of these skills in a different but still appropriate context, such as taking turns getting on a school bus. In an academic example, students may learn to compute division problems accurately and fluently on worksheets. Application would refer to their performance of these skills in response to word problems. Generalization would refer to the use of these skills in a mainstream classroom or in determining the price of one slice of pizza at a restaurant outside the school setting.

Some type of application or generalization is the end goal of special education. In most cases, it is important for teachers to directly teach the application of acquired basic skills and facts in their intended contexts. Generalization, however, is a more complex phenomenon that resists even precise definition in many instances. Most people agree, however, that generalization can occur across settings, time, stimuli, and behaviors. Although appropriate generalization is nearly always desirable, it has proven to be much more difficult to teach than application.

Summary of Levels of Learning

In summary, attention to different levels of learning is critical in special education. Identification and production refer to different behaviors that may be expected from students in specific content areas. Whenever instruction is designed, teachers should consider whether students must produce a correct response or whether identification is a more appropriate objective. Additionally, performance criteria should be assessed at various levels. Acquisition refers to accuracy criteria only, while fluency refers to accuracy plus rate of performance criteria. Fluency is of particular importance in basic skill areas such as reading, writing, and arithmetic. Application and generalization refer to the context in which these skills are applied. An example of an application task is when students are trained to use their decoding skills on an unfamiliar reading passage. Generalization, as used here, is somewhat broader and refers to the use of learned skills in untrained settings, such as the use of appropriate social skills in a grocery store. Figure 2.4 provides examples of application and generalization, and Figure 2.5 describes strategies for promoting generalization summarized from Scruggs and Mastropieri (1984b, 1994) and Stokes and Baer (1977). These strategies are described with respect to particular curriculum materials and tasks throughout this book.

In addition to levels of learning, a consideration of the type of learning is critical for optimal design of instruction. In the sections that follow, different types of learning and their implications for instruction design are described.

Behavior (acquisition / fluency)	Application	Generalization
Passages read correctly from reading textbook.	Reads correctly in classroom literature book.	Reads correctly in mainstream history textbook.
Long-division algorithms computed on worksheet.	Computes long-division word problems in class.	Computes long-division word problems on mainstream achievement test.
Roman numerals on worksheet.	Solves classroom problem with Roman numerals.	Reads Roman numerals on museum during field trip.
Role-plays "please" and "thank you."	Says "please" and "thank you" to neighboring student.	Says "please" and "thank you" to physical education teacher.
Spells *kn* words correctly on spelling test.	Spells *kn* words correctly on sentence writing.	Spells *kn* words correctly in mainstream homework assignment.
Role plays ignoring inappropriate behavior.	Ignores teasing of neighboring student.	Ignores teasing on school bus.

FIGURE 2.4.   Application and generalization tasks.

TYPES OF LEARNING

Most learning that takes place in school settings can be classified as: (a) discrimination learning, (b) factual learning, (c) rule learning, (d) procedural learning, (e) conceptual learning, and (f) problem solving and thinking skills. Examples of these types of learning are found in Figure 2.6. These are described separately in the sections that follow.

Discrimination Learning

Discrimination learning refers to learning that one stimulus is different from another stimulus or set of stimuli. One of the more obvious examples in special education is in learning to discriminate between reversible letters, such as *b* and *d*. Such reversal problems are commonly reported in students who are classified as learning disabled or reading disabled. However, such reversals are also commonly observed in nearly all beginning readers. A student has learned a *b/d* discrimination when he or she can correctly identify the *b* from the *d*. In later stages of learning, students will be required to write (produce) a *b* or *d* correctly. Other examples of discrimination tasks include learning differences between or among colors (e.g., "Point to the red ball"), shapes (e.g., "Show me the triangle"), arithmetic

1. *Train sufficient examples.* Teach students to respond correctly to a number of different examples.

2. *Train loosely.* Allow a wide variety of acceptable responses and conditions, and do not rely exclusively on overly structured situations.

3. *Use "indiscriminable contingencies."* Set up situations in which students are less certain exactly *when* their appropriate behavior will be rewarded. This will make them more likely to display appropriate social and academic behavior at all times.

4. *Use role play activities.* Set up situations that are likely to occur in external settings (e.g., use of appropriate social skills during job interviews), and have students act out the roles of different participants.

5. *Train specific strategies.* Teach students the necessary procedures for accomplishing specific tasks in other environments or circumstances.

6. *Promote self-monitoring.* Teach students how to monitor and regulate their behavior in a variety of situations.

7. *Reinforce generalization.* Provide explicit, positive feedback when behavior is successfully generalized. Discuss with the student how this was accomplished, and encourage future generalization efforts.

8. *Retrain.* Directly reteach the desired social or academic behavior in the generalization setting or conditions, or in as many as possible.

FIGURE 2.5.   Strategies for promoting generalization.

symbols (e.g., "Which one means add?"), and appropriate social responses (e.g., "Which student said the right thing?"). Once students have learned to accurately discriminate sets of stimuli, they generally will need to learn to produce individual stimuli fluently. Discrimination learning may be the initial stage of other types of learning, particularly concept learning, and should not be considered exclusive from the types of learning that follow. When planning instruction, it is important to attend carefully to discrimination learning, particularly at the earliest stages of skill development or in the introduction of new content where, for example, initial discriminations between different types of minerals may be difficult. Discrimination learning plays a role in many types of learning that follow.

Factual Learning

Factual learning refers to the making and establishment of basic associations and always follows a stimulus–response paradigm (pattern). An obvious example of factual learning is in the acquisition of foreign language vocabulary. In learning that the Spanish word *casa* means *house*, students are provided with the stimulus term *casa* and are expected to produce the

Type of Learning	Reading	Arithmetic	Social
Discrimination	p vs. q	+ vs. −	cooperate vs. compete
Factual			
Associative	l = ell	5 + 2 = 7	Laughing at other people is rude.
Serial list	a, b, c, d, e . . .	2, 4, 6, 8, 10, 12 . . .	School song or motto.
Rule	If two vowels appear together, say the long sound of the first vowel.	To divide fractions, invert and multiply.	Do unto others as you would have others do unto you.
Concept	vowel	prime number	courtesy
Procedure	1. Read title 2. Self-question 3. Skim passage 4. Self-question 5. Read carefully 6. Answer questions	1. Count decimal places in division. 2. Move decimal point in divisor that many places to the right, insert caret. 3. Place decimal point directly above caret in quotient.	1. Walk quietly in line. 2. Take tray, utensils, and napkins. 3. Put lunch on tray. 4. Take carton of milk. 5. Walk quietly to lunch table.

FIGURE 2.6. Types of learning.

response *house*. In basic skill areas factual learning includes the acquisition of basic math facts, such as 5 + 3 = 8, and basic decoding skills, such as learning appropriate sound–symbol relationships. Students can be required to produce a relevant fact when asked to identify the correct fact in, for example, a multiple-choice format. Although accuracy, application, and generalization of a learned fact is important, particularly in test-taking situations, the fluency rate expected may vary in importance. For example, it is critical that math facts be learned to a high rate of fluency; however, a rapid rate of responding may be of less importance in some content area learning.

Factual learning is so pervasive in schools on all levels that efficient factual learning is critical for school success. One potential problem with the teaching of facts is that it is sometimes possible for students to answer factual questions correctly without comprehending the content. Many undergraduate students, for example, can recall memorizing facts from textbooks without any real understanding of the facts being tested. Although such memorizing may be helpful in increasing test scores, it may not increase learning in any real sense. However, this associative stage may represent the first step in catching on to important content and, in this sense, is a critical component of learning. For example, in studying statistics, students might simply memorize the fact that r^2 is equivalent to "the proportion of variance accounted for" and be able to produce (or identify) such a response on a test. Although learning this fact may represent an important first step, it is also important for this fact to be "understood" (i.e., that underlying concepts be learned). Understanding of this type can be assessed in application or generalization tasks, in which students are required to use the fact in some novel context. In other instances, factual learning may require only one response. For example, it may be important to know that the capital of Maryland is Annapolis. Given that a student understands what is meant by capital, learning that Annapolis is the capital of Maryland may be the only objective. In some cases, students may need to learn facts in a specified sequence, such as the days of the week, the months in a year, amendments to the Constitution, and the presidents of the United States. This type of factual learning, as well as memorizing sequences such as the letters of the alphabet, is referred to as serial list learning. In other instances, factual learning represents the prerequisite building blocks for concept learning, which is described later in this chapter.

Rule Learning

Learning basic rules is critical for success in school. Many times students are referred to special education because they lack an understanding of rules. For example, a student may have failed to learn the application of inconsistent rules found in reading. A second example may be the lack of acquisition of classroom rules for social behavior. An example of a rule is "When two vowels go walking (appear together), the first one does the talking (says its name)." Another example is "Raise your hand and wait to be called upon before speaking."

Rules appear across all skill and content areas. In some areas, however, rules are inconsistent. Inconsistent rules are those that have unpredictable exceptions. These are particularly common in reading and spelling. For example, the *i* before *e* rule lists as an exception when these vowels appear after the letter *c*. However, the word *financier* is itself an exception to this exception, subject to a different rule. Such inconsistent rules can be particularly difficult for special education students.

In contrast, rules in mathematics are typically highly consistent. For example, when dividing fractions the rule that specifies that the divisor be inverted is constant. Most rules in mathematics can be taught without respect to inconsistencies.

Many rules follow an if–then paradigm. This is often true in social behavior, which can be of particular difficulty for special education students. Such rules may vary from situation to situation and also may be applied inconsistently. For example, the rule, "If you are not in your seat when the bell rings, then you must obtain a tardy slip," may be inconsistently applied by different teachers and even by the same teacher. Although it is important for teachers to be as consistent as possible, it is also important for students to understand sources of inconsistency.

Rule learning can incorporate knowledge of facts and discriminations. For example, the "in-seat" rule above presumes that students can discriminate in-seat from out-of-seat and have learned the meaning of "tardy slip." Such facts and discriminations must be mastered prior to learning the relevant rules. In some cases facts and rules can be combined sequentially in procedural learning, which is described in the following section.

Procedural Learning

Many activities in school require the execution of a series of skills in sequence. This type of learning is referred to as procedural learning. Procedural learning, such as the procedures involved in long division, is very common in mathematics. In long division, students must execute a series of steps in order to accurately compute the solution of the problem. To execute this procedure, students must know the underlying facts and understand the rules that constitute the specific steps.

Procedures are also common in reading comprehension and study skills. In order to read and study effectively, students must learn to execute a series of steps to monitor their understanding of a passage, such as prereading/skimming, identifying critical information, executing appropriate learning strategies, reviewing, and self-questioning. To be effective, such strategies must be executed in sequence and require the use of procedural learning.

Students who are taught to use a learning strategy independently (such as the *cover*, *copy*, and *compare* strategy for learning spelling words) must use a three-step procedure. First, students must *recognize* the situation for which a particular strategy is appropriate. Second, students must *recall* the steps of the strategy in correct order. Finally, students must correctly *execute* the strategy for the specific task. Many different learning strategies are presented throughout this book, but students using these strategies independently must always use this three-part procedure.

Other important procedural tasks are commonly found in vocational areas. For example, many students in special education are taught assembly tasks according to a certain procedural sequence. Finally, knowledge of procedures is important for general school functioning. Students must learn daily routines, such as entering a school cafeteria, many of which must be performed in sequence. In some cases, daily schedules are variable, and such schedules may be particularly difficult for mainstreamed special education students. To a large extent, the application of learned skills represents a knowledge of relevant procedures. It is important for special education students to be taught skills and the procedures by which they are applied.

Conceptual Learning

Concepts form an integral component of all knowledge. Although difficult to define precisely, conceptual learning has occurred when a student can provide a correct response to a novel instance of the concept. For instance, while learning colors, students may have learned that a certain pencil is red. However, it cannot be determined that students have mastered the concept of *red* until they can identify red flowers, red crayons, and red chairs that they had not seen previously. Likewise, students may have learned that a specific geometric form has been given the name *triangle*. However, students have not mastered the concept of *triangle* until they have demonstrated that they can identify or produce many forms of triangles. At the higher grade levels students learn more complex concepts, such as *amphibian*. To have mastered this concept thoroughly, students must have first acquired concepts for frog, toad, salamander, and newt. The knowledge of such a concept must be assessed across a wider domain of instances than the simpler concepts described above.

Concepts can be taught through rule learning or through discrimination-learning paradigms. Many concepts follow the if–then rule-learning paradigm. Using the previously described triangle example, an if–then rule can be applied, as in the statement, "If a geometric figure has three straight sides that enclose a space, then it is a triangle." Students demonstrate knowledge of this concept by applying the rule in novel instances. As another example, students could be taught the following rule to learn the concept *insect*: "If an animal has six legs and three body parts, it is an insect." Students who have learned this rule can also learn to apply it to different types of animals.

Concepts also can be taught through discrimination-learning paradigms. In such cases, students are provided with multiple instances and noninstances of the concept until they can identify the appropriate features in novel instances. A common use of this paradigm is in the teaching of locative prepositions. Locative prepositions refer to spatial orientation and include such prepositions as *above, below, on, in,* and *behind.* These concepts are difficult to teach with rule-learning paradigms and in special education are typically taught by means of instances and noninstances. For example, to teach the concept *on,* students could be shown a cup which in some cases is on the table and in some cases is not on the table. After students have been provided with sufficient examples, they should be able to identify or produce instances of the concept *on.* To identify the concept *on,* students should respond correctly to the following question: "Is the cup/ spoon/fork on the table?" To produce an example of the concept *on,* students should respond appropriately to the following command: "Put the cup/spoon/

fork on the table." Other concepts resist precise or simple definitions and generally are taught through discriminations of instances and noninstances. Such concepts include *freedom, justice,* and *appropriate.* In such cases, instances and noninstances are provided by statements such as "Running may be appropriate on the playgrounds but not appropriate in the halls."

In many cases, concepts are taught by the provision of rules and examples. To teach the concept *fish,* teachers may first introduce a general rule: "If an animal lives in the water and has gills and scales, then it is a fish." After students have demonstrated knowledge and familiarity with the rule, they are taught to apply the rule to various instances and noninstances. For example: "This animal is a dolphin. It lives in the water. It does not have gills, and it does not have scales. Is it a fish?"

Concepts are an integral component of school learning. Concepts are interrelated with other types of learning such as factual learning and generally are taught through the use of rules and discriminations of instances and noninstances.

Concepts can range from very simple (e.g., *red, triangle*) to complex (e.g., *torque, covalent bonding*). The more complex concepts build on simpler concepts and require more prerequisite knowledge. Nevertheless, several considerations can facilitate acquisition of any concept. First, initially emphasize the critical features of the concept, and describe less relevant attributes later. Second, link the new concept to things that students already know. Third, provide lots of examples of the new concept, and include instances as well as noninstances.

Problem Solving and Thinking Skills

Problem solving and thinking skills are different from the types of learning described earlier. Problem solving, as used here, refers to students finding an answer or a solution in the absence of an immediate strategy or means for solving the problem. To this extent, it refers less to strategy-based math problem solving than it does to constructing proofs in geometry, such as the Pythagorean theorem, or solving the "magic square" problem (insert the numbers 1 through 9 into a nine-chambered square such that the diagonals, rows, and columns all have the same sum). However, problem solving can occur on less formal tasks, such as finding the simplest solution to the problem

$$\frac{375 + 375 + 375 + 375 + 375}{5}$$

or in finding a way to keep newts from using the water-heating apparatus to crawl out of the aquarium.

Thinking skills is a broader term and includes the use of active reasoning in solving problems or in acquiring or understanding new concepts. Thinking skills and problem solving are involved with the processes of learning more than the products of learning (such as facts and concepts). Nevertheless, there is good reason for considering thinking skills and problem solving in special education. Most students with mild disabilities are not active reasoners (they frequently have been characterized as "passive learners"); however, it has been argued that information is not truly learned (i.e., at the application and generalization levels) until it has been actively elaborated upon, questioned, and reasoned through. Therefore, instructional activities that promote active reasoning through new information are more likely to serve application and generalization objectives than are activities that do not promote active reasoning. Further, there is reason to believe that students who have been encouraged to use thinking skills and problem solving strategies will ultimately become more thoughtful, reflective learners.

Thinking skills and problem solving are best taught through modeling, prompting, and active coaching. It may be a good overall policy to not answer some student questions until the students have demonstrated that they have actively thought about the question themselves. Often some prior knowledge must be brought to bear upon the task, and teachers can help prompt the retrieval of this relevant information. Thinking skills or problem-solving strategies are acquired best with reference to a specific subject. Such skills do not transfer easily across knowledge domains, and the best thinking usually occurs within a content that is well known to students.

Summary of Types of Learning

Types of learning can be subdivided into learning of discriminations, facts, rules, procedures, and concepts; problem solving; and thinking. It is important to note that these categories are not mutually exclusive and that many learning tasks include several different types of learning. Nevertheless, types of learning play an important role in the design of instruction and lend themselves to more appropriate delivery systems. The sections that follow describe how to use previously discussed variables in the design of instruction.

APPLICATION TO INSTRUCTIONAL DESIGN

Everything covered up to this point needs to be taken into consideration during the design of instruction, which is discussed in this section, as well as in the delivery of instruction. Before proceeding with specific design strategies, review the following variables on teacher effectiveness: (a) engaged time on task, (b) content covered, (c) teacher presentation, (d) questioning, (e) feedback, (f) guided and independent practice activities, and (g) formative evaluation. Review the following variables on objectives: (a) behavior, (b) conditions, and (c) performance criteria. Review the types of behaviors and levels of learning: (a) identification, (b) production, (c) accuracy, (d) fluency, (e) application, and (f) generalization. Also, review the types of learning: (a) discrimination learning; (b) factual learning, including simple associations and serial lists; (c) rule learning; (d) procedural learning; (e) conceptual learning; and (f) problem solving and thinking skills. At this point, producing definitions and examples of all of the above variables is required. The next section describes how to examine an objective and how to integrate the above variables into an optimal lesson design.

DESIGNING INSTRUCTION

Design of instruction involves the systematic examination and organization of all curricular and teaching variables. Effective instructional design incorporates (a) specification of long-term objectives, (b) development of specific short-term objectives and sequencing of skills, (c) selection of appropriate materials and instructional procedures, and (d) specification of decision-making systems and evaluation procedures. These components will be discussed separately.

Specification of Long-Term Objectives

As a first step toward designing any instruction, teachers should specify the content that should be learned by the end of the instructional sequence. An instructional sequence could consist of content that will be covered in a unit, quarter, semester, or year. Clearly stated long-term objectives are necessary in order to maintain appropriate levels of attention by teachers and students to required curriculum areas.

Long-term objectives may include statements such as "Students will count coins to a specific value, given pennies, nickels, dimes, quarters, half dollars, and silver dollars with 100% accuracy in less than 30 seconds." Another example of a long-term objective is "Student will exhibit school-appropriate behavior during cafeteria lunch period without prompting for 3 consecutive weeks." Long-term objectives for special education students typically are derived from students' IEPs. However, the IEP objectives usually can be subdivided into several levels of long-term objectives. To maximize instructional efficiency, such long-term objectives are linked to school-district-wide curriculum scope and sequences. In addition, materials that link instructional procedures with instructional objectives should be available. When curricular materials are linked to long-term objectives, curriculum-based assessment can be more readily implemented.

Specification of Short-Term Objectives

Once long-term objectives have been clearly designated, short-term objectives provide the behavior, conditions, and performance criteria that form the framework of daily lessons. The subdivision of long-term objectives is sometimes referred to as *task analysis*. Task analysis is the subdivision and sequencing of instructional steps at the optimal level of difficulty for students. Similarly, *conceptual analysis* refers to the subdivision and sequencing of instructional steps necessary to teach concepts. The optimal size of the instructional step is often determined by teachers based on previous formative evaluation data. Clearly specified short-term objectives are necessary in order to attend appropriately to the essential components of instruction.

Short-term objectives are similar in format to long-term objectives but generally describe very specifically the components of individual lessons. An example of a specific short-term objective, derived from the above long-term objective on coin counting, is "Student will identify the following coins: penny, nickel, dime, quarter, with 100% accuracy." Another possible short-term objective could be "Student will count from 1 to 20 nickels with 100% accuracy at a rate of 1 nickel per second."

Task analysis procedures also can be applied, and short-term objectives specified, in the area of social behavior. For the long-term objectives for cafeteria functioning presented earlier, cafeteria skills could be broken into tasks involving the procedures of going through cafeteria lines, seating, cleanup, and social behaviors relevant to appropriate interpersonal interaction in cafeteria settings. When such a task analysis is complete, short-term objectives could include the following: "Given a mainstream cafeteria setting, student will exhibit appropriate social behaviors while standing in cafeteria line for 3 consecutive weeks to a 100% criterion. Appropriate social behavior as defined here includes speaking in a tone of voice that does not carry intelligibly for more than 5 feet and refraining from teasing or making inappropriate physical contact with another student."

Like long-term objectives, short-term objectives are typically derived from IEPs, although they are often stated on a higher level of specificity than is appropriate to individual lesson presentations. For efficient delivery of instruction these objectives should also interact with appropriate curricular materials. Appropriate interactions can lead to curriculum-based instruction and assessment on a task-specific level.

Selection of Appropriate Materials and Instructional Procedures

Once objectives have been clearly specified, it should be easy to identify the types and levels of learning required. Teachers should be able to
state whether they expect students to identify or produce correct responses,
whether they expect learning to be produced at a level of accuracy or fluency, and whether students are expected to apply or generalize learned
information. Objectives should clearly state the level of learning that is
expected. In addition, teachers should be aware of the type of learning that
is expected to be produced. For example, many of the initial tasks in a coin-
counting curriculum require fluent production of factual responses. Later
on, students may need to produce rules and procedures for counting coins
at specified levels of accuracy or fluency. In previous lessons, discrimination of one type of coin from another, as assessed in identification tasks,
may have been necessary. For other learners, teaching relevant concepts
such as money may be important.

Once teachers have clearly determined *what* is to be taught, they must
determine the most appropriate materials and instructional procedures.
Instructional procedures refer to the manner in which instruction is implemented. For example, discrimination knowledge of the type needed for identification of specific coins typically is taught in special education through
a series of instances and noninstances (e.g., "This is a nickel. This is *not*
a nickel. Is this a nickel?") and feedback on match-to-sample tasks (e.g.,
"Point to the nickel in this group of four coins"). For serial-list factual
learning of the type used to teach counting by 5s, rehearsal is often used
("5, 10, 15, 20. . . . Now you say it"). To teach the procedural information
involved in cafeteria line behaviors, repeated teacher-led modeling, prompting, and feedback is typically used (e.g., "First I pick up my tray, then I pick
up a napkin, knife, fork, and spoon and put them on a tray. Now you do it").

The type of teaching procedure may also reflect the level of learning.
For example, teaching to accuracy criteria may include prompting and feedback for deliberate, careful work, while teaching to fluency criteria may
involve prompting and reinforcement for rapid and efficient performance.
Similarly, while teaching to application levels, teachers may employ more
deliberate models and demonstrations, and generalization instruction may
involve explicit instructions prior to the execution of the expected behavior
(e.g., "Now tell me what you are going to do when you get to the playground"). Some further examples of instructional procedures are given in
Figure 2.7.

In addition, it is mandatory that the instructional objectives and instructional procedures be accommodated to specific instructional materials. Materials should directly address specific objectives. Materials should not be
selected based upon convenience but because they include content directly
relevant to instructional objectives. When materials are not relevant, teachers

Objective	Instructional Strategies*
	Type of Learning
Discriminations	Presentation of instances and noninstances. Using models, prompts, and feedback.
Factual	Rehearsal and repetition, using drill and practice techniques; teaching meaningful elaborations; presenting information in manageable chunks.
Rules	Drill and practice; application of examples.
Concepts	Presentation of instances and noninstances; provision of rules; provision of multiple examples.
Procedures	Drill and practice; application activities; modeling, prompting, and feedback.
	Level of Learning
Acquisition	Models; demonstrations; slow pace; reinforce accuracy.
Fluency	Fast pace; reinforce speed of accurate responding; alter reinforcement procedures.
Application	Multiple examples; modeling, prompting, and feedback.
Generalization	Prompts; provision of rules; role play; multiple examples.

*Models, direct questions, and feedback can always be employed.

FIGURE 2.7. Instructional implications for different types of learning and levels of learning.

should adapt existing materials or create new materials that are directly relevant to instructional objectives. As students approach reintegration into regular classrooms, it is important that curricular materials and corresponding objectives closely resemble those used in regular classrooms. In fact, if a specific curriculum is used districtwide, teachers can more easily develop districtwide objectives and corresponding curriculum-based assessment materials that can be shared across teachers within school districts. Additional information on designing curriculum-based measures is presented in Chapter 3. Selection, evaluation, and adaptation of curriculum materials are discussed in Chapters 5 through 8.

In summary, teachers must attend to levels of learning and types of learning in order to develop instructional procedures and select appropriate curricular materials. The next section will discuss the specification of instructional decision-making systems and evaluation procedures that are used with instructional design.

TABLE 2.1.   Table of Specifications for Initial Reading Decoding.

CONTENT	BEHAVIOR				
	Identification	Production			
	A. Acquisition	B. Acquisition	C. Fluency	D. Application	E. Generalization
1. *Consonants*	1A	1B	1C	1D	1E
2. *Vowels (short)*	2A	2B	2C	2D	2E
3. *CVC words (cat, pat, mat)*	3A	3B	3C	3D	3E
4. *CVCE words (cake)*	4A	4B	4C	4D	4E
5. *CCVC words (blab)*	5A	5B	5C	5D	5E

Sample Objectives:

1A   Students will correctly point to the correct consonant from a list of 10 distractor consonants with 100% accuracy after hearing the teacher say either the consonant name or sound.

2B   Students will correctly say the vowel name and short sound upon request with 100% accuracy.

3C   Given a list of CVCE words, students will read each word accurately within 1 second.

4D   Given a passage from the reading series, students will orally read the passage and pronounce each CVCE word accurately.

5E   Given a passage from the weekly newspaper, students will pronounce all CCVC words correctly.

Tables of Specifications

When completing either a task analysis or conceptual analysis, it may be beneficial to construct a table of specifications. A table of specifications subdivides content and behavior and can actually be a composite of the task/conceptual analysis, the expected levels of behavior (learning), the types of learning (e.g., discriminations, facts, rules, procedures), the performance criteria, and the conditions under which the behavior is expected to occur. In other words, a table of specifications organizes behavioral objectives. Some educators (e.g., Bloom, Hastings, & Madaus, 1971; Howell & Kaplan, 1980) have proposed that these tables be used to design test items. The purpose of using tables of specifications is to enable teachers to evaluate their students' work more systematically. This table of specifications also can function as a record-keeping and lesson-planning device, because the combination of subdivisions of behavior and subdivisions of content form tasks or instructional objectives. Table 2.1 provides an example of a table of specifications for beginning reading decoding instruction. Content is arranged in order down the vertical axis, and behavior is arranged in order across the horizontal axis. For instance, the table of specifications subdivides the basic tasks involved in decoding skills into:

1. consonants

2. vowels

3. CVC words (consonant–vowel–consonant words, such as *cat*)

4. CVCe words (consonant–vowel–consonant–silent *e* words, such as *cake*)

5. CCVC words (consonant–consonant–vowel–consonant words, such as *slap*)

Concomitantly, the levels of behavior and learning are subdivided along the horizontal axis into (a) identification behavior at an acquisition level, (b) production behavior at an acquisition level, (c) production behavior at a fluency level, (d) production behavior at an application level, and (e) production behavior at a generalization level. As seen from Table 2.1, each cell can be made to represent an instructional objective that specifies the tasks and behaviors required. In order for the objectives to be complete, teachers need to supply the conditions under which the behavior is desired, as well as the performance criteria that are considered necessary for success. For example, examine cell 1A. Here the content, consonants, is combined with the acquisition level of identification behavior. This means that an instructional objective similar to the following can be generated at the intersection of that content and behavior: "Students will correctly point to (notice that *point to* is an identification level of behavior) the correct consonant (the content level) from a list of 10 distractor consonants with 100% accuracy after hearing the teacher say either the consonant name or sound." Note that the performance criterion of 100% has been incorporated into the objective and that only accuracy and not fluency behavior is emphasized.

Now, examine cell 1B. This cell designates the same content (consonants) but at a different level of behavior. This time the objective is "Students will correctly say (produce) the consonant name and/or sound upon teacher request with 100% accuracy." Note that the only change was the substitution of production behavior for the identification behavior used in cell 1A. Additionally, notice that the objective for cell 1C would add fluency criteria to the objective that was designed for cell 1B, as in the following: "Given a list of consonants, students will say each sound or name each sound accurately within 1 second upon teacher request." Notice that cell 1D alters the behavior to the application level. A good example of the objective might be "Given a listing of words containing CVC (consonant–vowel–consonant) letter patterns, the student will accurately say (produce) all the consonant sounds." Typically, when this objective is expected, teachers also will have introduced instruction on vowels; consequently, the application level of behavior would incorporate the correct reading of the entire CVC word. Cell 1E adds the generalization component to the objective. A good generalization objective might be similar to the following: "Given a newspaper, a basal reader, or a common product label, students will be able to say the consonant sounds and/or names."

Incorporating all of the instructional objectives above, teachers can design lessons to teach students each one of the objectives. Sometimes it may be desirable to subdivide the amount of the content included in each objective into either smaller or larger chunks. In other words, based upon the students' needs, teachers may find that they need to cover fewer consonants in a lesson. In fact, most teachers probably introduce only a few, rather than all, consonants at a time. Additionally, teachers may find that their students can proceed to producing the behaviors rather than spending the time on practicing identification. As will be seen throughout the remainder of this text, it is assumed that teacher judgment will play a critical role in the design and delivery of effective instruction. Several tables subdividing content and behavior are provided in this text as models for teachers to use in altering instruction to meet their students' needs. It is recommended that teachers use this systematic procedure to examine precisely what they are teaching. However, the tables of specification that are presented in this text are intended to be used as models for the design of instructional units based upon student needs. It is not recommended that teachers simply adopt the tables as presented, unless they match students' needs.

During initial planning phases of instruction, teachers may wish to transfer the instructional objective to a lesson plan format similar to the one in Figure 2.8. Notice that this form also includes a column of time allocated for each objective. More examples of tables of specification and lesson plans are given later in the chapters on specific curriculum areas (see Chapters 5 through 8, 10, and 11).

Evaluation Procedures and Decision-Making

Formative evaluation, discussed in the following chapter, is critical for teachers to use to determine whether their instruction is having the desired effect. Since virtually any instruction is likely to produce *some* effect, it is important for teachers to develop certain standards by which they can determine whether their students will be able to meet long-term objectives. In order to accomplish this, teachers must specify the steps necessary for meeting long-term objectives and determine the rate at which content should be covered. If content is not being mastered at an appropriate rate, teachers must modify their instructional procedures to increase the rate of learning.

Date: _____   Student: _____
Session # _____   Group(s): _____

Schedule of Instruction (Allocated Time)	Objective	Anticipated Teacher Behaviors	Anticipated Student Behaviors	Materials	Evaluation Procedure	Instructional Decisions

FIGURE 2.8. Sample lesson plan.

In order to modify instructional procedures effectively, teachers must carefully examine their current instructional considerations. These considerations include:

1. amount of engaged time on task;

2. rate at which content is covered;

3. instructional procedures, including review activities, type and length of teacher presentation, questioning and feedback procedures, type and length of practice activities, method of instructional delivery, and type of classroom management;

4. curricular materials and objectives;

5. instructional strategies used, such as rehearsal or elaborations;

6. procedures to increase motivation, such as verbal praise, class privileges, or tangibles; and

7. evaluation procedures.

First, teachers need to determine if each of these aspects is accounted for in their current lessons. If they are not, teachers need to design and add the missing element(s) to their planning and delivery of lessons. If all of the elements are accounted for, teachers need to determine whether any element can be altered to increase the rate of learning. The most obvious modification is to increase the amount of engaged time-on-task. However, engaged time may be optimal, but specific allocations of engaged time may not be optimal. For example, teachers may find that students are spending more time than necessary on seatwork activities, while time allocated to teacher presentation is insufficient for covering desired amounts of content; or teachers may find that allocations are optimal, but students are not catching on to new content at a sufficient rate. If this is the case a modification in the type of instructional strategy may be called for. Furthermore, the instructional procedures may have become monotonous, and, consequently, student motivation may have decreased. In such a case, alterations in presentation or reinforcement procedures may be optimal modifications.

Finally, it is important that the evaluation procedures themselves be evaluated. For example, learning may be occurring, but the evaluation procedures being used may not be sensitive enough to evaluate the behavior being observed. It is also possible that the evaluation procedure being used does not match the level of behavior specified in the objectives. For example, students may be taught simply to identify correctly spelled words and yet are asked to produce correctly spelled words in writing for spelling tests.

Task Analysis and Meaningfulness

Effective special education teachers are highly skilled at subdividing learning and behavioral tasks, as well as curriculum elements, into component parts. There are some important advantages to this type of task-analytic teaching. First, it allows teachers to know exactly what they are teaching and what learners are expected to learn. Second, it allows for direct, objective evaluation of learner progress. Third, it allows teachers and students to proceed along a specified sequence of task difficulty. Finally, it allows teachers to specify precisely where difficulty occurs and determine exactly what appropriate remedial techniques should be applied. This type of teaching, based on task analysis, specific objectives, and continuous monitoring of progress toward larger goals and objectives, is commonly employed in special education and, correctly applied, has been highly successful.

Nevertheless, there are some potential disadvantages to this model. The tables of specification described previously and used throughout this text are intended as guidelines to facilitate decision-making in special education. However, as tasks are broken down into subcomponents, they may become less meaningful to learners and, as such, more difficult to teach. Research over the past several years has demonstrated the necessity of preserving meaning in curriculum. Therefore, it is important for teachers to consider carefully the role of meaningfulness of the curriculum when applying table of specifications objectives. For example, when particular phonics rules are taught, learners always should be aware of the purpose of learning these rules. Additionally, they should apply them to words, and the meanings of those words, as soon as possible. Likewise, when early math skills or facts are taught, students should be aware of the purpose of the instruction and begin to apply this new learning in meaningful, problem-solving contexts as soon as possible. Finally, teachers should integrate learning across traditional discipline areas as application and generalization objectives. For instance, reading and language arts should employ similar materials whenever possible. Students can, for example, write stories from books they have read or employ their math skills on vocational tasks. Overall, the most effective instruction is that which is able to use careful task-analysis techniques without sacrificing the meaningfulness of the learning tasks.

Summary of Instructional Design

Instructional design encompasses all of the relevant teaching variables. Appropriate instructional design is based on long- and short-term objectives and incorporates both levels (identification/production, accuracy, fluency, application, and generalization) and types (discrimination, fact, rule, concept, procedural) of learning as well as teacher-effectiveness variables. An effectively designed instructional sequence includes goals and objectives, appropriate instructional methods and materials, and the use of effective procedures for evaluating the success of instruction.

RELEVANT RESEARCH AND RESOURCES

Much of Chapter 2 is concerned with establishing a model for instructional design. This model is based on previously applied and validated models of instructional design. One of the most widely used texts on instructional objectives is that of Mager (1962). The model of discriminating levels of learning is based generally on the model provided by Haring, Lovitt, Hansen, and Eaton (1978). A research-based orientation to different types of learning, such as discrimination, conceptual, factual, etc., can be found in any textbook on learning theory. A widely read text on learning is Bower and Hilgard (1981). A review of research on types of learning and learning disabilities is provided by Scruggs (1988). Much of the research that validates the application of this model is described at the end of Chapter 1. Problems in generalization of learned behavior and strategies for facilitating generalization outcomes are described by Scruggs and Mastropieri (1984b, 1994) and Stokes and Baer (1977). Information on tables of specifications is provided by Bloom, Hastings, and Madaus (1971) and Howell and Kaplan (1980). Information on instructional design is provided by Gagne (1965, 1970) and Gagne and Briggs (1974). Texts on curriculum-based assessment include Howell and Morehead (1987) and Salvia and Hughes (1990). Recent articles on IEPs include Smith (1990a, 1990b). Majsterek, Wilson, and Mandlebaum (1990) provided guidelines for evaluating IEP software.

Computer Software and Technology

Software that may be helpful in generating student IEPs is available from Western Psychological Services (WPS Automated IEP System) and from EBSCO Curriculum Materials (IEP Generator). See Appendix B for a list of addresses of producers and distributors of software and curricular materials.

CHAPTER 3

✥ ✥ ✥

Evaluation

THIS CHAPTER IS CONCERNED WITH THE EVALUATION OF BOTH INSTRUC-
tion and student behavior. Evaluation, as stated earlier, is a critical component of effective instruction. It can be further subdivided into *summative*
and *formative* evaluation. Summative evaluation is typically given only
once or twice in a school year, while formative evaluation is given frequently throughout the year. Additionally, the types of evaluation measures
or tests used can be norm-referenced or criterion-referenced measures. These
types of tests provide valuable but different information for special educators (see Figure 3.1). A variety of procedures for collecting information for
both types of tests have also been developed. These procedures include
development of permanent products, such as probes and paper and pencil
tasks, and recording of behavior through procedures that include direct
observation, continuous recording, time sampling, and duration and event
recording. A probe is a relatively short test that requires only a few minutes

Features	Norm-Referenced Tests	Criterion-Referenced Tests
Compares	Observed behavior to behavior of others.	Behavior to an existing standard (criterion).
Form of information	Percentiles and grade equivalents.	Proportions of standards mastered.
Common uses	Helpful for classifying and labeling students.	Helpful for designing and deliver-ing instruction.
	Can be used to help evaluate edu-cational programs.	Can be used to help evaluate spe-cific educational treatments.
Limitations	Must be reliable and valid.	Must be reliable and valid.
Frequency of usage	Commonly administered once or twice a year.	Commonly administered frequently throughout the year.

FIGURE 3.1.   Features of norm-referenced and criterion-referenced tests.

to complete; for instance, a listing of multiplication facts 0 through 9 could be considered a probe. Once completed by students, the resulting probe plus written answers can be called a permanent product. Permanent products can be collected, saved in a portfolio, and referred back to over time. Additionally, many record-keeping techniques have been used to successfully monitor progress. Such techniques include a variety of graphic displays, including precision teaching charts. Each of these evaluation procedures are presented in the following sections.

RELIABILITY AND VALIDITY

In order to be valuable, all tests must possess certain psychometric properties, such as reliability and validity. All tests must be reliable and valid, or they should not be used. Reliability can be determined by test–retest reliability procedures or by internal consistency procedures. Both procedures determine whether or not a test is providing the same information consistently and/or over time. For example, test–retest reliability describes whether a test provides similar results over a 2- or 3-week time period. Test performance needs to be stable over relatively short periods of time, or the test is not very reliable. Reliability would be considered very low, for example, if the same achievement test were administered 2 weeks apart and yielded dramatically different results (e.g., 30th percentile scores and 90th percentile scores for the first and second test administrations, respectively).

Internal consistency describes whether all of the individual test items are measuring the same "construct," such as personality or intelligence. In determining internal consistency, statistical procedures are used to determine whether, for example, all of the odd-numbered items are highly related to all of the even-numbered items. For example, if students scored at the eighth-grade level on the odd-numbered items and at the second-grade level on the even-numbered items on a test, that test would have low internal consistency. The teacher can determine the reliability of norm-referenced tests by examining the tests' technical manuals. Acceptable total-test reliability coefficients (scores) should be in the .80s and .90s. When scores are lower than that, tests should be viewed as suspect.

Validity helps to determine whether tests are measuring what they purport or intend to measure. Validity, for example, ensures that tests are measuring constructs, such as intelligence or reading achievement. Validity is typically determined by assessing performance on one test with performance on a highly related test. If both tests are considered valid, scores obtained on both tests will be comparable. For example, suppose that two reading comprehension tests are available. If both tests have high validity, students' performance on both tests should be very similar. Again, test validity coefficients should be available in the technical manuals that accompany tests. Both high reliability and validity are necessary prerequisites for tests to be considered adequate for use. It is mandatory for teachers to examine the reliability and validity coefficients of a test prior to its adoption. Additionally, teachers should question the reliability and validity of tests that have been administered by other school personnel. For example, several tests that purport to diagnose learning disabilities have extremely low reliability and validity. Consequently, little faith can be placed on these tests' results.

NORM-REFERENCED TESTS

Norm-referenced tests are tests that have been standardized, or "normed," on a large sample of students. Students' scores are compared to the scores of this larger normative sample. When these tests are administered, the results are interpreted on a comparative basis. In other words, it is possible to determine how well a particular student performed in relation to the larger sample. Intelligence tests, personality tests, achievement tests, and more recently, competency tests are typically norm-referenced tests. Such tests provide valuable information on an individual student's performance as compared with the general population's performance. These test results allow educators to make judgments concerning how well their student, classroom, school, or state is doing in relation to other students, classrooms, schools, and states. Typically, such norm-referenced achievement tests are administered on a yearly basis. The results can be used to assist in making policy decisions, such as the type of curricular materials and the type of in-service teacher-training programs that could be implemented on a school-district-wide basis.

Norm-referenced tests have been used mostly as summative evaluation measures. In other words, norm-referenced tests are usually administered only at the beginning or the end of the school year. When used in such a manner, the results summarize students' performance up to a certain point in time rather than assist in guiding effective instruction throughout the school year. However, as will be discussed later, any test can be normed (even criterion-referenced tests); therefore, it is incorrect to assume that all norm-referenced tests are summative tests.

The purpose of this section has not been to provide extensive information on norm-referenced tests, but to present a summary of the following facts:

1. Norm-referenced tests provide information that compares an individual's performance against a normative performance.

2. Norm-referenced tests are typically summative measures that provide a final or summary evaluation of performance.

3. High reliability and validity are critical for tests to be considered adequate.

CRITERION-REFERENCED TESTS

Criterion-referenced tests are tests that assess performance in relation to a particular criterion or curriculum. Criterion-referenced tests typically correspond to a particular set of skills or a specific curriculum. Therefore, a score on this type of test specifies how much of the curriculum or skill has been mastered, regardless of how well all the other students have performed. These types of tests can provide teachers with information on how well students have mastered the content covered to date, how rapidly content is being covered and mastered, how many students have mastered the objectives to date, and which students have not mastered which objectives.

Criterion-referenced tests are usually administered on a formative basis (regularly or continuously), rather than on a yearly or summative basis. If criterion-referenced tests are designed to correspond with a specific curriculum, they are referred to as curriculum-based tests. Sometimes these tests are used as placement tests at the beginning of the school term or year. In other words, teachers can administer a curriculum-based U.S. history pretest to determine where in the U.S. history curriculum they should begin to introduce new content. For example, if all of the students have previously learned and mastered the content of the discovery of America and pre-Revolutionary War units, instruction can begin at the Revolutionary War unit. Such curriculum-based tests can be used to monitor students' progress throughout instruction and to guide instructional practices throughout the year. For example, suppose a series of tests that correspond to the entire U.S. history curriculum had been developed. Assume that the items on these tests directly assess all of the content that is considered necessary to know upon completion of the U.S. history course. Then, as content was introduced and covered, formative tests could be administered to determine students' progress in mastering that particular content. Additionally, as mentioned in previous chapters, teachers could keep systematic records of their own teaching performance during these lessons, such as engaged time on task, types of guided and independent practice activities, and types of questioning and feedback activities. Results on the formatively administered curriculum-based tests can provide teachers with information on student progress and teaching effectiveness, and effective instructional decisions can be made based upon actual data (records or performance).

Many special educators have recently suggested that most evaluation in special education classes should be curriculum-based (Fuchs & Fuchs, 1986a, 1986b). It makes sense to link the scope and sequence of the objectives in specific content areas with curriculum-based tests. Some school districts have begun to develop curriculum-based tests to match their curriculum areas. Such tests can assist teachers not only in linking their instruction to curriculum but also in guiding the instructional decision-making process.

Curriculum-based tests also should have good reliability and validity data and be standardized or normed. As the development of curriculum-based tests expands, it is likely that techniques for assessing the reliability and validity of these tests will develop. It would be very useful for teachers to know, for example, that students have mastered half of the necessary objectives in a content area and that all seventh graders typically reach that point in mastery of the curriculum at about that same time of year.

Curriculum-based tests can also be designed to match IEP objectives and can then be used to designate when those objectives have been met. Ideally, IEP objectives will correspond closely to regular education objectives and will, therefore, facilitate the mainstreaming process. When students master those objectives, they will be ready for mainstreaming.

Additionally, curriculum-based tests can be devised for virtually any curriculum area, ranging from reading and writing to vocational skill areas to the social skills area. The first consideration in developing a series of curriculum-based tests is to precisely define the curriculum in terms of specific behavioral objectives and into a scope and sequence (or hierarchy or order in which the objectives should be met). Once this is completed, individual tests need to be designed to match each objective or series of objectives. Recall that since objectives specify the expected behavior, the conditions under which the behavior should be performed, and the performance criteria, designing a test is simply a matter of generating a pool of items that test each objective. It is critical that the behavior, conditions, and performance criteria in the objective match those of the test item. In other words, if the objective specifies production behavior at the fluency level of learning, then test items for this objective must also require production behavior at the fluency level of learning. If application or generalization behavior is specified in the objective, then test items also need to assess application or generalization.

Several researchers in special education, including Fuchs (1986), Fuchs and Fuchs (1986a, 1986b), and Deno (1986), have conducted research on issues related to curriculum-based measurement for over a decade. Results of these research efforts have been consistently positive. Some guidelines for constructing and using curriculum-based devices are briefly described below.

Constructing a Curriculum-Based Measure

The first step in constructing a curriculum-based assessment is to select a target curriculum area. It is generally a good idea to begin with a content area that most of the students take. Typically, special educators select reading first; however, any content area is suitable. For the remainder of this discussion, assume that a basal reading series such as the *Houghton Mifflin Reading Series* (1976) has been selected.

The second step involves the random selection of reading passages from the targeted reading series. Any passage can be chosen if it contains typical narrative material. It is generally wise to avoid selecting passages that contain an overabundance of dialogue or atypical material such as poems. Each passage should contain at least 100 words. At some of the lower reading levels, such as the primer and preprimer levels, this may be difficult if not impossible; however, alternative suggestions for these levels will be provided later. At the third-grade level and beyond, it is fairly easy to find appropriate target passages.

If the purpose of designing curriculum-based measures includes both placement and monitoring progress, a minimum of 10 passages should be selected from the beginning third of a level, 10 from the middle third of a level, and 10 from the final third of a level. If teachers find that their long-term goals for the majority of their students consistently fall within a particular third of a level, it is recommended that two or three times as many passages be selected from that portion of the text. At present, there is no standard for a precise number of passages, but it is important that an adequate number be selected so that a sufficient number of different, randomly selected measures can be administered while progress is being monitored.

Once the passages have been chosen, two copies of each passage should be made and each copy labeled. A good labeling system includes a symbol representing the curriculum series (e.g., HM if Houghton Mifflin were selected), a symbol representing the level of the text (e.g., A through O for Houghton Mifflin), a symbol identifying the particular section of the level (e.g., B for beginning third; M for middle third; and F for final third), and a number representing the ordinal relation within a particular level for each test (e.g., 1, 2, 3, etc.). If the labeling system is implemented at the beginning, time and effort are saved later.

Each labeled 100-word passage can be marked off with slash marks (/ /). If the 100-word passage ends in the middle of a sentence, a bracket ( ]) can be placed at the end of that sentence. Recall that two photocopies of each passage were made. One copy will be the teacher's copy; the other will be the student's copy. Some teachers like to count the number of words per line for each passage and write that number along the left side of the passage on the teacher's copy. As will be discussed later, this may or may not be necessary.

Some educators consider the process of test construction for reading to be complete at this time; however, other educators have emphasized that each passage should also include approximately five comprehension and recall items. It has been recommended that the comprehension items include the following:

1. Three factual or literal recall items. (Factual recall items require students to answer with information that is explicitly stated in the passage.)

2. One sequential factual item. (Sequential factual items require students to respond with information that is explicitly stated but

also requires thinking about the order of the events in the passage.)

3. One inferential recall item. (Inferential items require students to respond with information that is not stated explicitly but rather is implied or implicit within the text.)

Specific examples of how to construct these types of questions are discussed in Chapter 5. However, if comprehension items are desired, both the questions and appropriate responses should be written on the teacher's copy of the tests. These types of questions can provide information on students' recall. The next section briefly discusses how to administer the curriculum-based measures.

Administering a Curriculum-Based Measure

If the curriculum-based test is being used for initial placement, randomly select a passage from the third of the text level in which the student is expected to function well. If, however, the test is being used to monitor student progress, randomly select a passage from the section of the text that contains the long-term objective for that student. Then, place the student's copy in front of the student and place the teacher's copy in front of the teacher. (Acetate can be placed over the teacher's copy to facilitate reuse of tests.) Say to the student, "When I say go, begin reading aloud at the top of this page. [Point.] Try to read each word all the way down to this slash mark. [Point.] Ready? Go." Begin timing the student with a stopwatch. Make a slash mark at the end of 1 minute, stop timing, and record the total amount of time in seconds taken to read the 100-word selection. During the reading, circle any decoding errors that the student makes. If there are comprehension questions that accompany the passage, teachers should now verbally ask students to answer each item. Responses can be recorded as correct or incorrect.

Scoring a Curriculum-Based Measure

To compute the student's reading accuracy rate per minute, first determine accuracy by taking the total number of words read correctly (e.g., here, assume 94) and dividing that number by the total number of words read (e.g., in this case, $94 \div 100 = 94\%$). Second, determine reading accuracy per minute by multiplying the accuracy percentage by 60 seconds and dividing by the total number of seconds required to complete the reading task. In the above example, $.94 \times 60 = 56.4$, divided by 95 seconds equals .59.

If, on the other hand, you stop the student after 1 minute, you simply count the number of words read correctly within that 1 minute. Advantages of this procedure are that the student is required to read for only 1 minute and the teacher does not have to perform as many calculations to determine the accuracy rate per minute. One disadvantage, however, is that the student may have read an insufficient amount of content to answer any recall or comprehension questions.

After either procedure, a student's accuracy performance should be graphed. Teachers are better able to observe students' performance and progress over time when the data are displayed in a graphic presentation (refer to Figure 3.2 as an example). In order to monitor progress effectively, it has been recommended that teachers administer one of these curriculum-based tests once or twice a week. Recall that it was recommended that the tests be (a) selected from the long-term goal level of the text and (b) selected randomly. In many instances, students have been taught to graph their own performance data. This accomplishes two purposes: teachers save time and students become aware of their own progress toward long-term goals.

When initial placement in the curriculum series is the major purpose of assessment, teachers should assess student performance at several dif-

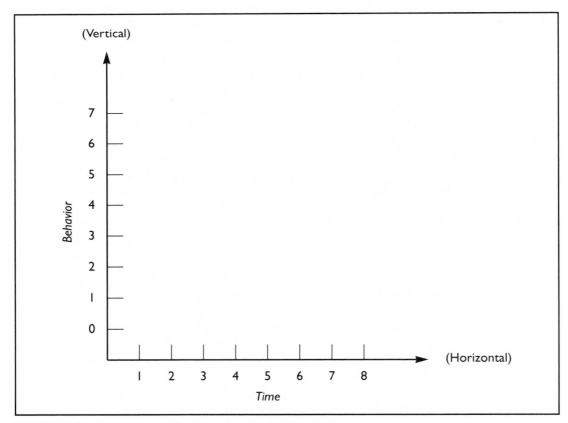

FIGURE 3.2. Typical layout of a chart reporting behavioral data.

ferent levels for 3 consecutive days. General rules to use as guidelines for placement in the curriculum include:

1. Examine the median (middle) accuracy score for the 3-day performance in all levels assessed.

2. Select the level in which reading accuracy is 95% or better.

3. Select the level in which students in Grades 1 and 2 read 20 to 29 words per minute correctly or students in Grades 3 through 6 read 30 to 39 words per minute correctly.

4. Select the level in which the average comprehension score is 80%.

Similar procedures can be established for all curricular domains. In some school districts, special educators have worked cooperatively together to develop measures for specific content areas.

Little research currently exists to document the optimal length of curriculum-based tests. Many educators advocate short, frequent tests rather than longer, infrequent tests. The main advantage of short, frequent tests is better knowledge of daily to weekly student performance and progress, which, in turn, may help keep students and teachers on top of their performance. More specific information regarding the design of formative tests and concomitant decision-making rules and error-analysis procedures is presented in each content area chapter.

Portfolio and Performance Assessment

Two types of assessment that have recently received much attention are portfolio and performance-based assessment. Both of these are highly relevant to curriculum-based assessment. Student portfolios include permanent products from the student's work throughout the school year, including audiotapes of oral reading, samples of written work, samples of laboratory booklets and notes, summaries of student performance, copies of summative exams, teacher observations, and videotapes of student presentations or demonstrations. All these products should be evaluated with respect to some predetermined standard (performance criteria), so that progress throughout the school year can be documented and instruction can be modified if satisfactory progress is not being made.

Performance assessment refers to assessment of student performance with respect to a specific, usually hands-on, curriculum. Performance assessment is particularly appropriate for hands-on science, math, social studies, or vocational curricula. In a performance assessment, students demonstrate what they have learned using "real" materials, rather than paper and pencil. They can, for example, complete electrical circuits in science, solve math problems using base ten blocks, construct a model of an urban center, or solve a problem using drafting materials.

Performance assessment can be particularly useful in special education settings, where many students have difficulties with paper and pencil tasks and also may exhibit problems with test-taking skills (see Chapter 9) used on traditional tests. Performance assessment allows students to exhibit their acquired skills (on the application or generalization level) without overreliance on language or literacy skills when these are not primarily being tested. As with portfolio assessment, teachers must evaluate performance assessment results with respect to specific criteria.

PROCEDURES FOR COLLECTING FORMATIVE DATA

Much data (information) collected in classroom situations is referred to as behavioral data, meaning observable activity that the student engages in. Generally, such data are collected one of two ways, which are described in this section. The first method for collecting data is by direct observation of the student. The second involves the scoring of permanent products, by which is meant things such as completed worksheets and tape-recorded students' responses.

Direct Observation

Direct observation procedures are generally employed for behaviors that are easily observed in classroom situations and for which there is no written product. However, for such observations to be accurate and systematic, it is important for the target behavior to be precisely *operationalized* prior to observation. After operationalizing a target behavior, teachers select one of several procedures appropriate for observing and recording these behaviors. Operationalizing behavior and appropriate recording systems are described below.

Operationalizing behavior

If a target behavior is not described precisely enough, it may not be recorded accurately. For instance, on-task behavior might be defined differently by different people, which could result in different operational descriptions. One way of defining on-task is "students visually or manually engaged with classroom materials." Such a description effectively operationalizes the behavior so that it can be observed and recorded accurately. Although different observers might define on-task differently, the above definition describes on-task in such a way that different individuals could record the occurrence of the behavior similarly.

Behavior	Sample Operational Definition*
Talking out	Student speaks to another student, the class in general, or the teacher without being called upon.
On-task	Student's eyes engaged on teacher or task. Manual engagement with classroom materials and writing utensils when appropriate.
Teasing	Student verbally referring to another student in a derogatory manner; inappropriate and unsolicited physical contact with another student.
Verbal courtesy	Student says "please" upon making a request and "thank you" upon receiving a favorable response to a request.
Arguing	Student questions a teacher's direction or judgment with expressions such as "Why?", "For what?", "No, I didn't," and "So?"
Good sitting	Student in seat with feet flat on the floor in front of desk and sitting up straight with body centered with respect to the desk and arms on desk top.
Daydreaming	Student's eyes looking away from academic task and not directly focused on any classroom object or person; no normal engagement with academic task.
Positive social interaction	Verbal exchange in which student comments favorably on another student or positively describes a shared experience, and student's comments receive favorable verbal response.

*Other definitions are also possible.

FIGURE 3.3. Operational definitions.

Different definitions of on-task may exist, however, depending on the characteristics of the task and the expectations placed on the student. For instance, during a handwriting activity, it may be appropriate for students' eyes and hands to be in contact with writing materials at all times (except to ask relevant questions or attend to teacher feedback). During a writing composition activity, however, students may need to reflect upon their writing without being physically in contact with writing materials. Any operationalization of this type of on-task behavior needs to reflect the specific task demands. Furthermore, some students may have enough initial difficulty staying on-task to make a less restrictive definition necessary at first. Such an operationalization could be "hands, feet and eyes directed away from other students and all verbalization directly relevant to the task." In all cases, it is important for teachers to precisely specify the nature of the behavior to be observed. Additional examples of operational definitions are provided in Figure 3.3. Teachers know that the behavior has been effectively operationalized when two different observers independently record the same behavior of the same student.

Recording Procedures

Once behavior has been operationalized, it cannot be recorded until an appropriate recording procedure has been chosen. These procedures, which include (a) continuous records, (b) duration recording, (c) interval recording, and (d) time sampling, are described below. Examples of these procedures are in Figure 3.4.

Continuous Records

Sometimes teachers wish to have a record of all behavior that a student exhibits during a specific period of time. For instance, a teacher may know that a certain student often has problems getting along with other students during recess periods but does not know specifically what is happening during these periods that is related to the problem. Such descriptive records of all student behavior are called continuous records.

Recording Procedure	Circumstances	Examples
Event	Behaviors are discrete.	Swearing
	Behaviors last similar amounts of time.	Homework assignments completed
	Knowledge of total frequency is desired.	Tardy to class
		Says "please"
Duration	Behaviors vary in length.	Out of seat
	Knowledge of total time is desired.	Off task
		Minutes in transition
	An observer's total attention is available.	Time in restroom
		Tantruming
Interval	Behaviors may vary in length.	Sitting quietly
	Total duration is not as important as estimate of percent of total time.	On task
		Appropriate social interaction
Time Sampling	Total duration is not as important as estimate of percent of total time.	On task
		Time spent in various activities
	Several students are observed at one time.	In seat
	Behaviors vary in length.	Cooperative play

FIGURE 3.4. Sample recording procedures.

When teachers take continuous records, they record all observed behavior exhibited by a specific student during a specific time period. All behaviors recorded are also described with respect to the time the behavior occurred. A continuous record may be written somewhat like the following:

10:09 a.m. Student takes one worksheet, passes remaining worksheets to student seated in back.

10:10 a.m. Student takes pencil from desk and begins writing on worksheet.

10:12 a.m. Student looks around the classroom, makes a face at another student (who does not respond), returns to work.

10:15 a.m. Student opens desk and manipulates objects in desk.

10:17 a.m. Upon prompt from teacher, student returns to work.

10:20 a.m. Student still working.

10:21 a.m. Student begins kicking the desk in front of student. Student in front whispers, "Stop it."

10:22 a.m. Student replies, "What?" and returns to work.

Such a record can be helpful when detailed knowledge of student behavior is desired. Continuous records can also be helpful in certain circumstances to demonstrate that IEP objectives have been met. For example, suppose a student had the following IEP objective: "Student will ignore inappropriate teasing by others 90% of the time." Continuous records could help indicate when teasing occurred and exactly how the student responded.

One difficulty with continuous recording, as with many of the observation procedures described in this chapter, is that it demands the undivided attention of the observer. If the teacher is also the observer, the observation process can detract from other, equally important classroom activities. However, there are some procedures for making the observation process less demanding of teachers' time. These include the use of peers, classroom aides, volunteers, other teachers, or school personnel in the collection of observational data. If such observers are used, however, they need to understand exactly how the behavior is operationalized and how it is to be recorded. Another way of making observations more efficient is by using videotape-recording equipment. Not only can behavior be observed and recorded at a later date, but target students can be shown their own behavior on tape. If the behavior is largely oral, such as talking out of turn, the behavior could be tape-recorded for later entry into a continuous record.

Continuous records can be helpful when teachers want more information regarding a range of student behaviors. The procedures that follow are appropriate when teachers want detailed information on specific, operationalized behaviors.

Frequency Recording

Sometimes it is important to know the number of times a particular behavior is occurring. For instance, teachers may want information regarding the number of times specific students speak without raising their hands. To record this type of behavior, teachers can simply tally the number of occurrences of talking out-of-turn. For example, if students "talked out" 10 times in an hour on one day and 15 times in 2 hours the following day, their rate of talking out decreased the second day (10 times per hour versus 7.5 times per hour). If the time of observation is not the same each day, the behavior must be divided by the amount of time in the observation. On the other hand, if the amount of observation time remains constant, no calculations are necessary.

Other behaviors that may lend themselves to frequency recording include questions, trips to the bathroom, homework assignments completed, temper tantrums, socially appropriate verbalizations, or occasions that students are out-of-seat. It is important to note that frequency recording provides no information regarding the level of intensity of the behavior or the length of time the behavior was exhibited. For instance, in counting frequency of out-of-seat behaviors, it is important that such behaviors are generally about the same duration (length of time), such as the amount of time to get a drink or sharpen a pencil. For frequency recording to accurately represent target behaviors, the behaviors being tallied must all be highly similar. For example, out-of-seat behavior may occur for 30 seconds during one event and 30 minutes during the next. If this problem occurs, some other recording procedure may be more efficient.

Duration Recording

Duration recording is used when teachers are interested in the length of time in which a behavior occurs. For instance, teachers may not be interested simply in whether a student was out-of-seat but also in the total length of time a student was out-of-seat. To conduct duration recording, the targeted behavior is operationalized (for instance, out-of-seat is defined as the seat of the student's pants not being in direct contact with the seat of the desk), and the teacher measures the amount of out-of-seat time exhibited using a stopwatch or other timing device. Such a procedure can be effective when the frequency of events is less important than the total time of occurrence of the behavior. The use of duration recording is appropriate when teachers would rather know how much time the student was out-of-seat than know how many times the student was out-of-seat. Other classroom behaviors that may be suitable for duration recording are minutes tardy and minutes off-task.

Interval Recording

Some teachers or other personnel may wish to record the behavior of several students at one time. This type of recording can be very difficult if event or duration procedures are used. One alternative is the use of interval recording. To use interval recording, the behavior to be observed is first operationalized. For instance, kicking could be operationalized as "student's foot in contact with forward desk, delivered with sufficient force to register sound at a radius of 20 feet." (Other operational definitions of kicking are, of course, possible). The observer then sets an interval for which the occurrence or nonoccurrence of the behavior is to be recorded. As an example, suppose the interval is 15 seconds. Using a clock or stopwatch, the observer records whether the behavior (in this case, kicking) occurs or does not occur during the interval. This occurrence or nonoccurrence is then recorded on a recording sheet that was developed prior to the observation session (see Figure 3.5). During interval recording, the total number of occurrences is not noted, as it is in event recording. Only the fact that the behavior has occurred at all during the interval is noted. If the behavior does not occur, the observer records a zero or another figure denoting nonoccurrence and moves on to the next interval, but this is a cumbersome procedure as it requires the observer to observe both the student and the clock. A procedure that is generally considered more optimal is to tape-record a series of quiet beeps or clicks at the end of each prespecified interval. With headphones, the observer can hear these beeps and know when each interval has ended.

Interval recording can be helpful when the behaviors being observed are variable in duration. For example, "talking out" could be operationalized as "any verbalization directed toward another student without explicit permission from the teacher." Such talking-out behavior could conceivably occur either as a simple exclamation or an extended discussion. Using interval recording procedures, the observer simply records whether or not the behavior has occurred during each interval. Occurrence of the behavior across several intervals may suggest extended conversation, while separate, distinct occurrences are recorded in separate intervals.

Interval data are generally summarized as percent data. For example, if 240 intervals of 15 seconds are recorded (that is, a 60-minute sample), and the student exhibited talking-out behavior during 90 intervals, the corresponding score could be summarized as 37.5% (90 ÷ 240) of total intervals. Generally, the reliability of such observations are computed as interobserver reliability. In the case of interval recording, two observers would independently observe the same behavior in the same student at the same time. If the behavior has been well operationalized and the observations are accu-

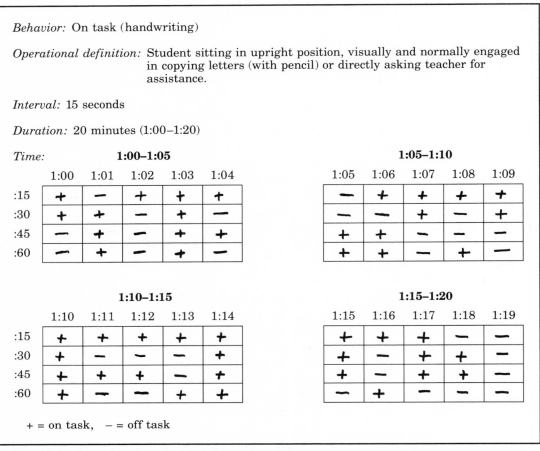

Behavior: On task (handwriting)

Operational definition: Student sitting in upright position, visually and normally engaged in copying letters (with pencil) or directly asking teacher for assistance.

Interval: 15 seconds

Duration: 20 minutes (1:00–1:20)

Time: **1:00–1:05** **1:05–1:10**

+ = on task, – = off task

FIGURE 3.5. Recording sheet for interval recording.

rate, the two observers should agree on most observations. Usually, such agreement is recorded as:

$$\frac{\text{Number of agreements}}{\substack{\text{Total number of observations}\\ \text{(Agreements and disagreements)}}}$$

The resulting proportion is then expressed as a percent. For instance, in the above example, if two observers agreed on 220 of the 240 items but disagreed on 20 items, the corresponding interrater reliability could be computed as:

$$\frac{220}{220 + 20} \quad = \quad \frac{220}{240} \quad = \quad 91.7\%$$

Generally, reliability over 90% is considered acceptable, but attempts should be made to resolve any inconsistencies or disagreements in observations. In some cases, however, reliability figures can be misleading. For example, in the above example, what if the 20 disagreements represented the only instances of occurrence of the behavior? The observation obviously was not reliable (i.e., observers never agreed on occurrences) and yet the reliability coefficient would be relatively high. In such cases, it is important to compute reliability of observation of occurrences separately, particularly if the behavior occurs only rarely.

As stated above, one advantage of interval recording is that several students can be observed at one time. If three students are being observed, for example, observers may first direct their attention primarily to the student who is most likely to exhibit the target behavior. Once this behavior has been exhibited, the student need not be observed for the remainder of the interval, and the observer can focus entirely on the other two students for the remainder of the interval. With interval recording, it is also possible to record several different behaviors for one student. For instance, intervals could be scored as on-task (+), off-task verbal (–v), off-task motor (–m), or off-task daydreaming (–d). This type of recording can determine more precisely what students are doing when they are off-task.

Time Sampling

The last recording procedure discussed here is time sampling. Like interval recording, this procedure provides only an estimate (sample) of relevant behavior. However, in most cases, time-sampling procedures can provide reliable and accurate information.

Like interval-recording procedures, time sampling involves setting time intervals that can be noted with clocks, stopwatches, or tape-recorded sounds. Unlike interval recording, however, observed behavior is recorded only at the instance of the time sample. For instance, if out-of-seat behavior is observed using a time-sampling procedure with samples taken at the end of every 1-minute period, only the behavior observed at the instance the second hand (or beep) registers the 1-minute mark is recorded. Although less behavior is directly observed this way, it is possible to record many different students at one time. With longer sampling periods, it is possible to assess an entire classroom at a time. For example, to give themselves a better idea of how students are spending their time, teachers could record what activities different students are engaged in at the end of every 10th minute.

Time-sampling procedures make use of recording sheets similar to those used in interval recording. Data are also usually summarized as percents of "times sampled." Reliability is also computed using generally the same procedures as interval recording. Although time-sampling procedures typically involve observing and recording of a smaller sample of behavior per student, many teachers find this method very practical for routine classroom use.

Summary of Observational Recording Procedures

Continuous records; event, duration, and interval recording; and time-sampling procedures are all used to gain an objective measure of student behavior. Objective evidence is often more useful to teachers than subjective impressions of a student's personality or attitude. For instance, it may be more valuable for teachers to know that a student was off-task for 40% of a math period than to hear someone's perception that the student has a "bad attitude" or suffers from "math anxiety." Off-task information, if appropriately combined with other relevant behavioral information, can lead teachers directly to making appropriate interventions to change such behavior. For instance, if off-task data were combined with information that the student was performing at a very low level of accuracy on math problems, such information could lead teachers to believe that the difficulty level of the problems was not appropriate. On the other hand, pronouncements about the student's attitude may not be reliable or valid and are of little use in planning interventions.

In addition to the accuracy of recorded information, it is important to remember that students often behave differently when they know they are being observed. Particularly at first, observers must be unobtrusive so that students are not aware that they are being directly observed. If observation becomes more a part of normal classroom routine, however, students are likely to take less and less notice of these procedures.

Finally, it should be noted that observational procedures are only helpful if they directly reflect classroom objectives and are specifically relevant to IEP objectives. For instance, if a student's IEP objectives state that a student will "be out-of-seat no more than four times during the day at prespecified periods, and with teacher approval," observational recording is necessary to demonstrate whether the student has met or is making progress toward meeting the objective.

On many occasions, a teacher's judgment can accurately reflect student behavior. On other occasions, however, a teacher's perception may not be accurate. In special education (or regular education), some students exhibit behaviors that teachers regard as annoying or offensive. As familiarity with the student increases, teachers may begin to react less strongly to the behavior. It may appear to the teacher that the student's behavior is improving when, in fact, the teacher is simply getting used to it. In such cases, observational data provide opportunities for more objective evaluation.

GRAPHIC DISPLAY OF DATA

Teachers can collect a large amount of data over a school year. In order for this data to be meaningful, however, it is usually necessary to present the

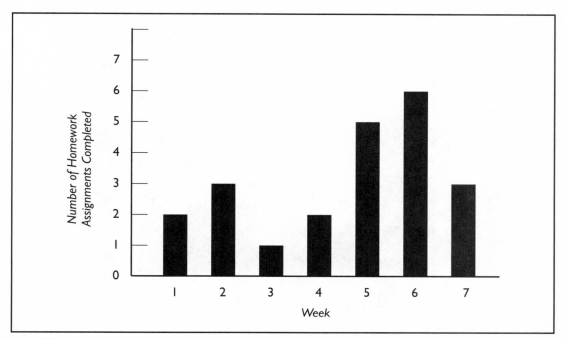

FIGURE 3.6. Example of a bar chart showing number of weekly homework assignments completed.

data on some type of chart. Charts typically consist of a vertical and a horizontal axis with data displayed between the axes. Usually, the occurrence of behavior is specified on the vertical axis, and the horizontal axis reflects the passage of time (see Figure 3.2). The rest of this section will describe the use of several types of graphic displays.

One way in which data can be presented is in a bar chart. For example, Figure 3.6 shows a graphic presentation of weekly homework assignments completed. In some cases, it may be more helpful to present the percentage of homework assignments completed (see Figure 3.7), because the total number of assignments may vary. Figure 3.8 shows how both sources of information can be included in one graphic display.

In other presentations, it may be more efficient to represent a data point with a dot, as in Figure 3.9. These dots can be connected to suggest possible trends in the data, such as the increase of desirable behaviors (e.g., rate of division problems solved correctly) or the decrease of undesirable behaviors (e.g., number of talk outs). Such data displays can be enormously helpful in determining whether students have met (or are meeting) IEP objectives.

In some cases, teachers record data on semilogarithmic charts. Semilogarithmic refers to the fact that the horizontal axis is linear, the same as other charts, but the vertical axis increases geometrically in value; that is, the vertical distance from 0 to 10 is the same as the vertical distance from 10 to 100, which is the same as the distance from 100 to 1000. Since some

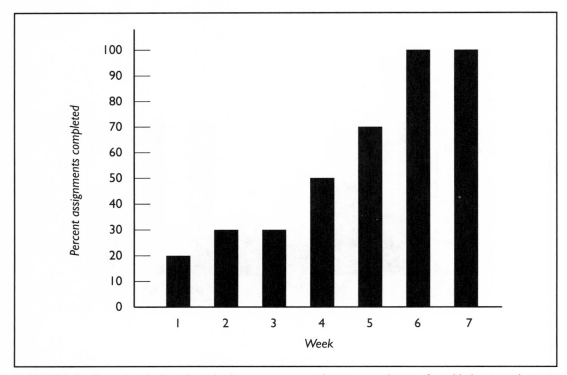

FIGURE 3.7. Example of a bar chart displaying percentage data on completion of weekly homework assignments.

behavior might increase geometrically as it is learned (e.g., the rate of learning increases over time), semilogarithmic charts display such behavior in a linear manner that can be helpful in making predictions. In addition, it is easy to represent a wide range of behaviors on the same semilogarithmic chart, including behaviors that occur only once or twice in a 7-hour day, as well as behaviors that can occur at a high rate, such as word-reading fluency. The use of such semilogarithmic charts in instructional decision making is sometimes referred to as *precision teaching*. And although precision-teaching charts, such as the one shown in Figure 3.10, may look complicated at first, they are really quite simple to use, as a little practice will show.

Validating Intervention Effectiveness

In most cases, IEP objectives do not specify *how* an objective is to be met. The type of treatment (intervention) used to meet the objective is usually a decision made by the special education teacher. While graphic presentation does not always demonstrate that the behavior change was due to the intervention, charts can be constructed to demonstrate this. First, teachers can collect preintervention observational data and record it in what is known as a *baseline phase*, as shown in the first part of Figure

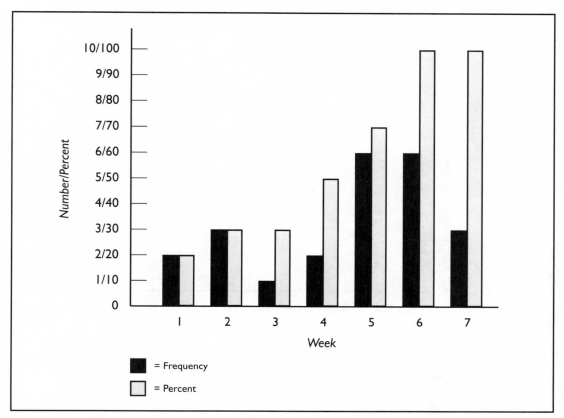

FIGURE 3.8. Example of a bar chart displaying both frequency and percentage data on completion of weekly homework assignments.

3.11. A baseline phase documents the occurrence of the behavior prior to the intervention. For example, a teacher may think that a student's late arrival to class each day is a problem. The teacher can observe and record the minutes the student is late each day for a certain period of time (e.g., 6 days). If this information verifies a teacher's suspicion that tardiness is a problem, the teacher can implement an intervention. An intervention for tardiness could involve positive reinforcement, such as tokens for prompt entry into the classroom. These tokens could be redeemable at a later date for prizes or privileges. The intervention could also involve punishment, such as informing the student that all class time lost through tardiness will be made up during recess, free time, or after school. On the day the intervention is to begin, the teacher draws a vertical line and labels the intervention, as in Figure 3.12, and begins to collect data. If the resulting data look like those in the second part of Figure 3.11, the teacher may conclude that the intervention was effective. Looking at the chart in Figure 3.11, it does seem likely that the treatment succeeded. If the teacher wanted to be more certain that treatment, and not some other event, was responsible for the change in behavior, the teacher would attempt to show control over the

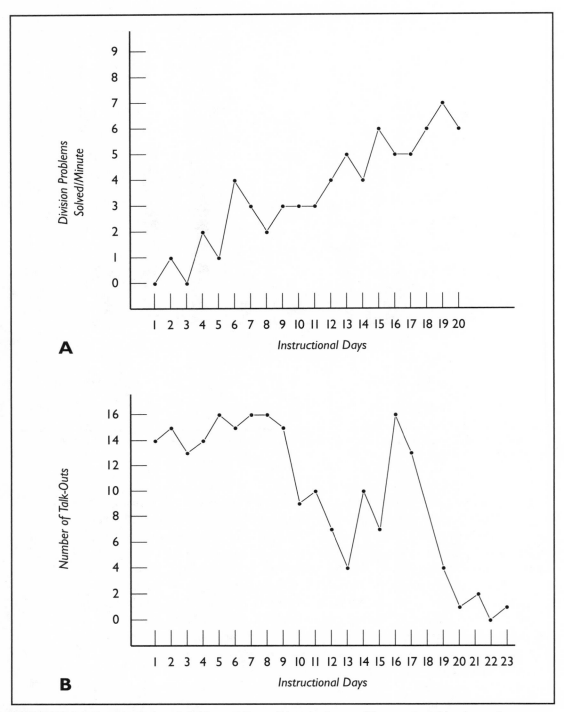

FIGURE 3.9. Graphic display of division problems (A) and talk-outs (B) represented by data points connected by lines to show trends.

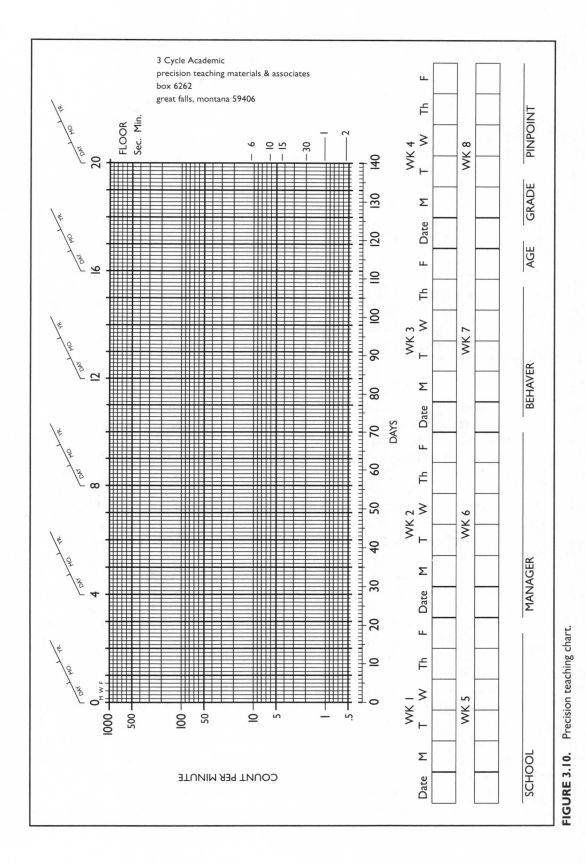

FIGURE 3.10. Precision teaching chart.

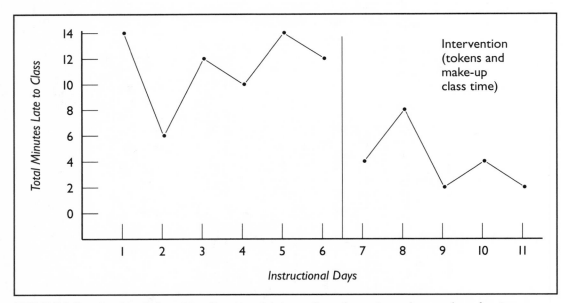

FIGURE 3.II. Graphic display of baseline data and data collected on minutes late to class after intervention using tokens and make-up time.

behavior by first returning to baseline, in which the intervention is not used, and reinstating the intervention at a later date, as in Figure 3.12. If the recorded behavior varies with treatment phase, as is shown in Figure 3.12, it can be more safely concluded that the treatment was responsible for the behavior change. This type of demonstration of experimental control over behavior, sometimes referred to as *behavior modification* or *applied behavior analysis*, has been demonstrated to be helpful in special education settings. The type of experimental design described above is referred to as a *reversal* (or ABAB) design, because the intervention is reversed in the return-to-baseline phase.

In some cases, however, it is not possible or desirable to return to baseline. Such cases include those in which learned behavior cannot be unlearned (behavioral trapping), such as with multiplication tables. For practical reasons, behavior that is highly destructive should not be returned to higher levels of intensity. In such cases, experimental control can be demonstrated with use of the *multiple baseline*, as shown in Figure 3.13, which depicts the use of a token reinforcement system for learning math facts. The baseline phases are of different lengths for different students, but the fact that each student increases in learning after implementation of the token system suggests that students are responding to the treatment.

Teachers do not always need to demonstrate experimental control over student behaviors. In most cases, it is sufficient to demonstrate that progress is being made and that objectives are being met at a satisfactory rate. In some cases, however, teachers may be uncertain of the effectiveness of a specific treatment or may wish to be more certain that a specific treatment

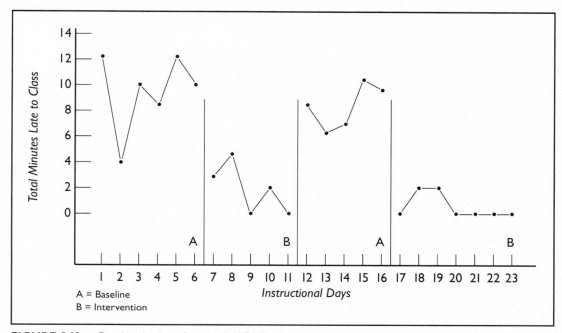

FIGURE 3.12. Graphic display of reversal (ABAB) data showing experimental control over behavior.

is effective before using it with other students. In such cases it may be helpful to employ reversal or multiple baseline designs.

Summary of Graphic Presentation of Data

Graphic presentations of permanent products or behavioral observations can be very helpful in determining whether instruction is effective. Although summative data are also helpful, teachers cannot afford to wait until the end of the school year to determine whether or not treatment has been effective. Graphic data displays, one type of formative evaluation, can provide this important information. Teachers need to decide for themselves how much time must be devoted to collection of student performance data. Research has supported the contention that records of student performance should be taken regularly and examined frequently in order to make effective decisions about instruction. Teachers should be able to judge when changes in instruction are *not* necessary as well as when they are necessary. Whether data should be collected, charted, and evaluated daily may depend on a consideration of the task, the learner, and other responsibilities of the teacher. It is known, however, that careful, accurate, and regular collection of student performance data and the use of these data in making instructional decisions is a critical component of effective teaching.

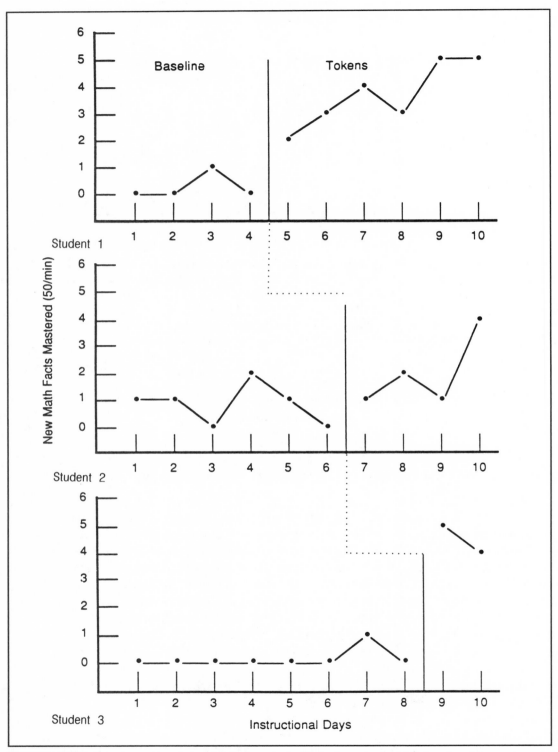

FIGURE 3.13. Demonstration of experimental control of behavior using multiple baseline data on three students.

MULTICULTURAL ISSUES

At least two issues in special education evaluation and assessment are directly relevant to multicultural and linguistically diverse students. First, students from multicultural and linguistically diverse backgrounds may be overrepresented in some special education settings. A discussion of the assessment procedures used for determining classification of students with respect to a particular category of disability (e.g., learning disabilities) is beyond the scope of this book. However, the concern that some minority groups may be overrepresented in special education suggests that special educators, as members of multidisciplinary referral teams, should help ensure that special education classification is the best possible educational option for individual students from multicultural or linguistically diverse backgrounds. Regular education classrooms also should be accommodating of student diversity; students should not be placed in special education programs simply because their culturally based cognitive or behavioral patterns are incompatible with rigid "monocultural" classroom instructional models (Franklin, 1992).

Another important issue involves fairness in assessment of academic progress. Generally, assessment should be based on culturally relevant and meaningful curriculum materials that are in turn meaningfully associated with relevant instructional objectives. Fair assessment is best made on relevant curriculum to determine whether acceptable progress is being made and to inform instructional decision making.

RELEVANT RESEARCH AND RESOURCES

Additional information on norm-referenced tests, criterion-referenced tests, and basic issues of reliability and validity is provided by Salvia and Ysseldyke (1981). Implications of the use of criterion-referenced assessment are described by Popham and Husek (1969), and a further description of direct observational systems is provided by Cooper (1981). Additional information on graphing observational data is provided by Tawney and Gast (1984). This text also describes experimental designs that are helpful in validating behavioral interventions.

An issue of *Exceptional Children* (Vol. 52, No. 3) (Tucker, 1985) was devoted to curriculum-based assessment. Articles by Deno (1986); Germann and Tindal (1986); Marston and Magnusson (1986); Peterson, Heistad, Peterson, and Reynolds (1986); Gickling and Thompson (1986); and Blankenship (1986) are of particular interest and describe supporting research data. In the same issue, Galagan (1986) described what he terms the "legal imperative" of the use of curriculum-based assessment in special education.

L. S. Fuchs (1986) wrote a review of research supporting the use of formative evaluation procedures. A meta-analysis of such findings is given in Fuchs and

(continues)

(Relevant Research and Resources continued)

Fuchs (1986b), and individual research reports on the effectiveness of curriculum-based assessment can be found in Deno, Marston, and Mirkin (1982); Deno, Mirkin, and Chiang (1982); Fuchs, Deno, and Marston (1983); Fuchs and Fuchs (1986a); and Fuchs, Deno, and Mirkin (1984). Applications of curriculum-based measurement are given by Fuchs (1987); Fuchs, Fuchs, Allinder, and Hamlett (1992); Fuchs, Fuchs, Hamlett, and Ferguson (1992); and Fuchs, Fuchs, Hamlett, and Whinnery (1991).

Curricular Materials

Curriculum Associates publishes the *Brigance Diagnostic Comprehensive Inventory of Basic [and Essential] Skills*, which can be useful in criterion-referenced testing. A Spanish version is also available. Many curriculum-based, performance, or portfolio assessments must be developed by teachers to target specific classroom activities. However, *Full Option Science System* (Encyclopedia Britannica) and *Science and Technology for Children* (National Science Resources Center) seem very suitable for many students with mild disabilities and include materials for performance assessment of science learning.

Computer Software and Technology

Computer software programs have also become available to assist with assessment. For example, PRO-ED publishes a series of curriculum-based measurement computer programs in reading, spelling, and math that generate tests, score tests, and graph performance. Teachers may also want to become familiar with some of the many word-processing programs, data base programs, spreadsheet programs, and graphics programs, such as The New Print Shop (Brøderbund Software) and Harvard Graphics (Software Publishing Corporation), that can be adapted to record, store, and graph student performance data. Software has also become available for scoring norm-referenced tests, including the KeyMath–R ASSIST (American Guidance Service) and WRMT–R ASSIST (Woodcock Reading Mastery Tests–Revised) (American Guidance Service) and COMPUSCORE for the Woodcock-Johnson Psychoeducational Battery (Developmental Learning Materials). See Appendix B for a list of addresses of producers and distributors of software and curricular materials.

CHAPTER 4

Classroom Management

EFFECTIVE MANAGEMENT OF STUDENTS' CLASSROOM BEHAVIOR IS A CRITical component of effective teaching in special education or any other educational setting. Research has shown that the teachers who are the most effective in managing classroom behavior are also usually the most effective in improving classroom achievement. The reasons for this are obvious. Teachers who spend an excessive amount of time lecturing students on their behavior or continually exhorting students to "be quiet," "sit down," or "keep your hands to yourself," are losing valuable instruction time. Additionally, if student achievement is to be maximized, it is critical for the classroom atmosphere to be friendly and cheerful but also businesslike and work oriented. The classroom atmosphere set by teachers gives a strong message to students regarding what is expected of them. Students who have been classified as behaviorally disordered or emotionally disturbed may have been so classified precisely because regular education teachers have had difficulty managing their behavior. In this regard, these students may prove to be particularly challenging. It must also be remembered that some students who have been classified as having learning disabilities or mild mental retardation and students who have a history of school failure also may present classroom behavior problems. The techniques for managing classroom behaviors are similar across all categories of special education; however, the level of intensity of the behavioral problems exhibited may vary from student to student or from classroom to classroom.

The first section of this chapter describes basic behavioral terminology. Next, applications of behavior management principles to the management of individual behavior are described. Following that, procedures for the management of whole classrooms are discussed. Finally, methods for room arrangement and scheduling relevant to effective classroom management are described.

Behavioral Terminology

As discussed previously, *behavior* is usually defined as the directly observable movements of a student (or other organism). Behavior is what we observe, measure, and intervene upon. Behavior is often changed by applying contingencies (consequences). In behavior management, these contingencies are often applied as *consequent events*, that is, after the behavior has been exhibited. Contingencies are intended to alter the future exhibition of the behavior.

Reinforcement and Punishment

Generally, the most effective contingency used in changing or modifying behavior is positive reinforcement. Positive reinforcement is any desirable consequent event that increases the desired behavior. What is reinforcing to one student may not be reinforcing to another student, simply because the preferences of individuals differ. Generally, positive reinforcement includes social reinforcers (e.g., verbal praise), tangible reinforcers (e.g., stickers and awards), and primary reinforcers (e.g., candy). It is important to remember, however, that whether or not something serves as a reinforcer depends on whether it increases future behavior and not simply that it is desirable. For example, the teacher may feel that public social praise could be used to increase a certain student's on-task behavior. The teacher could then use statements such as "I like the way you are working so hard on your assignment" to positively reinforce on-task behavior. If the on-task behavior does not increase as a result of using this praise (perhaps because the student is embarrassed by it), it cannot be said to function as a positive reinforcer.

Negative reinforcement, on the other hand, refers to undesirable consequent events that result in increased levels of future behavior. Negative reinforcement, which should not be confused with punishment (described below), involves the presentation of an undesirable stimulus that can be stopped by exhibition of the target behavior. A good example of negative reinforcement is the buzzer used in cars to remind riders to buckle seat belts. One buckles the seat belt not out of expectation of positive consequences but in order to stop the negative consequences of the buzzer. Another good example of negative reinforcement is nagging. Parents often nag children to clean up their rooms. Children comply not out of the expectation of a reward but in order to stop the parents' nagging. Similarly, infants often use crying as a negative reinforcement for parental attention. Parents attend to the infants so that they will stop crying. Although the examples given above show how negative reinforcement can be used, it is almost never the best treatment in classroom situations. Most of the time it is better to use positive reinforcement to change behavior in the classroom. A classroom situation in which negative reinforcement is often used is lining up to go to the cafeteria or recess. The teacher informs the class that they will wait in line as long as it takes for everyone to stand quietly and behave appropriately. Standing in line is used as a negative reinforcement for appropriate behavior. Students know that if they behave appropriately as a group they will not have to continue standing and waiting. Although using such contingencies may sometimes be necessary, it is also possible to provide positive reinforcement, such as an additional few minutes of playground time, for prompt and efficient lining up.

In contrast to positive and negative reinforcement, both of which serve to increase behavior, punishment refers to consequent events that are intended to decrease future behavior. Although positive reinforcement is more desirable and effective as a means of behavior management, punishment may sometimes be necessary, particularly when the behavior is infrequent and more positive methods have failed. Different types of reinforcement and punishment are described in Figure 4.1.

Consequent Event	Description	Examples
Positive reinforcement	Provision of reward to increase desired behavior	Verbal praise
		Tokens, exchangeable for trinkets
		Privileges, such as leaving seat without permission
		Free time
		Longer recess
		Popcorn parties at end of week
Negative reinforcement	Cessation of negative event to increase desired behavior	Nagging
		Teasing, such as "chicken," "fraidy-cat"
		Staying in from recess until a specific assignment is completed
Punishment	Provision of negative consequences to decrease undesirable behavior	Verbal criticism
		Time-out
		Loss of privileges
		Overcorrection, such as cleaning every student's desk for writing on own desk
		Response cost, such as loss of earned tokens

FIGURE 4.1. Consequent events.

Schedules of Reinforcement

Teachers need to attend not only to the types of reinforcement used but also to schedules of reinforcement. Schedules of reinforcement refer to the rate at which reinforcement is delivered. For example, in the initial stages of behavior change, it may be necessary to use *continuous reinforcement* with some students. Reinforcement is continuous when it follows every observed instance of the target behavior. For example, every time students arrive in class before the tardy bell rings, they are provided with a reward, such as a sticker or token that counts toward other prizes or privileges. Reinforcement can also be applied on an interval basis. *Interval reinforcement* refers to the time intervals during which reinforcement is provided. *Fixed interval reinforcement* is reinforcement that is provided at regular, known intervals. For example, students are provided with reinforcement for being on-task at fixed 5-minute intervals. This type of reinforcement tends to result in increased levels of performance immediately preceding the established interval. In contrast, *variable interval reinforcement* is provided at differing time intervals that are unknown to the student. Reinforcement could be delivered after 5 minutes, then after 8 minutes, then after 1 minute. Use of variable intervals of reinforcement can provide higher and more consistent levels of performance than use of fixed intervals of reinforcement.

In addition to interval schedules, some reinforcement is applied on a ratio basis. *Ratio reinforcement* refers to the number of responses required for reinforcement and is often applied to behavioral events. For example, students are given positive reinforcement for every third time a homework assignment is completed accurately. This is an example of a *fixed ratio* schedule of reinforcement. Like a variable interval schedule, a *variable ratio* schedule applies to a schedule of reinforcement that is not fixed. For example, students are reinforced on the 3rd, 11th, and 13th occasion of homework completion. This type of schedule also tends to produce higher and more consistent levels of behavior than a fixed ratio schedule.

This section has described some of the more common terms associated with behavior management. The application of these principles and additional terminology is provided in the sections that follow.

MANAGEMENT OF INDIVIDUAL STUDENT BEHAVIOR

Teachers in general, and special education teachers in particular, need to remain aware of the fact that classrooms are composed of individuals. These individuals often have different needs and may respond differently to the same treatment. The following section describes procedures that can be applied to individuals to manage appropriate classroom behavior.

Rules, Praise, and Ignoring

A necessary prerequisite to good classroom behavior is an awareness of the expectations for classroom behavior. Expectations should be directly and clearly communicated by posted classroom rules and teacher reminders. If students show problems discriminating between acceptable and unacceptable behaviors (e.g., acceptable and unacceptable tone of voice), they must be taught these discriminations (by explicit provision of instances and noninstances) before they can be expected to produce the desired behavior. Provision of rules by classroom behavior and understanding are necessary prerequisites for behavior management.

Rules are often ineffective, however, if they are not supported by contingencies or are inconsistently enforced. Research has shown that provision of rules alone may have little effect upon student behavior. One way rules can be enforced is through the use of praise and ignoring. Social praise for following classroom rules (e.g., "I like the way Jimmy has kept his hands to himself this period") can be effective in emphasizing that students are expected to follow rules. Teachers should seek out opportunities to provide social praise, particularly for students whose behavior is typically not praiseworthy. This type of activity is referred to as "catch them being good." Generally, this is a more effective way of positively changing behavior than frequent nagging or criticism. Likewise, teachers can choose to ignore one student's inappropriate behavior while simultaneously praising another student's good behavior. For example, if Tyler is off-task, but Ramona is on-task, the teacher could say, "I like the way Ramona is working hard and staying on-task." Frequently, this statement of praise for Ramona will help Tyler become on-task, too. Research has also demonstrated that soft reprimands may be more effective in controlling disruptive behaviors than loud reprimands. Many times it is possible for teachers to speak softly, in tones audible only to the disruptive students, rather than loudly so that the entire class hears.

In addition to using rules and praise, it is often helpful to ignore some types of inappropriate student behavior. Of course, behavior that is potentially harmful to other students must be attended to immediately. For many behaviors, however, the teacher can ignore the undesirable behavior and instead respond positively to another student who is exhibiting a positive instance of the behavior. For example, rather than reprimanding a student for squirming in his or her seat, the teacher can turn to another student and say, "I really appreciate the way Mary is sitting quietly. It makes it so much easier to get our work done." When coupled with rewards for appropriate behavior, ignoring undesirable behavior can be effective in managing classroom environments. If behavior is shown to decrease after it is ignored, the process is referred to as *extinction*. Teachers can also extinguish positive behaviors if they forget to reward them. Figure 4.2 provides an example of praising and ignoring.

Ms. A observed that one of her third-grade students, Sydney, was spending a good deal of her time off task (e.g., daydreaming, looking out the window, looking in her desk). Instead of intervening directly with Sydney's off-task behavior, Ms. A decided to ignore the off-task behavior and praise the instances in which Sydney was working well. In addition, Ms. A openly praised the on-task behaviors of a hard-working student, Joe, who sat near Sydney, with statements such as "I like the way you're working so hard, Joe. You're one of my very best workers!" Formative data collected by Ms. A indicated that Sydney's on-task and assignment completion behaviors increased sharply and that Joe's already high engagement rate became even higher.

FIGURE 4.2.   Praise and ignoring.

Direct Appeal, Proximity, and Public Posting of Behavior

Direct appeal, proximity, and public posting of behavior are procedures that are simple to implement and often very successful at changing inappropriate behaviors. In implementing direct appeal, teachers can meet individually with a student who is misbehaving and ask that student to try hard to behave appropriately. For example, assume one student (Robbie) has been very disruptive by teasing another student (Wanda) repeatedly during social studies class. After class, ask Robbie to remain and speak directly to him regarding the problem. During the discussion state something like "It has been difficult for you to complete your work during social studies because you have been teasing and bothering Wanda. I want you to try especially hard tomorrow and try to complete all of your work. If I see you start to tease Wanda I will signal you with my hand like this. [Demonstrate hand signal.] When you see that signal, it will remind you to get back to work and to leave Wanda alone."

Proximity is another procedure that usually results in appropriate behavior change. When a teacher sees a student acting inappropriately, the teacher can walk over next to that student. Usually the teacher's close appearance acts as a sufficient reminder to the student and the inappropriate behavior ceases. Many times teachers can combine proximity with a signal (such as establishing eye contact) which serves as a reminder for the student.

Finally, teachers can post good students' behavior. A chart including all students' names with spaces for inserting their respective accomplishments can be placed prominently in the classroom. Each day teachers can praise students by selecting to read the names of some of the accomplished students to the class. The accomplishments can vary and include items such as working hard, completing a task, and putting forth extra effort. Additionally, teachers can select the biggest accomplishment for the week, such as the Super Effort Award.

Tangible Reinforcement

Social praise or the granting of privileges can function as positive reinforcement in managing a student's behavior. Sometimes, however, social praise is insufficient and a more tangible type of reinforcement is required. Tangible reinforcements include things such as stickers, stars, toys or primary reinforcers such as food and drink. Although many teachers do not like the idea of providing tangible rewards for behavior that is expected in mainstream settings without reward, in some instances the provision of tangible reinforcement can represent an important first step toward meeting the goal of independent functioning in the mainstream. In some cases, students have learned patterns of behavior that are at first difficult to change. Tangible reinforcement may be helpful in making some of these initial changes. Students' preferences and interests can be surveyed so that teachers can select reinforcers that are appropriate for all students, including those from culturally and linguistically diverse groups. Tangible reinforcement can also be paired with social praise. In this way, students learn that the social praise is also important, and over time the tangible reinforcements can be faded out and replaced with social praise. Later, the reinforcement can be faded out, for example, by moving from continuous reinforcement to different levels of variable ratio or variable interval schedules.

One way to build in fading of tangible reinforcement is through the use of a token system. Token systems make use of things such as points or chips that are redeemable at a later date for actual tangible rewards. For example, a recording sheet, such as the one in Figure 4.3, is developed that describes a series of target behaviors for each period. As seen in Figure 4.3, a student can earn points for starting each period efficiently, working hard (on-task), staying in-seat, not talking out of turn, finishing work, and cleaning up. The student is given from 0 to 5 points at the end of each period, depending on the level of appropriate behavior exhibited. Points are totaled at the end of the day and added to points previously earned. Students may use these points to "purchase" more tangible reinforcers, such as toys and games. If a particularly strict behavior-management system is used, it may be necessary at first for students to be able to purchase reinforcers for a relatively small number of points. As inappropriate behaviors come under greater levels of control, however, the "price" of reinforcers should be increased so that students must exhibit higher and higher levels of appropriate behavior to purchase tangible reinforcers. As students begin to exhibit higher levels of behavior control, their performance can also be monitored less closely.

Tangible reinforcers are often included as reward components of individual behavioral contracts. A contract is a signed agreement between students and teachers specifying certain behavioral outcomes and rewards. In designing a contract, the teacher and student meet, select an obtainable behavioral goal, specify the conditions and time for meeting the goal, spec-

Period	Starting	Working Hard	In-Seat	No Talk-outs	Finish/Cleanup	Total
1. Reading	1	0	1	1	0	3
2. Math	1	1	1	1	1	5
3. Recess	1	1	1	1	1	5
4. Writing	1	0	1	0	1	3
5. Lunch	1	1	1	1	1	5
6. Science	1	0	0	0	0	1
7. Spelling	1	1	1	1	1	5
8. Recess	1	1	1	1	1	5
9. Class Meeting Social Skills	1	1	1	0	1	4
Totals	9	6	8	6	7	36

FIGURE 4.3. Sample classroom recording sheet for token systems.

ify the reward, and sign and date the contract. Contracts can be very effective at increasing positive academic and social behavior.

Tangible reinforcement has been shown to exert powerful control over many behaviors in special education settings. However, tangible reinforcement should be used only if milder forms of reinforcement do not prove successful.

Punishment

It would be nice to say that all classroom behavior can be managed through the use of positive reinforcement alone. Almost any special education teacher will agree, however, that some degree of punishment also is necessary to maintain order and keep the classroom functioning efficiently. This does not mean that teachers should be negative in any way toward their students. Although a stern, direct reprimand may sometimes be helpful in communicating expectations, excessive criticism can be very harmful to a classroom environment. As with any intervention, whenever punishment is used, formative data should be collected so that the consequences of using punishment can be evaluated. The following sections describe three types of punishment: time-out, response cost, and overcorrection.

Time-out

Time-out is sometimes referred to as "time out from positive reinforcement" and so defined may not be a literal example of punishment. In most cases, however, time-out serves as an undesirable condition that is intended to decrease future behaviors and, as such, can be considered punishment. Time-out, then, like any administration of punishment, must be considered in the context of the procedures and principles of the school environment.

Time-out generally refers to some type of separation of the student from the normal classroom environment and is usually applied following a disruptive event for which time-out was prespecified as a consequence. Sometimes time-out is used to provide a cooling-off period when students may have lost control of their tempers.

Although time-out is described as a unitary situation, it can be applied at several different levels. The mildest level, sometimes referred to as *contingent attention time-out*, involves removing a student from the immediate classroom activity but allowing the student to observe other students involved in the activity. In a higher level of time-out, the student is required to turn away from observing the classroom activities.

Some special education classrooms are equipped with time-out rooms in which students are completely isolated from the rest of the class, a procedure referred to as *exclusionary time-out*. Before using time-out procedures, several considerations should be made. First, it should be established through formative evaluations that reinforcement and milder levels of punishment have not been effective. Exclusionary time-out is then regarded as necessary, if not desirable. Second, exclusionary time-out should be brief. Five or 10 minutes is usually the maximum limit for such exclusionary procedures. Finally, most states, and common sense, require that lights be turned on and the door to a time-out room be unlocked. Exclusionary time-out, while considered a form of punishment, should be regarded as a type of intensive feedback for misbehavior and a brief period for a student to reflect upon this misbehavior. It should not be considered a form of incarceration.

Finally, as students leave the time-out room, they should be "debriefed" concerning the reasons they were put in time-out and given appropriate behavioral alternatives for the future. If loss of privileges (e.g., recess) is associated with time-out, these contingencies should also be specified. On the other hand, if students are consistently praised for positive competing behaviors, disruptive behaviors requiring time-out may decrease. As with any type of punishment, the student should be made aware that it is the behavior and not the student that is unwelcome in the classroom. Examples of debriefing procedures are provided in Figure 4.4.

Overcorrection and response cost

Overcorrection refers to requiring compensation beyond the level of behavior. For example, a student who has defaced a desk top with crayon is required to clean all desks in the classroom. Overcorrection also refers to the overlearning of appropriate behaviors. For instance, a student who throws food in the lunchroom is required to spend an afternoon appropriately carrying a tray of food to and from a lunch table.

Response cost involves the removal of previously earned rewards, such as tokens. For example, a student who misbehaves during one school period may not only earn no points for that period but also loses points previously earned that day. Like all punishment procedures, it is important to be certain that more positive efforts are not effective before implementing overcorrection or response cost procedures.

Self-monitoring

Self-monitoring refers to self-evaluation, recording, and reinforcement of behaviors by the student. Basically, teaching self-monitoring involves teaching the student to use the same principles that the teacher uses to modify his or her behavior. First, a student is taught to operationalize a target behavior, for example, teasing. Then the student is taught to record instances of teasing in his or her own behavior. Finally, the student is taught how to reward himself or herself for exhibition of a predetermined criteria of behavior after confirmation by the teacher.

An example of how self-monitoring can be used is given in Figure 4.5. Self-monitoring can be an effective procedure for helping students to function

Teacher: Your time-out is over. Before you go back to the classroom, we must discuss what happened. Why were you sent to time-out?

Student: I was bad.

Teacher: Can you tell me what you did?

Student: Johnny made faces at me so I threw my pencil at him.

Teacher: Were you sent to time-out because Johnny made faces?

Student: No.

Teacher: You were sent to time-out because you threw something at another student.

Student: Yes.

Teacher: Do you know why I cannot allow students to throw things?

Student: Somebody might get hurt.

Teacher: That's right. Somebody might get hurt. And some day that somebody might be you. Now, what can you do the next time you think Johnny is making faces?

Student: Ignore him.

Teacher: That's right. If you ignore him, he will stop. What else can you do if you think you are not going to be able to ignore him?

Student: Tell you.

Teacher: You can come and tell me, and I will make sure you don't get in trouble and also that no one teases you. Can you do that next time?

Student: OK.

Teacher: Just remember, you don't have to throw things. You can *ignore* and you can *tell me*. And remember, it's the *behavior* I don't like. But I like you and I know you can do better. Can't you?

Student: Yes.

Teacher: Good. Now let's go back to class and show everybody how well you can behave.

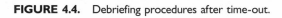

FIGURE 4.4. Debriefing procedures after time-out.

Ms. S had a student (Jill) who had a great deal of difficulty keeping herself on task during independent practice activities. Furthermore, the student often maintained that she had been working consistently throughout the period. Ms. S's judgment told her that Jill was probably off task much more often than the student realized. It also seemed that when Jill was off task, she was usually watching some other student. In order to increase Jill's on-task behavior, as well as her awareness of her own behavior, Ms. S provided Jill with a self-monitoring sheet. This sheet showed a stick figure drawing of a student working at a desk and another picture of a student looking around the room. Below these figures were boxes and time intervals as shown below:

Ring	On-task	Off-task
1	☐	☐
2	☐	☐
3	☐	☐
4	☐	☐
5	☐	☐
6	☐	☐
7	☐	☐
8	☐	☐
9	☐	☐
10	☐	☐

Jill was told that a timer would ring at random intervals and that Jill should check the box that described what she was doing at that moment, regardless of what she had just done or what she felt she was about to do. Ms. S then set the timer to ring at random intervals, on a variable interval of about 5 minutes. At first, Ms. S monitored each of Jill's self-recordings. At the end of the first period, Jill was forced to admit she was visually off task considerably more frequently than she had thought. Ms. S then told her to continue her self-recording, and Ms. S would do the same. When Jill achieved 9 out of 10 on-task checks on three consecutive self-monitoring sheets and her observations agreed with her teacher's observations, she would be entitled to 15 minutes with her favorite library book. Ms. S found that Jill's self-monitored on-task behavior went from 30% to 90% in a very short period of time and that Jill became much more capable of monitoring her own behavior.

FIGURE 4.5. Self-monitoring scenario.

in mainstream settings. Training in self-instruction and self-management, two components of self-monitoring, are described below.

Self-instruction training

Self-instructions or self-questions are self-directed statements that function as guidelines for students to follow throughout a problem-solving process. Each self-instruction represents one step toward the solution of the problem. Researchers typically have used a format that includes five self-instructions, beginning with the definition of the problem or a statement like "What should I do?" The second statement examines all potential solutions by asking a question like "What are all the possible options?" The third statement facilitates the focusing of attention to the problem at hand. A sample self-question or statement might be "I'd better think about my goal for right now." The fourth statement enables the student to select the optimal solution by asking a question or making a statement similar to the following: "I think this is the best solution . . . ." The fifth and final statement builds in self-reinforcing or coping statements. Statements such as "I chose the right answer" or "Oops, I made a mistake. Next time I'll get the right answer" are examples of self-reinforcement and coping statements, respectively. This series of problem-solving statements assists students in (a) identifying the problem and its attributes, (b) generating strategies or series of steps to solve the problem, (c) examining all possible solution options, (d) implementing the optimal solution, and (e) rewarding himself or herself upon completion of the solution.

A major goal of training in self-instruction is for students to internalize the self-instructions so that they are able to think through solutions to all problems. Generally, researchers and clinicians recommend that the following sequence of self-instructional procedures be implemented with all students:

1. The teacher models the task performance and overtly verbalizes the steps while the student observes and listens.

2. The student executes the task and overtly verbalizes all steps.

3. The teacher models the task while whispering the self-instruction.

4. The student executes the task and whispers the steps.

5. The teacher models the task again but this time uses *covert* self-instructional steps.

6. The student implements the procedure using covert self-instructional steps.

Teachers often add a self-monitoring component to self-instructional procedures. In other words, worksheets that list the questions or self-statements in sequential order are placed on a student's desk. During the initial implementation procedures, students can check off each question or statement as they think through the problem. As the procedures become more automatic, the monitoring sheet can be removed. An example of a self-monitoring checklist is provided below.

Check each step as you think it through.

1. What should I do? ☐

2. What are all the possible solutions? ☐

3. What is my goal for now? ☐

4. What is the best solution? ☐

5. Did my solution work? ☐

Procedures such as these can be beneficial for decreasing inattentive behavior and increasing performance on academic tasks. Further applications of self-instruction and self-monitoring are discussed in the content area chapters.

Reinforcement and punishment procedures are helpful tools for managing the behavior of individual students. The section that follows describes procedures for managing the behavior of students or classrooms.

Attribution training

Many students fail to attribute their classroom behavior to effort or choice on their own part. They can be said to have an "external locus of control" because they feel that people or events external to themselves are in control of their success or failure in the classroom. Students who are said to have an "internal locus of control" feel that they themselves are in control and that they can make the decisions about conduct that will enable them to succeed. The purpose of attribution training is to teach students to attribute success or failure in the classroom to decisions they make themselves.

Negative attributions are those that attribute success or failure to external forces. Examples are "I got sent to the office because the teacher doesn't like me," "Those other boys got me in trouble," and "I got rewarded because the teacher felt sorry for me." Positive attributions, on the other hand, are those that attribute success or failure to forces the student can control. Examples of positive attributions are "I lost points because I didn't control my talking" or "I get to take a 'happy-gram' home because I ignored the other students when they tried to tease me." Whenever students are given feedback on their classroom behavior, either positive or negative, teachers should be certain that the students realize they are in control of the behaviors they choose to exhibit and the consequences these behaviors will receive. Teachers should not accept negative attributions, which attempt to place the cause of success or failure on others. Figure 4.4 provides an example of a student's attempt to use a negative attribution and the teacher's refusal to accept it. Likewise, when students have a good day, teachers should remind them of the positive decisions they made that contributed to their success.

Attribution training is also very helpful for academic learning, where student success or failure is attributed to effort and execution of appropriate learning/study strategies. Attribution training for academic learning is discussed further in Chapter 9.

GROUP MANAGEMENT TECHNIQUES

All of the techniques described to manage individuals' behaviors can be adapted to modify a group's behavior. These techniques are especially beneficial for teachers. Recall that the major difficulty new teachers have in keeping students engaged on-task is classroom management. Most of the techniques described in the previous section for use with individuals will be described for application with small and large groups of students. Additionally, several techniques for large groups of students have been developed and found to be extremely effective in managing classroom behavior. Modifications of a classroom-level system have been used, as well as assertive discipline procedures on both classroom and schoolwide bases.

Motivation

The best overall strategy for managing classroom behavior is to create an environment in which students are motivated to learn and do not wish to create disturbances. In such environments, teachers and students are partners in a situation that is positive and beneficial for all. Both classroom behavior and academic learning can be greatly improved with motivational strategies.

Researchers often distinguish between *extrinsic* and *intrinsic* motivation. Extrinsic motivation generally refers to rewards or reinforcements given to students who work well and complete assignments accurately. In these cases, students work diligently not because they find the task satisfying but because of what they will earn if they work hard. Intrinsic motivation generally refers to efforts students put into tasks because they enjoy the learning activities or feel good about what they are learning. Overall, students are more intrinsically motivated to participate in experiential learning activities, such as those found in hands-on science experiments, than they are to participate in activities intended to improve basic skills functioning. Unfortunately, in special education basic skills learning is much more common, and therefore teachers must rely on more external sources of

1. *Be as positive as possible.* Students work harder to gain rewards than they do to avoid punishment. Teachers can tape-record their interactions with students to ensure they are being positive whenever possible.

2. *Teach enthusiastically.* Use a rapid pace, varied inflection, and positive tone of voice. Use animated eye movements, frequent gestures, dramatic body movements, and emotive facial expression. Use variety in choice of words, and openly and positively accept ideas or suggestions made by students.

3. *Use exciting demonstrations and examples.* Show students how exciting learning can be.

4. *Choose topics and activities that interest students.* Even for basic skills learning, choose application examples that reflect student interest. For example, for math application activities, calculate data from the Indianapolis 500.

5. *Set realistic expectations* that you think students can meet, and be very positive when they meet them.

6. *Monitor progress toward goals,* and let students know how much progress they are making.

7. *Intensify rewards,* using a variety of social and promotional rewards (e.g., public posting of achievement) and special class privileges in addition to more tangible awards.

8. *Promote positive attributions.* Students are more motivated, and more likely to succeed in the future, when they attribute their success to their own persistence of effort.

FIGURE 4.6. Strategies for increasing motivation.

support to help motivate students. Figure 4.6 lists general recommendations for increasing motivation.

Rules, Praise, and Ignoring

Classroom rules should be simple. Rules should be discussed with the entire class, and instances and noninstances of the rules should be covered. Ideally, rules should be posted in clear view of the entire room. Rules should be stated positively rather than negatively. An example of a positively stated rule is "Good, courteous student behavior is expected at all times." "Misbehavior such as teasing and poking is not tolerated" is an example of a negatively stated rule. Since teachers should emphasize positive student behaviors, it is better to write the rules positively.

It is especially important for teachers to reinforce students who follow class rules with open verbal praise. In this way, teachers publicly praise good behavior, and all students notice that praise. Research has demonstrated that rules alone do not always mean that good classroom behavior will automatically follow. However, when rules are accompanied by open praise of appropriate behavior and slightly inappropriate behavior is ignored, overall classroom behavior will improve. Assume that a class rule includes "good sitting behavior and paying attention." If a teacher notices that one student is not sitting appropriately and is staring out the window instead of paying attention, an appropriate response by the teacher is to ignore that particular student's behavior and to publicly praise a nearby student for the appropriate behaviors by stating, "I like the way Johnnie is sitting appropriately and paying attention." Often, such an open, public statement of praise for desired behavior will alter undesirable behavior. Another positive statement teachers can make to assist in turning off-task behavior to on-task behavior is to say, "I like the way (student's name) is working." Public praise of appropriate behavior is especially beneficial at the elementary age levels. A scenario for recording and evaluating classroom interventions is provided in Figure 4.7.

Interestingly enough, research has shown that most teachers tend to accentuate negative behaviors in their comments instead of positive ones, in spite of the fact that the positive approach has been demonstrated by research to be more effective. This is not meant to say that teachers can never say things like "Stop poking with that pencil." Sometimes it is necessary to deliver immediate feedback to stop inappropriate behaviors. However, comments on negative behavior should be linked to more than a single

---

Mr. L noticed that he was having more and more difficulty controlling talk-outs in his classroom. He wanted an objective evaluation of talk-outs in his classroom but was unable to find any school personnel with time to spare to do it. Besides, he was concerned that the presence of an outside observer in the classroom would change the class behavior in some way. As a result, unknown to his class, he tape-recorded several different class periods. After school, he prepared a table of all the talk-outs that had appeared on the tapes, including his own or other students' responses after each talk-out. What he found was that he was attending verbally (albeit negatively) to almost every talk-out, and in most cases, so did other students. Mr. L found that this attention seemed to be reinforcing talk-outs, rather than inhibiting them. He also found that many students (in fact, the majority) never talked out and also received almost no attention from him. Mr. L decided to change his teaching style so that he attended positively to students when they did not talk out and ignored students when they did talk out. Analysis of these recordings showed that all students but one had virtually eliminated their inappropriate talking-out. For the student who had not, he implemented a token system, whereby the student earned his recess minutes by making positive contributions in class. After this intervention, his tape-recordings showed him that instances of talk-outs had been virtually eliminated.

FIGURE 4.7. Praise and ignoring scenario.

event, and, if possible, an attempt should be made to accentuate some positive point. For example, a comment that might stop the pencil-poking behavior is "Why don't you show me you can control your behavior by yourself without me speaking to you?" If the comment is followed by the appropriate behavior, the teacher can then add, "See, I knew you could behave appropriately by yourself. I'm glad you are sitting the right way."

Class rules, as well as school rules, need to be accompanied by consequences. Teachers should be very specific not only with verbal praise for appropriate behavior but also with negative consequences for consistently inappropriate behavior. For instance, most high schools have rules and consequences. For unexcused tardiness, students may have one detention, 1 hour spent sitting quietly after school. Classroom rules and consequences may closely parallel school rules and consequences. The most critical aspect of consequences is that they be implemented fairly and consistently across all students. One of the worst things teachers can do is to provide idle verbal threats to students. Students tend to be very aware of when and which teachers consistently follow through with negative consequences. The most appropriate behavior is delivered when students know the rules and consequences and when the consequences are delivered fairly and consistently.

It is recommended that new teachers (a) determine what school rules and consequences exist; (b) parallel their own system with that of the school; (c) clearly communicate these rules and consequences to students, parents, and school administrators; (d) consistently use praise of appropriate behavior; and (e) consistently administer negative consequences, if necessary. Remember that positive comments should be used rather than negative ones and that consistency is a key to good classroom management. Other specific techniques, which are described in the next section, can be implemented in conjunction with rules, praise, and ignoring to establish excellent classroom management.

Class Contingencies

Research has shown that classwide contingencies, both positive and negative, can facilitate obtaining desired behaviors. These procedures can help teachers to enlist the support of good students in promoting desired classwide responses. For example, suppose a classroom goal is to achieve a certain performance level in overall good behavior in the school. Teachers can designate a class reward, such as a group popcorn party, a group movie, or an extra free period, that is dependent on the group's overall performance. Many times good students will help share the behavior of weaker students by providing them with verbal reminders and prompts. In such cases, the class as a whole benefits from the appropriate behaviors. Conversely, the class as a whole does not receive the positive reward if the goal is not met. If such procedures are used, it is critical that the goals be realistic ones for the group. Students will readily detect unobtainable goals and stop trying.

Another technique that has been successful in some classrooms consists of variations of the following scenario. Teachers state that every time they catch students doing something well they will put a marble (or chip or paper clip) into a jar on their desk (in full view of all class members). Conversely, every time something inappropriate is seen, one marble or chip will be taken out of the jar. When the jar is full, the entire class will receive a reward, similar to the ones described above. As the jar becomes full, all students tend to remind one another of good behaviors and to self-monitor their own behaviors better in anticipation of the group reward. In resource room programs, where different students are present each period, teachers can label a separate jar for each period and, thus, have several group competitions simultaneously. In a self-contained classroom setting, the teacher can designate specific periods or times of the day that "count" and others that do not.

The Good Behavior Game can promote cooperative behavior management within a class. Students are assigned to groups, and points are awarded to groups for prespecified behaviors by individuals. At the end of the activity, the group with the most points wins. In this type of behavior management system, students can be working individually or in cooperative groups.

These techniques can be combined with other forms of behavior management. Self-management and self-monitoring periods can be implemented and rewarded when performance is in accordance with specified rules. Extra privileges can be delivered to those students who effectively follow through with their respective self-monitoring plans.

Finally, teachers can use these procedures to reinforce different levels of learning with the class. Extra privileges assigned for good group work can provide the incentives necessary to keep progress at a desired rate.

Token Systems

Token systems can also be implemented on a groupwide basis. In such cases, the general rules for obtaining and exchanging tokens will be the same for the entire class. However, teachers occasionally may need to keep certain behaviors of some individuals on a continuous reinforcement schedule, while the behaviors of others are on a ratio or interval reinforcement schedule. In any event, teachers need to document the effectiveness of the reinforcement schedules that are being used.

Token systems or general point systems can be used most effectively when teachers have a classroom aide available to assist in recording behaviors and disseminating the tokens or points. Typically, an aide can be trained to carry a clipboard, pencil, and stopwatch and to accurately record student behaviors. Since most self-contained classrooms have either a part-time or full-time aide, these procedures can be easily implemented in many self-contained settings.

Tokens can be awarded for appropriate social behaviors, such as attending behavior, appropriate tone of voice, and appropriate social interactions, as well as for academic task completion and performance. Academic performance should be rewarded only if students possess the academic knowledge necessary to complete the task. Reinforcement alone cannot be a substitute for instruction; it can, however, supplement instruction. Variations on token and point systems have been extremely effective in shaping desired behaviors and responses.

Level Systems

Level systems are variations on Hewett's (1968) original "engineered classroom." Level systems consist of a series of steps or levels that have corresponding rights, responsibilities, and privileges associated with them. Level systems have been successfully implemented in separate-setting schools, self-contained settings, and resource settings at both the elementary and secondary levels.

To design and implement a level system, teachers must first prioritize the expected behaviors (social and academic) from most restrictive to least restrictive in terms of setting. For example, assume that the full-time mainstream setting was assigned level 5 and that the full-time special education setting with continuous monitoring and no privileges is assigned level 1. Levels 2, 3, and 4 are assigned behaviors and privileges arranged in a continuum between levels 1 and 5. For instance, level 2 could require students to sit in their seats during work periods and follow class rules, as in level 1; however, level 2 students would be allowed to get up and go to the water fountain on their own after their assignments were completed. Each succeeding level adds not only more privileges but also more student responsibilities. Many teachers have successfully implemented level systems and prefer them to token or point systems. Additionally, it is easier to implement self-monitoring procedures as a natural component of level systems than token or point systems.

After designing each of the levels, teachers must clearly define criteria for passing from one level to another. Sometimes teachers incorporate the mastery of both social and academic behaviors to a specified criterion prior to moving students up a level. Conversely, when students fail to maintain adequate performance at their current level assignment, they can be moved down a level. This type of system affords teachers flexibility in assigning privileges. Additionally, programming for generalization and mainstreaming can be built into certain levels. For example, teachers can partially mainstream students and monitor their progress daily in the level prior to full mainstreaming. Such a system helps to build successful experiences into students' schedules. Additionally, level systems can be used effectively to remediate learning and behavior problems. However, as with any of the procedures described, teachers must carefully monitor the programs and student progress to ensure that the program is progressing effectively and efficiently. An example of the use of a level system is provided in Figure 4.8.

Assertive Discipline

Canter's (1979) assertive discipline programs have been implemented and adopted by school districts across the country. This program works equally well with special and regular education classes. It operates best on a schoolwide basis, in which all teachers and building administrators use the same rules and contingencies. One of the major assumptions of assertive discipline programs is that all students and their parents are carefully informed of all the rules and contingencies. Once the ground rules have been established, if a student disobeys a rule during class, no discussion takes place. The teacher simply writes the student's name on the blackboard. If a second infraction occurs, the teacher places a check mark next to the name. If a third occurs, the teacher writes a second check mark on the board. Typically, from this point on, variations of the assertive discipline program are implemented. In some cases, after two check marks, students miss 10 minutes of their recess period. In other cases, students are immediately removed to a time-out area, which is occasionally the classroom next door or the vice principal's office. In most cases, after a certain number of infractions have occurred, the student's parents are called and asked to follow through with a reprimand at home. Most teachers find some adaptation of the program successful because the process eliminates the opportunity for discussion on the student's part. There is no opportunity for the student to say, "I didn't really do that" or "I didn't mean to . . . ." In any event, an assertive discipline program can be successful only if it is consistently implemented and all of the ground rules are understood prior to implementation. It is also important to implement positive goals so that the program does not become overly primitive. Additional guidelines for assertive discipline (summarized from Canter [1979]) are shown in Figure 4.9. Schools interested in implementing these procedures should acquire all the necessary training materials.

Behavior Management Lessons

Good behavior can be taught to students using the same instructional delivery systems that are used to teach lessons in reading and other academic content areas. First, identify the behavior management plan that will be implemented. Second, identify the objectives to be covered and estimate the number of lessons necessary to teach the management plan. Then, design lessons to teach students the rules for that management plan using the variables for effective instruction. Figure 4.10 offers a sample lesson on teaching students one form of behavior contracting, while Figure 4.11 provides a sample

The behavior-management system used in this classroom involved the assignment of each student to one of three levels, each calling for different responsibilities and privileges. The different levels were color coded; gray was the lowest, blue was the middle, and red the highest. Each student was given a colored name tag that matched the level he or she was in. These were traded in with each level change.

Students were evaluated each day to determine their levels for that day. To raise to the next higher level or to remain on the same level, students had to obey all of the rules of their level, including the 85% rules that were common to all of the levels (see below). Any infraction of the rules automatically dropped the student to the next-lower level.

Rules Common to All Students:

1. Maintain an average of 85% accuracy on assignments.
2. Maintain an average of 85% completion on assignments.
3. Breaking rules drops to next level.

Each level also had a set of rules and freedoms to go along with them.

Rules for Each Level:

Level	*Rules*	*Freedoms*
Gray	1. Be in seat at all times. 2. Raise hand before speaking. 3. Be prepared for class.	1. Upon completion of assignments, may read book of choice at own seat.
Blue	1. Raise hand to speak. 2. Be prepared for class.	1. May leave seat to obtain teacher assistance. 2. May use pencil sharpener or get drink of water during study time.
Red	1. Be prepared for class.	1. May study at table with other red-level students. 2. May talk to other red-level students. 3. May leave room for restroom break. 4. May negotiate with teacher for other freedoms.

Formative data collected on four students, including reversal, indicated that implementation of this level system had a positive effect on accuracy of responses, assignment completion, and level of on-task, socially appropriate behavior.

FIGURE 4.8. A level system.

Following are some examples from Lee Canter's Assertive Discipline, a schoolwide program. Additional information is given in Canter (1979):

1. Give expectations for teaching and learning

2. Provide rules:
   a. follow directions
   b. remain seated
   c. keep hands and feet to self
   d. raise hand before speaking
   e. no swearing or teasing

3. Provide discipline plan:
   a. first infraction—name written on board
   b. second infraction—check mark after name—15 minutes after school
   c. third infraction—two checks—30 minutes after school
   d. fourth infraction—three checks—phone to parents/guardians
   e. fifth infraction—four checks—exclusion to another room for 30 minutes, plus a more severe consequence determined by principal

4. Positive consequences
   a. verbal praise
   b. positive contact with parents/guardians
   c. other rewards determined by teacher and school

Schoolwide Implementation
Rules are schoolwide, with specific rules for playground, lunchroom, assembly, and hallway behaviors. They are implemented similarly by all teachers.

Discipline Card
Students who prove to be a behavior problem for several teachers may be issued a discipline card. All infractions made throughout the day are noted by each teacher, and consequences are administered by the final teacher.

FIGURE 4.9. Guidelines for introduction of assertive discipline to students.

contract. Once students completely understand the management plan being implemented, they will be more likely to behave appropriately.

SCHEDULING

One of the first and most difficult tasks that confront special education teachers every fall is the scheduling of their students, a task that must be completed rapidly at the beginning of each new year. Since the problems encountered in self-contained versus resource programs are slightly different, each is described separately in the sections that follow.

Daily Review

T: "Yesterday we seemed to be having a little trouble with getting our home-work done. It seemed that we had forgotten our classroom rules. Just to see if you remember, what are some of our rules?"

Delivery of Information

T: "Today I am going to show you a system to help both you and I follow rules and get rewarded for it. This is called a contract system. Can anyone tell me what a contract is?"

S: "That is when someone signs a piece of paper and promises to do what they are supposed to do in the contract."

T: "Good. A contract contains rules or promises that the students who sign it promise to do. They must follow these rules for a period of time. We are going to write out individual contracts that we agree on so we can all get along and do our best. The purpose of this contract is to help you follow rules and to make sure that you are rewarded for your efforts and good behavior.

"Here is a student named John. (Put sheet on overhead.) He is a fairly good student but sometimes has a tendency to talk too much. He does his work, but it usually takes him 5 to 10 minutes to get started, so, in the end, he is rushing to finish. And finally, during small group work, he likes to touch other students' materials.

"We then write out a contract for John and the teacher. In this con-tract, John and his teacher will talk about his difficulties, how to solve them, and what his reward will be if he successfully does everything on the contract. What is the first thing John should write out in his contract?"

Guided and Independent Practice

T: "What I want you to do now is think of things you personally can improve on in school. If you can't think of anything, I will help you. I want you then to come up with a contract to help solve these problems."

The students will then write out what they feel are the best solutions on their contracts. After they have finished with their contracts, students and teacher then agree on a reward system and sign the contracts.

Evaluation

Teacher evaluates students' contracts on their adequacy in addressing a school-related problem and on their effectiveness in promoting better behav-ior. For those whose contracts are not working, the teacher will go over a new contract with them on a one-on-one basis.

FIGURE 4.10. Sample behavior management lesson, written by Jennifer De la Vega.

Self-Contained Classrooms

Typically, self-contained classrooms at the elementary level consist of students with learning disabilities, behavioral disorders, or mild mental disabilities who spend their entire academic day with a special education

During the 1993–1994 school year, I promise to follow these rules. If I follow these rules in the resource room, a token will be given to me each day. At the end of the week, if I have 4 to 5 tokens I will get 15 minutes of free time.

I, Vinnie Smith, promise to

1. follow the class rules;

2. talk only when the teacher gives permission;

3. touch other students' materials only when they give me permission; and

4. begin my assignment on time.

If I do not follow these rules, I may lose class privileges.

Vinnie Smith (student)   _Jennifer De la Vega (teacher)_

FIGURE 4.11. Sample behavioral contract, written by Jennifer De la Vega.

teacher. Similar programs are sometimes referred to as _extended resource_ programs, because students attend nonacademic periods such as lunch, physical education, and recess with typical age peers although they receive all their academic work with a special education teacher. Many times students in self-contained settings also attend nonacademic periods with their age-appropriate peers. In either case, special educators are directly responsible for scheduling and teaching all academic subjects. Since classroom scheduling typically revolves around the total school's schedule, most programs share more commonalities than differences in overall schedules. Typically, an opening exercises period contains morning announcements and some type of short paper–pencil task. Reading is often scheduled for the first hour, during which students are divided into three or more groups based on ability. During this hour these reading ability groups may need attention by one teacher and one aide. Each group's activities might also be subdivided into three 20-minute periods including (a) 20 minutes of instruction with the teacher, (b) 20 minutes of instruction and/or guided practice with the aide, and (c) 20 minutes of independent practice and/or peer-tutoring practices. This breakdown allows for maximal use of teachers and aides during the reading hour.

Following reading, many teachers schedule a restroom/water fountain break, followed by an arithmetic hour. Again, ability groupings can be made, and instruction can follow some version of the reading period format. A recess and lunch period usually follows. After lunch, many teachers include a social skills period for the entire group, a language (written and oral) period, and a science and social studies period. Typically, physical education, art, and music classes are interspersed on weekly and biweekly bases.

Teachers in self-contained classrooms at both the elementary and secondary levels can usually determine their own schedules. Scheduling becomes more difficult, however, when they attempt to reintegrate their students into optimal regular education classes. This is discussed in more detail in Chapter 12.

Resource Rooms

Elementary resource teachers probably have more difficult scheduling demands than teachers in self-contained classrooms. If scheduling has not been completed by the building administrators, resource teachers must not only adequately schedule all of their students but also satisfy the scheduling needs of regular educators. Since most students attend resource rooms for reading and math instruction, an optimal first step is to complete ability grouping for all students in those skill areas. Additionally, in order to maintain good rapport with regular educators, it is important for resource teachers to consider regular classroom schedules when attempting to "pull out" resource students. Since it is almost impossible to please everyone 100% of the time, remember to be as pleasant as possible during communications regarding scheduling.

Once students have been assigned time periods for the resource room, it is critical to determine the daily routine for each student. Consider the teacher-effectiveness variables, especially active participation and formative evaluation, during the routine design of daily formats. An example of a resource room schedule is given in Figure 4.12.

Since most secondary programs now use computerized scheduling, secondary resource teachers may not have to complete their own scheduling. At the secondary level, guidance counselors can assist in scheduling by having students sign up for third-hour reading and fourth-hour study skills. Optimal scheduling is discussed in more detail in Chapter 12.

Effective scheduling, like effective behavior management, requires thoughtful planning and good interpersonal skills. Generally, it is important to design schedules with the intention of providing the best possible service to the largest number of students, particularly because this service relates to other activities in the school day. In many cases, special education services constitute the most important part of the student's school day. However, care must be taken to ensure that all of a student's needs during a school day are being met.

Time	Instructional Group (led by teacher)	Guided / Independent Practice Group (monitored by paraprofessional)
8:30– 9:00	Reading Level I	Reading Level II
9:00– 9:30	Reading Level II	Reading Level I
9:30–10:00	Reading Level III	Reading Level IV
10:00–10:30	Reading Level IV	Reading Level III
10:30–10:40	Recess/Break	Recess/Break
10:40–11:00	Math Level I	Math Level II
11:00–11:20	Math Level II	Math Level I
11:20–11:40	Math Level III	Math Level IV
11:40–12:00	Math Level IV	Math Level III
12:00–12:30	LUNCH BREAK	LUNCH BREAK
12:30– 1:00	Language Arts Level I	Language Arts Level II
1:00– 1:30	Language Arts Level II	Language Arts Level I
1:30– 2:00	Social Skills (all levels)	open*
2:00– 2:30	Study Skills Level I	open*
2:30– 3:00	Study Skills Level II	open*

*Paraprofessional is available to assist with the main instructional group or to work with other small groups on an as-needed basis.

FIGURE 4.12.   Daily resource room schedule.

MULTICULTURAL ISSUES

Students from some multicultural backgrounds may be referred disproportionally for behavior problems. Some researchers (e.g., Anderson, 1992) have argued that differences in cultural backgrounds, particularly with respect to language usage, can result in misunderstandings that are interpreted incorrectly by teachers as behavior problems. Teachers of students from multicultural or linguistically diverse backgrounds should be certain that judgments made about students' classroom behavior are not based on misunderstandings about the use of language or on overly rigid notions about how all students should behave. Certainly, classroom behavioral expectations should be the same for all students, regardless of background. However, teachers should be certain that their behavioral expectations do not favor, consciously or unconsciously, students from one particular cultural background. Teachers should consider the diversity in their classroom when establishing behavioral expectations. Establishing and maintaining dialogue with students, parents, and community members can help establish fair and appropriate behavioral standards.

RELEVANT RESEARCH

Information on behavioral terminology is provided in several texts, including Sulzer-Azaroff and Mayer (1977) and Martin and Pear (1978). These texts also provide details of behavioral techniques used in classroom management. Schedules of reinforcement are also described in these texts but were first described by Ferster and Skinner (1957). A discussion of behavioral methodology is provided by Scruggs (1992).

Published studies on effective management techniques for classroom behavior now number literally in the hundreds, only some of which can be mentioned here. Support for the relative effectiveness of positive reinforcement is provided by Mastropieri and Scruggs (1985–1986) and Scruggs, Mastropieri, Cook, and Escobar (1986). An early and widely cited study on rules, praise, and ignoring is provided by Madsen, Becker, and Thomas (1968), and similar support for the use of these variables in classroom behavior management is given by Becker, Madsen, and Arnold (1967); Broden, Bruce, and Mitchell (1970); O'Leary, Kaufman, Kass, and Drabman (1970); Hachett (1975); and Mitchell and Crowell (1973). The effectiveness of tangible reinforcement, including token systems, in special education classrooms is documented by Baker, Stanish, and Frazer (1972) and Jenkins and Gorrafa (1974). Forness and MacMillan (1972), however, cautioned against the overuse of tangible reinforcement. Punishment procedures are reviewed by Mac-Millan, Forness, and Trumball (1973) and Hewett and Forness (1984). Time-out interventions are validated by Spencer and Gray (1973), and time-out intervention for students labeled behaviorally disordered is reviewed by Rutherford and Nelson (1982). Positive support for the use of a level system is provided by Mastropieri, Jenne, and Scruggs (1988), and positive support for cooperative behavior management is given by Brigham, Bakken, Scruggs, and Mastropieri (1992). Self-monitoring procedures are validated by Broden, Hall, and Mitts (1971) and Glynn, Thomas, and Shee (1973). Kendall and Braswell (1985) provided a thorough review of cognitive-behavioral interventions with special education students, and Kerr and Nelson (1983) reviewed successful strategies in that area. The effectiveness of group contingencies is reported by Wolf, Hanley, and King (1970) and Greenwood, Hops, and Delquadri (1974) and reviewed by Liton and Pumroy (1975). Successful self-management and self-monitoring research is reported by DiGangi and Maag (1992); Hughes, Ruhl, and Misra (1989); Shores, Gunter, and Jack (1993); DiGangi, Maag, and Rutherford (1991); Prater, Joy, Chilman, Temple, and Miller (1991); and Etscheidt (1991). Finally, a comprehensive review of self-recording research is reported by Lloyd and Landrum (1990), and a review of self-management research is reported by Nelson, Smith, Young, and Dodd (1991).

❖ ❖ ❖

CHAPTER 5

Reading

READING IS PERHAPS THE MOST IMPORTANT ACADEMIC SKILL STUDENTS learn during their years in school. Reading ability is a necessary prerequisite for most school-related instructional activities. For example, a student typically cannot be expected to succeed in a history class without reading skills, since most information in history classes is conveyed through textbooks. In special education, students commonly exhibit serious deficits in reading skills. Not only do these deficits limit their attendance in reading instruction in regular classrooms, but they may also prevent students from participating in other mainstream courses that require reading skills, including science, drama, history, geography, English, foreign languages, health, civics, language arts, and, possibly, areas such as art and physical education. Thus, reading is a skill essential for school success.

There are many ways to teach reading, and there has been much debate over the best methods. Some educators have maintained that reading should be taught using a code-emphasis (phonics) approach. This approach teaches students to use word-attack skills to decode familiar and unfamiliar words. Other educational leaders have argued for a meaning-emphasis approach in teaching reading. This approach stresses the building of sight words and the use of contextual clues in deciphering unfamiliar words. In reality, however, there are few code-emphasis programs that do not also incorporate meaningfulness, and there are just as few meaning-emphasis programs that do not also teach decoding skills. In most cases, the issue of reading instruction concerns the degree of emphasis teachers should place on word-attack versus word-meaning instruction. Research in special education has generally supported the effectiveness of programs that emphasize phonics, probably because many students with disabilities are deficient at *phonemic awareness*, the knowledge of speech sounds and how they are combined to form words. However, it is also critically important that the meaning of words and passages be emphasized at all stages of the teaching process and that students learn to read a variety of materials. In addition, research has shown that specific instructional strategies have been effective in promoting reading comprehension, an area sometimes neglected in special education settings. Although phonetic instruction has been shown to be of critical importance, it should not be taught to the exclusion of the central purpose of reading, the extraction of meaning from written text.

This chapter first provides an overview of reading instruction that incorporates the application of effective teaching practices described in previous chapters, including maximizing engaged time-on-task, pacing, questioning, feedback, practice activities, and formative evaluation. The sections that follow describe practices for teaching phonetic analysis. The final section of the chapter describes strategies for improving reading comprehension.

Recently, a meaning-based approach referred to as *whole language* has been widely promoted for reading instruction in regular education classrooms. Advocates of this approach recommend: (a) de-emphasis of phonics instruction in favor of emphasis on meaning and context in learning new words, (b) use of a wide variety of reading materials, and (c) integration of reading, writing, and other language arts activities. Although the latter two components can be very useful in helping students meet application and generalization objectives, at least some direct instruction in phonics and phonemic awareness is very likely to be necessary for students with mild disabilities. At present there is little, if any, convincing research that supports the use of the whole language approach with students with mild disabilities (e.g., Gersten & Dimino, 1993; Mather, 1992), and in fact some recent research (e.g., Rudenga, 1992) suggests that the whole language approach may not meet the needs of these students. Therefore, teachers who wish to rely exclusively upon this method should be very careful to collect formative data that document its effectiveness with individual students.

TEACHING READING: AN OVERVIEW

Teaching reading is one of the most important activities of a special education teacher. Most students enter special education with a history of failure in reading. In order to maximize student learning during reading instruction, teachers should attend carefully to the components of reading instruction. The section that follows describes strategies for (a) selecting a reading program, (b) initial assessment and placement, (c) grouping for instruction, (d) teaching new information, (e) monitoring guided and independent practice, and (f) monitoring and adjusting instruction based upon formative evaluation data.

Selecting a Reading Program

The reading programs that have been most successful in special education have generally emphasized phonics or word-attack skills. These programs are easily identified by their systematic use of controlled letters and letter combinations that repeat the same sounds. In this approach, students are provided with repeated practice on words containing similar letters and similar sounds. For example, when introducing the sound *ound*, as in *found*, a code-emphasis program provides a reading passage containing several different instances of the sound by using words such as *pound, bound, found, sound,* and *mound*. Exceptions to this pronunciation (e.g., *wound*, meaning injury) do not appear until much later in the program. Additionally, sound patterns are not introduced until all individual sounds in the pattern have been covered. For example, *cat* would not be introduced until the three separate sounds, *c, a,* and *t,* had all been introduced. Examples of code- and meaning-emphasis programs are given in Figure 5.1.

Although code-emphasis programs may differ with respect to specific formats, use of illustrations, and the sequence in which skills are taught, they share the common feature of introducing specific sounds and word patterns in a systematic and controlled fashion and avoiding exceptions to phonetic rules when rules are first being learned.

Once a code-emphasis reading series has been identified, other features need to be considered before selecting a specific series. It may be impossible to locate a series that addresses all of the features listed below; however, when one or more of these features are lacking in a series, teachers need to supplement the deficits with other material.

1. *Interest level.* Has the series sacrificed interest level for phonetic regularity?

2. *Age-appropriateness.* Are poorer readers likely to be insulted by content intended for younger students?

(list continues)

Reading Passages	Explanation
Code Emphasis	
Dan ran to the big hill. He ran up the big hill. On top of the hill he ran to a big pit. He sat on top of the pit. In the pit he saw a dog. The dog was sad	Includes sight words *the* and *to,* but all other words are regular pronunciations of short vowels (e.g., *Dan, ran, hill, pit, dog*).
Meaning Emphasis	
Dan thought he would like to know what was on top of the great hill behind his house. One day he climbed up to look for himself. He found a small dog caught in a pit	Reads more like conversation but contains phonetic irregularities (e.g., three *ou* words [*thought, would, house*] that are all pronounced differently).

FIGURE 5.I. Code versus meaning emphasis in reading passages.

3. *Breadth of reading activities.* Does the series provide sufficient examples of reading under different formats, such as fiction, nonfiction, poetry, and current events?

4. *Compatibility with district's scope and sequence.* Does the series scope and sequence provide instruction on the skills that are required in mainstream classrooms?

5. *Sufficient opportunity for practice.* Does the series provide sufficient practice for students with learning problems, particularly at fluency and mastery levels?

6. *Comprehension instruction.* Does the series emphasize particular comprehension strategies and skills?

7. *Validation data.* Does the series provide some evidence that it has been successfully implemented with students with disabilities?

8. *Instructional component.* Does the series provide teachers with specific instructional guidelines that correspond with the teacher-effectiveness literature?

9. *Evaluation component.* Does the series provide a format by which student performance and instruction can be monitored and adjusted on a regular basis?

10. *Diversity.* Does the series provide sufficient representation of diverse cultures and gender roles?

No series will possess all of the above features, and in some cases, one or two of these features may be of little concern. For example, if the materials are used only with primary-age students, then a lower interest level may be appropriate. However, prior to adopting a series, all of the above questions need to be answered satisfactorily. Eventually, it is the teacher's responsibility to incorporate all of the above features into reading instruction. For example, if a series does not provide adequate comprehension instruction, teachers will have to supplement the series with reading comprehension instruction. If the series does not provide sufficient breadth of reading activities, teachers will need to obtain additional materials. Likewise, if a series does not include a formative evaluation component, teachers will need to develop an appropriate evaluation system on their own.

In many cases, teachers do not have the luxury of selecting their own reading programs. When this occurs, selection must be made from existing district materials. Teachers must then select the materials that contain most of the above features. Any features that are lacking should be supplemented by teachers. Probably the greatest problem encountered in the use of existing school district materials is that such materials may not provide controlled skill development and vocabulary. In such cases, teachers must adapt instruction to emphasize the phonetic regularities that do exist and de-emphasize the irregularities. Even with such adaptations, instructional materials may be far from optimal. Teachers can use other means to acquire phonetically based materials, such as contacting district libraries or the libraries of other districts and nearby universities. Publishers will often provide sample materials to teachers upon request.

Reading Assessment

When students enter special education settings, they typically bring assessment data, including evaluations of reading ability, with them. Assessment data are usually normative, which means the scores compare a student's functioning with that of other students in terms of percentiles, grade equivalents, or stanines. Such information is useful in determining the nature and extent of the academic deficiency and in assisting in special education placement decisions. Furthermore, normative data may provide some general insights into the student's reading abilities. Typical normative data, however, do not provide what can be regarded as the most critical component of assessment—placement of the student along the continuum of scope and sequence objectives.

Curriculum-Based Assessment

In order to determine a student's level within a reading program, it is necessary for curriculum-based assessment to be implemented. Curriculum-based assessment, as described in Chapter 3, refers to the direct evaluation of a student's skills with respect to an instructional curriculum. Given that the curriculum objectives parallel those of the district's scope and sequence, as well as those of the IEP, a curriculum-based assessment simply locates the instructional "starting place." For example, if the desired level of fluency is defined as 120 words per minute read orally with no errors, teachers should find the latest place in the curriculum at which this level of performance can be achieved. The first section of the curriculum at which this level of performance is not achieved is the optimal place to begin instruction. As another example, if successful reading comprehension, defined as answering correctly three factual-recall questions and one inferential question per page, is desired, then an appropriate level to start is the point in the curriculum at which the student fails to meet these criteria. As stated earlier, such performance criteria should be determined by the evaluation of acceptable performance levels in mainstreamed settings. These can be obtained by consultation with regular classroom teachers or similar evaluation of more typical students' performances.

It is important for teachers to develop standardized curriculum-based assessment procedures. To do this, teachers should select samples from passages of relatively low, moderate, and high difficulty from each level in their reading series. Performance criteria for decoding and comprehension should also be established for each level. As teachers develop a set of assessment devices, they will begin to have a systematic procedure for instructional placement in their reading curriculum. These procedures assist teachers in making instructional grouping decisions.

Instructional Grouping

Curriculum-based assessment provides important information for instructional grouping. Instructional grouping is necessary to maximize teaching effectiveness. When students are matched appropriately for instruction, the potential for all students to be engaged on-task is maximized. Instructional grouping is achieved by scheduling students who perform at similar levels with respect to a specific curriculum together. The more similarly the students perform, the more efficient the instructional group. In practice, however, it is not always easy to schedule perfectly matched instructional groups. Although instructional grouping is a way of maximizing instructional performance, it is also important to attend carefully to the instructional needs of individual students, particularly those whose performance is somewhat higher or lower than the majority of the group. Formative evaluation can help to ensure that all individuals are meeting instructional goals.

Once groups have been formed, teachers must ensure that assignment to groups remains dynamic and flexible. Research has shown that instructional groups have a tendency to remain static and stationary with respect to individual group membership. This is not always in the students' best interests. Group performance over time is a dynamic process, and this process should be carefully attended to by teachers. Membership within groups should be changed whenever performance warrants it. For example, if a student seems to progress more rapidly through the curriculum than other members of the group and seems insufficiently challenged, the student should be moved to a more appropriate instructional group. In other cases, it may be advisable to move a student from one group to another simply for the purpose of morale or group dynamics. Although research has shown that a student may benefit from being in a group with somewhat better readers, more caution should be applied in placing a student in a group with poorer readers.

The optimal number of students to be placed in a group cannot be precisely specified, but some considerations can be taken into account. These include:

1. total number of students needing instruction;

2. ability of students to work independently;

3. total time allocated for reading instruction; and

4. instructional resources available, including space, materials, and aides, tutors, or other paraprofessionals (e.g., parents, volunteers).

All of the above factors should be considered when deciding the size of instructional groups. Generally, groups of two seem inefficient, while groups larger than eight may be cumbersome. Just as assignment to group membership should be dynamic, assignment of group size should also be dynamic. If the size of a group appears problematic, it should be adjusted accordingly.

Reading Instruction

Chapter 1 presented the most important functions of teachers during instruction. These include (a) daily review, (b) presentation of objectives and material to be learned, (c) guided practice, (d) independent practice, (e) weekly and monthly reviews, and (f) formative evaluation. These functions are described with respect to reading instruction. During reading lessons, teachers should emphasize that the purpose of reading is comprehension and enjoyment. When decoding skills and oral reading fluency are primary objectives, teachers must make extra efforts at showing students that understanding is the underlying objective. This can be accomplished by making statements reiterating that the purpose of reading is to understand what the printed letters mean and by always including comprehension questions in lessons, such as "What does that mean?", "Can you think of another way to say that?", and "Why . . . ?" A sample reading lesson is given in Figure 5.2.

Daily review

Each reading lesson should begin with a review of the content covered in the previous lesson and a review of the purpose of reading. For example, if the previous lesson emphasized discrimination of words containing *b* and *d*, the next lesson should begin with a review of this discrimination and direct questioning of students to determine whether or not the discrimination has been mastered. Comprehension questions on the meanings of those words should also be included. If the discrimination is not found to be firm, additional instruction should be provided. For another example, if students had previously been taught a rule for decoding consonant–vowel–consonant–silent e (CVCe) words, the rule should be reviewed prior to proceeding to the next lesson. Review not only provides the teacher with an opportunity to determine whether or not the information has been acquired, it also provides students an opportunity for overlearning previously acquired information. Overlearning activities promote long-term retention, as well as help set the stage for future learning activities. If homework has been

Component	Examples
1. *Daily Review*	"Yesterday we learned some new words and their meanings from our book. Let's go over them together. What is this word? [Point to board.] Good. And what does [that word] mean? Can you think of a sentence using [that word]? . . . Who remembers how [that word] was used in the story? . . ."
2. *State Purpose*	"Today we are going to learn some more new words. These words all have *r*'s in them. First, we are going to learn how to say the words and what they mean. Then, we will practice using the words when we read our stories and when we write the words, their pronunciations, and their meanings in our reading logs."
3. *Deliver Information*	"These three letters plus *r*—[write on board] *ir*, *ur*, and *er*—all make the /r/ sound when they are together. When we see these letters in words we know that we should make the /r/ sound. Everybody, say the sound with me. [Signal.] . . . Good. Now look at the words that I have on the overhead. Most of these words have those letters plus *r*. How do we say the sound of those letters plus *r*? Let's go over this list together. The first word is [say word]; repeat after me. [Signal.] Now let's go over the definitions of each of these words that contain the special letters plus *r*. Does anyone know the meaning of the first word?" [Call on students and provide definitions when necessary.] . . .
4. *Guided Practice*	"Now I want you to get with your tutoring partners. I have a set of flash cards containing these words, their pronunciations, and their meanings. Each of you should take a turn as the tutor and as the tutee. Remember to use the correct tutoring behaviors and to record each other's performance. . . ."
5. *Independent Practice*	"Good job working hard during tutoring. It looks like everyone has learned our new words. Stay with your partners, put the flash cards away, and take out your books. We are going to read and discuss the third chapter of our book. This chapter contains many of the words that have the /r/ sound we have just practiced. The students who were the last ones to be tutors will read first to their partners. After a page, switch roles. You should help each other with the new words. Jot down the words that you have trouble saying. We'll discuss the chapter together. . . ."
6. *Formative Evaluation*	"When you think you can say each of the new words, use each one in a sentence, and tell me what happened in Chapter 3. Raise your hand and I will let you take your quiz."

FIGURE 5.2.   Sample reading lesson on *r*-controlled vowels.

assigned, this is the time to emphasize the importance of the homework and to check it to ensure that assignments have been completed accurately.

Presentation of material to be learned

Presentation of new content in reading should follow the teacher-presentation model presented in Chapter 1. When introducing new content, such as new letter sounds or a comprehension monitoring procedure, teachers must first state the objectives and main points to be covered. In the case of a letter sound, teachers make it explicitly clear that the lesson's goal is to learn that letter sound. Similarly, teachers make it clear that a specific procedure for monitoring comprehension will be learned. Next, teachers should include a step-by-step presentation of the new material. In the above examples, teachers would provide the letter and corresponding sound or present the comprehension-monitoring strategy in a step-by-step fashion. Next, teachers should model and demonstrate the new skill. Finally, after repeated questioning and practice, teachers should monitor students' understanding and adjust instruction accordingly. These procedures will be described in more detail later in this chapter.

Guided practice

In reading instruction, guided practice often takes the form of students reading orally in small group settings. Oral reading can be either from word lists or passages of story books that contain instances of the material previously introduced. A major goal of teachers at this point in instruction is to maximize engaged time-on-task for all students. This is done by ensuring that all students actively participate, even when they are not reading aloud. There are several means by which teachers can ensure that all students are covertly participating while one student is reading aloud. The most obvious method is to call on students to read in a random, rather than a systematic, manner. If students can deduce that they will not soon be asked to read, they are less likely to attend to the reading passage. Students also can be reinforced with praise, points, or tokens for knowing the correct place in the reading passage when called upon. When asking questions, the teacher should mention the student's name *after* and not before the question is asked (e.g., "What do you think the character is going to do next, Willie?"). If students think they might be called upon, they are more likely to think actively about the answer. Another active participation strategy is to have all students respond simultaneously after a teacher's signal. It is also helpful to occasionally have all students orally read simultaneously. Likewise, teachers can ask questions that require all students to respond with their thumbs (or hands) up or down.

Students can also read to each other in pairs rather than one at a time. Teachers can monitor the performance of several pairs of students with little difficulty, particularly if the nonreader of each pair assists in identifying errors. This activity can be very helpful in large groups that contain students of different reading levels.

Generally, it should be assumed that any procedure that facilitates or reinforces the active participation of all students at all times is likely to maximize learning. It is easy to understand how a reading group of four students, all of whom are actively engaged in reading, will be four times as effective as a similar group in which only one student at a time is on-task. The most critical aspect of guided practice is to provide students with many opportunities to respond correctly. Guided practice is most appropriate when students have been introduced to new skills and are in the process of strengthening these newly acquired skills. Although errors are expected at this stage, teachers need to provide immediate corrective feedback so that only correct responses are strengthened. When students are responding at a high level of accuracy, guided practice is less necessary, and instruction can proceed to a more independent level.

Independent practice

Independent practice in reading typically takes the form of independent seatwork, which may consist of silent reading with written responses to questions and completion of workbooks or worksheets. Independent practice is not as closely monitored by teachers, who are often engaged with other students, as guided practice. When students are engaged in independent practice, it is important that the activities closely parallel the goals of the lesson and be directly relevant to the guided practice activities that were previously completed. The teacher should reinforce quick, quiet, and accurate performance. Finally, independent practice activities need to be evaluated regularly. If a student is not performing accurately, additional guided practice or reteaching may be necessary. Conversely, if students are consistently exhibiting superior performance, they may need to proceed through the curriculum at a faster pace.

Independent practice can provide opportunities for overlearning in a context removed from a teacher-directed group setting. This may include developing mastery of skills. Independent practice is also helpful as a context for reinforcing independent study and work habits. It also provides an opportunity for students to develop a sense of responsibility for their own learning. However, research has generally shown that special education students learn at a slower rate from independent seatwork than they do from teacher-led instruction and guided practice. Although some benefits can be gained from independent practice, it is important for teachers to maximize the time spent in direct, teacher-led instructional contexts.

An alternative to the seatwork activity described above is the use of peer tutoring. Research has shown that special education students can function effectively as tutors and often gain fluency building skills in the process. In addition, tutoring has sometimes been seen to improve students' attitudes toward school and the content areas being tutored. Tutoring may also prove advantageous in that it provides students with additional practice in active responding. If peer tutors are employed, however, teachers must ensure that tutors use appropriate feedback procedures and that formative data are collected to ensure that both tutor and tutee benefit from the process. Since effective reading instruction demands a great deal of independent reading practice, tutoring can be an effective means of reaching this goal. Figure 5.3 presents additional information on peer tutoring, summarized from Scruggs, Mastropieri, and Richter (1985).

Another alternative to worksheet activities is computer-assisted instruction (CAI). Like peer tutoring, CAI provides students with immediate feedback. Additionally, a tutor is not required, and several contemporary programs include collection of performance data. One drawback of CAI is that computers at present are unable to monitor students' oral reading performance. CAI can be helpful in providing practice with feedback on phonics and reading comprehension.

Weekly and monthly reviews

In special education, it is critical to continuously review previously covered material in order to ensure long-term retention of the material. For this reason, teachers should review acquired reading skills on a weekly and monthly, as well as a daily, basis. For example, weekly and monthly reviews of phonics rules or comprehension skills learned to date help to make these skills more concrete as well as reinforce students' knowledge of the overall scope, sequence, and purposes of reading instruction. To enhance students' confidence in their progress, teachers can provide students with examples of their previous levels of performance. For example, students can be required to keep alphabet books, dictionaries, or daily logs that contain records of new letters, sounds, words, meanings, books read, and strategies learned during reading. These logs can become part of a student's portfolio and can document the amount of learning that has occurred. It is also helpful to record learning gains on graphs or charts and by playing audiotapes or videotapes of students' previous reading performances.

Formative evaluation

As in all areas of instruction, formative data should be collected regularly, graphed, and used to guide the instructional decision-making process. Figure 5.4 provides an example of a formative evaluation procedure that indicates that the student is performing and progressing at an optimal rate.

Chapter 3 presented information on how to design, administer, and use curriculum-based measures (CBM) to monitor progress in reading. Research results have indicated that students will exhibit greater performance under the following conditions:

Procedures for Peer Tutoring Programs

1. Select pairs that are likely to work well together.

2. For drill and practice activities using flash cards, students can be of similar ability. If a great deal of correction is likely or judgment is called for, however, the tutor should be of higher ability.

3. When acting as tutors, students should use the same teaching procedures as the teacher, except that they should generally not be used to introduce new content. Correction of errors should be immediate and positive and require restatement of the correct response by the tutee (e.g., "No, the word is pronounced _____ . You say it. [Response.] Good").

4. Even though research has shown that tutors can often learn from tutoring, they should not be overused in this capacity. Formative evaluation should be used to show that all students' objectives are being met.

5. All tutoring activities should be relevant to specific instructional objectives.

Potential Benefits of Tutoring

1. Tutees can gain the benefits of additional individual engaged time-on-task (e.g., greater levels of accuracy and/or fluency).

2. Students who are accurate in a skill can gain fluency by acting as a tutor.

3. Students who are engaged in tutoring can gain a sense of responsibility for themselves and others and can gain improved attitudes toward the class and the content area taught (e.g., reading). However, tutoring may not fulfill global, more difficult-to-measure constructs such as self-esteem.

4. Formative evaluation can determine whether the above potential benefits have, in fact, been realized.

FIGURE 5.3. Peer tutoring.

1. Teachers administer CBM at least twice a week.

2. Teachers select CBM based upon students' long-term goals.

3. Teachers examine the results of the CBM and make relevant instructional decisions based on performance data (e.g., increase time on task, alter instructional grouping).

For example, students can be administered timed readings of 100-word selections that reflect long-term objectives from their curricular materials twice a week. Teachers can record reading rate, number and type of reading errors (decoding, omission, insertion, etc.), and comprehension scores (answers to factual and inferential questions about the passage). Examination of this

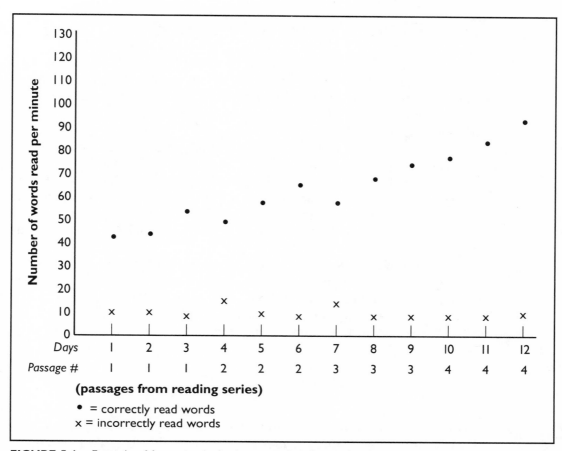

FIGURE 5.4. Example of formative evaluation procedure for reading.

data recorded over time can provide important information on student progress and instructional needs.

This section has presented an overview of reading instruction and described components common to all aspects of reading instruction. In any reading program, at any stage of instruction, it is important to review previous material, present new information clearly and concisely, provide guided practice on new material, provide independent practice activities, and periodically review cumulative information. It is also necessary to collect formative data and to regularly monitor and adjust instruction in accordance with formative data. At all times, it is important to maintain very high rates of on-task engagement.

The remainder of this chapter is devoted to applications of these procedures to specific areas of reading instruction. The next section discusses strategies for teaching word-attack skills (phonics), while the last section discusses strategies for improving reading comprehension.

TEACHING PHONICS SKILLS

As stated earlier in this chapter, most research indicates that children with learning difficulties learn to read most easily under instruction that is systematic, well-paced, and phonetic in orientation. If teachers provide intensive instruction and practice on critical word-attack skills, most students with learning difficulties can learn to read.

It was also stated earlier in this chapter that good word-attack skills are only one part of the total reading process. Without such skills, however, most special education students will not learn to read effectively. During phonics instruction, it is also important to emphasize meaning. At the earliest stages of reading instruction, students are primarily concerned with "cracking the code" of reading, but teachers need to emphasize the meaning of the printed words.

Word-attack or phonics instruction can be divided into several different components. These include (a) letter–sound correspondences, (b) sound blending, (c) phonics rule learning, and (d) learning of irregular sight words. Examples of these components are shown in Figure 5.5, and they are described separately in the following sections.

Letter–Sound Correspondence

Letter–sound correspondence, or the learning of sound–symbol relationships, is the first major step in the reading process. During this component of reading instruction, students are taught that written language is composed of individual letter symbols and that the clues to the reading process are in these symbols. This initial concept about decoding should develop as students learn more about sound–symbol relationships.

Fact learning

Letter–sound correspondence is one form of fact learning; that is, to learn that the letter *b* is associated with the *buh* sound is to learn a fact. There is no general rule that will tell a student what sound a certain letter represents. These sounds and corresponding letters must simply be memorized, and the more time students spend actively practicing these sounds, the faster they will learn. Students also must learn to discriminate different letters, especially ones that differ only in spatial orientation, such as *b* and *d*. Such discriminations are necessary for accurate reading.

Sound versus names

The teaching of sound–symbol correspondence should not be confused with learning the names of the letters of the alphabet (e.g., *a, bee, cee, dee,* etc.). Many students enter school having learned their ABCs as a serial list,

Phonics Components	Examples
Letter–sound correspondence	*a* as in hat
	b as in bat
	c as in cat
	d as in dog
Sound blending	cat = cuh-a-tuh
	hill = huh-iii-luh
Long vowels	
CVC+e	*o* as in vote
	a as in bake
vowel digraphs	*ea* as in beat
	ai as in bait
	oe as in toe
Diphthongs	*oi* as in voice
	ou as in sound
	ow as in brown
Consonant blends	*br* as in break
	bl as in black
	gr as in ground
	scr as in script
Long and short *oo*	
Long *oo*	*oo* as in book
	oo as in cook
Short *oo*	*oo* as in too
	oo as in tool
r-controlled vowels	*ur* as in hurt
	ir as in shirt
	er as in water
	ar as in star
	or as in actor

FIGURE 5.5. Phonics examples.

but many of them have no idea what these letter names represent. Their parents have simply reinforced them for reciting them in the correct sequence. In fact, research has not demonstrated that learning to recite the alphabet is helpful in learning to read. However, in some cases it may promote early success and improve a student's attitude toward learning to read.

Most common sound

When learning letter–sound correspondence, students must learn the most common sound associated with each letter first. Most consonants, other than *c* and *g*, have highly regular sounds associated with them. Vowel sounds are usually taught by providing the most common short sounds associated with them (e.g., *a* as in *apple, e* as in *bed, i* as in *bitter,* etc.). Letters are usually introduced one at a time after a review of previously learned letters. Students can be grouped easily for letter–sound knowledge, because there are only a certain number of letters to be learned. When grouping for instruction or while delivering instruction, teachers need to determine the rate (fluency) at which students can identify letters, as well as their level of accuracy. At any given time during the instructional process, students should be able to read a list of letters previously taught at a rate of 100 or more per minute. Such automaticity of responding is necessary so that students can concentrate on other reading skills at a later date.

Teaching letter sounds

As stated earlier in this chapter, a reading lesson should begin with a review of previously learned information. In the case of letter sounds, the teacher should first review any previous learning and homework assignments (e.g., relevant phonics worksheets or records of guided practice with parents or sibling tutors). Next, the teacher should clearly state the objective for the day's lesson (e.g., "Today we are going to learn two new letter sounds"). Students can be asked to repeat this information on cue to ensure attention (e.g., "What are we going to learn, everybody?" [Signal.]) When the teacher feels the group understands the purpose of the lesson, the first letter can be displayed or drawn on the board while the teacher says, "The letter we are going to learn today is *m*. [Point.] Everybody say it with me: *m*." The students should repeat the letter sound on cue from the teacher, both as a group and individually, until the teacher feels the initial part of the association has been established. Students should then be given practice in discriminating the letter from other, previously learned letters. This can be done both as an identification task (e.g., "Point to the letter that makes the *m* sound") and as a production task (e.g., "Read these letters as I point them out to you"). It is important that students learn to read the individual letter first, then learn to read it in the context of previously learned information. It is also important to include reading sounds in the context of words, words in sentences, and sentences in stories as early and as often as possible. This will help reinforce that the purpose of reading is comprehension, not simply saying sounds of letters or reading words in isolation. If students begin to forget previous information, instruction may be proceeding too rapidly. If students *always* know all previously and presently introduced content, instruction may be proceeding too slowly. Daily probes (timings) of previously and presently taught information can help determine the optimal rate of instruction. An example of a probe sheet used to assess decoding skills could include a list of the letters and words being taught or even short passages containing the target information.

Like instruction in other areas, lessons should be positive, rapidly paced, allow for much overt student responding, and allow for a high level of correct responses. Errors should be acknowledged but not emphasized unless an error was due to carelessness, inattention, or flippancy. At such moments, teachers need to emphasize paying attention and putting forth effort.

Sequence of instruction

In most cases, the sequence of introduction of new letter sounds, word patterns, and words will parallel the curriculum. The teacher's guide that accompanies the reading series will generally identify which new letter sounds, word patterns, and words are being introduced. Teachers should be overt about introducing the new sound (even if the text is not) and make sure that the sounds are applied correctly in any application or generalization exercises (e.g., reading the new sound in context of words, sentences, and paragraphs).

Special problems

Sometimes students will exhibit difficulty learning letter sounds. At such times, it is important to conduct an error analysis to try to determine the source of difficulty and attempt to correct it. Usually, letter–sound correspondence errors involve errors of discrimination learning or fact learning.

Discrimination learning.

Many beginning readers, as well as students with learning difficulties, have problems discriminating between letters that differ only in orientation (*b* versus *d*, and *p* versus *q*). In order to avoid such problems initially, such letters should not be introduced consecutively. Several letters should be taught between the introduction of *b* and *d*, and sufficient practice should be provided to ensure that the first letter sound is completely mastered before the second is introduced. If difficulties persist, direct teaching of the discrimination may be necessary. Relevant activities include identification tasks in which students circle the *b*'s in a random series of *b*'s and *d*'s. Formative data, such as the daily percent of *b*'s and *d*'s correctly read, will help the teacher determine whether the student is making progress. In general, increasing engaged time-on-task helps develop the discrimination. In addition, some type of mnemonic (memory-enhancing) elaboration may prove helpful. For example, the student can be told to visualize a poster bed viewed from the side as a reminder that the *b* has the vertical line on the left side and the *d* has the vertical line on the right side. As with any mnemonic, however, the teacher must be careful to ensure that the students understand the purpose of the strategy and that the strategy is helping reinforce learning.

Factual learning.

Sometimes students exhibit difficulty remembering previously learned letter sounds. In this case, errors are not simply the substitution of letters with similar appearances but rather covert errors (e.g., "I don't know") or confusion with dissimilar letters (e.g., *s* for *t*). In these cases, the student must be provided with additional practice on problem letter sounds. If the group as a whole is having difficulty, it may also be helpful to slow the pace of instruction or increase time-on-task variables. Providing the student with a tutor for a few extra minutes a day or enlisting the aid of parents or siblings in the evenings may also be helpful. Finally, some recent research has suggested that a letter–sound mnemonic may be helpful in the initial acquisition and retention of letter–sound correspondence. For example, showing a picture of the initial letter sound (e.g., a picture of a flower for *f*) has not been found to be particularly helpful in teaching the *f* sound. However, making the *f represent* a flower

may be helpful in enforcing the sound–symbol relationship. In any case, formative data can help determine whether instruction is producing a desired effect.

Letter–sound correspondence is a principal component of the reading process and is taught by factual and discrimination paradigms, using procedures common to all effective teaching, including review of previous learning, statement of goals, introduction of new content, guided practice, independent practice, and weekly and monthly review. Generally, individual letter sounds are not taught independently but are taught in conjunction with other reading skills such as sound blending real words, which is described below.

Sound Blending

As students learn the sounds of individual letters, they must also learn to blend these sounds together to produce the sounds of letter combinations. This procedure, which is necessary in learning how to read words, must be taught overtly. Sound blending should begin as soon as students have learned enough letter sounds to begin to pronounce consonant–vowel–consonant (CVC) trigrams, such as *cat, big,* and *tan.* Students can also be taught to decode nonsense CVC trigrams such as *biv, lub,* and *pom.* The occasional use of nonsense words can help ensure that students are attending to the letter sounds and sound-blending procedure and have not simply memorized individual sight words. However, since nonsense words are devoid of meaning, they should be used sparingly.

Teaching sound blending

As in all lessons, students should first be informed of the purpose of the lesson (e.g., "We are now going to learn to read some new words"). Students are then asked to provide the sounds of the individual letters (e.g., "Everybody, what is this sound? [Point to *c*.] What is this sound?" [Point to *t*]). Students are then asked to blend them along with the teacher (e.g., "Everybody, say them together with me: kuh-aaa-tuh. What's the word? [Response.] Good! The word is *cat*. What does *cat* mean?"). Students should repeat this procedure several times with the teacher, as a group and individually, to ensure the word is learned accurately. As they learn new trigrams, the students should practice all words together to ensure that they learn to make appropriate discriminations between trigrams with different letter sounds. Teachers can help by providing students with flash cards or probe sheets on which appropriate CVC trigrams have been written and by timing students' responses to verify that the skills can be produced with fluency. Again, it is important to emphasize the meanings of the new words, too. Although teachers must use judgment when determining appropriate rates, 60 correct responses per minute is a good minimum rate to aim for before proceeding.

When students have produced sound-blending skills accurately and fluently, the teacher can assess the students for application of these skills by having them read the words in a passage from the curriculum materials. Again, the goal should be for the students to read these materials at accuracy and fluency rates similar to those of mainstream students who are using similar materials. During story and passage reading, teachers also should emphasize the meaning of the information. After fluency practice, students can be asked to think about what happened in the story, to describe what the story was about, to predict what could happen next, and to reread as necessary to confirm their answers. Students should not proceed to a new reading passage until they have read the current passage accurately and fluently. Just as a music teacher would not ask a pupil to sight-read a new piece on the piano each day, a reading teacher should allow the student time to develop the appropriate reading skills for the passage.

Onsets and rimes

Stahl (1992), describing the work of Treiman (1985) and Adams (1990), presented the teaching of *onsets* and *rimes* as an alternative to the teaching of individual phonics rules. The onset is the part of the syllable before the vowel, and the rime is part of the syllable from the vowel onward. This also can be a useful strategy in promoting written language.

Analysis of phonics regularities by Adams (1990) has indicated that rimes are much more regular than individual letters and combinations of letters. For example, the digraph *ea*, supposedly pronounced as long "e," is often irregular. However, with the exceptions of *–ead* (bead, head), *–eaf* (sheaf, deaf), and *–ear* (dear, bear), it is very regular. The rime *–ean,* for example, is almost always pronounced with the long "e" sound. In addition, rimes such as *–ack, –ing, –ide, –ight, –oke,* and *–ump* are very regular in pronunciation and are found in a large number of words.

Instruction based on these principles is used in several successful reading programs, including the Benchmark School, a school in Pennsylvania for children with reading difficulties that was recognized in 1986 for Excellence in Education by the U.S. Department of Education (Gaskins et al., 1988). When students encounter unfamiliar words (e.g., *wheat*), they are encouraged to compare them with words that are familiar to them (e.g., *meat*) to help their decoding and then to cross-check to ensure the new word as read makes sense in the passage. Instruction based on onsets and rimes has limited research support in special education settings at present. However, the research that exists supports its effectiveness. Further, the principles on which such instruction is based are well validated by research.

Formative data

Data can be collected on sound blending and word reading in several ways. Teachers can ask students to read lists of trigrams containing letters that have been learned and time the reading rate for both correct and incorrect responses. These data can be displayed on a graph or chart. Some teachers prefer to use precision-teaching charts, which were discussed in Chapter 3, for this purpose. Graphic presentations are helpful in determining whether students are making progress in acquiring reading skills. Students' reading logs also can be updated regularly to contain newly learned materials.

Another method for collecting formative data is the use of tape recordings. If tape recordings of reading performance are made regularly, they can provide another measure of reading progress. Reading performance data collected from tape recordings can also be quantified by recording the rate of correct versus incorrect performances. In addition, tapes made previously can be played back to students to provide them with additional feedback on their progress. When students have read a specific passage to a prespecified level of fluency, they should move on to the next lesson. If the passage has not been read fluently, however, additional practice should be provided.

Special problems

Sometimes individual students will demonstrate difficulty with sound blending. At such times, it may seem simpler to teach the words as sight words rather than sound blending. This temptation should be avoided, however, because a firm knowledge of sound blending is much more likely to serve the student's long-term reading needs. The first thing a teacher can do when sound-blending problems are encountered is to carefully analyze the task. The teacher may be teaching too much information too rapidly, or the student may not have sufficiently mastered individual letter sounds. In the latter case, it is necessary to go back to letter–sound instruction until the student demonstrates a high rate of fluency on letter sounds. If difficulties in blending letter sounds persist, the teacher will need to intensify the instruction, either by increasing the total time on task or by providing more intensive one-on-one instruction, directed by either the teacher or another student who is deemed "expert" in sound blending. If motivation appears to be a problem, the teacher should make an effort to increase incentives to learn, either by additional teacher praise and attention or by awarding points or tokens redeemable for awards or privileges.

Phonics Rule Learning

Blends

After students have mastered letter sounds and sound blending, they must learn a series of rules for the correct pronunciation of groups of letters. The simplest examples are consonant blends, because these are special cases of sound blending. Because sounds derived from consonant blends are regular and directly reflect the sounds of the letters, they are generally taught after CVC blending. Examples of consonant blends are *br*, *str*, and *bl*. Consonant blends are different from previously covered blending in that there are only a certain number of blends and the sequence is invariant. For instance, one cannot pronounce blends such as *lpf* or *mtl*. Blends are introduced one at a time in the context of words, and opportunities for practice and feedback, both on individual blends and in the context of other blends, are provided. Ultimately, consonant blends should be recognized and pronounced as readily as individual letter sounds.

Diphthongs

Diphthongs are vowel pairs that produce two merged sounds. The diphthongs are: *oi*, *ow*, and *ou*. These sounds are regular and should be taught as separate phonics facts and practiced in the contexts of words and their meanings.

Other phonics rules

Many word-attack strategies include the application of explicit rules for decoding. One of the first rules to be taught is the rule governing the pronunciation of CVC + e words. Such CVCe words include *hope, tape,* and *bite*. This rule states that in CVCe patterns, the internal vowel is pronounced with the long sound (e.g., says its name) while the final *e* is silent. Students must be taught (a) to repeat the rule from memory, (b) to discriminate a letter pattern that calls for application of the rule, and (c) to correctly apply the rule to the letter pattern. If all three of these rule-learning components are not in place, it is unlikely that the word can be read correctly. When rules such as the CVC + e rule are taught, as in other word-attack skills, they should first be explicitly introduced (e.g., "Today we are going to learn a new rule"). Next, the rule should be explained and practiced with the group as a whole. After this, students should be given guided and independent practice in identifying CVCe patterns and in applying the rule. Students should be able to easily discriminate words such as *hop* from words such as *hope* and to clearly explain the rule that governs their pronunciation. An example of teaching the CVCe rule is given in Figure 5.6.

Another important phonics rule is the rule governing the pronunciation of double vowels, such as those in *hail*, *each*, and *reason*. In this case, the instructional procedures parallel those for other rule-learning situations.

When students have demonstrated accurate and fluent identification and production of phonics rules, they should be provided with guided opportunities to master these rules by learning to apply them in the context of reading passages. At all levels of learning, collection of formative data can help ensure that all learning objectives are being met.

Teacher (T): How do you say this word? [Points.]

Student (S): Hop.

T: Hop. Good. Now, watch me. [Writes an *e* at the end.] Now the word is *hope*. How do you say it?

S: Hope.

T: Good, hope. Now, here's the rule: when you add *e* to a word like *hop*, you don't pronounce the *e*, but the *o* says its name. So, you say ō instead of ŏ. How do you say the word?

S: Hope.

T: Good, you say hope. What's the rule?

S: If you add *e*, you say *o*.

T: Right, if you add *e* to a word like *hop*, the vowel says its name. Let's try it with another word. How do you read this word? [Writes *cap*.]

S: Cap.

T: Cap, good. Now, I'm going to add an *e*. [Adds *e*.] How do you read it now?

S: Cape.

T: Correct, cape. How did you know to say cape?

S: Because you said it says its name.

T: What says its name?

S: The *a*.

T: Right, the *vowel* says its name, in this case, the *a*. Now let's try some more. Then let's review what these words mean.

FIGURE 5.6. Teaching a phonics rule.

Special problems

Research has shown that many special education students have difficulty with rule learning. Generally, when problems occur, task-and-error analysis shows that the problem lies either in (a) recall of the rule, (b) identification of the relevant letter patterns, or (c) correct application of the rule. The source of the error can be uncovered by questioning (e.g., "What kind of word is this? What is the rule you use for this kind of word? How should you read this word?"). Students should then be given additional guided practice on the difficult components. Sometimes, rules can be stated in a way that aids in their recall. A familiar example is the rhyme, "When two vowels go walking, the first one does the talking." Although this rhyme is easy to memorize, it is critical that students know what is meant by "vowels," "go walking," "first one," and "does the talking." Otherwise, memorizing the rhyme will be of little use to students.

Teachers should introduce phonics rules as they are introduced in the curriculum materials. A good reading program will consist of regularly sequenced word-attack skills and include a great deal of practice on each new skill. If the new skills to be taught are not provided explicitly in the teacher's guide, the teacher must determine the requirements of the new task and introduce them in reading lessons. A table of specifications for some decoding skills is given in Table 5.1.

Irregular Sight Words

Unfortunately, many words in the English language cannot be pronounced by the accurate application of word-attack skills. These exceptions include words such as *heir, was,* and *research* and are found on all levels of reading difficulty. In general, it is wise to avid the introduction of irregular words until regular phonics rules have been learned and mastered.

Irregular sight words must be taught as facts; that is, learning how to read the word *through* is not useful for anything other than reading the word *through*. This is very different from learning individual phonics rules that can be applied to a large number of individual words. When teaching irregular words, it is best not to elaborate on the nature of the words other than to state that these are special words that must be read in a special way. They are taught by using extended drill and practice, using flash cards, writing on the blackboard, or picking them out of reading passages.

If students demonstrate difficulty in learning specific sight words, the teacher should first determine whether the word was ever explicitly taught. Often sight words that a student has never encountered appear in a new reading passage. In this case, a student with good word-attack skills will attempt a phonetic reading of the word or attempt to deduce the sound of the word through contextual cues. If a sight word has not been taught,

TABLE 5.1.   Table of Specifications for Reading Decoding.

CONTENT	BEHAVIOR				
	Identification	Production			
	A. Acquisition	B. Acquisition	C. Fluency	D. Application	E. Generalization
1. *Consonant sounds (b, c, t . . .)*	1A	1B	1C	1D	1E
2. *Vowel Sounds (a, e, i, o, u)*	2A	2B	2C	2D	2E
3. *CVC words (cap, hop)*	3A	3B	3C	3D	3E
4. *CVCe words (cape, hope)*	4A	4B	4C	4D	4E
5. *Sight words (saw, what)*	5A	5B	5C	5D	5E
6. *Consonant blends (bl, st)*	6A	6B	6C	6D	6E
7. *Vowel digraphs (ai, ea)*	7A	7B	7C	7D	7E
8. *Word endings (−ing, −er, −est)*	8A	8B	8C	8D	8E
9. *Compound words (into)*	9A	9B	9C	9D	9E
10. *R-controlled vowels (ir, ar)*	10A	10B	10C	10D	10E

Behavioral Objectives:

3B   Students will orally read 10 CVC words [list words] from a list with 100% accuracy.

4C   Students will orally read 10 CVCe words [list words] from a list with 100% accuracy in 10 seconds.

9D   Students will orally read passages from their reading book that contain compound words with 100% accuracy.

10E Students will orally read passages from their geography texts that contain r-controlled vowels with 100% accuracy.

explicit instruction should be provided. Unless they are teaching students how to use contextual cues to read new words, however, teachers should not surprise students with unfamiliar irregular words. Teachers should be able to identify new sight words in reading passages and teach them to accuracy and fluency before students are asked to apply them in context.

If a student is having trouble reading sight words that have been previously taught, additional drill and practice must be provided. In some cases, teachers may decide that too many new words have been introduced in too short a time period and, consequently, may reduce the pace of instruction. Another approach is to increase the amount of time-on-task in active responding to the sight words. This can be provided either by the teacher, an aide, parent, or a peer tutor who is familiar enough with the words to provide corrective feedback. If individuals other than the teacher deliver instruction, care must be taken to ensure that specific objectives are being met, since the teacher may not be able to observe all of the instruction. In all cases, formative data can help to determine whether or not objectives are being met.

Summary of Phonics Instruction

In the preceding section, phonics or decoding instruction was divided into letter–sound correspondence, sound blending, phonics rule learning, and irregular sight words. These components were described with respect to the teaching of relevant facts, rules, discriminations, and procedures. Although phonics instruction has been divided into several components, it must be remembered that the overall goal is to tie all these components into clear, efficient reading of text. Providing guided practice of all previously learned skills on reading passages is an opportunity to ensure that all previously learned skills have been effectively integrated. If problems occur, teachers should be able to identify the source of the problem and provide corrective instruction.

Although good decoding skills are critical for the reading success of special education students, these skills alone do not guarantee that students will become competent readers. To become competent readers, students also need to develop skills for comprehending what they read. Reading comprehension skills are discussed in detail in the next section.

READING COMPREHENSION

Reading comprehension is the ultimate goal of reading instruction. All of the phonics and decoding skills discussed previously are necessary prerequisites for successful reading comprehension. In the past, little instruction in reading comprehension took place in classroom settings. However, recent research has advanced our understanding not only of what processes occur during reading comprehension but also of how to facilitate the explicit instruction of reading comprehension. It is now generally agreed that reading comprehension involves an interaction of several variables, including the learner, the background (or prior knowledge of the topic and schema) of the reader, the strategies (or metacognitive skills) the learner possesses, and the text material itself. Additionally, it is known that readers employ strategies to facilitate comprehension before reading, during reading, and after reading. In the following sections, each of these variables is described and discussed in relation to how reading comprehension can be taught.

The Learner

The reading level of the learner must be determined. As mentioned previously, after completion of a curriculum-based assessment, learners can be placed at an appropriate level of difficulty in the text material. It is important to match the learner with the appropriate difficulty level and to maximize the learner's attentional and motivational levels. Teachers can maximize attention and motivation by stressing their importance to instruction or by manipulating classroom contingencies based on performance. Ultimately, teachers want students to be accountable for their own learning; therefore, a combination of teacher emphasis and contingencies may be used initially, followed by a fading out of the contingencies.

Prior Knowledge and Schema

Research has shown that the amount and type of background knowledge students bring to reading passages influences the amount and type of information that is recalled or comprehended. This is sometimes referred to as prior knowledge or *schema*. Schemata (plural) are considered to be networks of conceptual knowledge about the world in which one lives. This conceptual knowledge assists people in understanding and thinking about events encountered in reading. For example, the phrase "I am going to a birthday party" evokes a birthday knowledge system or schema. Even if a more detailed description of the birthday party is missing from the reading passage, most readers would be able to describe a birthday party scenario without much difficulty. Likewise, upon encountering a passage that describes a highway scene with an ambulance and blocked-off traffic, most readers would be able to describe an accident schema.

Prior knowledge can be directly evoked by teacher questioning. For example, immediately prior to reading a passage about beavers, the teacher can ask students to discuss and elaborate upon what they already know about beavers. Activation of prior knowledge can lead to enhanced comprehension of the passages. As the students read the passages, the teacher can remind students or ask students to describe how the passage interacts with students' prior knowledge as discussed before reading the passage.

Such schemata, or meaningfully oriented clusters of information, allow readers to interact with elements in the text material. Typically, readers tend to form hypotheses about the text based on the schemata or prior knowledge they bring with them. These hypotheses are usually refined after the reading of a story has been completed. For example, when introducing a book about dinosaurs, the teacher could say, "This book is about dinosaurs. Everyone, think about what you know about dinosaurs. [Pause for thinking time.] What do you know about dinosaurs, Tommy? . . ." Students can then form hypotheses about the book, and upon completing the book the teacher could say, "Who remembers what they predicted would happen in this book? Were you right? How did your predictions change? What new information do you have about dinosaurs?" This interactive view of the reading process relies upon two components. First, readers construct hypotheses based on their schemata and the text. Second, readers refine those hypotheses to comprehend, interpret, and evaluate the text material. In order for refinement of hypotheses to take place, readers must employ comprehension-monitoring strategies. A table of specifications for comprehension monitoring is given in Table 5.2. Such strategies are also referred to as metacognitive strategies and are described below.

Metacognitive Strategies

Comprehension-monitoring skills

Comprehension monitoring refers to the ability to monitor understanding of text as it is being read. Comprehension monitoring can include understanding (a) individual words, (b) particular sentences, (c) relationships among sentences, and (d) the entire text or story. Recently, numerous types of self-monitoring and self-questioning strategies have been taught to students, and, when the strategies have been used effectively, students' comprehension performance has improved. Several of these strategies will be described briefly. As in all the instruction techniques discussed, students can be required to identify these strategies prior to producing them.

Self-questioning

Self-questioning is a global strategy that can encompass many of the more specific strategies. In its basic form, self-questioning simply means asking questions of oneself while reading. In the initial teaching stages, students are usually required to state their self-questions aloud so that teachers can monitor their performance. As students become more proficient at self-questioning, they are sometimes required to use a self-monitoring sheet and either check off or write down the questions when they ask them. Ultimately, when students consistently and accurately employ the self-questioning strategies, even the self-monitoring sheets can be phased out. A simple example of a self-questioning strategy is teaching students to ask themselves the question "Do I understand what I just read?" If students are able to answer affirmatively, they can proceed with reading the passage. However, if they answer negatively, they are required to go back and reread

TABLE 5.2. Table of Specifications for Reading Comprehension.

CONTENT	BEHAVIOR				
	Identification	Production			
	A. Acquisition	B. Acquisition	C. Fluency	D. Application	E. Generalization
1. Who, what, when, where, how, why	1A	1B	1C	1D	1E
2. Facts and details	2A	2B	2C	2D	2E
3. Titles	3A	3B	3C	3D	3E
4. Sequencing events	4A	4B	4C	4D	4E
5. Paraphrasing and summarizing	5A	5B	5C	5D	5E
6. Main ideas	6A	6B	6C	6D	6E
7. Inferences	7A	7B	7C	7D	7E
8. Predictions	8A	8B	8C	8D	8E
9. Deductions	9A	9B	9C	9D	9E

Behavioral Objectives:

1A After reading a paragraph and being given multiple-choice questions, students will circle the correct answer to questions like the following: Who was in the story? When did the story take place? All questions will be answered correctly.

2B After reading two paragraphs, students will write every fact and detail that occurred in those paragraphs with 100% accuracy.

3C After reading a story, students will immediately be able to provide an appropriate title for the story (within 15 seconds).

4D After reading a story in the basal reading series, students will be able to successfully sequence all the events.

6E After reading Chapter 7 in their free-time books, students will be able to tell the main ideas of all the stories.

the passage until they are able to answer correctly. An example of this type of self-monitoring strategy is given in Figure 5.7 (see also Graves, 1986). Other specific skills that could be used during self-questioning follow.

Paraphrasing and summarizing

Another strategy that can be incorporated into self-questioning is paraphrasing. Paraphrasing is simply restating in one's own words what was just read. Paraphrasing can be used for words, sentences, paragraphs, or

		Yes	No
Paragraph 1	Do I understand what I read? If yes, continue reading. If no, reread the part I just read.	☐	☐
Paragraph 2	Do I understand what I read? If yes, continue reading. If no, reread the part I just read.	☐	☐
Paragraph 3	Do I understand what I read? If yes, continue reading. If no, reread what I just read.	☐	☐
Paragraph 4	Do I understand what I read? If yes, continue reading. If no, reread what I just read.	☐	☐

FIGURE 5.7. Sample self-monitoring sheet. *Note.* This model can be adapted to prompt students concerning specific information (e.g., Why did the bird fall out of the tree? Where did Jose go after school?).

entire stories. Teachers also can ask students to summarize a story. In this case, a summary would be similar to a paraphrase. The critical aspect of this task is for students to restate in their own words what they have read. Summarization strategies can involve students asking themselves, "Who or what is the passage about?" and "What happened in the passage?" Summarization can also include deleting unnecessary information, finding a higher-order (superordinate) term to describe a list of actions or items, and identifying or inventing a paragraph topic sentence.

Sequencing events

Another strategy, which is best used near the end of a story, is sequencing the events that have occurred. This task is particularly helpful when the chronological order of events is important to remember. For example, students may be required to know the sequence of events that led to the United States' involvement in Vietnam or to list the events that occurred in the plot of a novel. In the initial stages of learning sequencing, instruction may take the form of requiring students to identify which of two events occurred first. Later, the production of events would be required, and, finally, students may be required to sequence the events silently through self-questioning.

Main ideas

Main ideas of sentences, paragraphs, and stories need to be identified and produced by students. A main idea is a condensed one- or two-sentence version of the passage. When students are asked to generate the best title of a passage, they are being required to name a main idea. Typically, this skill is the first step required prior to summarizing entire passages. A sample lesson on main idea instruction is given in Figure 5.8.

Some researchers have hypothesized that students should be taught to identify the main idea in pictures prior to being required to identify the main idea in paragraphs or groups of sentences. If these types of activities are practiced first, teachers can be sure that students really understand what a main idea is. As in any identification stage of instruction, students can be required to select the best main idea from several choices. After mastery of the identification-stage objectives, students can be required to produce the main idea from illustrations. Instruction can then proceed to requiring students to identify and produce main ideas, first from sentences, then from paragraphs and increasingly larger reading selections.

Review	T: Remember all last week and yesterday we practiced identifying the main ideas from paragraphs after we read them? Who can tell me what the main idea is? [Signal.]
	S: The main idea is a summary statement of the story.
Goal statement and teacher presentation	T: That's right, the main idea tells us in one sentence what the paragraph is about. The main ideas we identified yesterday were selected from multiple-choice items. Today we are going to practice coming up with the main ideas on our own. First, watch how I do this example. [Reads paragraph out loud while students follow along silently.] Now, the main idea of that paragraph is [states main idea] because it tells us in one sentence what that paragraph is about. Remember, the main idea is not simply a fact or detail from the story. The main idea tells more of the general idea of the whole paragraph. Let's read the second paragraph together. [Signal; everyone reads.] Now, what would be a good main idea statement?
	S: [States main idea.]
	T: That's a fact in the paragraph. How can we change that to a statement that summarizes what the paragraph is about? [Signal.]
	S: [States main idea.]
Summary and review	T: Let's review the answers to the examples you just completed. [Reviews answers.] Today we practiced writing the main idea after we read passages. Remember the main idea is a summary statement telling us what the passage (or paragraph) is all about.
Formative evaluation	T: [Distributes sheets.] Now I will give you a 5-minute quiz. Please read the next three paragraphs silently. After each paragraph write the main idea. Any questions? Ready? Begin.

FIGURE 5.8. Sample lesson to teach the main idea.

Following directions

The ability to follow directions accurately is a necessary prerequisite for most comprehension activities. Directions can be written or verbal but must be followed correctly if the task is to be completed.

Identifying and producing who, what, when, where, how, and why

Literal recall represents the factual (stated) information contained in passages. Answers to who, what, when, where, how, and why questions are usually stated explicitly in passages, and their recall is therefore considered literal. The successful recall of answers to these questions means that students have recalled or comprehended important information from passages. Students can be required to go back to the narrative and locate precisely where the answers to questions are located. Sometimes these answers are referred to as the major facts and details of passages. An example of a self-monitoring sheet for such facts and details is given in Figure 5.9.

Understanding vocabulary

In order to fully comprehend a passage, it is typically necessary to understand the meaning of the vocabulary words contained in the passage. Sometimes vocabulary meanings can be determined by understanding the context in which they are used. Other times, new words can be figured out from word-analysis skills, such as decoding the prefix, suffix, or root words. Still other times, the exact meaning may not be necessary for complete understanding of the passage, while other instances may require students to ask someone else the meaning or look it up in a dictionary or glossary.

Highlighting

Highlighting typically refers to underlining or highlighting with a colored marker the major points, events, or characters in a narrative. Sometimes it is impossible to write in texts; at other times it is permissible. It may be necessary to teach students how to identify the components that need highlighting.

Recalling nonexplicit information

Exact information is sometimes not stated explicitly, but answers can be either deduced or inferred from the facts that are presented. Deductions are made based upon knowledge of a general rule and follow logically from that rule. For example, after reading a passage that first presents general information on the hibernation of bears during the winter months and then

Paragraph 1

1. Can I tell where this story takes place?
   ☐ Yes   ☐ No
   If yes, where? _____
   If no, reread paragraph.

Paragraph 2

2. Can you tell me who is in this story?
   ☐ Yes   ☐ No
   If yes, who? _____
   If no, reread paragraph.

Paragraph 3

3. Can you tell me what the con man gave the robber?
   ☐ Yes   ☐ No
   If yes, what? _____
   If no, reread paragraph.

4. Can you tell me who dressed in the robe?
   ☐ Yes   ☐ No
   If yes, who? _____
   If no, reread paragraph.

Paragraph 4

5. Can you tell me who has the robe?
   ☐ Yes   ☐ No
   If yes, who? _____
   If no, reread paragraph.

6. Can you tell me who has the core?
   ☐ Yes   ☐ No
   If yes, who? _____
   If no, reread paragraph.

FIGURE 5.9. Self-monitoring sheet designed to accompany a specific reading story, by DeAnn Umbower and Mary Taylor.

presents information on a particular bear, readers could deduce that the particular bear would also hibernate during the winter months. Sometimes the general rule or premise is stated explicitly in the text, while other times readers may need to possess the appropriate prior knowledge in order to know the general rule. In either case, once the general rule is known, a specific instance or fact usually can be deduced based on the knowledge and application of that rule. Teachers can assist students in identifying specific rules and in deducing the correct but not explicitly stated information.

Another type of information that is not explicitly stated in texts is called inferential information. Inferential comprehension is made by taking all of the specifically stated facts into consideration and then using that information to infer the answer. A question like "How did Susie feel?" is an inferential question. In order to answer the question effectively, readers must refer back to specifically stated facts and details, such as "It was her birthday party" and "She had her favorite cake and ice cream," in order to infer that Susie was excited and happy and not sad and disappointed. Teachers can assist students in recognizing inferential questions and in locating the specific facts that will aid them in inferring the correct answer based upon the facts provided. A sample lesson on inferential comprehension is excerpted in Figure 5.10.

Typically, comprehension of nonexplicitly stated information is the most difficult aspect of reading comprehension for students with learning difficulties. With specific, direct instruction and practice using the principles of teacher effectiveness in these areas, however, special education students can make progress.

Imagery

Imagery is the imagining of a picture of what has occurred. Occasionally, imagery has successfully augmented students' ability to recall information from prose passages. Typically, students are told to imagine and think about events in a story. After such instructions, students think about the events and make up a picture in their minds to facilitate recall of those events later on. Imagery has been more successful with older students than younger students.

Previewing and reviewing activities

Previewing the material prior to reading can help activate prior knowledge and schemata. A preview can consist of examining the title, major subheadings, summaries, and illustrations included in the stories. Previewing allows readers to get ready for the topic through self-questioning such as "Do I know anything about this topic?" or "Is it related to something else I know?" Additionally, taking time to review the material upon completion can facilitate recall. For example, students can ask questions like "Can I summarize the story? Do I know the correct sequence of events? Can I answer all the who, what, when, where, how, and why questions?" Both previewing and reviewing activities can facilitate recall.

Uses of metacognitive skills

Recall that this section's premise is that reading comprehension involves an interaction of learners with their schemata strategies and metacognitive skills. Metacognitive skills enable the reader to determine which of the abovementioned skills are appropriate for the type of reading. In other words, sophisticated readers not only successfully employ all of the skills presented but, more importantly, know when to execute the particular skills independently.

Review	T: Remember that we have been practicing reading passages, thinking about what was happening in those passages, and answering questions such as who was in the story and when and where the story took place. Remember that whenever we've had comprehension questions to answer we've been able to go back to the passage and locate the answer. Let's do an example together. Everybody read the passage in your book silently with me. [Signal.] Raise your hand when you have the following answers: Who? What? Where? When? Now, raise your hand when you can locate the answer for each of the following questions. . . .
State goal and teacher presentation	T: Today we are going to read passages and learn how to answer comprehension questions for which you can't go back to the passage and find the exact answer. In order to answer questions like these, you need to have read the passage and thought about what was happening in that passage just like before. However, you also have to infer or try to figure out the answer from the information that was provided in that passage. Let me give you an example. [Teacher reads passage.] Now can we answer the following question: How did Cindy feel? That information is not stated exactly in the story. However, we can figure out the answer from the information that was presented. First, we know that the score in the volleyball game was a tie. We also know that Cindy's first serve was an ace. Do you know what an ace means?
	S: Cindy's team scored another point because no one could return her serve.
	T: Right. We also know that Cindy's second serve was another ace and she smiled. How did Cindy feel? Who can figure out how she felt and why she felt that way?
	[Teacher presents several similar examples.]
Guided practice	T: [Distributes papers.] Now we are going to practice answering some similar questions. [Teacher leads students, provides corrective feedback as necessary.]
Independent practice and then formative evaluation	T: Since you have all done well on these, I want you to try the next ones by yourselves. Ready? Begin.

FIGURE 5.10. Lesson on teaching inferential comprehension skills in reading comprehension.

Successful readers consciously and spontaneously employ strategies to recall the sequence of events, summarize passages as they read, or deduce outcomes and make predictions based on the reading passages. Since poor readers are less likely to execute these tasks, direct teaching and practice of these skills using modeling, prompting, feedback, and formative evaluation is necessary. Additionally, the use of verbal self-questioning can assist in this teaching process. Figure 5.11 presents an adaptation of a reading com-

I. Literal Recall
    A. Details
    B. Main Ideas
    C. Sequences
    D. Comparisons
    E. Cause and Effect Relationships
    F. Character Traits

II. Inferential Recall
    A. Supporting Details
    B. Main Ideas
    C. Sequences
    D. Comparisons
    E. Cause and Effect Relationships
    F. Character Traits

III. Evaluation and Judgment
    A. Reality and Fantasy
    B. Fact or Opinion
    C. Adequacy of Validity
    D. Appropriateness
    E. Worth, Desirability, or Acceptability

IV. Appreciation
    A. Emotional Response to Content
    B. Identification with Characters
    C. Reactions to Language
    D. Imagery

FIGURE 5.11. Taxonomy of reading comprehension.

prehension hierarchy summarized from Baumann (1986). Notice that this hierarchy subdivides reading comprehension skills in a fashion very similar to that found in Table 5.2. Teachers need to determine the optimal sequence of instruction for their students.

Before, during, and after reading

As mentioned earlier, many of the strategies students can be taught to facilitate reading comprehension are employed at three distinct times: before reading, during reading, and after reading. Figure 5.12 presents a summary listing of many of the strategies that teachers can teach their students to use at each of these time periods. As with all instruction, the collection of formative data can help determine whether or not instructional objectives are being met.

Before Reading	During Reading	After Reading
Examine Text	*Summarize Key Issues*	*Summarize Entire Selection*
1. preview organization	1. determine main ideas	1. integrate information
2. examine charts, illustrations	2. organize main ideas	2. concisely summarize all elements of text
Mobilize Prior Knowledge	*Make Predictions*	*Determine Achievement*
1. examine/think about content	1. generate hypotheses	1. confirm/refute predictions
2. examine/think about vocabulary	2. refine predictions	2. answer questions
Determine Purpose of Reading	*Clarify Hypotheses*	*Apply Learning*
1. select strategies	1. confirm hypotheses	1. study information
2. generate questions	2. refute hypotheses	2. rehearse information

FIGURE 5.12. Comprehension strategies undertaken before, during, and after reading.

Text Material

The particular text material used can either augment or detract from reading comprehension instruction. It is important to take the following features into consideration when selecting text material: (a) readability; (b) sequencing of skills and context; (c) type of print; (d) type of illustrations; (e) type of diagrams, maps, and/or charts; (f) types of stories, passages, and poems; (g) types of practice activities, (h) amount and type of supplemental practice/workbook activities; and (i) type of instructional practice and guidance on reading comprehension. Some criteria for selection of texts are given in Figure 5.13. Since the learning strategies and study skills chapter presents more detailed information on text and supplementing textual materials with text-embedded adjunct aids, such as maps and advance organizers, this section will simply recommend that teachers choose text that is the appropriate reading level and that allows sufficient opportunities for practice at reading comprehension activities that include literal and inferential questioning. It is also advisable to select a wide variety of reading materials, including children's literature, to the extent that students are able to read this material fluently. A variety of reading material can help students meet application and generalization objectives and also can help students develop an appreciation and enjoyment of books and reading. All the comprehension strategies discussed in this chapter can be used with a variety of materials.

Putting It All Together: Reading Comprehension Instruction

Explicit direct teaching needs to be done on all of the components discussed up to this point. Once the reading material and students have been

Readability	• clear organization
	• appropriate difficulty level
	• controlled vocabulary
	• consistent vocabulary
	• controlled development of concepts
	• clear and effective use of subheadings
	• appropriate type size
	• clear introductions and summaries
	• comprehension practice activities
Illustrations	• relevant to content
	• organize content
	• descriptive pictures of key parts
	• visual charts to show how content is organized
	• maps or diagrams
Adequate practice activities and teacher instructions.	

Look for formative data documenting the efficacy of these materials with special populations.

FIGURE 5.13.   Criteria for selecting text material.

matched, specific objectives for teaching all of the comprehension monitoring skills need to be developed and taught using the teacher-effectiveness model. Additionally, students can be taught directly how to use their prior knowledge and how to activate it during reading. For example, assume a lesson's objective is to introduce deductive-reasoning strategies and to review recalling facts and details from reading passages. As in all lessons, teachers would first review procedures for recalling facts and details from passages. When it is determined that the review was sufficient, teachers would introduce deductive reasoning, probably by stating the rules of deductive reasoning and providing positive and negative examples. During this instruction, teachers would demonstrate examples, model, prompt, and provide corrective feedback on the use of deductive reasoning. All students would be actively engaged during this teacher presentation and student participation activity. When it is determined that students are ready for a guided practice activity, teachers would go through several step-by-step examples with the entire group prior to allowing students to practice on their own. Teachers would then carefully circulate around the students and provide immediate corrective feedback on their performances. When it is determined that the skill has been practiced to an extent that the students are executing it accurately, they would be ready to receive an independent practice activity. Finally, near the end of the lesson, teachers could require students to complete a short assignment on the skill in order to have a measure of their daily performance.

Eventually, reading comprehension instruction could involve a more complex group process, such as the reciprocal teaching model proposed by Palincsar and Brown (1984). Throughout this model various reading comprehension questions and strategies are discussed verbally, and all students take turns participating as group leader in a dialogue. Initial results using this model with low-performing students were positive.

The major strategies practiced include (a) summarizing, (b) question generating, (c) clarifying, and (d) predicting. It is hypothesized that summarizing facilitates students' ability to identify and integrate the most salient parts of the text. Question generating provides students with the opportunity to pose questions about the text and to self-test. Students are taught to clarify text content so that they become aware that many aspects of the text, such as vocabulary or new concepts, can influence comprehension. Finally, students are taught to make predictions about what will happen next in the text. Making predictions is thought to assist students in (a) seeing a purpose for reading, (b) using the structure of the text (e.g., subheadings), and (c) confirming or refuting their hypotheses. The critical aspects necessary for success appear to be the direct teaching, modeling, and guided practice in effective use of summarizing, question generating, clarifying, and predicting.

As mentioned previously, in the past teachers concentrated more on the teaching of decoding skills than on the teaching of comprehension skills. However, in special education, it is necessary to emphasize the instruction of both, so that students meet the ultimate objective of reading—deriving meaning from print. Most of the research on teaching reading comprehension to special education students has occurred over the past decade.

This section has discussed the skills and procedures necessary to teach reading comprehension. It was stressed that reading comprehension is the end goal of reading and that it involves the interaction of the learner, the learner's prior knowledge and schemata, the learner's metacognitive abilities and use of comprehension-monitoring skills, as well as the text itself. It was emphasized that (a) the learners and texts must be matched at the appropriate difficulty level, (b) the learners' attention and motivation on the task are critical, (c) the learners be instructed to activate their prior knowledge and schemata on topics being covered, (d) direct instruction using the teacher-effectiveness model take place on all comprehension-monitoring skills, and (e) the learners be provided with ample guided and independent practice at executive comprehension-monitoring strategies. Finally, learners should use these comprehension skills over a wide variety of printed materials, including newspapers, magazines, literature, lab manuals, and trade books.

Special Problems

Sometimes special education teachers encounter students, particularly at the upper elementary or secondary level, who have struggled unsuccessfully with reading skills for many years. Because of this history of failure, they may be particularly unwilling to continue to work on skill acquisition (either phonics or comprehension skills), even though this may be the approach most likely to lead to literacy development. If this motivational problem seems so severe that the student appears to prefer accepting failure to making an effort, it may be helpful to try a different approach. In the authors' own experience, particularly recalcitrant learners may be successfully motivated to try an approach similar to what has been named "language experience." Using this method, students dictate stories in their own words to the teacher or into a tape recorder. The stories can be about the students' own lives or about a special interest, such as basketball. The teacher or aide then transcribes the stories on the typewriter or word processor and meets with the students individually to read the stories they have "written." Students who have had little success with reading may be positively encouraged by seeing their own stories in "print" and may be positively motivated to learn how to read them. Since the stories are in the students' own language, there should be little difficulty with vocabulary. Similarly, inferring, predicting, and using context cues should hold little difficulty. As students read the passages successfully, they can create an "anthology" of their own writings.

The drawback of this method is that it essentially compels the teacher, at least at first, to abandon the type of sequenced skill acquisition that typically is very helpful for disabled readers. Further, since the passages may be learned simply as sight words, generalization of reading skills may be limited. Although this approach was found by the authors to be successful in specific instances, it has little if any research support for students with mild disabilities. Teachers who choose to employ this approach are advised to introduce relevant skills as soon as possible and to validate its effectiveness using formative evaluation methods.

RELEVANT RESEARCH AND RESOURCES

Reviews of the issues involved in whole language reading instruction for students with learning disabilities are presented by Mather (1992) and Gersten and Dimino (1993). Reviews of research on the teaching of reading are written by Calfee and Drum (1986), Paris and Oka (1989), and Weisberg (1988), while Ciborowski (1992) and Gaskins and Elliot (1991) described comprehensive implementation procedures for reading instruction. Support for the role of a code-emphasis approach to reading is described by Chall and Stahl (1982), Stahl and Miller (1989), and Williams (1979). For reviews of the failures of psycholinguistic and perceptual-motor approaches to teaching reading, see Kavale and Forness (1985). Evaluation of engaged time-on-task in special education studies is made by Haynes and

(continues)

(*Relevant Research and Resources continued*)

Jenkins (1986); Leinhardt et al. (1981); and Zigmond, Vallecorsa, and Leinhardt (1980). Support for a direct instructional, phonics-based approach to reading instruction in special education is provided by many researchers, such as Deshler, Alley, Warner, and Schumaker (1981); Hendrickson, Roberts, and Shores (1978); Pany and Jenkins (1978); Pany, Jenkins, and Schreck (1982); Pflaum and Bryan (1982); Roberts and Deutsch-Smith (1980); Schworm (1979); Stein and Goldman (1980); Blackman, Burger, Tan, and Weiner (1982); and Meyer (1982). A phonological reading study is reported by O'Conner, Jenkins, Leicester, and Slocum (1993). Fluency-developing activities are described by Bos (1982) and Weinstein and Cooke (1992). Jenkins, Stein, and Osborne (1981) and Schumaker, Deshler, Alley, Warner, and Denton (1982) described effective teaching of reading comprehension.

A variety of strategy instruction studies have been completed over the past decade, and all have reported positive effects for training students with mild disabilities in the strategies. These strategies include the following: the effects of peers and adaptations of reciprocal teaching (Bruce & Chan, 1991; Englert & Mariage, 1991), repeated readings (O'Shea, Sindelar, & O'Shea, 1987), word-identification strategies (Lenz & Hughes, 1990), peer previewing (Salend & Nowak, 1988), variations of summarization and self-monitoring (Malone & Mastropieri, 1992), paraphrasing (Jenkins, Heliotis, Stein, & Haynes, 1987), summarization (Gajria & Salvia, 1992), summarization and attributional retraining (Borkowski, Weyhing, & Carr, 1988), vocabulary instruction and interactive instruction (Bos & Anders, 1990a, 1990b), self-questioning (Griffey, Zigmond, & Leinhardt, 1988; Simmonds, 1992), informed strategy training (Rottman & Cross, 1990), and program variations (Jenkins & Jewell, 1993; O'Conner, Jenkins, Cole, & Mills, 1993). Studies investigating the effects of imagery are described by Chan, Cole, and Morris (1990); Clark, Deshler, Schumaker, Alley, and Warner (1984); Ferro and Pressley (1991); and Rose, Cundick, and Higbee (1983). Studies investigating the effects of various types of text structure include Bacon and Carpenter (1989); Simmons, Kameenui, and Darch (1988); Pickering, Pickering, and Buchanan (1988); and Gurney, Gersten, Dimino, and Carnine (1990). Reports of the benefits of attribution and strategy training are described by Borkowski, Weyhing, and Carr (1988); Fulk and Mastropieri (1990); and Schunk and Rice (1992). Wong (1979, 1980); Wong and Wong (1986); and Wong and Jones (1982) provided additional information on teaching reading comprehension in special education settings. Wong (1986b) provided a review of special education research on metacognition, while Palincsar and Brown (1984) and Graves (1986) provided additional support for the use of metacomprehension training as a facilitator of prose recall. Vellutino (1979) provided a review of research on reading problems. Spatial organizer research is provided by Mastropieri and Peters (1987), while activating prior knowledge research is provided by Gaffney (1984) and Snider (1989). Support for the use of mnemonic illustrations in reading is presented by Scruggs, Mastropieri, McLoone, Levin, and Morrison (1987); Mastropieri, Scruggs, and Levin (1987b); and Goin, Peters, and Levin (1986). Additional information on self-monitoring in reading is provided by Hallahan, Marshall, and Lloyd (1981). Much of the above

(*continues*)

(Relevant Research and Resources continued)

information is reviewed and synthesized by Lewis (1983). Tutoring interventions in reading are described by Osguthorpe and Scruggs (1986); Scruggs, Mastropieri, and Richter (1985); Scruggs and Richter (1985); Cook, Scruggs, Mastropieri, and Casto (1985–86); Scruggs and Osguthorpe (1986); and Scruggs, Mastropieri, Tolfa, and Osguthorpe (1986). Studies investigating the effects of computers and reading decoding, fluency, and/or comprehension are described by Swanson and Trahan (1992); Torgesen, Waters, Cohen, and Torgesen (1988); and Cohen, Torgesen, and Torgesen (1988). Finally, the lack of support for some alternative models of reading instruction in special education is discussed by Arter and Jenkins (1977).

Curricular Materials

Some code-based reading series include the following: *Reading Mastery* (Science Research Associates [SRA]), *Corrective Reading–Decoding* (SRA), *Corrective Reading–Comprehension* (SRA), *Merrill Linguistic Readers* (Charles E. Merrill Publishing), *Basic Reading* (J.B. Lippencott), *The Palo Alto Reading Program* (Harcourt Brace Jovanovich), *Sullivan Reading Program* (Webster/McGraw Hill), the *Edmark Reading Program* (Edmark Corporation), and *Open Court Series* (Open Court). Several companies also publish commercially available skill series, which include programs by Science Research Associates *(SRA Reading Labs)* and the *Barnell Loft Specific Skills Series* (Barnell Loft). These can be helpful as practice activities; however, be careful that students have learned and are applying relevant strategies while using these materials.

Books that have low readability levels but high interest can be obtained from Fearon Janus Quercus, Lakeshore Lifeskills, and LinguiSystems (the *Abridged & Accessible Classics Activity Program* and *Victory*). The Dolch Reading Materials (Developmental Reading Materials [DLM]) have books that teach basic sight words but that also have high-interest/low-vocabulary materials available (*The Essential Sight Words Program* [DLM]).

Science Research Associates also publishes a series called *Learning Through Literature* that can be used to integrate literature learning in reading programs. LinguiSystems also publishes materials that attempt to combine skill-based and whole-language approaches to reading instruction. Similarly, reading lists of books that can be used by beginning readers have been published by advocates of Reading Recovery (Clay & Watson, 1987). Similarly, Allyn & Bacon publishes a listing of regularly patterned books that can be used in teaching reading when attempting to control the vocabulary and word patterns. These lists include books such as those published by Putnam Publishers, including *The Very Hungry Caterpillar*. These literature, trade, and picture books can be used in integrating books within reading programs for students with disabilities.

Curricular materials highlighting cultural diversity can also be integrated within reading and social studies classes. These materials include *The Peoples of North America* and *Black Americans of Achievement* (Curriculum Associates);

(continues)

(Relevant Research and Resources continued)

American Cultural Literacy: Famous Firsts, Nuevas Fronteras / New Frontiers and *American Mosaic Reading for Multicultural Literacy* (SRA); and the *Hopes and Dreams I and II* and *Nation Builders Biographies* (Fearon Janus Quercus).

Computer Software and Technology

Computer programs are also commercially available and can be used for practice activities for students with mild disabilities. Many programs have been developed, and availability of new programs will undoubtedly increase in the future. Okolo, Bahr, and Reith (1993) provided a comprehensive review of computer-based instruction in special education. Church and Bender (1989) provided a description of how to integrate computers within the curriculum and provided a listing of available software for reading, writing, and mathematics. Programs can usually be classified as drill and practice, games, tutorials, problem solving, simulations, or production programs. Teachers are encouraged to evaluate the programs to determine suitability for meeting students' needs and IEP objectives. Some programs currently available for basic reading practice are Listening to Learn, Bouncy Bee Learns Letters, Bouncy Bee Learns Words, and Missing Letters (International Business Machines [IBM]), and Stickybear Reading (Cambridge Development Laboratory). Vocabulary and skill practice is available on Clue In On Phonics and Rush Hour Rally: A Game of Sequence (Gamco Industries), Word Attack! and Word Attack Plus! (Cambridge Development Laboratory); and IBM Vocabulary Series: Levels II–IV (IBM). Practice on reading comprehension is provided in Main Idea Gold Rush, Sherlock Holmes and the Masters of Mystery, and The Incredible Adventures of Quentin (Cambridge Development Laboratory); IBM Reading for Meaning: Levels I–IV (IBM); Super Solvers Midnight Rescue and Treasure Dive: Reading for Meaning (Gamco Industries); and Mickey's Magic Reader (Sunburst Communications). The Readable Classic Tales (Cambridge Development Laboratory) are classic texts that can be read on the computer. Finally, Bilingual Reading Comprehension (Educational Resources) is a reading comprehension program that translates English and Spanish.

See Appendix B for a list of addresses of producers and distributors of software and curricular materials.

✥ ✥ ✥

CHAPTER 6

Language Arts

MOST STUDENTS ENROLLED IN SPECIAL EDUCATION EXHIBIT DIFFICULTY in language arts-related areas. Therefore, systematic, high-quality instruction must be delivered in these areas to ensure that students' development in language arts skills parallel advances they are making in reading and other skill areas.

Language arts involves a series of interrelated skills. Four major components of language arts are to be discussed in this chapter: (a) spelling, (b) handwriting, (c) language, and (d) written composition. The application and generalization of integrated language arts skills are critical to overall success in school.

SPELLING

In some ways, spelling is a more difficult activity than reading. Reading requires students to recognize letters and letter patterns and recall corresponding sounds, which are then verbalized. In spelling, students are required to *produce* the corresponding letters. Recall of the correct spelling of words requires a type of serial list learning (e.g., recall of letters in a series) in the context of application of phonics rules.

Ideally, spelling should be regarded as an essential element of a well-integrated reading/language arts curriculum. That is, students should learn to spell words as they learn to read them. Generally, it is inappropriate to give students spelling words that are not a part of their reading vocabulary. Like reading instruction, spelling instruction in special education should progress systematically along a continuum of phonic analysis and sight word skills with high levels of engaged time-on-task devoted to rehearsing the spelling words.

Training

An example of parts of a spelling lesson is given in Figure 6.1. Like any other lesson, teachers should review previous words and explicitly state the

Lesson Section	Teacher Dialogue
Review	We have been learning how to spell four *oa* words. Can you remember what those four words were, Mary? [Mary responds.] Yes, the words were: *soap, goat, boat,* and *float.* Now, let's all spell them together. Everybody ready? Everyone spell *boat.* [Signal.] Good. B-O-A-T. Boat. . . .
State purpose	Today we are going to learn three more *oa* words and one word that is *not* an *oa* word. . . .
Present information	Everyone watch while I write them one at a time on the board. The first word is [writes] *coat.* Everyone, spell it with me. [Signal.] C-O-A-T. Good. Coat. . . .
	Now, the last word we are going to learn has the *oh* sound, but it is not an *oa* word. This word is *pour.* Watch while I write it. [Writes.] OK, let's all spell it together: P-O-U-R. Now, you spell it for me, Bob. [Spells.] Good. What is different about this word, Mary? [Answers.] Right, it is not spelled with *oa;* it is spelled with what, George? [Answers.] Right, it is spelled with *ou.* . . .
Guided practice	Now, everybody write these words on the paper I am giving you. I want you to study these words using the study strategy you have used before. Remember, look at the word and spell it, cover the word and spell it, then check your spelling. If you are right, go to the next word. What do you do if you are wrong, George? [Answers.] Good. If you are wrong, study the word again. When you think you know the four words, ask me or ask your neighbor to give you a written test. . . .
Independent practice	OK, everybody go back to your desks now and study the four words from today plus the four words from before. In 10 minutes you will all take a test.
Formative evaluation	OK, everybody put your words away and take out a clean piece of paper. Get ready to spell all eight words. . . .

FIGURE 6.1. Excerpts from a daily spelling lesson on one-syllable *oa* words.

purpose of the lesson (e.g., "Today we are going to learn three new spelling words taken from your reader"). The teacher then presents the first word and models the spelling. If the word is a CVC word, such as *cat* or some other highly regular word, the teacher should review the component sounds by asking, for example, "What letter makes the *kuh* sound? What letter makes the *tuh* sound? What letter makes the *aaa* sound?" When letter sounds are clearly understood, students should be asked to spell the word orally (e.g., "Everybody, how do you spell *cat*?" [Signal]). If phonics rules other than letter–sound correspondence are used, these rules should be explicitly stated, and their use in spelling the word should be described. It is also helpful to group words with similar spellings and those that follow similar rules. If irregular words are being taught, teachers should simply state the spelling and ask students to repeat it. A possible table of specifications for spelling is given in Table 6.1.

TABLE 6.1. Table of Specifications for Spelling.

CONTENT	BEHAVIOR				
	Identification	Production			
	A. Acquisition	B. Acquisition	C. Fluency	D. Application	E. Generalization
1. CV words	1A	1B	1C	NA	NA
2. CVC words	2A	2B	2C	NA	NA
3. CVC+e words	3A	3B	3C	3D	3E
4. Words with internal vowel digraphs: (1) oa (2) ou (3) ae (4) ie (5) ei	4(1)A 4(2)A 4(3)A 4(4)A 4(5)A	4(1)B 4(2)B 4(3)B 4(4)B 4(5)B	4(1)C 4(2)C 4(3)C 4(4)C 4(5)C	4(1)D 4(2)D 4(3)D 4(4)D 4(5)D	4(1)E 4(2)E 4(3)E 4(4)E 4(5)E
5. Words with diphthongs: (1) oi (2) ou (3) ow	5(1)A 5(2)A 5(3)A	5(1)B 5(2)B 5(3)B	5(1)C 5(2)C 5(3)C	5(1)D 5(2)D 5(3)D	5(1)E 5(2)E 5(3)E
6. Words with two-letter initial blends: (1) st (2) sp (3) sl (4) br (5) bl	6(1)A 6(2)A 6(3)A 6(4)A 6(5)A	6(1)B 6(2)B 6(3)B 6(4)B 6(5)B	6(1)C 6(2)C 6(3)C 6(4)C 6(5)C	6(1)D 6(2)D 6(3)D 6(4)D 6(5)D	6(1)E 6(2)E 6(3)E 6(4)E 6(5)E
7. Words with three-letter initial blends: (1) str (2) spr	7(1)A 7(2)A	7(1)B 7(2)B	7(1)C 7(2)C	7(1)D 7(2)D	7(1)E 7(2)E

NA = not applicable

Sample Objectives:

2A Given 20 pictures representing CVC words, student will correctly identify each correct spelling from four choices with 100% accuracy.

3B Student will correctly spell, in writing, 20 orally presented CVC+e words.

4(2)C Student will correctly spell, in writing, 10 orally presented words containing the vowel digraph *ou* with 100% accuracy in one minute.

6(3)D Student will correctly spell all words containing the initial blend *bl* in journal entries.

7(2)E Student will correctly spell all words containing the initial blend *spr* in mainstream class written assignments.

Guided Practice

Once students understand the initial process of spelling new words, guided practice should be provided. Practice can take the form of small-group oral rehearsal of new words or active monitoring of tutor pairs using flash cards. It is also helpful to provide frequent written tests of new spelling words, especially when students check their own work after the test and immediately correct errors. These errors should then be the focus of additional practice.

Independent Practice

When students begin to demonstrate accuracy in spelling performance, they should receive additional independent practice in order to develop fluency and to promote overlearning for long-term retention. Several types of independent practice activities can be helpful. One obvious approach is to provide flash cards to pairs of students on the same spelling level who can drill each other on the words and record levels of accuracy or fluency performance. It is also helpful to teach students a strategy for independent study of spelling words: (a) read and spell the word; (b) cover the word; (c) spell the word aloud; (d) check for correct spelling; and (e) retest errors or, if correct, move to the next word. When students have performed this procedure accurately, they can repeat the procedure writing rather than saying the spelling word. Students who are studying independently should be provided with specific goals relative to their abilities (e.g., "You should be able to spell these four words by the end of class"), and their performances should be evaluated.

In general, having students copy spelling words or use words in various workbook or practice activities, such as matching shapes, unscrambling letters, or locating them in word-search activities, is less likely to enforce learning than is direct drill and practice. Some of these activities may be helpful in meeting other objectives, however, such as developing handwriting skills by copying. A list of spelling activities that are supported by research (Loomes, 1982) is provided in Figure 6.2.

Evaluation

As stated earlier, spelling activities should parallel progress made in reading. Many spelling curriculum materials show little relation to reading materials. In such cases, the teacher should select words carefully to match the reading sequence. It is also helpful to attend to school scope and sequence to ensure that students are meeting school objectives.

Students should be retested frequently on words covered to date to ensure that spelling words are not forgotten. Teachers can compile a list of

---

Students learn to spell more effectively when they:

- Increase engaged learning time
- Use self-monitoring strategies
- Check their own spelling and make corrections
- Use learning strategies such as clustering, rehearsal, and elaboration
- Study similar words together
- Frequently review previously learned words

FIGURE 6.2. Spelling techniques supported by research.

spelling words learned to date in order to provide students and teachers with information on student progress and to compare this progress with the student's IEP objectives. An example of a formative evaluation procedure for spelling is given in Figure 6.3.

Special Problems

If students present problems in learning spelling words, teachers should use error analysis to determine whether the errors are due to a lack of understanding of a phonics rule. If this is the problem, the rule should be retaught and its relevance to the spelling word made explicit. If the student exhibits understanding of relevant phonics rules, additional drill and practice should be provided. If retention of previously learned words is a problem, the student should engage in more overlearning activities or move more slowly through the curriculum, perhaps by limiting the number of words learned at a time. Another possibility is to provide additional time-on-task through tutors, self-study, or homework assignments. Since spelling is rarely regarded by special education students as a self-reinforcing activity, teachers may also want to ensure that sufficient motivation has been provided for spelling performance. To this end, some type of goal setting, in which the learners help set their own spelling goals, may be helpful.

Finally, research has supported the use of a spelling mnemonic, particularly at the upper elementary or secondary levels. Spelling mnemonics are useful in cases in which memory of phonics rules is not helpful for recall of, usually, one difficult part of a word. For example, some students have difficulty remembering the vowels that appear in the word *cemetery*, although recall of the consonants does not pose a problem. In this case, the student can be provided with or asked to generate an interactive sentence, such as "She screamed, 'E-E-E' as she walked by the cemetery," to help recall the vowels. For another example, to remember the spelling word *villain*, the

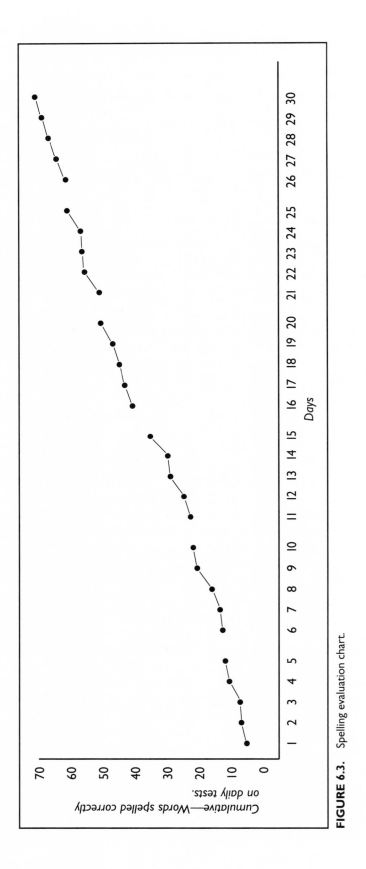

FIGURE 6.3. Spelling evaluation chart.

Word	Example
privilege	Special priVILEges are VILE.
laboratory	A LABORatory is for LABOR.
judgment	GM (General Motors) made a judGMent.
stationery	LettERs are written on stationERy.
bargain	You GAIN from a barGAIN.
feminist	The feMINIst would not wear a MINI skirt.
relevant	The ANT was relevANT to the science class.
obedient	If you are not obeDIEnt, you will DIE.
sacrilegious	SacRILEgious people RILE me.
grammar	Bad gramMAR will MAR your reputation.

FIGURE 6.4. Spelling mnemonics.

sentence, "The *villain* had a *villa in* the town," could be used. For such an elaboration to be helpful, however, the student must know the meaning, as well as the spelling, of all of the words in the elaborative sentence. Mnemonics are useful when the student has overall knowledge of the spelling but is having difficulty on just one or two letters. Additional examples of the use of mnemonics (Shefter, 1976; Suid, 1990) are given in Figure 6.4.

HANDWRITING

Handwriting is an important skill for students to master. It has been argued that students can use typewriters or computers in place of learning good handwriting skills; however, it is the position of these authors that students need to become fluent at handwriting, too. As with all skills, if teachers do not provide students with adequate instruction and practice, they are essentially denying students the opportunity to choose to use these skills later in life.

There has been a debate in handwriting instruction as to whether manuscript (printing) or cursive (handwriting) should be taught first. Many schools tend to introduce manuscript in first grade and cursive in third; however, some school districts have introduced cursive first. Additionally, some schools have adopted a particular handwriting system, such as D'Nealian (Thurber & Jordan, 1981), *Better Handwriting for You* (Noble, 1966), or *Zaner-Bloser Handwriting: Basic Skills and Applications* (Barbe, Lucas, Hackney, Braun, & Wasylyk, 1984). It is recommended that special educators adopt the systems that are used in their school districts. Even though cursive writing is more regular and consistent, research has shown that the initial use of manuscript writing has several advantages, including: (a) being easier for young children to learn, (b) facilitating learning to read and spell, (c) not being detrimental to learning cursive writing, and (d) being generally more legible than cursive writing.

The following sections discuss handwriting assessment and instruction for acquisition, fluency, and application levels of learning handwriting. Instruction for manuscript and cursive writing is combined, as the teaching behaviors and practice activities differ only in whether the letters are manuscript or cursive in form.

Handwriting Assessment/Error Analysis

In both cursive and manuscript forms, handwriting can be informally assessed very easily. Several formal published handwriting assessment measures exist, such as the *Test of Written Language* (Hammill & Larsen, 1978) and the *Zaner-Bloser Evaluation Scale* (1986). It is recommended, however, that teachers use a scope and sequence that includes both manuscript and cursive letter formations for assessing and instructing handwriting. Additionally, the handwriting behaviors expected should follow a sequence from easy to difficult. In other words, the sequence of instruction/assessment should proceed as follows: (a) tracing models, (b) tracing faded-out models, (c) copying close models, (d) copying models from the blackboard, and (e) writing from memory as shown in Figure 6.5. Likewise, assessment should proceed from producing individual letters, words, sentences, and paragraphs to producing short narratives (a progression similar to the sample table of specifications shown in Table 6.2).

Student behavior critical to the handwriting process can be examined. It is recommended that teachers check the following student behaviors:

1. Is the student holding the pencil correctly?

2. Is the student positioning the paper correctly?

3. Is the student's posture and sitting position conducive to good handwriting?

4. Is the student motivated during handwriting exercises?

5. Is the student consistently using the same hand during writing exercises?

Occasionally, a slight modification in one of the behaviors listed above will dramatically improve a student's handwriting.

An analysis of the student's handwriting can also lead to appropriate instructional strategies. Teachers can attend to the following aspects of the student's handwritten products. (*See list on p. 167.*)

Task	Example
Tracing models	Student traces over: *cat*
Tracing faded-out models	Student traces over: *cat*
Copying close models	Student copies: *cat*
Copying models from blackboard	Same as 3, except from blackboard:
Writing from memory	No model.

FIGURE 6.5. Letter-copying sequence.

TABLE 6.2.   Table of Specifications for Manuscript Handwriting.

CONTENT*	Identification	Production			
	A. Acquisition	B. Acquisition	C. Fluency	D. Application	E. Generalization
1. *Lowercase letters*					
a–f	1(1)A	1(1)B	1(1)C	NA	NA
g–l	1(2)A	1(2)B	1(2)C	NA	NA
m–s	1(3)A	1(3)B	1(3)C	NA	NA
t–z	1(4)A	1(4)B	1(4)C	NA	NA
2. *Uppercase letters*					
a–f	2(1)A	2(1)B	2(1)C	NA	NA
g–l	2(2)A	2(2)B	2(2)C	NA	NA
m–s	2(3)A	2(3)B	2(3)C	NA	NA
t–z	2(4)A	2(4)B	2(4)C	NA	NA
3. *Words*					
2 letter	3(1)A	3(1)B	3(1)C	NA	NA
3 letter	3(2)A	3(2)B	3(2)C	NA	NA
4 letter	3(3)A	3(3)B	3(3)C	NA	NA
5 letter	3(4)A	3(4)B	3(4)C	NA	NA
4. *Sentences*					
2 word	4(1)A	4(1)B	4(1)C	4(1)D	4(1)E
3 word	4(2)A	4(2)B	4(2)C	4(2)D	4(2)E
4 word	4(3)A	4(3)B	4(3)C	4(3)D	4(3)E
5 word	4(4)A	4(4)B	4(4)C	4(4)D	4(4)E

*Other arrangements or analyses of content (e.g., single letters) are possible, depending on instructional goals and skills of the learner.

NA = not applicable

Sample Objectives:

1(1)A   Student will correctly point out 20 cursive letters from a list of 40 cursive and manuscript letters *a–f* with 100% accuracy.

2(2)B   Student will legibly write 30 instances of cursive letters (*g–l*), as assessed by comparison with a written standard, with 100% accuracy.

3(2)C   Student will legibly write 30 three-letter words in cursive, as assessed by comparison with a written standard, with 100% accuracy at a rate of five words per minute.

4(3)D   Student will legibly write (as compared with a written standard) cursive four-word sentences in daily journal entries.

4(4)E   Student will write (as compared with a written standard) cursive five-word sentences in answering questions on readings in mainstream settings.

1. Letter formation

2. Letter size

3. Letter alignment

4. Letter spacing

5. Letter orientation

6. Letter omissions, additions, and/or substitutions

7. Rate or speed at which handwriting is completed

These considerations are discussed in relation to instruction at the acquisition, fluency, and application levels in the following sections.

Acquisition Instruction

During acquisition instruction, the major goal is for students to produce accurately all of the letters in isolation and in combinations that form words and sentences. The first stage of handwriting instruction corresponds to the letter identification stage in reading. Typically, students are required to trace letter shapes. Since handwriting is a production task, it is assumed that students can accurately identify all of the letters and can discriminate among difficult letters. However, since the first stage in writing is tracing models, teachers can reinforce the similarities and differences among many letter shapes (e.g., *b* and *d*, *p* and *q*). Teachers should use the same instructional procedures for teaching difficult letter discriminations that were discussed in Chapter 5. During this stage, it is critical for teachers to model, demonstrate, and provide corrective feedback on the correct posture and pencil and paper positioning, because this is the stage in which good habits as well as bad habits are formed. Although the sequence of instruction can follow established scope and sequence objectives, a sample sequence for instruction is given in Figure 6.6.

It is recommended that the following steps be practiced for forming specific letters: (a) tracing entire letters, (b) completing letters that consist of dashed lines, (c) copying letters from close and distant models, and (d) producing letters without using models. Corrective feedback is critical. Students need to be provided with sufficient practice opportunities in order to acquire these skills with 100% accuracy. Although "neatness" with 100% accuracy is a somewhat subjective standard, teachers can assist students in evaluating their own performances by clearly stating the evaluation standards. Standards, which typically include letter size, letter shape, letter orientation, and letter closure, can be displayed with the use of models. One particularly effective self-checking procedure is the use of transparent overlays that accurately display all the critical attributes of the letters and are

Sequence	Groups	Examples
1.	point	*i t*
2.	loop	*e l f*
3.	circle	*o p q g*
4.	mound	*m n*

FIGURE 6.6. Instructional sequence for cursive letters.

available for students to superimpose over their completed work. This self-checking process helps students to recognize and correct their own errors and has been shown to improve writing performance.

In teaching students handwriting, teachers should (a) design an instructional objective that matches the students' ability to the instructional materials and performance criteria used and (b) use the teacher-effectiveness variables during the design and delivery of the lesson. Teacher presentation should be clear and concise, and modeling demonstration and feedback should be given. Students' active participation should involve all of the students all of the time, and all students should have many opportunities to practice newly learned letters, first under the teacher's guidance and then independently. Optimal practice activities are directly related to the objective. In other words, all involve practice in writing (tracing or copying) the letters to be mastered.

The key to success at this level is a sufficient amount of guided and independent practice. When students can accurately produce all the letters without a model, instruction can proceed to fluency-building activities. Formative evaluation can help to determine whether students need more or less time-on-task. An example of an acquisition lesson is given in Figure 6.7.

Fluency Instruction

The goal during fluency instruction is to increase the rate at which students are able to accurately produce manuscript and/or cursive letters. Again, it is important to reinforce good posture, pencil holding, and paper position during these instructional periods. Teachers can spend their review time on reinforcing accuracy of letter formations, as well as good posture and positioning. During the teacher presentation phase, teachers should stress fluency while maintaining accuracy. This type of instruction requires a great deal of practice activity. Teachers can also reinforce good independent word habits during these practice activities. Since fluency instruction

Lesson Section	Teacher Dialogue
Review	Last week we started to learn cursive writing. What was the group of letters we learned last week, everybody? [Signal.] Correct, the *e* group. The *e* group was letters *e, h,* and *l.* Everybody write cursive *e, h,* and *l* on a piece of paper.
State purpose	Today we are going to learn two letters of the *i* group. These letters are *i* and *t.*
Present information	Everybody watch me write an *i* on the board. [Writes.] Do you see how I did it? I start at the line, go up, and come back down. What did I do last, Raymond? [Answers.] Correct, I put a dot on the *i.*
Guided practice	I'm going to give you a worksheet now to practice the letters *i* and *t.* On the first line, you write right over the letters. What do you do on the first line, George? [Answers.] Good. Write right over the letters on the first line. Everybody try it.
Independent practice	I can see everyone is doing very well on the letters *i* and *t.* Now I want you to go back to your desks and write *i* and *t* slowly and neatly, just like we practiced. Write each letter 25 times.
Formative evaluation	Everybody hand in your papers now, and I'll tell you how well you did.

FIGURE 6.7. Excerpts from a sample acquisition lesson.

emphasizes the rate at which students can write accurately, practice activities should involve extra incentives for fast yet accurate completion. During this phase of instruction, teachers may want to alter reinforcers in order to maintain student motivation. The majority of activities during this phase will be independent practice activities that require handwriting and emphasize speed as well as accuracy.

Additionally, several investigators have shown that self-instruction procedures and self-correction procedures can be added to handwriting instruction to increase handwriting performance. Self-instruction components include the following:

1. Student says aloud the letters or words that need to be written.

2. Student names the letters that need to be written.

3. Student repeats each letter name as it is written down.

4. Student describes verbally the motions of the pencil while forming the letter (e.g., "verbal description for writing the letter *a* . . . start at the middle line; go around, down to the bottom line; back up to the beginning; retrace down the bottom line." [Graham, 1983, p. 233]).

Self-correction procedures require students first to identify their own errors by circling incorrectly formed letters and then to produce accurately formed letters. A combination of self-instruction, self-correction, and the teacher-effectiveness variables can be quite successful in promoting good handwriting.

Application and Generalization Instruction

Application instruction in handwriting refers to instruction aimed at allowing students opportunities to apply their handwriting skills on a variety of tasks. This instruction can be combined with instructional assignments in other areas, such as creative writing, homework assignments, and mathematics work. Once students have become fluent in handwriting, they can be reminded that they are expected to demonstrate these skills on all written work. This is also an opportune time to remind students to use self-correction procedures. At times it may be necessary to remind, prompt, and correct minor problem areas.

Special Problems

Most handwriting problems reflect either insufficient task analysis, insufficient engaged time-on-task, or content being covered too rapidly. If motor or other problems are so severe that handwriting problems affect other skill areas, it may be wise to substitute a typewriter or word processor for essential writing activities while continuing to practice handwriting as much as time allows.

Further analysis of handwriting problems may indicate that the total number of letters being miswritten are less than expected. Research has shown that only four symbols—*a*, *e*, *r*, and *t*—account for about half of all misformed letters. Additional attention to these letters, or other specific letter misformations, can bring about disproportionate gains in handwriting performance.

ORAL LANGUAGE

Special education teachers encounter a wide range of variability in spoken (oral) language abilities. Although nearly all students classified as moderately or severely disabled are in need of language training, many students classified as mildly disabled, including students exhibiting learning disabilities, behavior disorders, or mild mental retardation, do not exhibit serious spoken language problems and may not have language development included in their IEP objectives. Furthermore, students who do exhibit severe language problems are usually referred to specially trained speech and language teachers for remediation.

Many mildly disabled students, however, do exhibit difficulties in some aspects of oral language. For example, Kavale and Forness (1987) completed a critical analysis of research on subtyping in learning disabilities and reported that 60% of the students classified as learning disabled exhibited some type of language problem. Consequently, teachers may wish to provide some language instruction for these students. Some published materials that provide scope and sequence for several aspects of language development are available for this type of instruction. When using these materials, teachers should choose the aspects of the materials that most directly correspond to specific instructional objectives.

Most language training for students characterized as mildly disabled includes instruction in vocabulary, syntax, and semantics. In all aspects of language training, teachers must attend to the receptive (identification) versus expressive (production) functions of language use as well as to the general accuracy, fluency, and application stages of learning. Some programs, for example, attend mainly to training receptive vocabulary at the accuracy stage of learning. Although this in itself is a worthwhile objective, teachers must make certain that the materials used teach what the student needs to learn. If the material does not, additional lessons must be developed or otherwise acquired by the teacher.

Vocabulary

Most mildly disabled students have vocabularies that are less well developed than those of students in mainstream settings. Several standardized assessment materials are available for overall vocabulary functioning, although it should be noted that these tests typically assess only receptive vocabulary; that is, students are asked to indicate which of several pictures represents a particular word supplied by the examiner.

Vocabulary Training

Students with vocabulary deficiencies should receive training both on whole words and meaningful word parts, such as common prefixes and suffixes with standard meanings (e.g., *anti–*). Generally, only vocabulary words that are directly meaningful and relevant to the students' life and school experiences should be taught. During acquisition, students should first learn to identify word meanings. If students have acquired relevant concepts, this is often accomplished by rehearsal. For example, if a student is learning that *corridor* is another word for *hall*, corridor can be taught as a fact. That is, whatever was previously associated with *hall* can now be associated with *corridor*. However, if a student is acquiring the vocabulary word *pugnacious* but has not learned the relevant concept (i.e., does not know the meaning of *aggressive*), the student must first be taught this concept, usually by provision of a verbal description or rule followed by presentation of instances or noninstances (e.g., "Children who are aggressive fight with and bully other children. What do aggressive children do? [Answer.] Good. In this picture [show picture], is the boy being aggressive?"). Once they have learned the concept of *aggressive*, students can be taught synonyms (words with similar meaning) as facts (e.g., "Another word for *aggressive* is *pugnacious*"). Once students have acquired accuracy and fluency levels of performance with vocabulary words, they can learn to apply the new words to their own expressive vocabularies. This can be accomplished by asking students to use words in contextual sentences (e.g., "Say 'She is an aggressive student,' using a different word for aggressive"). Also, students should be reinforced for using the new words spontaneously in classroom conversation. As in the acquisition of spelling words, vocabulary words should be overlearned and assessed frequently and cumulatively to ensure that words are not being forgotten. It is also helpful to compile a list of vocabulary words learned to use for review, training, and feedback for students as well as for teachers' records. Teachers can also evaluate the rate of acquisition of vocabulary words with respect to IEP goals and objectives. If, for example, a student has learned 15 new vocabulary words in the first 3 months of school and an IEP objective states that the student will learn 200 new words over the year, this objective will probably not be met without more intensive, faster-paced instruction.

Special Problems

If students have difficulty learning new vocabulary words, teachers should first ascertain whether relevant concepts are being mastered. If not, conceptual learning should be intensified. If relevant concepts have been acquired (i.e., the student can explain the concept but cannot produce the appropriate vocabulary word), additional drill and practice should be provided, perhaps using a peer tutor. If students initially acquire vocabulary word meanings but do not retain them over time, more overlearning activities may be indicated. It is also helpful to use new words as often as possible during class, especially when students show difficulty in applying the word in novel contexts.

One method of learning new vocabulary words that has received much research attention is the mnemonic *keyword method*. In the keyword method, the new vocabulary word is first changed into another word that is concrete and already familiar. For example, to learn that a *dahlia* is a type of flower, the word *dahlia* is first recoded to the keyword *doll*. *Doll* is a good keyword for *dahlia* because it sounds like the first part of *dahlia* and is easily pictured. The learner is then shown (or asked to imagine) a picture of the keyword and the referent interacting; in this case, the student perhaps can picture a doll sniffing a flower. It is important that the keyword be associated with the referent in the picture and not simply pictured with it. Thus, while a picture containing a doll and a flower may not be sufficient to facilitate the association, a doll sniffing, picking, or otherwise interacting with the flower is more likely to facilitate the association. Finally, the retrieval process should be explicitly described to the student: "When you hear the word *dahlia*, remember the keyword *doll*, remember the picture of the doll, and think of what else was in the picture. The doll sniffing the flower means that dahlia is a kind of flower." Additional examples of the keyword method are given in Figure 6.8, while Figure 6.9 presents a sample lesson for instructing students using this method.

The keyword method can be very helpful in vocabulary learning as well as in learning the facts in content areas such as science and social studies. Other applications of the keyword method are discussed in the

Vocabulary Word (Meaning)	Keyword	Picture or Image
Dahlia (flower)	doll	A *doll* sniffing a *flower.*
Viaduct (bridge)	duck	A *duck* walking on a *bridge.*
Marmalade (jam)	mama	A *mama* spreading *jam* for her child.
Toreador (bullfighter)	tornado	A *bullfighter* fighting a *tornado.*
Barrister (lawyer)	bear	A *bear* acting like a *lawyer.*
Celebrate (honor with a festive occasion)	celery	A *festive occasion* in which *celery* is served.
Persuade (convince)	purse	One woman *convincing* another to buy a *purse.*
Orbit (travel around heavenly body)	rabbit	A *rabbit traveling* around the earth.
Beacon (signal light)	bacon	A *signal light* shining on a pan of *bacon.*
Oxalis (clover-like plant)	oxen	*Oxen* eating *clover-like plants.*
Vituperation (abusive speech)	viper	*Viper* engaging in *abusive speech.*
Jodhpurs (riding breeches)	joggers	*Joggers* wearing *riding* breeches.
Dirigible (blimp)	deer	A *deer* with a *blimp* tied to its antlers.
Corsair (pirate)	core	A *pirate* eating an apple *core.*

FIGURE 6.8. Examples of the keyword method for learning vocabulary.

Today I'm going to help you learn some new vocabulary words. I want you to try hard, because at the end of our session, I will give you a quiz to see how well you remember the meanings of the words. I am going to teach you using a special method of remembering.

The first thing I am going to teach you is a keyword for each new vocabulary word. A keyword is a little word that sounds like part of the new vocabulary word and is easily pictured. For example, the keyword for *jodhpurs* is *joggers*. What is the keyword for jodhpurs? Good. Now I'm going to show you a picture that will help you remember the meaning of jodhpurs. [Show illustration.] (See Illustration A.) The keyword for jodhpurs is joggers. Jodhpurs are riding breeches. Remember this picture of joggers wearing riding breeches. Remember this picture of what? [Signal.] And jodhpurs means what? [Signal.]

JODHPURS (joggers)

Jodhpurs are riding breeches made loose and full above the knees and close-fitting below them.

Illustration A

[Remove illustration.] Now, when I ask you the meaning of the word, you need to do the following things. For example, if I said, "What does jodhpurs mean?" or "What are jodhpurs?" first you should think back to the keyword for jodhpurs. That is [answer]. Good. Then, you need to think back to what else was happening in that picture, which was [answer]. Good! Joggers wearing riding breeches. Therefore, we know that jodhpurs are riding breeches. Let's try the next example.

(continues)

FIGURE 6.9. Sample instructions for teaching new vocabulary words with the keyword method.

The keyword for *oryx* is *ore*. What is the keyword for oryx? [Answer.] Good. Now I'm going to show you a picture that will help you remember the meaning of oryx. [Show illustration.] (See Illustration B.) The keyword for oryx is ore. Oryx are a type of antelope with long horns that project backwards. Remember this picture of a type of antelope pulling ore out of a mine. Remember this picture of what? [Signal.] And oryx means what? [Signal.]

An oryx is any of a group of large African antelopes with long, straight horns projecting backwards.

ORYX (ore)

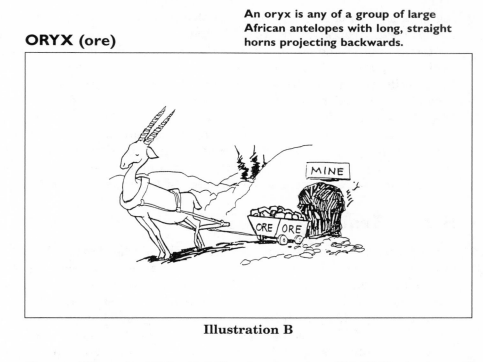

Illustration B

[Remove illustration.] If I said, "What does oryx mean?" or "What is an oryx?" first remember what the keyword for oryx is. [Answer.] Good! Then, you need to think back to the picture that has the ore in it and then think back to what else was happening in that picture. [Answer.] Good. Therefore, oryx means a type of antelope because the keyword for oryx is ore and the picture has a type of antelope pulling ore out of a mine. Do you have any questions?

FIGURE 6.9. continued

chapters that follow. For vocabulary learning, however, it must be emphasized that research has supported the use of the keyword method for the initial acquisition of vocabulary words. Other strategies are necessary to develop fluency and application of new vocabulary words to the student's oral language.

Syntax

Unlike reading, students typically enter school settings with well-developed language skills, which were acquired at home or in other extracurricular environments. Therefore, the teaching of syntax (grammar) in a special education setting may depend on a careful error analysis of specific students' spoken language. This can be done by tape-recording a conversation with a particular student, transcribing the student's dialogue, and looking for a pattern of errors in the student's grammar. Students may then be grouped with respect to identified instructional needs and taught specific syntactic skills. Some published materials are available for developing such skills and additionally provide a scope and sequence for the development of these skills. When using these materials, the teacher should be certain that specific student objectives are being addressed. In other words, any training in syntax should reflect student deficiencies observed in those specific skills. Much syntax training involves a type of rule learning in that students must first be able to identify specific grammatical rules that apply to specific situations. It should also be obvious that syntax must be learned on a level at which performance is fluent and easily applied to spontaneous oral language.

Syntax Training

Syntax can be subdivided into literally hundreds of areas. Major areas of instruction, however, include subject–verb agreement, verb tense, pronoun usage, sentence structure, adjective usage, and adverb usage. A sample table of specifications is given in Table 6.3. For lessons in subject–verb agreement, for example, the teacher can begin by reviewing previous learning and stating the lesson's objective: "We are going to learn how to say some new sentences." The teacher then displays a picture and provides modeling for subject–verb agreement: "Look at this picture. The cows *run*. You say it." [Signal.] After this sentence has been acquired, the teacher promotes the discrimination: "Now, look at this new picture. The cow *runs*. You say it." [Signal.] When the discrimination has been mastered, the teacher should promote fluent, unmodeled responses using a variety of stimulus cards. Students can be given guided and independent practice with workbooks, computers, or other instructional aides. The final goal, of course, is to develop correct subject–verb agreement in spontaneous spoken language. Progress toward this objective can be assessed by taking regular oral language samples, transcribing them, and evaluating the extent to which instructed syntactic features have been mastered. Teachers must also reinforce the use of correct syntax throughout the day.

Dialect

In some instances, students deviate from standard English not because of inappropriate language development but because the student speaks a

TABLE 6.3. Table of Specifications for Syntax.

CONTENT	BEHAVIOR				
	Identification	Production			
	A. Acquisition	B. Acquisition	C. Fluency	D. Application	E. Generalization
1. Subject–verb agreement	1A	1B	1C	1D	1E
2. Verb tense	2A	2B	2C	2D	2E
3. Pronoun usage	3A	3B	3C	3D	3E
4. Adjective usage	4A	4B	4C	4D	4E
5. Adverb usage	5A	5B	5C	5D	5E

Sample Objectives:

1E   Student uses correct subject–verb agreement to 100% criterion in mainstream class.

2D   Student always correctly applies verb tense when addressing the special education teacher or other classmates.

3C   Given a single cloze passage with 20 pronouns deleted, student inserts the correct pronoun in writing 100% of the time in 3 minutes or less.

4B   Given 20 simple sentences, student will supply an appropriate adjective in every case.

5A   Given 20 sentences containing correct and incorrect adverb usage, student will circle every correctly used adverb.

different dialect. Often, different dialects consist of language patterns that are regular within themselves but differ from standard English in many syntactical respects. Some argue that the language in the public schools and mainstream America is standard English and that all students should learn this way of speaking. Others argue that different dialects are necessary for cultural identity and should not be suppressed. A good policy for an individual teacher is to determine the school or district policy on dialect issues and to teach according to this standard. In the long run, it seems best to let the community decide how its children's educational needs, including dialect, can best be served.

Special Problems

In some instances, students have particular problems with syntax. Such problems should be addressed by careful task and error analyses, followed by more intensive instruction and additional time-on-task. With respect to syntax, or other issues relevant to oral language, the speech and language teacher may be able to provide assistance.

Semantics

Because it deals with meaning, semantics is the most important aspect of language in regard to how language is expressed and understood. With respect to semantics, expressive language reflects the individual's ability to be understood, and receptive language reflects the individual's ability to understand oral language. Training intended to facilitate language or listening comprehension is commonly thought to be highly related to reading comprehension.

Training

Typically, when teaching semantic understanding, teachers read sentences or paragraphs and question students on their meaning. These questions initially involve basic factual recall (e.g., "Who bought the sausage at the store?") and later advance to inferential and deductive reasoning based on the sentences heard. In this type of instruction, students are taught to solve analogies and syllogisms. Analogies are statements that require understanding of similarities (e.g., "*Bear* is to *cub* as *cow* is to _____"). Syllogisms are the basic elements of deductive reasoning and contain a major premise (e.g., "All men are mortal"), a minor premise (e.g., "Socrates is a man"), and a conclusion (e.g., "Therefore, Socrates is mortal").

When teachers teach semantic usage, their specification of objectives and sequences of teaching should be as systematic and explicit as any in any other instructional area. Previous information is first reviewed (e.g., "Yesterday, what did we say were the four *wh–* questions?"). Second, the purpose of the lesson is explicitly stated (e.g., "Today we are going to answer some different *wh–* questions"), followed by teacher-directed instruction (e.g., "Yesterday, Fred walked to town to use the telephone. You say it. [Signal.] Now, who walked? [Fred] Where did he walk? [Town] When did he walk there? [Yesterday] Why did he walk there? [To use the telephone]"). Students then receive guided and individual practice on the lesson, and formative data is collected on their performance. As with syntax, the overall goal is comprehension of the meaning of spoken language in everyday usage.

Special Problems

When students exhibit difficulty understanding the meaning of spoken language, teachers need to first determine whether students are attending appropriately. In many cases, attention and not receptive semantic language is the problem. If it is, students should be prompted and reinforced for attending. Often, it is not sufficient simply to ask the students to repeat what was just said. Students must demonstrate that they actively processed the information by restating the previous statement in different words or answering comprehension-type questions.

If attention is not a problem, teachers next need to assess whether relevant vocabulary is understood. If not, vocabulary instruction or the use of simpler vocabulary is needed. If students understand the vocabulary, teachers must then determine whether the difficulty involves literal recall or the ability to make deductions or inferences based on what was heard. Specific instructions in the area of difficulty should then be provided.

Students may also exhibit difficulty expressing meaning in spoken language. Teachers should try to determine what the students are attempting to communicate by questioning and then should model the appropriately verbalized sentence. If expressive vocabulary is a problem, these words should be taught. Overall, expressive semantic difficulties should be regularly evaluated and carefully monitored to ensure that progress is being made. With any case of persistent speech or language problems, the speech and language teacher should be consulted.

Finally, in special education settings, a student's expressive language is sometimes semantically correct yet notable because of its bizarre content. If a student's expressive language persistently reflects a different perspective on reality than other individuals' (e.g., repeated expression of unrealistic fears and fantasies accompanied by apparent lack of understanding of how these statements are received by others), it may be evidence of serious psychological problems for which more specific professional help is necessary. It is, of course, not up to the special education teacher to make such a diagnosis. However, teachers should record incidents of aberrant speech and be careful to reinforce more normal patterns of language. A continuous record of instances of bizarre speech and a listing of antecedent and consequent events may prove helpful in these cases. Additionally, special education teachers should consult with their respective school psychologists for advice in working with students who exhibit bizarre speech patterns.

WRITTEN LANGUAGE

Written language or composition requires the use of almost all of the skills covered in this text. Written language is an application of oral language that requires mastery of preskills including reading, spelling, thinking, syntax, semantics, and handwriting. Successful writing skills are among the most difficult skills to acquire since they require the application of so many prerequisite skills. Additionally, good writing instruction has rarely taken place in classrooms. Traditionally, teachers distributed blank paper to students and issued directions like "Write what you did on your summer vacation." Recently, however, researchers have begun to investigate optimal instruction in writing. In fact, the federal government has funded a National Institute of Education to study writing. Several formal and informal writing-assessment measures are also available. It is recommended that special education teachers determine what their district-level objectives and curriculum materials in the area of writing are and adjust their objectives accordingly.

As in most other curriculum areas, researchers recently have begun to emphasize the role of meaning in the writing process. This is accomplished by teaching such necessary skills as writing mechanics within the context of written products that are meaningful to learners. Further, the integration of writing with other relevant academic activities has been emphasized. This means that students should be encouraged to read what they and other students have written, that students should write about books or passages they have read, and that they should engage in relevant, interactive dialogue about what they and others have read and written. The most effective special education teachers are those that can conduct efficient, skill-based instruction, while at the same time emphasizing application and generalized use of these skills in meaningful and motivating contexts.

The next section presents a framework for examining written products and instructional strategies for writing instruction within the teacher-effectiveness model.

Examination of Written Products

Assessment procedures for formal and informal writing share common elements. Typically, students' written language is subdivided into common elements including:

1. *Mechanics*
   a. capitalization
   b. penmanship
   c. punctuation
   d. format
   e. spelling
   f. error monitoring

2. *Grammar* or *syntax*
   a. subject–verb agreement
   b. verb tense
   c. pronoun usage
   d. sentence structure
   e. adjective usage
   f. adverb usage

3. *Semantics*
   a. language usage
   b. vocabulary usage

4. *Organization*
   a. sequencing of ideas
   b. sequencing of sentences
   c. sequencing of paragraphs

5. *Content*
   a. relevance to topic
   b. breadth and depth of knowledge displayed
   c. originality
   d. degree of documentation

6. *Type of writing*
   a. declarative
   b. narrative
   c. expository
   d. letters

7. *Sophistication of writing*
   a. sentence length
   b. sentence variation
   c. sentence complexity
   d. sophistication of ideas

TABLE 6.4. Table of Specifications for Writing Mechanics.

CONTENT	BEHAVIOR				
	Identification	Production			
	A. Acquisition	*B. Acquisition*	*C. Fluency*	*D. Application*	*E. Generalization*
I. *Capitalization:* sentence proper name	I(I)A I(2)A	I(I)B I(2)B	I(I)C I(2)C	I(I)D I(2)D	I(I)E I(2)E
2. *Punctuation:* period comma	2(I)A 2(2)A	2(I)B 2(2)B	2(I)C 2(2)C	2(I)D 2(2)D	2(I)E 2(2)E

Sample Objectives:

I(I)A Given 10 sentences, student correctly identifies correct and incorrect capitalization in all cases.

I(2)B Given 20 proper and common names in dictation, student capitalizes with 100% accuracy.

2(I)C Given a paragraph of 10 run-on sentences, student puts periods in correct place in all cases in 5 minutes.

2(2)D In a classroom writing task, student correctly places commas in 15 of 15 instances.

2(2)E Student places all commas correctly in mainstream class writing assignment.

Table 6.4 provides a sample table of specifications for writing mechanics. Students' performance on the above elements can also vary as a function of student and situation variables such as (a) the particular assignment and purpose of writing, (b) amount and type of teacher directions, (c) amount of time allocated for the task, (d) background knowledge, and (e) motivation and attention given to the task. Several samples of students' written products should be evaluated in terms of both the elements listed above and student and situation variables. Once these evaluations are collected, an error analysis can be completed to determine specific subskill areas that need instruction or reteaching.

Instructional Strategies

This text's aim is to present the teacher-effectiveness model as a framework for incorporating all instruction, and this section presents that model as it is used with writing instruction. Sample lessons are presented first, based on the error analysis or examination of students' written products. Second, specific instructional strategies to increase sentence complexity or sophistication of writing are discussed. Third, prewriting strategies are discussed, followed by postwriting strategies. Finally, instruction in specific types of writing is presented.

Sample Lesson Designed From an Error Analysis

Using the method of examining writing products, teachers can determine very specific instructional needs. For example, if students consistently produce incorrect subject–verb agreements in their compositions, whether the tasks are timed or untimed, then a decision would be made to reteach correct subject–verb agreement. First, the teacher would develop an instructional objective or series of objectives reflecting the content to be taught. In this case, a good example is "Students will identify correct subject–verb agreement in sentences with 100% accuracy," followed by "Students will write the correct subject–verb agreement in sentences with 100% accuracy." A fluency (rate) application and a generalization objective, such as "Students will consistently use the correct subject–verb agreement in all of their writing assignments," are then specified. Notice that the first instructional objective emphasizes the identification of the correct grammar, followed by the production of the correct forms in contrived formats (accuracy and rate), and finally the application or generalization objective.

After specifying the objectives, the teacher can design the instructional lesson using all of the teacher-effectiveness variables. An example of each in the context of teaching subject–verb agreement is presented below.

1. *Review*. Teacher begins the lesson with a review of subjects and verbs. During this time, students respond to the teacher's questions, thus providing the teacher with information on how well past content has been retained. Decisions can then be made to either introduce new content or reinstruct old content.

2. *Teacher presentation*. Teacher verbally presents the lesson's objective, tells students the rules for subject–verb agreement, provides examples and nonexamples, and requires all students to participate in responding to direct questions on the rule and examples of the rule. Teacher provides corrective feedback to students during the presentation and keeps the pace of instruction moving rapidly enough to ensure that all students are participating.

3. *Guided practice*. During this portion of the lesson, students are actively engaged in a practice activity that is guided by the teacher. This ensures that students practice correct subject–verb agreements.

4. *Independent practice*. Once it is determined that students are able to practice subject–verb agreement activities successfully, the teacher allows students to continue to practice independently. However, the teacher continues to monitor students' work.

5. *Formative evaluation*. After students complete the independent practice activity, the teacher can give students a 1- or 2-minute quiz to

verify their mastery of subject–verb agreement. The quiz should include several items that match the specific objective covered in the lesson. In this case, since subject–verb agreement is being reintroduced, the teacher can decide whether more or less time is needed on this task.

The amount of engaged time-on-task, the type of teacher presentation, questioning, and feedback, the type and amount of guided practice and independent practice, and student performance can now be examined to determine if and how instruction should be monitored and adjusted.

Any pattern of deficiencies in students' written composition can be analyzed and reinstructed using the above model. Again, it is recommended that teachers use districtwide objectives and scope and sequences in order to maximize mainstreaming potential. Most importantly, systematic analysis of students' errors should be combined with effective instruction in those deficit areas.

Increasing Sentence Complexity

Many students with mild disabilities write very simple sentences consisting of a subject and a verb. To analyze the complexity of a student's writing, only a T-unit analysis can be conducted. A T-unit, or *minimal terminal unit*, is a main clause or a main clause and its accompanying subordinate clause. The number of words used per T-unit can be calculated (see Figure 6.10). Typically, the higher the number of words per T-unit, the more sophisticated the writing. The teacher can analyze the students' writing to determine the average T-unit length. If the T-unit length is low, teachers should teach sentence-combining activities. Through examples and practice activities, sentence-combining activities teach students how to write sentences that contain main clauses and subordinate clauses. For example, given the following series of simple sentences:

Tom went outside. (3 words, 1 T-unit)

He looked at the flowers. (5 words, 1 T-unit)

The flowers were dry. (4 words, 1 T-unit)

He got some water. (4 words, 1 T-unit)

He watered the flowers. (4 words, 1 T-unit)

and given sentence-combining instructions that recommend the combination of simple sentences to form a major clause and subordinate clauses by using words such as *when, whether, or,* and *however,* the above example can be rewritten to look like the following.

Knight Rider is my favorite TV show./ It is about a guy who has a special car./ He chases crooks in his car./ Sometimes he fights,/ but he always comes out OK./ He drives his car real fast.

Total T-units:	6
Total Words:	38
Words / T-unit Ratio:	6.33

FIGURE 6.10. Calculation of T-units.

Tom went outside to look at the flowers. (8 words, 1 T-unit)

Because the flowers were dry, he got some water and watered the flowers. (13 words, 1 T-unit)

Specific instruction and practice can be completed using sentence-combining activities. Again, specific objectives and the teacher-effectiveness variables should be incorporated into sentence-combining instruction.

Prewriting Strategies

Specific instruction also needs to be conducted on prewriting strategies. There is nothing more frustrating than to sit down with a blank piece of paper, a pencil, and no ideas about what to do or how to start doing it. Very specific instruction and practice can be given in the following areas:

1. brainstorming topic ideas

2. methods for getting started

3. narrowing topics

4. outlining major subheadings

5. outlining minor details

6. organizing ideas

7. writing first drafts

8. researching topics

Adequate instruction and guided and independent practice should be provided on all of the above prewriting strategies. Some examples for prewriting strategies are given in Figure 6.11. Harris and Graham (1992, p. 49)

Assignment: Write a persuasive paper on a school policy.

1. What is a school policy? (If you don't know, try to find out.)

2. List as many school policies as you can.

3. Which of these policies do you feel most strongly about?

4. Are you in favor of it or opposed to it?

5. List as many arguments as you can think of.

6. Can you think of any more?

7. List the arguments in order of importance to you.

8. What would happen if your ideas were accepted?

FIGURE 6.II. Prewriting strategies.

proposed the use of the TREE strategy for planning a simple opinion essay: note *T*opic sentence, note *R*easons, *E*xamine reasons (are they convincing?), and note *E*nding. For writing simple stories, Harris and Graham (1992, p. 49) recommended the SPACE strategy: note *S*etting, *P*urpose, *A*ction, *C*onclusion, and *E*motions. Each of these strategies can also be adapted to a postwriting self-monitoring strategy, as described in the next section.

Postwriting Strategies

Similarly, adequate instruction needs to be implemented on postwriting strategies. Effective use of postwriting strategies can make the difference between an excellent paper and a less-than-adequate paper. Postwriting strategies include:

1. proofing for spelling, mechanics, and general format

2. proofing for adequate organization of ideas and content coverage

3. revising based upon (1) and (2) above

4. re-editing and handing in assignments on time

Very specific error-monitoring and self-monitoring strategies can be combined not only to assist students in locating and correcting errors but also to ensure that checking skills are completed. Figure 6.12 contains a self-monitoring sheet for the story grammar strategy (cf. SPACE strategy, described previously) for organizing and sequencing ideas in narrative prose or stories (Harris & Graham, 1992, p. 30).

	Yes	No
Did I use the story grammar strategy (3-W, 2-What, 2-How)?	☐	☐
Did I include:		
• Who the main character and other characters are?	☐	☐
• When the story takes place?	☐	☐
• Where the story takes place?	☐	☐
• *What* the main character wants to do?	☐	☐
• *What* happens when the main character tries to do it?	☐	☐
• *How* the story ends?	☐	☐
• *How* the characters feel at the end?	☐	☐

FIGURE 6.12.   Story grammar self-monitoring sheet. Adapted from *Helping Young Writers Master the Craft: Strategy Instruction and Self-Regulation in the Writing Process* by K. Harris and S. Graham, 1992, Cambridge, MA: Brookline Books. Adapted with permission.

In the future, it is possible that word processors will be widely available for students' use. Some word-processing programs now contain spellers, which check for spelling errors, and counters, which tally total words and sentences. Computer programs like these can be invaluable for use in guided and independent practice activities for students. However, as with any instruction, their ultimate efficacy will depend on teachers' collection of formative data and teachers' judgments as to whether objectives have been mastered.

Specific Types of Written Products

Writing is an application of many skills. Additionally, there are many purposes for writing, the form for each of which needs to be explicitly instructed. For example, students may be required to write any of the following:

1. personal letters

2. thank you notes

3. letters to manufacturers requesting exchanges of merchandise

4. research reports

5. persuasive arguments

6. creative prose

7. poetry

8. technical manuals

All of these are easier to write if a concrete model is provided (see Figure 6.13). Be careful, however, that overreliance on a model does not inhibit creativity of ideas in the later stages of writing. All types of writing should be instructed using the proposed teacher-effectiveness model, and students' performance should be monitored. It is recommended that special educators determine regular education goals and objectives in writing and adjust them accordingly for their special-needs students.

Collaborative Writing

Researchers have recently begun to recommend student interaction and collaboration in writing. Students have improved the quality of their writing and their attitudes toward writing when they engage in collaborative activities with other students under teacher supervision. Students can meet in pairs or groups to brainstorm ideas, plan and organize written products, monitor and encourage progress toward task completion, and proofread and revise each other's work, perhaps using self-monitoring checklists. Although it is important to ensure that individual students have mastered the competencies necessary for independent writing, it also can be very helpful and rewarding to teach writing as a collaborative, interactive process.

Heading	Dear Grandma,
Thank-you	Thank you for the sweater. I like the color and
Elaboration (2 sentences)	it fits very well. I know I will be needing it now that the weather is getting cold.
Address the giver	I hope you had a nice Christmas.
Closing	Love,
Signature	Bobby

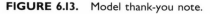

FIGURE 6.13. Model thank-you note.

Special Problems

When students exhibit difficulty with written language, teachers must determine where the difficulties lie. First, teachers may wish to determine whether the problem is primarily due to insufficient ability to manipulate paper and pencil. If this is the case, provision of fluency-building activities in handwriting may be desirable. Additionally, teachers may wish to determine whether the problem is due primarily to insufficient ability to generate novel ideas. To determine if this is the case, teachers can require students to write titles and descriptions of illustrations. A series of pictures depicting a story can be presented to the students, and students can be asked to write down the sequence of events from the illustrations. By implementing this type of procedure, teachers eliminate the generation of novel ideas component from the writing task. Teachers can then determine how accurately students can describe a sequence of events in writing.

A more precise evaluation of students' ability to use proper grammar, including sentence structure and punctuation, can also be made. Composition instruction can then proceed with the aid of such illustrations. The illustrations can eventually be phased out from instruction and replaced by verbal story starters.

Some teachers have found that requiring students to write on a daily basis in journals or logs greatly facilitates the performance of reluctant writers. Some teachers choose *not* to read or evaluate these written products so that students will write more freely and learn to enjoy writing more. Many teachers set aside a regular time for writing. This frequent practice sometimes enables students to gain confidence in writing. Additionally, it may be beneficial for teachers to add self-correction components to writing instruction. During self-correction activities, students can be required to identify their errors and then to produce the correct responses. When self-correction is explicitly taught, students may be better able to generalize error-monitoring strategies to their independent work.

SUMMARY

This chapter has presented instructional information on language arts, including spelling, handwriting, oral language, and written language. The emphasis has been placed on (a) determining specific instructional objectives from a larger task analysis or scope and sequence and (b) designing effective lessons based on the teacher-effectiveness variables. If teachers use the specified instructional model for delivery of instruction, they will be better able to monitor and adjust instruction based on student performance in each area. Language arts is a global area with imprecisely defined domains. For this reason, it is recommended that teachers determine the competencies emphasized in their particular school district and design objectives and lessons to coincide with them.

RELEVANT RESEARCH AND RESOURCES

Spelling

An overview of effective spelling practice is provided by Loomes (1982). Most of these techniques have been validated on students classified as learning disabled, behaviorally disordered or emotionally disturbed, and mentally retarded. Research on spelling in special education is reviewed by Graham and Miller (1979). Error analysis procedures are described by Ganschow (1984). Time-on-task as an important variable is discussed by Gerber (1984). The importance of list length and cumulative rehearsal/distributed practice is demonstrated by Gettinger, Bryant, and Fayne (1982); Gettinger (1984); Neef, Iwata, and Page (1980); and Weaver (1984). Gettinger et al. (1982) demonstrated the importance of grouping words with similar spellings. Self-monitoring and self-checking procedures are validated by Beck, Matson, and Kazdin (1983). Effective tutoring procedures are described by Higgins (1982) and Reith, Polsgrove, and Eckert (1984). Rehearsal techniques are described by Weaver (1984), while cognitive approaches are described by Wong (1986a) and Englert, Hiebert, and Stewart (1985). Finally, initial validation of the spelling mnemonic, albeit with students without disabilities, is reported by Negin (1978). Initial results that support a time-delay procedure are presented by Stevens and Schuster (1987). A recent review of research on spelling interventions for students with learning disabilities is written by Gordon, Vaughn, and Schumm (1993).

Handwriting

A review of remedial handwriting research is provided by Graham and Miller (1980). The use of task analysis, overlearning, monitoring, and verbal cues is described by Hagen (1983). Self-instruction and self-correction techniques are evaluated by Graham (1983); Kosiewicz, Hallahan, Lloyd, and Graves (1982); and Robin, Armel, and O'Leary (1975). Other techniques for improving handwriting performance are suggested by Connell (1983), Hanover (1983), and Ruedy (1983).

Oral Language

The general effectiveness of a direct instruction approach to oral language with children from lower income groups is described by Gersten, Woodward, and Darch (1986), who have also described similar interventions with students with disabilities. Lloyd, Cullinan, Heins, and Epstein (1980) provided support for direct instruction procedures in improving the oral and written language of learning-disabled students. Use of the keyword method in facilitating initial acquisition of

(*continues*)

(Relevant Research and Resources continued)

vocabulary words is supported in research described by McLoone, Scruggs, Mastropieri, and Zucker (1986); Mastropieri, Scruggs, Levin, Gaffney, and McLoone (1985); Mastropieri, Scruggs, and Levin (1985a); Scruggs, Mastropieri, and Levin (1985); Mastropieri, Scruggs, and Fulk (1990); Fulk, Mastropieri, and Scruggs (1992); McLoone, Scruggs, Mastropieri, and Zucker (1986); Mastropieri (1988); and Scruggs and Laufenberg (1986). Carlisle (1993) reviewed literature on vocabulary learning and reading disabilities. Additional suggestions for oral language training in special education are given by Bording, McLaughlin, and Williams (1984); Minskoff (1982); and Fisher, White, and Fisher (1984), while Bos and Anders (1987, 1990a, 1990b) described an interactive process for facilitating vocabulary.

Written Language

Additional information on assessment of written language is provided by Isaacson (1984, 1985a, 1985b) and Thomas, Englert, and Gregg (1987). A recent issue of *Learning Disabilities Research & Practice* (Vol. 6, No. 4), edited by Graham and MacArthur (1991), is devoted to writing. Reviews of research on writing instruction for mildly disabled children are written by Graham (1982) and Isaacson (1987). Additional information on teaching strategies is given by Marik (1982); Moran (1983); Nutter and Safran (1984); Weygant (1981); Giordano (1984); Walmsley (1984); Bridge and Hiebert (1985); Graham and Harris (1987); Hillocks (1984); Englert (1990); Englert and Mariage (1991); MacArthur, Graham, and Schwartz (1991); Zaragoza and Vaughn (1992); Graham, MacArthur, Schwartz, and Page-Voth (1992); Wong, Wong, and Blenkinsop (1989); and Dowis and Schloss (1992). The effective use of peers as collaborators in writing is described by MacArthur, Schwartz, and Graham (1991); Wong, Wong, Darlington, and Jones (1991); and Englert, Raphael, Anderson, Anthony, and Stevens (1991). The use of microcomputers in the writing process is described by Hine, Goldman, and Cosden (1990) and Malouf, Wizer, Pilato, and Grogan (1990). Curriculum-based measurement and the assessment of writing is discussed by Parker, Tindal, and Hasbrouck (1991); Deno, Marston, and Mirkin (1982); and Tindal and Parker (1989). Five (1992) described the integration of students with mild disabilities into a collaborative class writing program. Harris and Graham (1992) wrote an excellent book on teaching writing. Their research is reviewed by Graham, Harris, MacArthur, and Schwartz (1991).

Curricular Materials

Commercially available curricular materials exist in the language development area. A sample of these materials include: *Peabody Language Development Kits* (American Guidance Service), *DISTAR Language Program* (Engelmann & Osborne, 1976), and the *Clinical Language Intervention Program* (Psychological Corporation). Materials are also available to facilitate written communication. These include *Reasoning and Writing* (SRA) and *Story Starters* (Curriculum Associates).

(continues)

(Relevant Research and Resources continued)

Computer Software and Technology

Computer software is also available for supplementing instruction in the language area. Several word-processing programs are available, and teachers should select programs based upon availability at their schools. Most programs contain spell check components, and many newer programs also contain grammar checks (e.g., WordPerfect 6.0 [WordPerfect Corporation]). Software programs are described in detail by Church and Bender (1989). Scholastic distributes numerous software programs intended to facilitate composing and writing for students, including First Draft, Success With Writing, and Multiscribe I and IIGS. Mind-Play distributes Author! Author!, Ace Reporter, and Ace Detective, and DLM distributes The Writing Adventure. Programs that provide practice on specific skills components include the IBM Combining Sentence Series: Levels II–IV, the IBM Spelling Series: Levels I–III, the IBM Vocabulary Series: Levels II–IV, the IBM Punctuation Series: Levels II–IV, and the IBM Parts of Speech Series: Levels II–III (IBM). The Spider Hunt Spelling: School Edition, Word Munchers, Grammar Gremlins, and the Vocabulary Detective are available from Cambridge Development Laboratory, while the Mammoth Meltdown: A Parts of Speech Game, Blackout: A Capitalization Game, and Punctuation Baseball and Grammar Baseball are available from Gamco Industries. Additionally, some software is available in Spanish. For example, Voy A Leer Escribiendo (VALE) (I): Learning to Read and Write and Mi Editor Primario (I), a word-processor program, are available from IBM.

Finally, word prediction software programs are available. These programs predict the word after the author has typed a letter or a couple of letters. A listing of word options is displayed, and the author selects the correct option. According to Heinisch and Hecht (1993), more than 15 word prediction programs are available, including Predict It and Co:Write (Don Johnston Developmental Equipment), Mind Reader (Brown Bag Software), KeyWiz (Words + Inc.), and Handi-WORD (MicroSystems Software). See Appendix B for a list of addresses of producers and distributors of software and curricular materials.

❖ ❖ ❖

CHAPTER 7

Mathematics

LIKE READING, MATHEMATICS IS ONE OF THE ESSENTIAL BASIC SKILL AREAS. All children are expected to learn the vocabulary, concepts, computational skills, procedures, algorithms, and problem-solving strategies essential for successful mastery of mathematics. Some educators make a distinction between mathematics and arithmetic. The latter, often referred to as computational skills, is comprised of basic addition, subtraction, multiplication and division operations, and algorithms (or step-by-step procedures used for solving more complex computation problems). Mathematics is broader in definition, including arithmetic as well as numeration, number systems, fractions, decimals, problem solving, geometry, measurement, time, money, algebra, calculus, and interpretation of charts, tables, and graphs. Various educational approaches have been attempted in teaching mathematics. Some educators have proposed the teaching of basic skills that emphasize the mastery of certain math facts and operations. Others have proposed using inductive techniques that emphasize a reasoning and problem-solving approach. The debate in the approach to mathematics instruction is similar to the debate in various approaches to teaching reading (see Chapter 5). In reality, the skills emphasized in each approach are considered essential for a thorough understanding and generalization of mathematics. In special education, research has generally supported the effectiveness of programs that emphasize a direct drill and practice approach toward the teaching of all areas, including basic math facts, vocabulary, concepts, and problem-solving strategies. It is critically important for special educators to use the teacher-effectiveness variables in the delivery of mathematics instruction and, concomitantly, to examine the type of learner behavior expected (identification, production, and application), the level of learning (acquisition and fluency), and the type of learning (discriminations, facts, rules, procedures, and concepts) in order to design an optimal set of instructional strategies. It is also critical that students understand underlying mathematical concepts and that they learn to reason mathematically. It is not enough that they memorize math facts or that they mechanically apply strategies to solve problems they do not really understand.

Recent research has documented that very little instructional time is allocated to mathematics in the classroom. In fact, many elementary-age students spend less than 20 minutes a day engaged in relevant mathematics instruction. Students with mild disabilities desperately need excellent instruction in all areas of mathematics. Chapter 11 presents examples of the importance of mathematics skills in daily living. Students with special needs require excellent instruction in all areas of mathematics, especially in areas that emphasize the generalization and application of skills related to math.

This chapter first provides an overview of mathematics instruction, including the selection of a mathematics program, mathematics assessment and error analysis, instructional grouping, and the use of the teacher-effectiveness variables. The sections that follow describe practices for teaching beginning math skills, intermediate-level math skills, and advanced math skills.

TEACHING MATHEMATICS: AN OVERVIEW

The teaching of mathematics is a critically important activity for the special educator. As mentioned above, most special-needs students enter special education programs with specific skill deficiencies in mathematics. This section describes strategies for selecting a mathematics program, initial assessment and placement, general error analysis, grouping for instruction, presenting new information, delivering guided and independent practice activities, and monitoring and adjusting instruction based on formative evaluation data.

Selecting a Mathematics Program

School districts typically adopt a particular series for instruction in mathematics. Most series divide the teaching of specific facts, concepts, and algorithms into various grade levels. The series usually provides student textbooks, student workbooks, and a teacher's guide. Additionally, several remedial math programs have been published and are widely available, along with supplemental programs that are designed to provide additional practice in specific skill areas. (Several are listed at the end of this chapter.) Before selecting a specific mathematics series, teachers are recommended to first determine the district's scope and sequence for math skills and then consider the following features:

1. *Scope and sequence of math skills.* Has the series clearly identified a scope and sequence of objectives that matches the district's

scope and sequence? Is the content organized so that prerequisite preskills are taught prior to the applications of those skills? Are skills that could be easily confused introduced separately or simultaneously?

2. *Breadth of mathematics activities.* Does the series provide sufficient examples of math problems under different formats, such as vertical problems, horizontal problems, word problems, and applications to "real world" situations?

3. *Concreteness and meaningfulness.* Does the series make mathematics learning as concrete and as meaningful as possible?

4. *Sufficient opportunities for practice.* Does the series provide sufficient guided and independent practice activities for students with learning problems, particularly at the fluency and generalization levels? Does the series present sufficient types of formats within the practice activities, and are reviews that cover skills learned previously included?

5. *Strategy instruction.* Does the series provide the teacher with specific cognitive strategies for learning and applying new facts, rules, concepts, and procedures?

6. *Instructional component.* Does the series provide the teacher with specific instructional guidelines and formats for introducing new facts, rules, concepts, and procedures that correspond with the teacher-effectiveness literature?

7. *Evaluation component.* Does the series provide a format by which student performance and progress can be monitored and adjusted on a regular basis? Does the series provide a placement test?

8. *Validation data.* Does the series provide some evidence that it has been successfully implemented with special education students?

9. *Diversity.* Does the series provide sufficient representation of diverse cultures and gender roles?

Probably no material will possess all of the features listed above; however, prior to selecting a math series, all of the above questions need to be answered satisfactorily. It will be up to the teacher to supplement the series in any areas of deficit. For example, if a series does not provide adequate strategy instruction for solving word problems, then teachers will need to supplement the series by providing students with specific strategy instructions and corresponding guided and independent practice activities on applying those strategies. Likewise, if the series lacks sufficient practice activities, teachers will have to supplement it by providing additional relevant exercises.

Teachers must often select and use a math program from existing district materials. In such a case, teachers must select a program that addresses as many of the above features as possible and supplement their instruction with any missing features. The most frequently encountered problems include (a) material presented on too abstract a level with insufficient examples, (b) insufficient relevant practice activities, (c) inadequate strategic instructions, (d) insufficient instructions for the introduction of new concepts, (e) insufficient application and generalization examples (including practice using different formats), and (f) insufficient formative evaluation procedures. Teachers must adapt their instructional procedures to accommodate such inadequacies.

Mathematics Assessment

When students enter special education programs for mathematics instruction, they typically have been tested for current level of functioning or performance in math. This current level of performance is usually expressed as a grade equivalent score, a percentile score, or a stanine score from a norm-referenced test. This overall score provides information concerning how these students are performing in relation to all other students of that age and grade level. Although this information can be beneficial in determining the need for special education services, it usually does not provide information regarding specific skills the students have or have not mastered in relation to the curriculum materials used in a particular school. As mentioned in Chapter 5, it is recommended that special educators administer curriculum-based assessment to determine where along the scope and sequence of objectives in the curriculum the student needs to begin instruction.

Curriculum-Based Assessment and Instructional Grouping

Although many diagnostic tests are available and some can provide teachers with an analysis of skills students possess and lack, use of such tests should be linked to curriculum materials being used in the classroom. Otherwise, teachers should begin to develop their own curriculum-based tests to determine where along the curriculum students need instruction. As was emphasized in Chapter 5 for reading, when district objectives match curriculum objectives, and students' IEP objectives are based on these objectives, curriculum-based assessment locates the starting point for instruction. For example, assume that a specific mathematics series has been adopted for use. Next, assume that a series of curriculum-based tests that correspond with the adopted math series has been developed. The first step in implementing this assessment procedure involves selecting the test at the approximate skill level (first, second, third, etc.) of the new student. After completing the administration and scoring of the test, the teacher can identify specific skills that have or have not been mastered in relation to the curriculum. Appropriate placement for instructional purposes can then be completed.

Procedures such as these can also assist teachers in making instructional grouping decisions. Refer back to the above example, but instead of administering the test to one student, administer the test to all students who are required to receive mathematics instruction in the special education setting. After scoring all of the tests, teachers can determine how to form their instructional groups based on an examination of mastery of specific math skills.

Periodic readministration of such curriculum-based measures can provide teachers with the following information:

1. Are the originally formed instructional groups still optimal?

2. Are the students mastering the skills at an appropriate rate?

3. Are students retaining previously mastered skills?

4. Are the students ready to be mainstreamed back into regular education mathematics classes?

These curriculum-based assessment procedures can become an integral part of the instructional process. The tests focus attention on the specific mathematics skills students need to master and, therefore, assist teachers in designing and delivering instruction at levels appropriate for specific students. (For a discussion of all of the factors that need to be taken into consideration when forming instructional groups, see Chapter 5.) Additionally, teachers can obtain valuable information regarding students' mathematics performance by using the error analysis procedures described in the next section.

Error Analysis

Mathematics is well suited for use in error analysis procedures. As mentioned previously, error analysis is a technique that is used to analyze students' errors in an attempt to determine patterns in those errors. For example, typical systematic errors could include any of the following:

1. *Incorrect fact.* The student recalls an incorrect fact consistently (e.g., $7 \times 8 = 57$).

2. *Incorrect operation.* The student executes the incorrect operation (e.g., consistently performs addition when the operation should be multiplication).

3. *Incorrect execution of procedures.* The student applies the steps to an algorithm incorrectly. The procedure may not be known or may be executed in the wrong sequence, or a necessary step may be omitted (e.g., the steps necessary to execute a long-division problem or subtraction with borrowing).

4. *No pattern errors.* The responses are incorrect and appear to be random.

5. *Combinations of incorrect facts and incorrectly employed operations and/or algorithms.*

Typically, the first step in completing an error analysis is to obtain a sample of the student's work. Recent classroom assignments, classroom tests, or survey or curriculum-based tests may be used. Second, the work is corrected. The student's errors are then categorized by error type, using the classification suggested above. Special educators can also develop an informal checklist that incorporates all possible operations, facts, and algorithms. This checklist can be used to monitor students' progress toward mastery. Figure 7.1 presents a sample error analysis checklist. When students make errors, teachers should be able to determine the reason for those errors. It will probably be necessary to provide instruction in those areas. It is important to note that simply because a student appears to make an error, it does not necessarily mean that the student does not know that particular fact, operation, or algorithm. It may simply be a careless error. In fact, after completing an error analysis and determining specific error patterns, teachers can verify whether or not such errors are in need of remediation by asking students to explain the steps and procedures they used to arrive at their answers. That is why it is important to monitor instruction based on student performance data that is collected continuously.

Teacher Effectiveness and Mathematics Instruction

As in all of the content areas addressed in this book, the teacher-effectiveness variables can be combined with the content of mathematics instruction in order to maximize student achievement gains. The model that is presented next is based in part on teacher effectiveness research in mathematics (e.g., Good, Grouws, & Ebmeier, 1983), which was conducted over a period of several years and which demonstrated very impressive achievement gains in mathematics for the participating students. What

Content Area	Addition	Subtraction	Multiplication	Division
Basic fact knowledge (0–20)	8 + 7 —— 14	12 – 9	7 × 6 —— 45	81 ÷ 9 = 7
Basic operation knowledge	15 + 4 —— 11	17 – 9 —— 26	6 × 6 —— 12	9 ÷ 3 = 27
Basic procedural knowledge (regrouping, long-division steps)	27 + 6 —— 213	53 –36 —— 23	25 ×44 —— 80 80 —— 160	1R95 32⟌63 63 —— 32 95

Note: Only the major breakdowns are provided in this example. Additional subdivisions should be added as necessary.

FIGURE 7.I. An error-analysis checklist.

follows is an example of an application of the teacher-effectiveness functions during a mathematics lesson.

Daily Review

Each mathematics lesson should begin with a review of the content covered in the previous lesson. For example, assume a series of lessons/objectives on money was being covered as listed in the table of specifications shown in Table 7.1. Additionally, presume that lesson objectives covering the identification and naming values of all coins have been introduced and practiced previously and that the present lesson objective requires students to name values of different groups of coins (adding). (Refer to cell 1B in Table 7.1.) The lesson review would cover the identification and naming values of coins in isolation. Direct teacher questioning similar to the following would be appropriate. Teacher holds up a penny or an illustration of a penny and says, "What coin is this? [Signal response.] How much is a penny worth?" [Signal response.] Eventually, all of the coins that had been previously practiced would be reviewed. Corrective feedback would be provided, if necessary, and, based on student performance, teachers would know whether or not those objectives had been mastered. If homework worksheets had been assigned as an independent practice activity, this would also be the appropriate time to check students' performance for understanding.

TABLE 7.1. Table of Specifications for Basic Money Skills.

CONTENT	BEHAVIOR				
	Identification	Production (counting)			
	A. Acquisition	B. Acquisition	C. Fluency	D. Application	E. Generalization
1. *Coins*					
(1) pennies	1(1)A	1(1)B	1(1)C	1(1)D	1(1)E
(2) nickels/dimes	1(2)A	1(2)B	1(2)C	1(2)D	1(2)E
(3) quarters	1(3)A	1(3)B	1(3)C	1(3)D	1(3)E
(4) half dollars	1(4)A	1(4)B	1(4)C	1(4)D	1(4)E
(5) silver dollars	1(5)A	1(5)B	1(5)C	1(5)D	1(5)E
2. *Currency*					
(1) 1 dollar	2(1)A	2(1)B	2(1)C	2(1)D	2(1)E
(2) 2 dollars	2(2)A	2(2)B	2(2)C	2(2)D	2(2)E
(3) 5 dollars	2(3)A	2(3)B	2(3)C	2(3)D	2(3)E
(4) 10 dollars	2(4)A	2(4)B	2(4)C	2(4)D	2(4)E
(5) 20 dollars	2(5)A	2(5)B	2(5)C	2(5)D	2(5)E

Sample Objectives:

1A   Students will identify 15 coins, including pennies, nickels, dimes, quarters, half dollars, and dollars by pointing to the correct coin upon request when presented with the target coin and three distractor coins each, within 2 seconds, with 100% accuracy. (As written, this is a fluency-level identification objective. By deleting "within 2 seconds," the objective becomes an acquisition-level objective.

1(1)A Students will identify pennies when presented with pennies and three distractor coins, by pointing to the penny 10 out of 10 times.

2E   Students will accurately apply their math computation skills when presented with story problems that require students to make change using 1 to 20 dollars with 100% accuracy.

Presentation of New Materials

Presentation of the new content should parallel the procedures outlined in Chapter 1. Teachers must first clarify the goals and main objectives for the day's lesson. In this example, the teacher could say, "We have all learned how to identify pennies, nickels, dimes, quarters, half dollars, and silver dollars and how to tell the value of those coins. Today we are going to learn how to name (count the value of) different combinations of those same coins." The teacher would present several examples in a step-by-step fashion using the model–lead–test approach. In the present example, the teacher could say, "See this? [Point to nickel on blackboard.] What is it? How much is it worth? What is this? [Point to a penny.] How much is it worth? Now, one nickel and one penny are worth six cents together, because one nickel equals five cents and one penny equals one cent, and five cents plus one cent equals six cents. When you are asked to tell the value of several coins, first you determine the value of each coin, then you add all the values together." The teacher tells the students the procedures to use to determine the values of several coins and simultaneously presents an illustration.

Next, the teacher should present another example and lead the students through the procedures by asking students, "What is the first thing to do in adding coins together? What do you do after you determine the value of each coin?" Another example should then be provided. This format should be followed until it is determined that students are ready for a guided practice activity.

Guided Practice

Recall that the major goal of guided practice is to ensure that all of the students have opportunities to practice the new skills correctly and frequently with teacher feedback and monitoring. All teacher questions should be directly relevant to the instructional objective, in this case, relevant to adding values of different groups of coins. All or most of the students should participate in all or most of the guided practice activity. During the above lesson, the teacher might continue to present examples and require students to respond orally on signal. Students could also be required to solve problems individually, write the responses on individual slates, and hold up their slates on cue. Throughout this activity, students' performances can be monitored, and teachers can provide immediate corrective feedback whenever necessary. If students require additional review on the procedure, teachers can easily re-present the information just presented. Students need the opportunity to practice the newly introduced skills under constant teacher monitoring. This helps to ensure that students are practicing the skills correctly. When students have learned the new skill and are executing it accurately, teachers can proceed to independent practice activities.

Independent Practice

Independent practice in mathematics often consists of paper–pencil tasks that students are required to execute on their own. It is critical for teachers to initially guide students during this activity. In fact, it is recommended that teachers lead students through the first few examples to ensure that students understand the task demands. It is also important for teachers to monitor students' independent practice by circulating around the room. If students appear to be having difficulty, teachers can provide immediate corrective feedback and reinstruct the essential components of the new skill.

During this stage of the lesson, quick and accurate performance needs to be reinforced. Teachers can use independent practice activities to reinforce good, independent study behaviors. Most importantly, however, teachers need to ensure that such activities are directly relevant to the lesson's main objective. In the present example, the majority of the items on the practice activity should require students to practice adding and naming values of various groups of coins. Other items could require students to exhibit previously taught skills. These activities allow students opportunities to (a) practice the newly introduced skill, (b) become fluent at the new skill, and (c) overlearn the skill so that teaching applications of the skill can proceed.

Several alternatives to the typical seatwork activity provide viable independent practice activities too. Peer tutoring, computer-assisted instruction, and various other audiovisual aids (e.g., tape recorders) are all valuable procedures that, when implemented and monitored carefully, can be effective alternatives to independent seatwork. However, as in any procedure, teachers need to ensure that (a) the activities are directly relevant to the instructional objectives and (b) student performance is carefully monitored.

Weekly and Monthly Reviews

In special education settings, it is especially important to review previously taught skills. This is necessary to ensure long-term retention and to allow for easier application and generalization of those skills. Weekly and monthly reviews can be built into the introduction of new skills. Such reviews can also document the progress of mastery of IEP objectives. Reviews can be implemented using the procedures described for introducing new skills. Additionally, such review sessions can be optimal times for implementing peer tutoring. At these times it is important to inform students of their progress.

Formative Evaluation

In all instruction, teachers may implement formative evaluation near the end of the independent practice activity. A short test requiring students to execute the skills just practiced can assist teachers in adjusting their instruction based on students' performance. Remember that decisions to alter instructional procedures can include (a) increasing time-on-task, (b) reintroduction of new skills, (c) additional model–lead–test procedures, (d) adding more concrete and meaningful examples, (e) additional guided practice, and (f) additional independent practice. In order to be valid, however, decisions must be based on student performance data.

This section presented a very general overview of mathematics instruction and described the components of instruction necessary for all math skills. It is important to document student progress and to evaluate instruction based on that progress. Good instruction incorporates clear teacher presentations and active student participation in guided and independent practice activities that are directly relevant to instructional objectives. The remainder of this chapter presents specific strategies for teaching beginning, intermediate, and advanced mathematics skills.

BEGINNING MATH

Beginning mathematics includes skills and concepts in numeration, counting, one-to-one correspondence, equivalence, signs and symbols, addition concepts, addition facts, multidigit addition without regrouping, column addition, subtraction concepts, and multidigit subtraction without regrouping. Table 7.2 presents a possible table of specifications for beginning math skills, and each area is discussed separately in the sections that follow. Teachers are again reminded to consult their districts' math scope and sequence. District objectives may vary from those presented in Table 7.2. It is also important to point out that each content area listed can be further subdivided into its own table of specifications.

Numeration

One of the first skills students learn when they enter school is counting. Many students, in fact, have already mastered counting skills before they start school. Basically, counting involves *serial-list learning* (e.g., learning series such as 1, 2, 3, etc.), much like learning the letters of the alphabet. However, learning to count has little value unless students are also given instruction in the underlying concepts of numeration, which include one-to-one correspondence and equivalence. Although all components of numeration instruction should be mastered, these components are discussed separately in the following sections.

Counting

As stated above, counting involves serial-list learning and constitutes factual information. Counting is usually taught by providing direct drill and practice to develop acquisition and fluency. Teachers first review any previous learning and then teach the new information to be learned in short segments. For example, a teacher could review counting from 1 to 5, determine whether or not all students have learned this sequence, and then introduce the next three numbers: 6, 7, and 8. "Okay, we all know how to count to 5. Now we're going to learn to count to 8. Listen to me do it. 1, 2, 3, 4, 5, *6, 7, 8.* Everybody say 6, 7, 8 with me. [Signal.] [Repeat if necessary.] Good! Once more. [Signal.] Okay, now let's all count from 1 to 8. [Signal.] Now, you do it. [Signal.]" Provide corrective feedback as necessary.

Usually, many repetitions are required to learn counting fluently, and continuous monitoring on progress charts can be helpful in determining whether or not students are making satisfactory progress. It is also important to ensure that counting skills are learned cumulatively; that is, at any stage, students can go back to the first number and count consecutively to the last number learned. In most cases, students should eventually learn to

TABLE 7.2. Table of Specifications for Beginning Math Skills.

CONTENT	BEHAVIOR				
	Identification	Production			
	A. Acquisition	B. Acquisition	C. Fluency	D. Application	E. Generalization
1. *Counting*					
a. rote 1–10	1aA	1aB	1aC	1aD	1aE
b. rote 1–20 and higher	1bA	1bB	1bC	1bD	1bE
c. counting beginning at numbers other than 1	1cA	1cB	1cC	1cD	1cE
d. count "by's" 10, 5, etc.	1dA	1dB	1dC	1dD	1dE
e. count backwards	1eA	1eB	1eC	1eD	1eE
2. *Symbol skills*					
a. writes and identifies symbols 1–5, 6–10, teens, etc.	2aA	2aB	2aC	2aD	2aE
b. draws lines for numeration $(2 = //)$	2bA	2bB	2bC	2bD	2bE
c. signs (+, −, =)	2cA	2cB	2cC	2cD	2cE
d. reads and writes equations	2dA	2dB	2dC	2dD	2dE
3. *Operations*					
a. single-digit addition	3aA	3aB	3aC	3aD	3aE
b. single-digit subtraction	3bA	3bB	3bC	3bD	3bE
c. story problems	3cA	3cB	3cC	3cD	3cE
d. column addition	3dA	3dB	3dC	3dD	3dE
4. *Facts*					
a. +1 facts	4aA	4aB	4aC	4aD	4aE
b. +2 facts	4bA	4bB	4bC	4bD	4bE

(continues)

Sample Objectives:

1aA   Student will correctly point to the target digit (1–10) from a list of five distractor digits after hearing the teacher say the number.

2aB   Students will correctly write the symbol for the digits (1-10) after hearing the teacher say the number.

3cD   Students will correctly execute 10 simple story problems involving basic addition facts after hearing and/or reading the problems.

5cE   Students will correctly use and apply the concept of addition to real problems involving buying candy at the store.

TABLE 7.2. continued

CONTENT	BEHAVIOR				
	Identification	Production			
	A. Acquisition	B. Acquisition	C. Fluency	D. Application	E. Generalization
5. *Concepts/ vocabulary*					
a. one-to-one correspondence	5aA	5aB	5aC	5aD	5aE
b. equality	5bA	5bB	5bC	5bD	5bE
c. add, more than	5cA	5cB	5cC	5cD	5cE
d. subtract, less than	5dA	5dB	5dC	5dD	5dE

count at a fluency rate of over 100 numbers per minute. Additionally, students should receive instruction in "count by's." For example, students can be taught early on to count by 10s, 2s, and 5s in a manner very similar to that just described. This, too, involves serial-list learning and is factual information. Individual student needs and abilities can determine the amount of new information to be presented at one time. Often, during this type of instruction, it is a good idea for the teacher to set the pace for student responding by either clapping or snapping fingers whenever a response is desired. Figure 7.2 provides an illustration in which the teacher breaks the content into smaller chunks.

As counting skills are gained, it is important for students to learn to associate each number with its respective symbol (i.e., 1 = one, 2 = two, 3 = three). This type of factual learning is associative and can be taught concurrently with counting skills by means of drill and practice with flash cards. To be sure that associative components are being mastered, teachers should avoid always presenting number symbols in sequence. "Okay, now we are going to practice some numbers we learned last week. Everybody, what is this number? [Display 3; signal.] Three, that's right. Now, what is this number? [Display 6; signal.] Six, that's right." As students become fluent, they should be able to read these numbers almost as fast as they can count.

One-to-One Correspondence

One-to-one correspondence means that a student can apply counting and numeration skills to a set of similarly classified objects. In other words, a student, when asked, should be able to apply counting and numeration skills to items that he or she has not counted before, such as a group of blocks, boxes, or pennies. This application task ensures that the student has acquired the concept of one-to-one correspondence; that is, that num-

Lesson Objective: Students will orally count by 2s from 2 to 40 with 100% accuracy in 15 seconds (2s: 2, 4, 6, 8, 10, 12, 14, 16, 18, 20, 22, 24, 26, 28, 30, etc.)

1. Introduce the concept, using concrete objects and paper and pencil.

   | | | | | | | | | | =   10
     2   4   6   8   10   =   10

2. Break the information into the appropriate-size chunks.

3. Model the information (2, 4, 6, 8, 10).

4. Lead the students with you (Now, everyone say it with me when I say go. Go: 2, 4, 6, 8, 10).

5. Test the students by requiring them to respond without your assistance.

6. Provide corrective feedback whenever necessary. For example, if students respond 2, 4, 8, 10:

   T: No, listen: 2, 4, *6,* 8, 10
   S: 2, 4, 8, 10
   T: No, listen: 2, 4, *6*. Say it with me. [Signal.]
   S: 2, 4, *6*
   T: Again [signal]: 2, 4, *6* . . . 2, 4, *6* . . . 2, 4, *6*. Good, now listen: 2, 4, *6,* 8, 10. Say it with me [signal]: 2, 4, *6,* 8, 10.
   S: 2, 4, 6, 8, 10
   T: Good, again. [Signal.]
   S: 2, 4, 6, 8, 10

   First, try repeating the correct answer.
   Second, shorten the amount of desired information.
   Third, overemphasize the omitted response.
   Fourth, return to the original-size chunk if students respond correctly with the shortened response.

These procedures can be used with any other serial-list learning, associative task (e.g., 5s, 10s, 3s, 9s, days of the week, months of the year, etc.). It is recommended that students become proficient at one set of count-by's prior to introducing another set.

FIGURE 7.2. Count-by instructions.

bers can be applied, one to each set of things, in order to determine how many there are. As with other concepts, the test of acquisition is passed when counting skills can be applied to objects the student has not classified and counted before (e.g., "Charles, tell us how many chairs are in this room"). When students can apply skills in a variety of specific tasks, teachers can evaluate whether these skills can be generalized across other teachers, classroom settings, objects, or combinations. If not, teachers should prompt, reward, or reteach the counting skill in the new context.

Equivalence

Equivalence is a functional concept in mathematics that asserts that different sets with the same number of objects in them are in some way equivalent. As a concept, equivalence is tested in application tasks involving novel instances of the concept. For example, two sets of pennies can be placed side by side to show that they are equivalent. The teacher then can count each set and demonstrate that the numbers are equal. Following that positive example of "these two groups of pennies are equal," a negative example can be shown. In the present example, one penny could be removed and the teacher would say, "These two groups are not equal." Students can then be tested on these examples for understanding. Additional examples (e.g., pencils) can be used in a similar fashion. The equal sign (=) can be introduced here as an associative fact. As students begin to identify equivalence, they can be asked to determine equivalent numbers of different objects (e.g., "Here are six erasers. Show me the same number of pencils"). Once students have demonstrated this ability, independent practice activities, such as relevant worksheets, can help to reinforce this concept. Similarly, the concepts *more than* and *less than* can be introduced. The concepts are taught by provision of a general rule and specific examples and nonexamples, practiced and assessed by means of novel examples (e.g., "Does this row have *more* pennies than that row? Does it have *less* pennies? Good, this row has *less* pennies than that row"). Teachers must use the students' responses to determine whether additional practice activities on examples and nonexamples are required for thorough understanding.

Signs and Symbols

As students develop skills in math, they must learn the symbols that will direct them to the operations they will be conducting. Students may have already learned the equal sign (=) from equivalence lessons. As the need for new symbol identification arises, these symbols should be taught as simple associative facts. For example: [Display +.] "What does this symbol tell you to do? [Signal.] Right, it tells you to add." It is not generally helpful to teach symbols before they are needed.

Shapes, such as triangles, squares, and circles, are usually introduced in the primary grades as an initial stage of geometry. However, students usually do not make practical use of such information (other than identification) until several years later. Learning shapes is a form of concept learning, in that students must be able to identify a novel instance of the concept and discriminate it from noninstances. For example, when teaching what a triangle is, teachers could provide a rule and show how it could be applied. "A triangle is a closed shape with *three straight sides*. How many straight sides? [Signal.] Three, that's right. So if it has three straight sides, it is a triangle. That means [point to shape] this is a triangle, and this is a triangle, and this is *not* a triangle. Is this a triangle? Yes. Why is this a triangle, Mary? Right, because it has three straight sides. Why is this a triangle, Bill? Because it has three straight sides. Is this a triangle, Sue? Why not? Right, because it has four straight sides." Teachers can determine that the concept has been mastered when students can accurately identify a large number of triangles and describe relevant attributes. Figure 7.3 presents additional information on how teachers can assist students in learning the concept *triangle*.

When students begin to display knowledge of different shapes, teachers can introduce the initial concepts involved in fractions. Shapes are often employed in teaching initial fraction concepts because they are familiar, concrete, and easily divided. Teachers can select a circle and present it to the class as a single, whole thing. The circle can then be divided into two equal pieces, each of which constitutes ½ of a circle—the 1 representing the number of shaded-in pieces and the 2 representing the total number of pieces. As concepts, fractions must be taught using precise, multiple examples, and students must eventually demonstrate their ability to describe fractions they have not seen previously. Again, formative data recording the type and value of the fractions correctly identified can be helpful in determining whether the information is being learned efficiently.

Addition and Subtraction Facts

When students have mastered all necessary preskills, they usually begin to learn the basic addition and subtraction facts. This type of learning, involving the memorization of a large number of abstract facts, is often a long and tedious process for students with mild disabilities, particularly for many of those who have been described as having mild mental retardation.

The learning of basic addition and subtraction facts is associative, and there is little alternative but to provide as much direct drill and practice as possible to ensure that basic facts are being learned. It is important to collect formative data to determine whether sufficient progress is being made.

There are several things to consider when teaching addition and subtraction facts. First, the teacher must make an effort to make this portion

Preteaching Activities

1. Identify all essential and nonessential attributes of triangles.

Essential	*Nonessential*
enclosed shape	size
three straight sides	color
three angles	orientation in space

2. Design examples and nonexamples of triangle to demonstrate to students which attributes are essential and which are not essential.

3. Generate a clear, succinct rule statement that includes all of the essential information.

Teaching Activities

1. Tell the rule.

2. Show examples. (This is a triangle.)

3. Show nonexamples. (This is not a triangle.)

4. Test using examples and nonexamples. (Is this a triangle? Is this a triangle?)

5. Reteach and provide corrective feedback as necessary.

6. Provide a relevant practice activity that requires students to identify triangles.

7. Test for understanding.

FIGURE 7.3. Preteaching strategies for the concept *triangle*.

of the school day at least as enjoyable as any other portion of the school day. This can be done by a genuine attitude of enthusiasm on the part of the teacher and by communicating to the students that, although the task is not easy, it is nonetheless rewarding and something they should take pride in. Teachers should also be prompt to reward students for effort and progress and convey to students the importance of the task.

Second, teachers should carefully sequence instruction and use formative data to determine that content is not being covered too quickly or too slowly. Small chunks of content can be covered and mastered prior to the addition of new facts. New math facts, as they are introduced, do not require elaborate explanations; the most important aspect of the task is usually the use of rapid-paced, fluency-building activities that lead to a high percentage (80–90%) of correct responses. In order to maximize the total number of opportunities for correct responding, teachers can employ peer tutors with flash cards, drill and practice provided by computer software (some hand-held calculators provide this practice), or an independent study strategy in which the student self-prompts with a flash card, answers, and self-evaluates by examining the reverse side of the flash card. Students or tutors can learn to provide themselves with a series of trials (on facts for which they are 80–90% accurate) and to evaluate their performance on each trial. Such student-collected (or tutor-collected) data can help ensure on-task behavior and allow the teacher to evaluate progress. The teacher can also test periodically to ensure accuracy of self- or tutor-provided data.

As math facts are learned to fluency levels, they should be reviewed periodically to be certain they are not being forgotten as new facts are introduced. The overall goal of math fact instruction is automatic, fluent responses to problems.

Addition and Subtraction Concepts

As facts are being learned, it is important for students to be taught relevant concepts associated with addition and subtraction. Without instruction in the meaning of addition and subtraction, students will have difficulty applying math facts to problem-solving activities. Knowledge of math concepts per se, however, cannot be expected to facilitate fluency in math facts, although such knowledge can facilitate comprehension.

Addition and subtraction concepts are generally communicated through manipulation of concrete objects. For example, a teacher may say, "I have three paper clips. See, one, two, three. If I *add* two more paper clips, how many will I have? Count with me: four, *five*. If I add two paper clips to three paper clips, I will have five paper clips altogether. Now you try it. If you have four paper clips and add three, how many will you have altogether? [Prompt and provide feedback.]" Such activities in addition and subtraction can reinforce the relevant concepts for students. Figure 7.4 presents some strategies for teaching addition concepts. Like other concepts, a general rule or procedure is demonstrated, and students are prompted to demonstrate knowledge of the concept using novel instances. When students can effectively add and subtract quantities of real objects in a variety of instances, evidence of concept acquisition has been provided. It is important to remember, however, that such conceptual instruction is unlikely to facilitate the automatic recall of facts at a fluency level necessary for later complex operations. Conceptual understanding of such processes can lead students to determine the answers to addition and subtraction problems through other means, such as number lines or finger counting. A number line is simply a horizontal line with consecutive numbers marked off on it. To add 4 and 3, for example, students place their pencils on the number 4 and then move three more places to the right, to the spot indicated as 7. To subtract, students place their pencils on the number indicating the minuend and move the number of places to the left indicated by the subtrahend, which

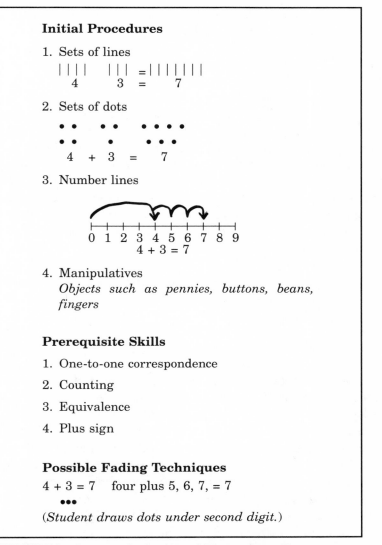

FIGURE 7.4. Strategies for teaching addition concepts.

will indicate the difference. Although such means provide evidence that relevant concepts have been mastered, they are long and tedious means for arriving at solutions. Optimal mathematics instruction involves an appropriate combination of factual and conceptual learning.

Problems in Beginning Math

Students can exhibit problems in any of the above areas of mathematics. In some cases in special education, problems can be remarkably persistent. In all cases, careful attention to content and components, formative performance data, and careful error analysis can be helpful in remedying such problems. Problems in mathematics functioning to this point can be viewed as either problems with facts or problems with concepts.

Math Vocabulary

Some students may have difficulty with mathematics procedures because they do not understand relevant vocabulary and therefore do not understand teacher explanations. In such cases, use of mnemonic techniques may be helpful. For example, to remember that the multiplier is the bottom number of a multiplication problem, teachers can present a keyword for multiplier (*pliers*) and show a picture in which an open pair of pliers represents the multiplication sign, displayed next to the multiplier. For multiplicand, the keyword *hand* could be shown pointing to the appropriate number. Similarly, divisors can be shown wearing *visors* (keyword for divisor), and *quotation marks* (keyword for quotient) can be placed around quotients. These visual keyword prompts can be removed as students remember the terms or learn to use imagery to prompt themselves.

Math Facts

Generally, facts in mathematics are taught using procedures similar to those used in any other type of factual learning. Math facts may prove to be difficult for students with mild disabilities to remember because of the abstract nature of numbers. If students demonstrate particular difficulty acquiring relevant facts, remedial procedures usually involve provision of additional engaged time for learning and smaller or more carefully sequenced steps. If no additional time is available during the school day, teachers can try to enlist the aid of parents or older siblings to provide additional practice at home. Teachers can also attempt to ensure that high engagement rates are operating at relevant times and that the student is properly motivated and has not become discouraged. If the student appears to be developing a negative attitude toward learning math facts, efforts must be made to manipulate the curriculum so that a very high rate of accurate responding is produced and the student is rewarded for maintaining that high level of performance, even if such manipulation requires slowing the pace of instruction.

Two additional methods have been proposed for assisting students' acquisition of math facts. Thornton and Toohey (1985) compiled a system of strategic computation. These include "counts ons" for +1, +2, and +3 facts, in which the student starts with the larger number and counts on 1, 2, or 3 additional numbers. Another is "zeros," which employs the simple rule of adding by 0. The "doubles" strategy is more complicated and involves thinking of pictures for adding doubles. For instance, the 2 + 2 fact employs a car picture, with two front and two back (= 4) tires. The 3 + 3 fact employs a picture of a grasshopper, with three legs on each side, while the 4 + 4 fact employs a picture of a spider. Five plus five uses a picture of two hands, 6 + 6 an egg carton, and 7 + 7 a pack of crayons. For facts that are "near doubles" (e.g., 5 + 6), students think of a double fact (e.g., 5 + 5) and add the remainder. So, in this case, 5 + 6 = (5 + 5) + 1 = 10 + 1 = 11. The "nines" strategy employs addition by 10 and then subtracting 1. These strategies can be helpful for students who have learned addition concepts but are having difficulty remembering facts.

Another method for computing facts is Touch Math (Bullock, Pierce, & McClelland, 1987, 1989). The system involves placing dots that represent quantity on numbers, for which students can later use imagery. For example, the number 1 has one dot in the middle of the number; 2 has a dot on the top and on the bottom left side of the number; 3 has dots on top, middle, and bottom left; four dots in a square pattern are placed on the number 4; and so on. For numbers 6 through 9, encircled dots, or *double touches,* are used. Six has three double touches, 7 has three double and one single touch (dot), and so on. Students are taught, for example when adding, to start with the higher number and count the additional numbers of dots on the other addend. In this way, Touch Math is a type of number line in which the markers are integrated into the physical structure of the numbers. For subtraction, students start with the minuend value and count backwards on the subtrahend. For multiplication, students use "count by's" (e.g., 3s), where each touch of the multiplier represents a count by of the multiplicand (e.g., 3, 6, 9, 12 for 3 × 4). For division, students count up from 0 by count by's of the divisor and write tally marks as they count. When they reach the dividend value, the number of tally marks represents the quotient. More complete information for using Touch Math is presented by Bullock et al. (1987).

These two types of strategies can be helpful in facilitating early math fact use. However, since they both focus more on computation than problem solving, effort must be made to ensure they are applied in relevant mathematical reasoning contexts.

There may come a time when teachers begin to regard the teaching of hundreds of math facts as hopeless for particular students. Math facts can appear to be a bewildering array of nonending, meaningless problems to many students, who appear completely incapable of learning more than a few at a time, only to forget those as soon as new facts are introduced. On the other hand, special education teachers typically are trained not to "give up" on any student. We do not intend to recommend any specific procedures for determining when the teaching of facts may not be beneficial or may be premature. Nevertheless, the dominant focus of mathematics should be on reasoning and problem solving, not memorizing facts. There are, in fact, alternatives to the learning of math facts, such as the use of calculators and number lines, and teachers may choose to employ these alternatives when memorization of facts does not seem to be a viable alternative. Before taking such a step, teachers should be certain that they have data that document insufficient learning progress over a significant period of time and over several documented attempts to remedy the problem. In addition, teachers should have the agreement of a principal or special education coordinator that such an alternative seems productive. Finally, teachers should not presume that the student will *never* learn math facts; renewed attempts to teach such information should be made at a later, specified date. The decision to discontinue drill on math facts for the time being should be made only because this drill is thought to inhibit overall mathematics learning at the present time.

Math Concepts

If students demonstrate persistent difficulties in acquiring simple math concepts, attempts should be made to enhance simple discriminations and to provide additional examples and nonexamples and practice. For instance, if a student has difficulty learning what a triangle is, the teacher should simplify the initial discrimination by pairing triangles of similar shape and size only with circles. As the student becomes proficient with this discrimination, other more similar shapes, such as squares, can be employed with different types of triangles. If students demonstrate difficulty learning *less than* or *more than*, initial discriminations can be simplified in the same way. For example, students can be shown two sets of the same objects that vary greatly in number (e.g., 2 versus 20 pennies). As the students gain accuracy in making this type of discrimination, objects and number differences can be varied. Additionally, a wide variety of manipulative math materials are available to assist in math concept development. As in all other cases, collection of formative evaluation data can be very helpful in determining whether or not students are acquiring important concepts. Since mathematics can be regarded as an essentially hierarchical sequence of skills, a firm foundation of initial facts and concepts is critical for later skill development.

INTERMEDIATE MATH

In this section, it is assumed that students have learned the skills described in the previous section to fluency, application, and generalization levels. Figures 7.5 and 7.6 present the typical instructional sequence for addition and subtraction problems. The next set of skills taught generally includes place value, regrouping in addition and subtraction, multiplication and division facts and algorithms (procedures), measurement, and word-problem solving.

Skills	Examples	
1. Adding single-digit numbers	$3 + 2 =$	$\begin{array}{r} 4 \\ +\ 3 \\ \hline \end{array}$
2. Adding single- or double-digit numbers together (no regrouping)	$\begin{array}{r} 23 \\ +\ 5 \\ \hline \end{array}$	$\begin{array}{r} 16 \\ +\ 11 \\ \hline \end{array}$
3. Adding three single-digit numbers	$\begin{array}{r} 2 \\ 4 \\ +\ 1 \\ \hline \end{array}$	$\begin{array}{r} 5 \\ 1 \\ +\ 3 \\ \hline \end{array}$
4. Adding multidigits together (no regrouping)	$\begin{array}{r} 123 \\ +412 \\ \hline \end{array}$	$\begin{array}{r} 473 \\ +\ 15 \\ \hline \end{array}$
5. Adding 2-digit numbers with regrouping in 1s column	$\begin{array}{r} 48 \\ +\ 19 \\ \hline \end{array}$	$\begin{array}{r} 67 \\ +\ 5 \\ \hline \end{array}$
6. Adding multidigit numbers with regrouping in 1s to 10s and/or 10s to 100s columns	$\begin{array}{r} 489 \\ +\ 19 \\ \hline \end{array}$	$\begin{array}{r} 357 \\ +261 \\ \hline \end{array}$
7. Adding multidigit numbers in columns with and without regrouping	$\begin{array}{r} 78 \\ 22 \\ +\ 13 \\ \hline \end{array}$	$\begin{array}{r} 688 \\ 123 \\ +437 \\ \hline \end{array}$

FIGURE 7.5. Typical sequence of addition problems.

Place Value

Place value refers to a student's ability to identify the relative value of numbers depending on their positions in a series. The concept of place value in our system revolves around the concept of base 10; that is, whenever we reach a factor of 10 in counting (10, 100, 1,000, etc.), we reflect this distinction by a change in place value.

The overall concept of place value in a base 10 system can be communicated by use of commercially available block materials or simple teacher-made materials. Blocks are composed of *units* (one single block), *longs* (composed of 10 units in a single line), *flats* (composed of a 10 × 10 ten-flat block of units), or *cubes* (composed of 1,000, or 10 × 10 × 10 units). Teachers can use these blocks to illustrate what groups of 10 or 100 blocks can be traded in for higher units. Teachers can model this procedure for counting or arithmetic tasks and ask their students to use the blocks. Concepts of place value can be learned when students are able to manipulate the blocks

Skills	Examples	
1. Basic facts (0–10)	9 – 6	7 – 4 =
2. Subtracting a single- or double-digit number from a double-digit number without regrouping	19 – 6	37 –12
3. Subtracting a single- or double-digit number from a double-digit number with regrouping from 10s to 1s	23 – 7	52 –29
4. Subtracting multidigit numbers from multi-digit numbers with regrouping from 10s to 1s and/or 100s to 10s	703 –192	821 –473
7. Subtracting involving all levels of regrouping	91,998 – 8,729	7,503 –4,767

FIGURE 7.6. Typical sequence of subtraction problems.

correctly in novel instances. Figure 7.7 demonstrates place value for the number 126. If 6 more units were added (126 + 6), they would be added to the units column. The 12 units are traded for 1 long (10) and 2 units. The long is placed in the appropriate column, making the sum 1 flat (= 100), 3 longs (= 30), and 2 units (= 2), or 132.

Manipulatives such as these can be helpful in facilitating the learning of a concept by making it more concrete. However, this does not necessarily mean that students will be able to independently apply such learning to operations on written numbers. In order for students to demonstrate that whole numbers should be lined up along similar rows of place values (1s above 1s, 10s above 10s, etc.) or that sums of 10 or larger will involve regrouping of places, examples will also need to be directly modeled, prompted, and corrected.

Regrouping

Understanding of place value is important for developing skill in regrouping. Regrouping, sometimes referred to as carrying in addition or borrowing in subtraction, refers to making use of higher-order columns when values exceed the relevant factor of 10 on a particular column. Although conceptual understanding of place value is important, regrouping is basically a rule-governed procedural task and should be taught as such. As with any

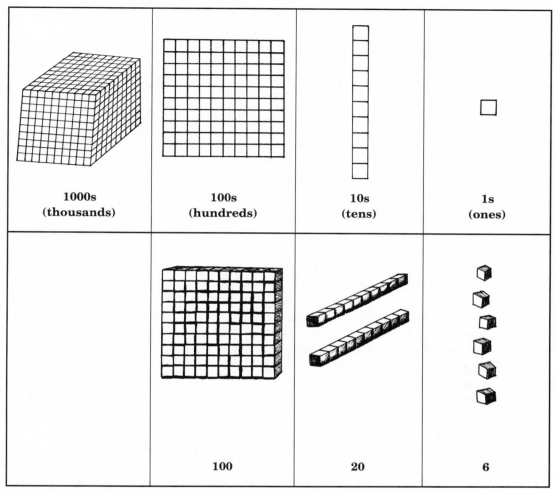

1000s (thousands)	100s (hundreds)	10s (tens)	1s (ones)
	100	20	6

FIGURE 7.7. Teaching place value concepts: *126.*

procedure, students must learn to (a) discriminate instances when the procedure is applicable from noninstances, (b) retrieve relevant procedural information, and (c) successfully execute the procedure. For example, in the simple regrouping problem

$$\begin{array}{r} 19 \\ + \ 3 \\ \hline \end{array}$$

students are first taught that regrouping (e.g., carrying) will be necessary. ([Show problem.] "Look at this problem. What does the sign tell us to do? [Signal.] That's right, it tells us to add. So, which number do we add first? Good, we add the number in the right column. So, we first add which two numbers? That's right, the 9 and the 3. What's the sum? Twelve, right.

Now, I am going to tell you something new. If the numbers add to 10 or more, you write the 1s number *under* the 1s column and write the 10s number *above* the 10s column. [Model procedure.] See, 9 + 3 equals 12, so I write the 2 *under* the 9 and 3 and write the 1 *over* the 1 in the 10s place. Now, I add the numbers in the 10s column: 1 and the 1 and write down the 2. Let's do it again with another problem." [Repeat procedure.])

Similar procedures are used to teach borrowing. After each procedure has been modeled, students must be given guided practice and feedback along every step. First, they must identify when the numbers in the 1s place sum to a value greater than 9. Then, they must remember the steps to execute. Finally, they must execute these steps accurately to compute the correct answer. As can be seen, students may at first perceive regrouping as a highly complex task requiring many different operations. When introducing this or any other procedure, the teacher must teach the separate steps carefully and determine that students have mastered each step before moving on. Figures 7.8 and 7.9 present specific steps for teaching regrouping in addition and subtraction. Teachers may find it beneficial to have students fluently recognize when the procedure is called for prior to practicing the execution of the specific procedures. Additionally, during the acquisition level of instruction, it may be necessary to write the steps necessary to execute the procedures on a separate sheet of paper. Students can then check off each step as it is executed. Many teachers have also successfully used graph paper instead of blank paper during the initial instruction periods. Graph paper helps students line up the numbers appropriately.

When students begin to exhibit high rates of correct responses, they can begin independent practice activities, usually in the form of worksheets. Because many commercially available worksheets do not contain sufficient examples of practice at all difficulty levels, special education teachers may need to construct their own worksheets. When students are completing worksheets independently, it is important that they be encouraged to work quickly, accurately, and efficiently. Students should have specific goals set for them (e.g., "By the end of the period, you should have finished these three pages") and be supervised frequently enough to ensure they do not practice errors. When students exhibit consistently high levels of fluent responding, they should be provided with opportunities to generalize these skills to other situations. This will be discussed further in the section on word problems.

Multiplication and Division Concepts

Students enrolled in special education classes often have difficulty at first in understanding the meaning of multiplication and division. These concepts should be taught using specific, concrete examples. Commercially produced materials are available, but teachers can also develop their own

Prerequisite Skills	**Rule**	**Example**	**Procedures**
Addition facts Place value 3-digit column addition	If, after adding two or more digits in a single column, the sum equals a 2-digit number, then regrouping must be completed.	26 +17 —	Add the two digits in the 1s column (6 + 7 = 13)
Vocabulary used in lesson (e.g., 1s column, sum, etc.) Concept of regrouping	Students must *recognize* (identify) that regrouping is necessary.	2|6 +1|7 |3	13 = one 10 and three 1s, and the 10 *cannot* be in the 1s column
	Students must *retrieve* the appropriate steps for regrouping.	1 26 +17	Place the one 10 at the top of the 10s column and
	Students must *execute* the steps in the procedure.	1 26 +17 3	Place the ones under the 1s column
		$1 + 2 = 3\begin{cases}1\\26\end{cases}$ +17 3	Add the first two numbers in the 10s column
		$3\begin{cases}1\\26\end{cases}$ (3 + 1) +17 43	Add the sum of the first two numbers to the last number and write the sum under the 10s column

FIGURE 7.8. Strategies to teach addition with regrouping.

materials using classroom materials such as paper clips. Using such objects, arrangements that portray multiplication or division concepts can be made. For example, the operation 3×2 can be demonstrated with the use of three groups of paper clips containing two paper clips per group. Students can then count the paper clips by 1s, 2s, or 3s to arrive at the total of 6. Like any concept, students can be said to have acquired it when they can demonstrate novel instances (e.g., "Using these pennies, show me what 4×3 means"). Similarly, division concepts can be taught by removing prespecified groups from a total and showing the answer in number of groups. For example, for the problem $6 \div 3$, students can be shown a group of six erasers while groups of three are removed. Since two groups of three can be removed, the answer is 2. Students have acquired this concept when they can apply it to novel instances.

Prerequisite Skills	Rule	Example	Procedures
Subtraction facts Place value Vocabulary used in lesson	After looking at the digits in a column, if the top number is smaller than the bottom number, then regrouping must be completed.	53 −28	Identify (recognize) that the bottom number in the 1s column is larger than the top number (8 vs. 3) and cannot be computed
Concept of regrouping (using money or other examples)	Students must *recognize* (identify) that regrouping is necessary. Students must *retrieve* the appropriate steps for regrouping. Students must *execute* the steps in the procedure.	4 5̸3 − 28	Borrow one 10 from the 10s column by crossing out the top number in the 10s column and reducing the crossed out number by one (4₅̸)
		4 1 5̸3 − 28	Add that borrowed 10 to the 1s column by placing a 1 to the left of the top right number (3 becomes 13)
		4 1 5̸3 − 28 ───── 5	Now subtract the two numbers in the 1s column
		4 1 5̸3 − 28 ───── 25	Subtract the two numbers in the 10s column
		4 1 5̸3 − 28 ───── 25 ───── 53	Check the problem by covering the top row of numbers and adding the bottom rows

FIGURE 7.9. Strategies to teach subtraction with regrouping.

Multiplication and Division Facts

The first facts to be learned in multiplication or division involve signs and terminology. For multiplication, students must be able to identify the × sign as representing multiplication and also learn such vocabulary as *multiplier, multiplicand,* and *product.* If such terms are not learned to a fluency level, communication with the student about multiplication will be difficult. For division, students must learn the ÷ sign, *divisor, dividend,* and *quotient.* If relevant division concepts have been learned, these terms will

Skills	Examples
1. Count by 5s, 2s, etc.	5 10 15 20 25 30 35 40 45 50
2. Basic facts (0–9)	9 7 × 3 × 7
3. Single-digit factor times double-digit without regrouping	22 31 × 3 × 7
4. Single-digit factor times double-digit factor with regrouping	27 58 × 4 × 6
5. Single-digit factor times multidigit factor with or without regrouping	672 235 × 9 × 6
6. Multidigit factors times multidigit factors with or without regrouping	672 23 × 89 ×32

FIGURE 7.10. Typical sequence of multiplication problems.

be easier to teach. Figures 7.10 and 7.11 present the typical instructional sequence for multiplication and division problems.

Teaching number facts in multiplication and division is similar to teaching number facts in addition and subtraction in that high levels of drill and practice are required for fluent performance. Again, teacher-led drill can be supplemented with computer programs, tutors, programmable calculators, and family involvement. Multiplication facts generally are taught first to fluency levels (at least 50 facts per minute from flash cards) before division facts are taught.

Learning multiplication facts can be facilitated by preteaching relevant counting skills. For example, students who have learned to count by 2s (e.g., 2, 4, 6, 8, etc.) have already established a set of responses for learning the 2s tables. As students learn their multiplication tables, progress can be displayed on charts so that students can be made more aware of their progress.

Division facts can be taught after multiplication tables have been learned. If multiplication facts have been learned to fluency levels, division facts should be acquired much more quickly, as the number patterns have already been learned in one sense (i.e., $2 \times 3 = 6$ is highly similar to $6 \div 2 = 3$). If students have clearly learned the similarities between multiplication and division concepts, division facts will be more meaningful.

Because division facts may be learned more rapidly than multiplication facts, teachers may be tempted to cover division facts too quickly. Although learning should proceed more quickly, it may not. The same pro-

Skills	Examples	
1. Basic facts (0–9)	$3\overline{)21}$	$18 \div 2 =$
2. Single-digit divisor and quotient with remainder	$2\overline{)19}\,^{R}$	$3\overline{)22}\,^{R}$
3. Single-digit divisor with multidigit dividend with and without remainders	$3\overline{)345}\,^{R}$	$2\overline{)68}$
4. Estimation and rounding skills to the nearest 10	$76 = 80$ $74 = 70$	
5. Double-digit divisors with dividends requiring estimation	$28\overline{)6800}$	
6. Multidigit divisors with multidigit dividends	$365\overline{)49,850}$	

FIGURE 7.II. Typical sequence of division problems.

cedures to carefully evaluate and monitor progress should be employed in division as in any other aspect of mathematics learning. Again, facts are learned through repeated drill and practice coupled with motivation- and confidence-building activities, a positive attitude, and continuous measurement and evaluation of progress.

Multiplication and Division Procedures

Procedural learning relevant to computations in multiplication and long division is viewed by many students as a complex and unrewarding task. If teachers appropriately analyze the tasks, provide sufficient appropriate instruction, and maintain a confident, positive attitude, procedural tasks can be regarded as rewarding and productive. Procedural learning, as stated earlier, involves three components: (a) identification of when the procedure is necessary, (b) recall of the steps in the procedure, and (c) accurate execution of the steps in the procedure. In order to teach these procedures efficiently, teachers must carefully attend to all three steps. In multiplication, for example, a number of instances that call for specific procedures must be identified: Does the multiplier (bottom number) have more than one digit? If so, the student must be able to execute the procedure for double-digit multiplication. Does the product of each fact contain more than one digit? If so, students must execute the regrouping procedure. A good first step to such instruction is to ensure that students have fluent ability to identify when procedures are necessary. This can be facilitated by providing practice on the identification step only. For example, students can be given sets of multiplication problems and asked to indicate instances in which regrouping procedures are necessary.

When students have demonstrated the ability to identify cases in which procedures are necessary, they should be taught to recall the steps involved in the execution of the specific procedure. Then steps are learned as a serial list. For example, in a long-division problem, one procedure involves (a) estimating a product, (b) completing and writing down the product under the appropriate portion of the dividend, (c) bringing down the next number, and (d) repeating the procedure as necessary. This procedure is a complex one, and students need to develop fluency in being able to describe the necessary steps in sequence. In order to do this, direct drill and practice are necessary.

Finally, when students can identify when a procedure is called for and list the steps involved, they should learn to effectively execute the procedure to obtain the correct answer. Because students are able to state the steps required, it should not be assumed that they will be able to execute the steps without difficulty. Direct teaching and guided practice are necessary to ensure that this final step can be carried out. Ultimately, students should be able to carry out all steps of mathematics procedures fluently and without hesitation. Figures 7.12 and 7.13 present the specific steps and procedures for teaching multidigit multiplication and long division. Graph paper can be used during acquisition instruction to assist students in proper alignment of the digits. Teachers may also find it helpful to list these steps on the blackboard and on students' individual monitoring sheets. Initially, students can be required to check off each step as it is implemented. Some teachers have found it beneficial to add additional prompts and cues, such as color codes, for steps during acquisition instruction. Once the skills have been acquired, these extra prompts can be removed. Again, formative evaluation techniques are helpful in determining whether or not students are computing problems at an adequate rate.

Measurement

Most measurement tasks at the intermediate level involve (a) conceptual and factual learning of units of equivalence and (b) procedures involved in making measurements (i.e., the application of measurement facts). First, concepts of equivalence can be demonstrated by use of measuring instruments. For example, two pint containers can be shown to fill one quart container. When students can demonstrate such operations reliably in novel situations, they have acquired the concept. Measurement facts can be taught using drill and practice techniques similar to those used in teaching multiplication and division tables. Finally, students can be shown, through modeling, prompting, and feedback, the procedure for measuring different units of length, volume, time, and so on. In these cases it is also important to reinforce knowledge of relevant facts and concepts.

Prerequisite Skills	Rule	Example	Procedures
Multiplication facts Place value Regrouping Addition facts	In completing multi-digit multiplication problems, always begin multiplying by using the multiplier in the 1s column and multiply all the numbers in the multiplicand from right to left.	27 ×32 ― 54	Multiply all the top numbers by the number in the lower 1s column (2 × 7 = 14, write down the 4, carry the 1, 2 × 2 = 4, + 1 = 5; write down the 5)
	Proceed to the digit in the 10s column of the multiplier and complete the same process.	27 ×32 ― 54 0	Place a zero in the 1s column under the 4, because we are now going to multiply by 10s
	Each time write the answer under the multiplier. After completing all multiplication, draw a line under the last row of numbers and add the columns to obtain your answer.	2 27 ×32 ― 54 810	Multiply all the top numbers by the number in the lower 10s column (3 × 7 = 21, write down the 1 next to the 0, carry the 2, 3 × 2 = 6, + 2 = 8; write 8 next to the one)
		27 ×32 ― 54 +810	Draw a line under 810, and place an addition sign next to 810
		27 ×32 ― 54 +810 ― 864	Add the columns, just like an addition problem (4 + 0 = 4, write down the 4, 5 + 1 = 6, write down the 6, 8 + 0 = 8, write down the 8) The answer is the bottom number, in this case, 864

FIGURE 7.12. Strategies to teach multidigit multiplication.

Problem Solving

Any amount of mathematics instruction is of little use unless students can use knowledge of concepts, facts, and procedures to solve problems. As such, word problems can be considered application tasks that involve the use of previous learning.

Prerequisite Skills	Rule	Example	Procedures
Division facts Multiplication facts Place value Regrouping Subtraction Addition	Estimate the number of times the divisor can go into the first one or two numbers of the dividend. Write that number above the dividend in the quotient space. Multiply this number by the divisor. Write that product below the first one or two numbers of the dividend. Subtract those numbers. If the remainder is less than the divisor, bring down the next number from the dividend and repeat the procedure. If the remainder is bigger than the divisor, redo the first part of the problem (i.e., the quotient should be a larger number). Repeat all steps as needed.	8⟌259	Read the problem: 259 divided by 8
		8⟌259 —	Underline the first part of the problem Read the underlined part: "8 goes into 25"
		3 8⟌259	Write the answer above the last underlined number (3)
		3 8⟌259 24	Multiply 3 × 8 = 24 Write the answer 24 under the underlined numbers
		3 8⟌259 24 1	Subtract (draw a line under 24 and complete regular subtraction: 25 − 24 = 1)
		3 8⟌259 24 19	Bring down the next number (9) Read the new division problem: "8 goes into 19"
		32 8⟌259 24 19	Write the answer (2) above the number you just brought down
		32 8⟌259 24 19 16	Multiply 2 × 8 = 16 Write the answer under the 19
		32 R3 8⟌259 24 19 16 3	Subtract to obtain the remainder. Write the remainder next to the answer Say the answer, "8 goes into 259 32 times with a remainder of 3" *(continues)*

FIGURE 7.13. Strategies to teach long division (single-digit divisor, multidigit dividend).

Prerequisite Skills	Rule	Example	Procedures
		32 × 8 ⎯⎯⎯	Check your problem by writing a multiplication problem out of your answer and the divisor
		32 × 8 ⎯⎯⎯ 256 + 3 = 259	Multiply and add the remainder to your answer
			Check your new answer. Is it the same as your dividend? If yes, you did everything correctly.

FIGURE 7.13. continued

In most cases, solving a word problem involves the three steps previously described in executing any procedure. After reading or listening to a problem, students must first determine which major procedure (i.e., operation) is called for to solve the problem. Students should be readily able to describe any problem as calling for addition, subtraction, multiplication, or division. They then need to retrieve the steps needed to execute the general procedure—for example, that one particular number must be divided by another and the quotient expressed with respect to a particular unit (e.g., pies, dollars, books, hours). Finally, the entire procedure must be accurately executed. Of course, the execution of this procedure (division) will involve, in turn, identification, recall, and execution of other procedures related to the division operation.

It may be helpful to teach these steps separately. For instance, students can be shown examples of word problems in which they are asked simply to indicate whether addition, subtraction, multiplication, or division is called for. Figure 7.14 presents a sample set of strategies to teach students typical clue words for problem solving. When they have mastered this objective, students can be given problems in which they are asked to indicate the operation and describe the steps necessary to execute the general procedure. Finally, if these two steps have been mastered, students can be asked to execute the procedures and solve the problem. Ultimately, students should be able to reason their way through two-part problems and problems for which obvious clue words are not included. Students can be said to have generalized this learning when they can solve similar problems in other classroom or in nonschool settings (e.g., dividing the cost of a pizza). Figure 7.15 provides a strategy for thinking through word problems.

Operation	Clue Word	Example
Addition	altogether both together in all	How much did it cost altogether?
Subtraction	left	How many are left?
Multiplication	Tells one, asks for a quantity.	Boxes. Each one weighs 3 lbs. How much do 5 boxes weigh?
Division	Tells quantity, asks for one (how much each).	Five equal boxes weigh 15 lbs. How much does one weigh?

FIGURE 7.14. Strategies for clue-word problem solving.

Peer and Cooperative Group Learning

Strategies that can be applied at any point in the math curriculum involve the use of peers, either as tutors or in cooperative groups. Peers can be used to learn math facts from flash cards, to check each others' work, or to reinforce newly acquired concepts. In cooperative learning groups, students can work collectively on problem-solving activities or on worksheets in guided practice activities. As with all peer-mediated activities, teachers should ensure that students can apply appropriate social skills to group situations and that individual as well as group progress is being made. Careful attention to curriculum demands as they impact on individual learners and to group dynamics can help ensure that peer and group learning activities are successful.

Cooperative learning has also been widely recommended as a mainstreaming strategy. In such situations, cooperative groups of students with differing skill levels (including students with disabilities) work together to learn skills and complete mathematics (or other subject area) assignments. Since each group as a whole is approximately equal, groups can compete fairly with each other to complete assignments, gain new skill levels, or solve particular problems. In such situations, higher-achieving students are motivated to help lower-achieving students so that the group as a whole will succeed. However, as with any cooperative group situation, teachers must ensure that all students have learned appropriate social skills for this type of interaction. Additionally, in mainstreaming situations, it is also important to ensure that regular class peers know how to interact with, and effectively assist, students with disabilities. In these situations, it is particularly important to gather formative data on the progress of mainstreamed students.

1. *Read* the problem.

2. *Think* about the problem.

3. *Decide* the operation sign.

4. *Write* math sentence.

5. *Compute* the problem.

6. *Label* the answer.

7. *Check* the problem.

Problems in Intermediate Math

Problems in mathematics fact learning on the intermediate level may parallel those that appear on the lower levels. When such problems occur, the solution is generally found in careful task analysis and increased drill and practice, whether teacher led or monitored by computers, calculators, peers, or family members. The decision to replace learning of multiplication and division tables with calculators or printed tables of facts should be made in conjunction with administrative personnel and only after repeated attempts to facilitate fact learning have been documented.

There is one procedure that has been helpful for learning of ×9 tables, shown in Figure 7.16. Additionally, many students can easily count by 5s and use this knowledge to facilitate learning of ×5 tables. Students who have a firm knowledge of addition facts and the concept of multiplication (as all students learning multiplication tables should) should be able to easily solve ×2 tables (e.g., $5 \times 2 = 5 + 5$). Finally, the answer to ×1 and ×0 problems should be obvious to students who know relevant concepts. If the student, then, can determine ×0, ×1, ×2, ×5, and ×9 tables and apply relevant equivalence concepts (e.g., $3 \times 6 = 6 \times 3$), there will be only 15 facts left to learn. Such an approach may make the task of learning multiplication facts more bearable for some students.

The 15 facts referred to in the previous paragraph are 3×3, 4, 6, 7, and 8; 4×4, 6, 7, and 8; 6×6, 7, and 8; 7×7 and 8; and 8×8. These can all be learned using a mnemonic technique known as the "pegword method." This method replaces a rhyming name for each number: 1 is *bun*; 2 is *shoe*; 3 is *tree*; 4 is *door*; and so on to 10 is *hen*. For numbers higher than 10, use 12 is *elf*; 18 is *aiding* (e.g., with an ambulance); 20 is *twin*; 30 is *dirty* or *thirsty*; 40 is *party*; 50 is *gifty* (i.e., gift wrapped); and 60 is *witchy*. Teachers can create pictures for each of the strategies. For example, for $3 \times 3 = 9$, students can say, "Tree to tree is line," and be shown (or think of) a line between two (different, not "twin," trees). For $3 \times 4 = 12$, students can say, "Tree door is elf," and be shown a picture of an elf behind a door in a tree. For $4 \times 8 = 32$, students can say, "Door to gate, dirty shoe," and be

1. Hold hands out with palms facing downward in front of you.

2. Number your fingers 1 to 10 from left to right (e.g., little finger on your left hand is number 1, thumb on your right hand is 6, while little finger on right hand is 10).

3. For a given 9s problem (e.g., 9 × 4 =), select the number that is not 9 (i.e., 4), count over on your fingers, beginning with number 1 (your left hand little finger) to that digit. In this example, you should count over to the index finger, or 4th finger on your left hand. Then, bend that finger down.

4. The number of fingers to the left of the bent finger represents the number of 10s in the answer, while the number of fingers to the right of the bent finger represents the number of 1s in the answer. In the case of 9 × 4, since three fingers are to the left and six fingers are to the right, the correct answer is 36. In the case of 9 × 5, the left thumb is bent. Four fingers are to the left and five are to the right of the bent thumb. The answer, then, is 45.

FIGURE 7.16. Steps for calculating 9s tables.

shown a picture of someone kicking a door and a gate with a dirty shoe. For 7 × 8 = 56, they can say, "Heaven's gate holds gifty sticks." Examples of all 15 strategies are given in Mastropieri and Scruggs (1991).

ADVANCED MATH

The mathematics learning described in this section is advanced relative to the skills covered in the previous sections. This section will describe the teaching of fractions, decimals, ratios, geometry, and simple algebra problems.

Fractions and Decimals

Concepts relevant to fractions have been described previously. The concept to be taught with respect to decimals is that the numbers represent 10ths, 100ths, 1,000ths, and so on.

Students have mastered this concept when they can identify such proportions in novel instances. The distinction between fractions and decimals is in notation and in procedural operations more than in concepts, which are essentially the same. Actually, decimals can be regarded as a special case of fractions.

Once basic concepts and vocabulary are understood, instruction usually involves teaching procedures for computation of decimals and fractions. Addition of fractions with like denominators follows a simple rule:

Leave the denominators constant and add the numerators. Beyond this simple application, procedures become more and more complex. In more complex procedures, it is helpful to teach the three steps to procedural learning for each new procedure. Students, for example, must learn to identify when the sum of two or more fractions results in a numerator that is greater than the denominator. This identification should access the retrieval of the appropriate procedure: (a) divide the numerator by the denominator, (b) record the quotient as the whole number, and (c) record the remainder as the numerator of the original fraction. Finally, students should demonstrate the ability to execute such a procedure.

A different set of procedures is necessary for reducing fractions. In executing the procedure, students should first attempt to identify the *largest* number that can be divided into both numerator and denominator. Students should master the identification step of this procedure to the extent that any fraction is automatically evaluated to determine whether it can be reduced. Figure 7.17 presents a sample lesson on the instruction of concepts in fractions. Figure 7.18 presents specific strategies and procedures for instruction in the operations of fractions.

Decimal operations are generally less complex than fractions if students have mastered all of the relevant preskills. For addition and subtraction, students must learn to arrange numbers vertically with reference to the decimal point rather than the digit placed farthest to the right. The decimal point is then added to its proper position in the sum or difference. Similarly, simple rules govern the placement of decimal points in products and quotients. Although such rules are basically quite simple, it is important to ensure students understand *why* they are performing these operations as well as *how* such operations are performed. Figure 7.19 presents strategies for instruction in operations involving decimals, and Figure 7.20 presents a sample lesson using self-monitoring in decimal operations instruction. These relevant concepts can be enforced both prior to and during the instruction of specific procedures.

Instruction of ratio and proportion concepts and procedures generally involves application of fraction knowledge. An example that is typically used for building the concept of ratios is recipes. Students can be shown how, in order to prepare a meal for twice as many people as specified in the recipe, a proportion of 2:1 must be followed for each ingredient. Students can be said to understand the concept when they can adapt proportion concepts to novel tasks, such as different recipes calling for different proportions. Finally, students need to apply previously learned skills in conjunction with proportions. Although many application tasks are not particularly difficult, it should not be assumed that students are able to execute proportion and ratio operations until they have exhibited this ability in several different cases. When students do so, teachers should make sure that all steps of the procedure are understood.

Component	Examples
Daily review	Last week in math we practiced addition and subtraction of whole numbers. Everyone write one addition problem and one subtraction problem . . . .
State objective and teacher presentation	Today, we are going to learn about fractions. Fractions are parts of whole numbers or units.
	[Draw a circle.] This is a circle in a whole unit. [Shade in half of the circle.] This shaded part *represents* one of the two parts or one-half of the whole circle. [Draw another circle, shade in a small portion—less than half.] This shaded part is not *half* of the circle. [Point to first circle.] This shaded part is *half.* [Point to second circle.] This is not half. Is this half?
	Here is a whole glass of water [show]. I can divide this glass in *two* [draw a line through middle and pour out the top part], and I will have one-half left. How much will I have left, Robert?
	Continue with several additional examples of whole versus half.
Guided practice	[Worksheets with the following examples are on all students' desks.]
	Now, we are going to practice some more items. Everyone put his or her finger on number 1. Look across at the three examples. Circle the one that is only half. Everyone hold his or her paper up when you've completed the first example . . . .
Independent practice	[Worksheets similar to the one used during guided practice are distributed.] Now, everyone, this sheet is just like the one we completed. Everyone put his or her finger on number 1. Circle the picture that shows half. Good. Now do the same for all the rest of the items on this page . . . .
	[Collect when done.] [Review.] Today, we . . . .
Formative evaluation	[Teacher distributes a similar sheet.] Okay, now when I say go, everybody begin this sheet just like the last one we completed. Any questions? Go. [After 1 minute,] Stop and hand in your papers.

FIGURE 7.17. Sample lesson for teaching initial fraction concepts.

Geometry

Basic geometry concepts involving shape have been described previously. Many of the operations in basic geometry involve the application of a formula, which is essentially a rule-learning task. For example, for students to compute the area (A) of a square, they must be able to retrieve the relevant formula ($A = B^2$). This formula involves the concept of the area of a

Skill Area	Prerequisite Skills	Rules	Procedures	Example
Addition of fractions with like denominators	Addition Fraction concepts Fraction vocabulary	If the denominators are identical, add the numerators.	Read the problem.	$\dfrac{3}{8} + \dfrac{2}{8}$
			If the denominators are equal (are the same number), just add the numerators.	$3 + 2 = 5$
			Write the sum of the numerators as your new numerator and carry over your denominator to the denominator spot.	$\dfrac{3}{8} + \dfrac{2}{8} = \dfrac{5}{8}$
			Read your answer.	$\dfrac{5}{8}$
Subtraction of fractions with like denominators	All of above plus subtraction	If the denominators are identical, subtract the numerators.	Read the problem.	$\dfrac{3}{8} - \dfrac{2}{8}$
			If the denominators are equal, just subtract the numerators.	$3 - 2 = 1$
			Write the difference of the numerators as your new numerator, and write the same denominator as your new denominator.	$\dfrac{3}{8} - \dfrac{2}{8} = \dfrac{1}{8}$
			Read your answer.	$\dfrac{1}{8}$
Multiplication of fractions	All of the above	Multiply the numerator by numerator to form a new numerator and multiply the denominator by denominator.	Read the problem.	$\dfrac{1}{3} \times \dfrac{2}{5}$
			Multiply the two numerators.	$1 \times 2 = 2$

(continues)

FIGURE 7.18.   Strategies for teaching fractions.

Skill Area	Prerequisite Skills	Rules	Procedures	Example
			Write the product as the new numerator.	$\dfrac{1}{3} \times \dfrac{2}{5} = \dfrac{2}{}$
			Multiply the two denominators.	$3 \times 5 = 15$
			Write the product as the new denominator.	$\dfrac{1}{3} \times \dfrac{2}{5} = \dfrac{2}{15}$
			Read the answer.	$\dfrac{2}{15}$
Division of fractions	All of the above plus division	If you see a fraction problem that requires division, invert the second fraction and then use the multiplication rule (i.e., multiply the numerators and multiply the denominators).	Read the problem.	$\dfrac{1}{3} \div \dfrac{2}{5}$
			Invert the second fraction (turn it upside down).	$\dfrac{2}{5} \to \dfrac{5}{2}$
			Change the sign from division to multiplication.	$\dfrac{1}{3} \times \dfrac{5}{2}$
			Multiply the numerators.	$1 \times 5 = 5$
			Write the product as the new numerator.	$\dfrac{1}{3} \times \dfrac{5}{2} = \dfrac{5}{}$
			Multiply the denominators.	$3 \times 2 = 6$
			Write the product as the new denominator.	$\dfrac{1}{3} \times \dfrac{5}{2} = \dfrac{5}{6}$
			Read the answer.	$\dfrac{5}{6}$

Note. Other skills involving fractions include some of the following: using mixed fractions in all operations, finding lowest common multiples, finding greatest common factors, and reducing fractions. As above, all skills need to be task analyzed and sequenced.

FIGURE 7.18. continued

Operations	Rules	Examples
Addition	Line up the decimals in the addends and place the decimal in line in the sum.	21.1 + 3.1 $\begin{array}{r} 21.1 \\ +\ 3.1 \\ \hline 24.2 \end{array}$
Subtraction	Same as addition.	35.01 − 19.10 $\begin{array}{r} 35.01 \\ -\ 19.10 \\ \hline 15.91 \end{array}$
Multiplication	Count the number of digits to the right of the decimal point in both the multiplier and multiplicand.	$\begin{array}{r} 3.1 \leftarrow 3 \\ \times\ .22 \leftarrow \\ \hline 62 \\ 62 \end{array}$
	Leave that many decimal places in the product.	$3 \rightarrow\quad .682$
Division	Move decimal in divisor to the right of the last number.	$.20\overline{)660.}$ $.20.\overline{)}$
	Move decimal in dividend an equivalent number of spaces to right.	$.20.\overline{)660.00.}$

FIGURE 7.19. Strategies for operations involving decimals.

square, which can be demonstrated by drawing a grid of the unit of measurement on the square and counting the square units represented. Computing the area from a formula also involves the knowledge that $B^2 = B \times B$, and the B stands for the length of any side of the square. When students have learned these concepts, they must learn the appropriate formula as a fact. Finally, they must learn to apply the formula to the particular area being computed. For example, when computing the area of a square with a side of 3 feet, students must first retrieve the appropriate formula ($A = B^2$) and apply it to the specific instance (i.e., $A = 3^2 = 3 \times 3 = 9$). Students must attend to every step in the sequence to arrive at the correct answer.

Similar procedures are necessary for computation of areas of other shapes, although the formulas are somewhat more complex. Additionally, for computations involving circles, students must additionally learn that the symbol π equals approximately $3\frac{1}{7}$ or 3.14 and that this number must be substituted in appropriate equations. Also, a number of other symbolic notations must be learned as facts (and concepts) before they can be applied to computation problems. These include such notations as r = radius, b = base, h = height, and so on. Careful task and conceptual analysis will help determine exactly what students already know and what they must be additionally taught to perform particular operations in geometry.

Review

Remember how we have practiced doing long division? Look at this example with me.

$$20\overline{)100}$$

Everyone compute the answer with me . . . .

State objective and teacher presentation

Today we are going to learn what to do when we have decimals in the divisor. We can't divide when there is a decimal in the divisor. These are examples of decimals in the divisor:

$$1.20\overline{)878} \qquad .7\overline{)82} \qquad .11\overline{)211}$$

Are these examples of decimals in the divisors?

$$.10\overline{)82}\ [\text{Yes}] \qquad 10\overline{)82}\ [\text{No}]$$

$$1.9\overline{)77}\ [\text{Yes}] \qquad 19\overline{)7.7}\ [\text{No}]$$

You must complete the following steps before you compute a division problem:

First, look at the divisor to see whether or not it contains a decimal.

Second, if there is no decimal in the divisor, divide as usual.

Third, if there is a decimal, move the decimal to the right of the last number in the divisor.

Fourth, move the decimal in the dividend an equivalent number of spaces to the right.

Fifth, now divide as usual.

Everybody watch me as I use those steps to help me divide. [Proceed through several examples.]

Now, when you see a division problem, go through the following steps on the self-monitoring sheet below:

Self-Monitoring Sheet for Division Involving Decimals

First, look at the divisor to see whether or not it contains a decimal.

Second, if there is no decimal, divide as usual.

Third, if there is a decimal, move the decimal to the right of the last number in the divisor.

Fourth, move the decimal in the dividend an equivalent number of spaces to the right.

Fifth, now, divide as usual.

FIGURE 7.20. Sample lesson for using self-monitoring instructions in teaching division involving decimals.

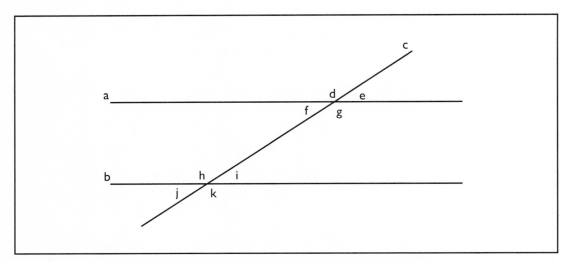

FIGURE 7.21. Problem requiring the use of prior knowledge and deductive reasoning.

Higher levels of geometry instruction typically involve deductive-reasoning paradigms, and many special education students experience difficulty using this kind of reasoning in problem-solving activities. Teachers should first be certain that students have mastered all of the relevant rules, concepts, and facts. A series of deductive reasoning steps can then be executed, based on all known information, to lead to the solution. For example, consider Figure 7.21 and the problem: Given that a, b, and c are straight lines, a is parallel to b, and angle d ($\angle d$) is 120°, what does $\angle k$ equal?

In order to approach this problem, students must first have demonstrated knowledge of the concepts of *straight line* and *parallel*. They must also know the fact that all straight lines equal 180°. Using this information, they must apply it to a procedure for determining the value of $\angle k$. This procedure involves a series of deductions based on prior knowledge. Given sufficient practice in solving similar problems, however, students will begin to recognize the deductive steps that lead to the solution:

1. line c = 180°

2. $\angle d$ = 120°

3. $\angle f$ = 180° − 120° = 60°

4. $a \| b$

5. $\angle f = \angle j$ = 60°

6. $\angle k$ = 180° − 60° = 120°

Many special education students have difficulty with this type of deductive reasoning, often because they are not certain how to proceed. Students should be given many instances for each type of solution so that prior knowledge of procedures can cue the student in problem solving. Students should then be taught a general procedure for solving such problems. This procedure involves first writing down everything that is known about the problem and, second, listing information that is not known but can be computed. Students should then examine all of this information with respect to prior experience with similar problems to determine the steps for solution. If a sequence of operations is not immediately forthcoming, students should attempt a trial-and-error approach in which attempts are recorded and systematically eliminated. Carefully structured teacher questioning, prompting, and coaching can help guide the students' thinking.

Algebra

Introduction to algebra can begin very early in mathematics instruction. For example, students can be introduced to algebraic notations with problems such as

$$2 + 3 = x$$

as an alternative to

$$\begin{array}{r} 2 \\ + \ 3 \\ \hline \end{array}$$

A different set of operations, of course, is required when students are asked to solve problems such as $2 + x = 5$. Although some students are able to use reasoning or trial-and-error approaches to solve such problems, instruction in these kinds of solutions requires teaching of equivalence concepts and specific procedures for problem solving. First, it must be explicitly taught that the equal sign (=) means that values on either side are identical and that overall operations applied to one side must be applied to the other. These concepts can be demonstrated through the use of real numbers or objects. Students must then be taught that operations should be employed to isolate x, or the unknown value, on one side of the equation. The other side, if free of unknowns, will reveal the answer. For example, to solve $2 + x = 5$ for the value of x, students must first determine that x can be isolated by subtracting the value 2 from both sides of the equation, an operation that results in $x = 3$, the answer.

As problems become more complicated, students must demonstrate knowledge of operational procedures; that is, for $5x + 2 = 12$, subtraction must be performed first, followed by division by 5 to produce the solution, 2.

Once solutions have been determined, students should be encouraged to check work for accuracy by substituting obtained values for unknown symbols.

Problems in Advanced Math

As can be seen in the preceding pages, advanced mathematics skills involve application of all previously learned skills on a higher conceptual level. Thus, many special education students, particularly those characterized as having mild mental retardation, can exhibit persistent difficulty in acquiring these skills. How far (or whether) to proceed with instruction in these areas is a decision that involves consideration of (a) the level of difficulty exhibited, (b) realistic educational goals for the student, and (c) instructional alternatives involving more practical applications that may ultimately prove more useful for the student. It is generally not sufficient, however, to perceive that a specific student will have difficulty learning a specific content. If preskills have been mastered, it should be documented that the student exhibits persistent difficulties over time and through instructional adaptations to the extent that specific instructional alternatives should be considered.

Fractions and Decimals

If students have mastered the necessary preskills, they should have little difficulty acquiring concepts relevant to fractions and decimals. If such problems are observed, demonstrations of relevant concepts should be made more concrete. As very specific, concrete examples are mastered, they can be enhanced by presentation of different, less concrete examples. Generally, the more opportunities students have to manipulate or operate on specific examples, the more likely they are to master the concept.

In general, students who are fluent on basic math facts should have little difficulty learning computation procedures. One source of difficulty that is frequently encountered is reduction of fractions after initial calculations. One source of this difficulty is that it is not easy to specify an exact procedure that students can use in every instance. Some general guidelines can be reinforced, however, and are presented below as questions the student should ask of any fraction.

1. Can the denominator be divided by the numerator (e.g., $\frac{4}{8} = \frac{1}{2}$)?

2. Do the numerator and denominator both end in 0? If so, divide by 10 (e.g., $\frac{20}{30} = \frac{2}{3}$).

3. Do the numerator and denominator end in 0 or 5? If so, divide by 5 (e.g., $\frac{15}{20} = \frac{3}{4}$).

4. Can the numerator and denominator be divided by 3 (e.g., $\frac{3}{9} = \frac{1}{3}$)?

If these steps are practiced over a period of time, reduction of fractions may become a less difficult task. Similar procedures applied to multiplication problems before computation reduce the need for later reduction:

$$\frac{2}{5} \times \frac{15}{16} = \frac{\overset{1}{2}}{\underset{1}{5}} \diagup\!\!\!\!\diagup \frac{\overset{3}{15}}{\underset{8}{16}} = \frac{3}{8}$$

Geometry

A number of materials are commercially available for reinforcing geometry concepts. Most difficulties students exhibit with geometry involve problems with vocabulary, formulae, or application to specific procedures. Careful task and error analysis should be employed in addition to questioning students to determine the exact nature of the problem. When problems are identified, they should be approached by additional drill and practice on specific facts and procedures, using a pace appropriate to the instructional sequence. If problems occur in geometry problem solving when essential vocabulary and concepts are well understood, high levels of guided practice are necessary. Because difficulties in this area can be a source of great frustration, it is particularly helpful to provide assistance in a manner that maintains a high level of correct responding.

Algebra

Once they learn relevant concepts, students have little difficulty solving very simple algebra problems. As problems become more complex and higher levels of deductions are required, however, problem solving can present great difficulties. When this point is reached, it is important to go back to the level of problems that did not present difficulty and reteach the more complex procedures using smaller steps and increased levels of direct teaching and guided practice. If peer or other tutors are employed, it must first be determined that algebraic procedures are being taught the same way by all tutors and the teachers. When students have overlearned a very specific set of procedures, the next should be introduced. If such a teaching strategy seriously hampers the rate of curriculum covered, teachers should determine whether the content learned will be sufficiently useful or whether different, more practical content should be covered.

RELEVANT RESEARCH AND RESOURCES

Overviews of mathematics instruction are written by Resnick and Ford (1981); Romberg and Carpenter (1986); Mastropieri, Scruggs, and Shiah (1991); Mastropieri, Bakken, and Scruggs (1991); Baroody and Hume (1991); and Mayer (1993). Applications of the direct instruction model for at-risk learners are reviewed by Gersten et al. (1986). Textbooks that present information on teaching mathematics include Silbert, Carnine, and Stein (1981); Baroody (1989); Cawley, Fitzmaurice-Hayes, and Shaw (1988); and Cawley (1984). The effects of the use of microcomputers on mathematics are presented by Shiah (1993) and Trifiletti, Frith, and Armstrong (1984). Some specific math strategies for learners with mild disabilities are described by Atkinson (1983), Blankenship (1978), Blankenship and Baumgartner (1982), McLeod and Armstrong (1982), and Coble (1982). Strategy training research in which special education students have been successfully taught sequences of steps (procedures) for problem solution is reported by Fleischner, Nuzum, and Marzola (1987); Englert, Culatta, and Hein (1987); Cullinan, Lloyd, and Epstein (1981); Lloyd, Saltzman, and Kauffman (1981); Grimm, Bijou, and Parsons (1973); and Rivera and Smith (1987). Various approaches and strategies for solving problems are described by Bottge and Hasselbring (1993); Case, Harris, and Graham (1992); Garnett (1992); Thornton and Toohey (1985); Montague, Bos, and Doucette (1991); Skinner, Bamberg, Smith, and Powell (1993); and Wilson and Sindelar (1991). Scott (1993) described the positive effects of Touch Math with students with mild disabilities. Montague and Applegate (1993) provided an analysis on problem-solving analyses of students with mild disabilities, while the effects of teaching math problems through a sequence of concrete to abstract procedures is described by Mercer and Miller (1992). The effects of strategy training on higher-level mathematic problem solving are described by Hutchinson (1993) and Zawaiza and Gerber (1993). For some concerns about the effectiveness of cooperative learning as a mainstreaming strategy, see Tateyama-Sniezek (1990).

Some self-instruction training techniques in special education are described by Leon and Pepe (1983). Peer-mediated instructional techniques and cooperative learning approaches are described by Slavin, Madden and Leavey (1984a, 1984b) and Beirne-Smith (1991). Finally, Good and Grouws (1979); Good, Grouws, and Ebmeier (1983); and Carpenter (1985) provided extensive information on the effective teaching model for mathematics.

Curricular Materials

Examples of math materials with clear scope and sequences that are targeted for students with mild disabilities include the *DISTAR Arithmetic Levels I–III* (SRA), *Corrective Mathematics Program* (SRA), and *Connecting Math Concepts* (SRA). Materials also available that emphasize problem solving include *Strategic Math Series* (Edge Enterprises), *Solve: Action Problem Solving* (Curriculum Associates), and *Project Math* (Educational Progress). *The Touch Math Program* (Innovative Learning Concepts) is available for teaching basic addition, subtraction, multiplication, and division. Manipulative materials are available from Delta

(*continues*)

(Relevant Research and Resources continued)

Education and include items such as the base 10 blocks and associated worksheet materials. Creative Publications also produces math and science manipulatives including fraction pieces, tangrams, learning links, linker cubes, play money, money stamps, pattern blocks, attribute blocks, and geoboards. Many of these items can be acquired as components of math manipulative kits for various age and ability levels, including Cuisenaire rods. Finally, calculators that can be used on the overhead projector (Calc-u-vue) and matching student solar-powered calculators are available from Learning Resources and Delta Education.

Computer Software and Technology

Computer software in mathematics has become widely available. Many programs could be used as supplements for practice activities for basic fact acquisition, and some for problem-solving activities. Some basic math skill programs include: Math Leap Frog, Math Wars, Milt's Math Drills, Number Munchers, Subtraction Defenders, Junior Math Class, Jumping Math Flash, Sports Math, Math Blaster Plus!, Robomath, Math Football, and Race Car 'Rithmetic (Cambridge Development Laboratory); and Number Sea Hunt, Number Maze, and Facts Arcade Games (Gamco Industries). Problem-solving programs that are available include: Super Solvers Outnumbered!, Math Blaster Mystery, and Mutanoid Math Challenge (Gamco Industries); and Gertrude's Secrets and Gertrude's Puzzles (IBM). Gamco Industries also produces some Spanish software including: Math Blasters Plus! and Decimal & Fraction Maze. Finally, some interactive videodisc materials containing math programs are also becoming more widely available. See Appendix B for a list of addresses of producers and distributors of software and curricular materials.

CHAPTER 8

✢ ✢ ✢

Science and Social Studies

THE TEACHING OF SCIENCE AND SOCIAL STUDIES IS OFTEN GIVEN A LOW priority in special education. Because special education students are in need of basic skills remediation, the additional time required to teach basic reading, math, and language often replaces time conventionally allotted to areas such as geography, history, or zoology. It is true that basic skills are of primary importance; however, it can also be asserted that special education students have as great a need as anyone else to learn about the world around them. If at all possible, time should be allotted for such pursuits to ensure that all students not only acquire basic skills, but also that they acquire a knowledge of, and curiosity about, their world.

Curriculum specialists have long advocated specialized teaching procedures for science and social studies. Science specialists have often recommended teaching by the discovery or inquiry method; that is, that teachers act as facilitators to the students' own "scientific discoveries" of basic principles. Such techniques, it is argued, provide an experiential basis to science and provide insight into scientific methods. Similarly, social studies curriculum specialists have advocated Socratic inquiry methods in which students are prompted to use their own reasoning to arrive at relevant concepts, relationships, and ethical or moral principles. Although each of these approaches has its particular strengths, it should be remembered that instructional procedures should reflect instructional objectives; that is, if specific deductive reasoning strategies are the instructional objectives, then deductive reasoning strategies should be taught. If learning scientific procedures is the objective, then scientific procedures should be taught. Likewise, if moral reasoning is an objective, that is what should be taught. However, content area instruction, including science, history, and geography, also includes as objectives the learning of facts (including classification systems), concepts, rules, and procedures, as does any other content area. Furthermore, these learning tasks must also be taught initially through accuracy levels to fluency, application, and generalization levels of learning. Teachers must consult with school administration and teaching personnel to help determine the most appropriate instructional objectives for their students.

A final issue for consideration concerns the primary setting for content area instruction. Special education students who exhibit difficulty on basic skills tasks, such as reading age-appropriate material independently, note-taking and study skills, and writing skills, may receive science and social studies instruction in a special education setting. Students who have learned basic skills to a certain level of efficiency but exhibit difficulty with study skills may receive mainstream instruction in these content areas and receive additional help in study skills from the special education teacher. The distinction here is between a special educator in a primary role of delivering content area information or in a secondary, supportive role of providing assistance in study skills. Consultation with parents, other teachers, administrators, and students themselves, as well as an objective evaluation of necessary prerequisite skills, can help determine the best placement for the student and the optimal role of the special education teacher.

Science and social studies comprise content areas of great scope, and it is certainly beyond the scope of this chapter to cover more than the basic elements of science and social studies instruction. This chapter will, however, provide a general overview of science and social studies content, followed by some general procedures for delivery of instruction in these specific areas.

SCIENCE

Most science content taught in elementary or secondary schools can be divided into *life science*, which is the study of living things and includes botany, zoology, and anatomy, and *earth and physical science*, which is the study of physical concepts and laws and includes geology, paleontology, chemistry, physics, electricity, and astronomy. These two areas will be described separately.

Life Science

Life science is fundamentally concerned with classification and description of living things, their interaction, and their environments. An outline of topics taught in life science is given in Figure 8.1. Concept learning and fact learning play important roles in teaching life science. For instance, the fundamental distinction made in classification of organisms is between *plants* and *animals*. These two *kingdoms* are actually concepts and must be taught as such. As described in previous chapters, concepts can be said to have been acquired when the learner can independently identify novel

I. Characteristics of Living Things

    A. Definitions

    B. Components of Life

        1. Molecules

        2. Cells

        3. Organs

        4. Individuals

        5. Populations

II. Properties of Living Things

    A. Genetics

    B. Metabolism

    C. Reproduction and Development

    D. Adaptation

    E. Responsiveness

III. Exploration of Extraterrestrial Life

IV. Theories About the Origin and Evolution of Life

    A. The Theory and Process of Evolution

    B. Prehistoric Plants and Animals

    C. Other Theories

V. Classification of Living Things, Lower Organisms

    A. Viruses

    B. Algae and Bacteria

    C. Yeasts, Molds, Algae, Fungae

    D. One-celled Organisms

VI. Classification and Characteristics of Plants and Animals

    A. Plants

        1. Mosses and Ferns

        2. Coniferous Trees (Gymnosperms)

        3. Deciduous Trees and Flowering Plants (Angiosperms)

(*continues*)

FIGURE 8.1. Outline of content in life sciences.

(*continued*)

  B. Animals

    1. Invertebrates

      a. Sponges and Worms

      b. Coelenterates (Jellyfish, Coral)

      c. Mollusks

        i. Gastropods (Snails and Slugs)

        ii. Bivalves (Clams and Scallops)

        iii. Cephalopods (Octopus and Squid)

      d. Arthropods

        i. Arachnids (Scorpions and Spiders)

        ii. Insects

        iii. Crustaceans (Shrimp, Crabs, Lobsters)

    2. Vertebrates

      a. Fish

      b. Amphibians (Newts, Toads, Frogs)

      c. Reptiles (Lizards, Snakes, Crocodiles, Turtles)

      d. Mammals (Dogs, Cats, Horses, Apes, Humans)

      e. Birds

VII. The Environment

  A. The Ecosystem

  B. Animal and Plant Communities

  C. Dangers to the Environment

FIGURE 8.I.   continued

instances and noninstances of the concept. In this case, the students have acquired the concepts *plants* and *animals* when they can accurately identify plants or animals that they have not seen before. Concepts are usually taught by providing a general rule or set of rules and providing sufficient practice on identifying instances or noninstances of the concept.

Animals

The discrimination between plants and animals is a relatively simple one (except in the case of some one-celled organisms called protists) that can usually be acquired simply by provision of instances and noninstances. More difficult concepts and definitions may require the provision of rules for aiding the discrimination. Table 8.1 provides a table of specifications for classification of animals. Note that this is a very general table that can be modified to address the needs of specific students (e.g., the table can be

TABLE 8.1. Table of Specifications for Classification of Vertebrate Animals.

CONTENT	BEHAVIOR				
	Identification	Production			
	A. Acquisition	**B. Acquisition**	**C. Fluency**	**D. Application**	**E. Generalization**
1. *Fish*	1A	1B	1C	1D	1E
2. *Amphibian*	2A	2B	2C	2D	2E
3. *Reptile*	3A	3B	3C	3D	3E
4. *Mammal*	4A	4B	4C	4D	4E
5. *Bird*	5A	5B	5C	5D	5E

Sample Objectives:

1A Given 20 drawings containing one fish and four nonfish animal distractors, student will correctly circle the fish in all cases.

2B Student will orally provide a correct definition of amphibian and describe common characteristics.

3C Within 30 seconds, student will orally provide a definition of reptile and describe common characteristics of reptiles.

4D Student will describe mammals and their characteristics after reading classroom materials about mammals.

5E Student will identify birds and describe relevant characteristics of birds on a class field trip.

expanded to include more detailed information). For example, the next major discrimination within the animal kingdom is between *vertebrates* and *invertebrates*. Students must be first taught that the vocabulary word *vertebrate* means backbone and, in the case of the vertebrates, generally refers to an internal skeleton. Specific rules can be of help in promoting the discrimination between vertebrates and invertebrates. For example, if it looks like a bug, worm, shellfish, or octopus, it is probably an invertebrate. One way of getting across the concept of vertebrates so that students can make appropriate discriminations is simply to teach the five classifications of vertebrates: fish, amphibian, reptile, mammal, bird. However, before this is done, it is simpler to provide general instances and noninstances of vertebrates until students have learned the concept in a general way. At first it might be helpful to display pictures or drawings of vertebrates in which the skeletons can be seen.

When students have learned the basic discrimination between invertebrates and vertebrates, they can begin to learn about different kinds of vertebrates and invertebrates. It may be easier to start with vertebrates because these animals are likely to be more well known to students than invertebrates. As stated above, the five classifications of vertebrates are fish, amphibian, reptile, mammal, and bird. The learning of this serial list may be promoted by the provision of a mnemonic, first-letter strategy, in this case the acronym FARM-B (F for fish, A for amphibian, R for reptile, and so on). They should be told to remember FARM-B for classification of vertebrates because most farm animals, such as cows, chickens, and horses, are vertebrates.

Following learning of the serial list, students must master the five classification concepts so that they can discriminate between the different kinds of vertebrates and state the important attributes associated with each classification. For example, attributes of fish are that they (a) are cold blooded, (b) breathe through gills, (c) have scales, and (d) live in the water. Drill and practice techniques are helpful in learning these attributes. Additionally, students should be regularly assessed on their ability to discriminate between different types of vertebrates and to state reasons for making the discriminations. For example, students can be provided a worksheet containing pictures of different kinds of vertebrates and asked to write the type of vertebrate beneath each picture. If students possess fluent writing ability, they can be asked to state why they classified each animal as a certain type of vertebrate. If students have not yet learned writing skills, they can be asked to state their reasons orally. Pictures, books, media, and living examples can also be very helpful. Drill and practice, cumulative review, and frequent formative data collection procedures will facilitate learning and allow the teacher to make instructional decisions.

When students have learned basic classification of vertebrates, they should be taught how invertebrates are classified. Initially, distinction can be made between *mollusks*, including small snails, bivalves (such as clams), and squid-like animals, and *arthropods*, including spiders, crabs and lobsters, and insects. Students should be taught to discriminate between mollusks and arthropods in the same manner as they were taught to discriminate between types of vertebrates: instances and noninstances of each concept should be provided, along with rules to guide the discrimination between mollusks and arthropods. Finally, guided and independent practice on making such discriminations should be provided, and formative data collected. Excerpts from a possible lesson are provided in Figure 8.2. When these discriminations have been learned, further subdivisions, such as the division of arthropods into arachnids (spiders) and insects, are taught. Since some spiders and insects are similar in appearance, provision of specific rules is necessary to promote discrimination; that is, that spiders have eight legs and two body parts, while insects have six legs and three body parts. In all instruction, it is critical to observe the principles of effective instruction used in previous areas: review, introduction, presentation, guided practice, independent practice, and formative evaluation.

Observational and Experiential Learning

Few educators would recommend that life sciences be taught simply as a list of facts and concepts without provision of observation or experience with the plants and animals being studied. There are three major methods

Component	Examples
Daily review	"Last month, we learned about vertebrates. Tell me what a vertebrate is, Michelle. [Answers.] Correct. A vertebrate has an internal skeleton. Now, last week we started talking about invertebrates. What is an invertebrate, Robert?"
State purpose	"Today we will learn about two kinds of invertebrates. One kind is called a mollusk. Everyone say it with me. [Signal.] Mollusk. The other kind . . ."
Deliver information	"Many mollusks have shells and live in the sea, like clams. [Show picture.] Some have shells and live on land, like snails. [Show picture.] Some live in the sea and don't have shells, like the octopus. [Show picture.] But, except for the shell, they all have soft bodies. What do they all have? [Signal.] . . ."
	"Now, the other kind of invertebrate I want to tell you about is the arthropod. Arthropods are animals like insects, spiders, and centipedes—like the animals in these pictures. [Show pictures.] Remember, animals that look like bugs are called arthropods. Hard-shelled sea animals are also called arthropods, like these crabs and lobsters. [Show picture.] But all arthropods have jointed legs. What do all arthropods have? [Signal.] Correct. All arthropods have jointed legs, like these. [Show pictures.] . . ."
	"Now let's try some more examples. [Show picture.] Is this animal an arthropod or a mollusk, Mary? [Answers.] Correct, it is a mollusk. How do you know it is a mollusk, Robert? . . . [Present several additional examples and question entire class.]"
Guided practice	"Now I'm going to give everybody a worksheet, and we can do this one together. First, look at picture number one. Now, everybody write the letter *M* under the picture if it is a mollusk and *A* if it is an arthropod. Do it now and we'll check your answers together . . ."
	"How do we know if an animal is a mollusk? [Signal for class response.] Correct. How do we know if an animal is an arthropod? [Signal for class response.] Correct. . . . Now, what is the answer to number one?"
Independent practice	"Now that we've gone over the directions and samples for the new worksheet, I want everyone to do these by themselves at their desks. . . ."
Formative evaluation	"Everybody clear your desk and we'll have a little test on arthropods and mollusks."

FIGURE 8.2. Lesson on mollusks and arthropods.

of providing experience outside of the regular curriculum materials: media presentations, outside activities, and exhibiting animals in the classroom.

Media presentations

Films, videotapes, videodiscs, and filmstrips can be extremely helpful in showing students a number of living things that they may not have had an opportunity to see for themselves. In addition, media presentations can be used to increase interest and curiosity about living things. All media presentations should enhance prespecified objectives for the science unit. Teachers should preview media presentations as well as become familiar with the machinery used to present the information. Class time should not be wasted with an irrelevant film, nor should class time be lost because the teacher is not familiar with a particular film projector or other instructional media equipment. If instructional media are to be used, the teacher should be able to specify the objectives involved in the presentation as well as the procedures by which the objectives can be evaluated. For instance, if the objective of presenting a particular filmstrip is to provide specific information on the distinction between frogs and toads and to provide several attributes unique to each type of amphibian, prior to the presentation the teacher should determine what types of questions students should be able to answer at the end of the presentation. Additionally, students should be made aware of the purpose of the presentation and the information they are expected to acquire. For example, a teacher could introduce the filmstrip by saying the following: "We have been learning about different types of amphibians. What do we know about amphibians? [Solicit responses and provide feedback.] Today we are going to see a filmstrip about two kinds of amphibians, frogs and toads. Who can tell us something about frogs and toads? [Solicit responses and provide feedback.] When the filmstrip is over, you should be able to tell me three ways of telling frogs and toads apart. Are you ready?" [Show filmstrip.] When the filmstrip is over, the teacher can determine, through verbal questioning or a worksheet activity, whether the information has been learned.

One particular shortcoming of media presentations in special education is that new information is typically presented only once, and students have no opportunity to practice the information. Teachers must make sure that important information has been practiced to the point where it will be remembered. Media presentations can be interesting and enriching experiences but are, in themselves, no guarantee that the information will be remembered. Additional instructional activities, possibly including repeated presentations, are necessary to ensure learning and retention.

Outside activities

In some cases, teachers may wish to take their students to a nearby field, pond, or other natural community to observe animals in their natural habitat or to collect specimens of insects or other animals. Such activities can be very helpful in extending the experiential base needed to make learned information more meaningful. However, as with media presentations, it is important that (a) objectives relevant to the activity be developed, (b) students be informed of the objectives, (c) activities be carefully planned and specified ahead of time, and (d) means be developed for evaluating whether objectives have been met. For example, "to observe a pond community" is an objective that has not been specified carefully enough and does not lend itself to more than the simplest evaluation of outcomes. Finally, such an objective does not impart to students a clear idea of what behavior is expected of them. If, however, the objective is for students to record their observations in a notebook, to collect as many observations as possible of insects, arachnids, and amphibians, and to classify them correctly, students and teachers are both aware of the purpose and expectations of the visit.

An activity like the one just described can be regarded as a generalization activity in that classroom knowledge is being applied in a real world setting. To this end, outside activities should be carefully specified and evaluated. It should also be remembered that outside activities are typically less structured and less familiar to students than routine classroom activities and, as such, have potential for influencing behavioral problems. To avoid such a situation, teachers should be certain that students are aware of the behavior expected of them as well as the consequences for appropriate and inappropriate behavior.

Classroom exhibits

Teachers may wish to exhibit, or allow their students or community to exhibit, animals from other settings. A wide variety of animals appropriate for classroom display are available from biological supply companies. Students may benefit experientially from the direct contact that such exhibits provide. As with other experiential activities, however, objectives for these activities should be specified ahead of time, along with the procedures by which these objectives can be monitored. Exhibits can be highly effective supplements to instruction; however, they should not be considered replacements for direct teaching of important concepts, facts, and rules.

Another typical experiential activity is the use of animals as classroom pets. Newts, fish, hamsters, rabbits, guinea pigs, and birds are frequently seen in classrooms. Such pets are not only a common source of enjoyment for students but can also provide opportunities for observation of the growth and behavior patterns of particular animals over time. Classroom pets can also form the basis for procedural learning of the care and feeding of such animals (see Figure 8.3). Important activities necessary for the care of the animal can be divided among the students, who can gain important insights concerning their own responsibilities to such animals. As with other activities, however, objectives should be clearly specified, and procedures for evaluating such activities should be developed.

Week	Student	Task 1	Task 2	Task 3	Task 4
1.	Roy	☐	☐	☐	☐
2.	Sam	☐	☐	☐	☐
3.	Maria	☐	☐	☐	☐
4.	George	☐	☐	☐	☐
5.	Jose	☐	☐	☐	☐
6.	Gail	☐	☐	☐	☐
7.	Katrina	☐	☐	☐	☐
8.	Tomas	☐	☐	☐	☐

Note. Task 1: Monday feeding; Task 2: Wednesday, add water; Task 3: Thursday feeding; Task 4: Friday, clean tank.

FIGURE 8.3.   Suggested list of responsibilities for the care of newts.

Plants

Instruction in classification and characteristics of plants can parallel instruction in animal life. As in the previous section, major classification systems of plant life are taught using procedures for facilitating discriminations and concept learning. Additionally, attributes of specific types of plants can be taught as facts. Enhancement of classroom learning can be achieved through media presentations, and outdoor activities can do much to enhance knowledge of plant life, particularly when such activities are undertaken with respect to specific instructional objectives (see Figure 8.4). Finally, plants of many different kinds can be raised in the classroom and cared for over time by all students assuming different roles. As in any special education instruction, objectives should parallel the scope and sequence of objectives in the regular classroom to as great an extent as possible.

Anatomy

Anatomy is the study of the structure and function of the human body. The study of anatomy is important to special education because of its relation of the study of anatomy to other areas such as health, nutrition, and physical education. The study of anatomy is also relevant to sex education, although this is a controversial topic in some school districts and should be taught with the approval of the school administration and parent groups.

Anatomy is concerned with the structure and function of different organs and organ systems of the human body. Usually, one organ system (e.g., respiratory, circulatory, nervous, digestive, or reproductive) is studied at a time. Unlike the study of plants and animals, organ systems do not form a particular hierarchy of classification. Additionally, the study of anatomy is finite in that there is only one example of a particular organ. Because

Component	Examples
Daily review	"We have been learning about oak, maple, and walnut leaves. [Hold up leaf.] Which kind of leaf is this one, Bill? . . ."
State purpose	"Today we are going to go outside, and I want each student to find three oak leaves from different trees, three maple leaves from different trees, and three walnut leaves from different trees. What are you going to do, Mary? . . ."
Provide information	"The first thing I want you to do when we start is to get your coats on. Then we will leave the classroom and the building quietly. Then I want everyone to follow me to the trees . . ."
Guided practice	[Outside] "Now, everyone look on the ground under this tree and see if you can find a maple leaf. Show me when you've found one . . ."
Independent practice	"Okay, now everyone finish by yourself: collect three maple, three oak, and three walnut leaves from different trees. . . ."
Formative evaluation	[Classroom] "Everybody put your leaves on the table in groups, and I'll check them. . . ."

FIGURE 8.4. Plant lesson with outdoor application activity.

of this, anatomy is more likely to emphasize the learning of facts rather than concepts, rules, or discriminations. For example, there is only one instance (in the human species) of a pancreas, while there are many different instances of amphibians. Teaching about amphibians, then, requires the teaching of rules, discriminations, and instances and noninstances of the concept *amphibian.* Teaching about the pancreas, however, requires the teaching of facts regarding the structure and function of this organ.

A typical anatomy lesson would be taught using the same teacher-effectiveness principles described in this and previous chapters. After the review of previous instruction, the teacher specifies the overall objective for the present lesson (e.g., "Today we are going to learn about the circulatory system of the human body") and the specific objectives (e.g., "We will learn the parts of the heart and how they work together to keep the blood flowing"). Following the introduction, the teacher presents the information to be learned, questions students, and provides feedback on their responses. Following this, a guided practice activity is provided; for example, students label the parts of a human heart on a worksheet. Students can complete such activities independently once they have reached a certain level of accuracy (about 90%). Generalization of this information can be developed by having students assemble a commercial model of a human heart and describe the relevant anatomical details as they do so. They could also draw and label points of a heart from memory or identify similar parts in a cow's or sheep's heart. Future lessons on the circulatory system could focus on the structure and function of blood and the blood vessels. For a related health activity, students could learn about cholesterol, its effects on the circulatory system, and what dietary changes can prevent cholesterol problems. Students can also receive lessons on the effect of cigarette smoking on the circulatory system. As in other areas in the life sciences, instructional media and models can be helpful in making the information more concrete and in enriching the experiential basis of learning. As with other uses of instructional media, however, teachers should be careful to demonstrate that specific objectives are being met by the presentation of such instructional media. Finally, the scope and sequence of instructional objectives should follow a specific table of specifications that parallels the district scope and sequence of objectives. The extent to which students have met these objectives should be documented by formative evaluation techniques.

Earth and Physical Sciences

Earth and physical sciences are generally more abstract and farther removed from students' everyday experience than life sciences and, consequently, may be more difficult to learn than life sciences, particularly for students who exhibit difficulty with abstract thinking. Teachers, then, should make the information as concrete as possible and incorporate evaluation techniques that address whether or not students demonstrate real understanding of the information being taught. For example, for students to demonstrate that they understand principles of electricity, they should not only be able to recite the principles but also be able to describe how a specific wiring diagram would be expected to produce a specific effect.

The earth and physical sciences include such fields of study as geology, astronomy, electricity, chemistry, and physics. The remainder of this section will describe geology and astronomy.

Geology

Geology is the study of history and structure of the earth as recorded in rocks. It encompasses the earth's structure, function, composition, surface features, and history. The study of fossils in the rocks, and the life forms they describe, is referred to as paleontology and can be studied in a manner similar to the life sciences. An outline of topics taught in earth science is given in Figure 8.5. Geology instruction in special education settings involves the classification and description of various rocks and minerals. A sample table of specifications for geology is given in Table 8.2. Minerals are homogeneous crystalline substances, like gold or quartz, while rocks are composed of different types of mineral or nonmineral substances. Generally, students can be taught the different classifications of rocks (igneous, metamorphic, sedimentary) and their specific attributes, including common or specific uses of different rocks and minerals. Instruction in this

I. The Earth's Physical Properties
   A. Gravity
   B. Magnetism

II. Composition of Earth's Interior
   A. Crust
   B. Core
   C. Mantle

III. Earthquakes and Volcanoes

IV. Rocks and Minerals
   A. Rocks
      1. Igneous
      2. Metamorphic
      3. Sedimentary
   B. Minerals
   C. Ore Deposits
   D. Mineral Fuels
      1. Coal
      2. Petroleum
      3. Oil Shale
      4. Natural Gas

V. Earth's Atmosphere

VI. Weather and Climate
   A. Condensation
      1. Dew
      2. Frost
   B. Clouds and Fogs
   C. Precipitation
      1. Rain
      2. Snow
      3. Sleet and Hail
   D. Storms
      1. Thunder and Lightning
      2. Thunderstorms
      3. Tornadoes and Waterspouts
      4. Cyclones
      5. Hurricanes and Typhoons
   E. Weather Forecasting

FIGURE 8.5. Sample outline for earth sciences.

TABLE 8.2. Table of Specifications for Geology.

CONTENT	BEHAVIOR				
	Identification	Production			
	A. Acquisition	B. Acquisition	C. Fluency	D. Application	E. Generalization
1. *Rocks*					
(1) Igneous	1(1)A	1(1)B	1(1)C	1(1)D	1(1)E
(2) Sedimentary	1(2)A	1(2)B	1(2)C	1(2)D	1(2)E
(3) Metamorphic	1(3)A	1(3)B	1(3)C	1(3)D	1(3)E
2. *Minerals*					
(1) Talc	2(1)A	2(1)B	2(1)C	2(1)D	2(1)E
(2) Barite	2(2)A	2(2)B	2(2)C	2(2)D	2(2)E
(3) Apatite	2(3)A	2(3)B	2(3)C	2(3)D	2(3)E
(4) Quartz	2(4)A	2(4)B	2(4)C	2(4)D	2(4)E
(5) Diamond	2(5)A	2(5)B	2(5)C	2(5)D	2(5)E

Sample Objectives:

1(1)A   Given two rock distractors, student identifies 10 igneous rocks with 90% accuracy.

1(3)C   Student describes in writing the causes and three characteristics of metamorphic rocks and gives three examples in less than 3 minutes at 100% accuracy.

2(2)D   Student applies knowledge of color, hardness, and use of the mineral barite in a written paper on minerals.

2(4)E   Student discusses the use of quartz in mainstream class.

area generally parallels instruction in life sciences; that is, initial classifications and discriminations are taught using discrimination, concept, and rule learning. They are also tested similarly in that students are expected to identify novel instances of such types of rocks as igneous or sedimentary. Specific types of rocks and minerals (e.g., quartz, feldspar, turquoise) can be described with respect to specific attributes (such as common colors or streak, hardness, luster, and use). The overall purpose of instruction is to teach students about the composition of the earth and the kinds of uses rocks and minerals have been put to in the world around them. A sample lesson is excerpted in Figure 8.6.

Another important aspect of geology is the overall composition and character of the earth itself. Instruction includes the composition of rocks and minerals in the different layers of the earth and the interaction of these layers, which is responsible for volcanoes, earthquakes, and mountain formation.

Astronomy

Astronomy is the study of the stars, planets, and other extraterrestrial phenomena such as comets, asteroids, and meteorites. One difficulty in teaching astronomy is that much of the information must be conveyed through pictures rather than direct observation. Heavenly bodies that can be directly

Component	Examples
Daily review	"Last Tuesday we talked about igneous rocks. Tell me what igneous rocks are, Arnold . . . ."
State purpose	"Today we are going to study sedimentary rocks . . ."
Delivery of information	"A sedimentary rock is one that is made of material that has settled at the bottom of an ocean or lake. It starts out as small particles, like sand, that get cemented together under pressure and time. Look at the screen, and I'll show you some examples of sedimentary rock . . ."
Guided practice	"Now I'm going to show you some specimens, and each of you write whether it is a sedimentary or igneous rock. When you have written each answer, we will check them together."
Independent practice	"Now turn to page 156 in your book. You will see a number of rocks pictured. Number your paper from 1 to 20 and write an *I* if the rock is igneous, and write an *S* if the rock is sedimentary. . . ."
Formative evaluation	"All right, trade papers with your neighbor, and we will check your work."

FIGURE 8.6. Sample lesson on rocks.

observed, including planets, constellations, the Milky Way, and the moon in different phases, cannot be seen during school hours and must be simulated in some way. Basic concepts and discriminations (e.g., meteor versus meteorite, star versus planet, galaxy versus nebula) can be taught using the procedures described throughout this book, including rule learning and provision of sufficient instances and noninstances of specific concepts. Again, a detailed table of specifications and formative evaluation procedures can ensure that objectives are being met.

Hands-On Science

Many professional science organizations today recommend the use of "hands-on" curriculum materials for teaching science. These materials deemphasize the use of books and paper-and-pencil activities in favor of direct manipulation of scientific phenomena brought into the classroom. For example, students observe cell structure with microscopes, grow plants under varying conditions and record growth rates, observe and record the properties of various rocks and minerals, create series and parallel electrical circuits and construct electric motors and telegraphs, predict and record the movement of a pendulum under different conditions, and recreate landforms in miniature. Instead of simply reading about science, students are provided with the opportunity to interact directly with science materials using scientific methods.

It has been argued that hands-on science activities are particularly helpful for students with mild disabilities because they place less emphasis on basic skills such as reading and writing, they present information at a high level of concreteness and meaningfulness, and they can be highly motivating for students who are often uninspired by textbooks and worksheets. Further, research has suggested that students with mild disabilities learn more with hands-on science materials and prefer them over the use of traditional textbook and worksheet activities.

Finally, mainstreaming students with mild disabilities into cooperative groups of nondisabled students doing hands-on science may be more successful than mainstreaming students with mild disabilities into traditional science classes. Because of the numbers of materials required in hands-on science approaches, it is usually necessary for students to work in groups and share materials. Sometimes different roles are assigned to group members. In the Full Option Science System (FOSS), groups consist of four members: the "reader," the "recorder," the "getter," and the "starter." Other models are more flexible, using smaller or larger groups when appropriate and planning for more helping or tutoring roles. These cooperative group situations potentially are more accommodating to students with special needs than approaches requiring independent work on textbooks and worksheets.

Proponents of hands-on science often emphasize teaching "process" skills over the learning of facts. These process skills include such things as observing, classifying, predicting, inferring, and hypothesizing. As applied to real world tasks, experience using these process skills could be very beneficial to students with mild disabilities. For instance, students can be presented with deflated balloons placed on each side of a balance. They can then be asked whether they think air weighs anything and asked to predict what would happen if one of the balloons were inflated and then replaced on one side of the balance. When they complete the activity, students describe their observations and explain why the outcome was different from or the same as what they had predicted. Such activities, appropriately structured, could help students develop their thinking skills and become more confident in their own ability to understand and explain the world around them.

However, there are also some potential drawbacks to the use of these materials. Students who have not learned appropriate social behavior may interact inappropriately with science materials and may interact inappropriately in cooperative group situations. Further, if, as sometimes occurs, unstructured "discovery" activities are employed with these materials (especially in mainstream class situations), students with mild disabilities may not be able to move through the activities, or the reasoning processes, as rapidly as their regular class peers.

Nevertheless, with appropriate modifications, these potential drawbacks often can be overcome. Teachers can determine the social skills prerequisites for such learning and ensure that individual special-needs students have learned these skills. Also, if the activities are sufficiently reward-ing, students' participation can be made contingent upon appropriate behav-ior. Likewise, if questioning is carefully structured, students can be coached through thinking processes, by teachers or trained peers, and led to make their own conclusions, rather than simply becoming confused or waiting for other students to answer. Research has suggested that such coaching, if done carefully, can increase learning and retention. For example, the teacher may have just pointed out from a picture or video that anteaters have long front claws. Rather than simply providing an explanation and asking the student to repeat it, the teacher may choose to coach the student through the explanation, as shown in the following dialogue:

TEACHER: Why do you think anteaters may have long front claws?

STUDENT: I don't know . . .

TEACHER: Well, let's think it through, using information we already know. What do you know about anteaters?

STUDENT: They eat ants?

TEACHER: Good! They eat ants. That's right. And where do ants live?

STUDENT: Ants live in holes in the ground.

TEACHER: Good. So, if anteaters eat ants, and ants live in holes in the ground, why do you think anteaters have long front claws?

STUDENT: Oh! So they can dig for ants.

TEACHER: Exactly.

Recent research has suggested that students with mild disabilities learn and remember information better if they are coached to think it through themselves than if they simply are told the information (e.g., Scruggs, Mas-tropieri, & Sullivan, in press).

Finally, time may be found to allow students with mild disabilities to repeat science activities and practice the necessary skills (e.g., measuring, using specific apparatus). It is important that individual students' contri-butions are carefully monitored, to ensure that all students are meeting their personal objectives.

Several different versions of hands-on science materials are currently available and are listed at the end of this chapter. Some things to look for in choosing hands-on science curriculum materials are: clear, explicit descrip-tion of classroom activities; sufficient information for teachers; and evalua-tion materials that help teachers determine that target information and skills are being acquired. When employing these activities, it is helpful to be certain students understand all rules and activity expectations before they begin handling the materials. It may also be found that some activities are learned best when they are undertaken more than once. With the first presentation, students can concentrate on mastering the required manipulative skills. With additional presentations of the same, or only slightly modified, activity, students can concentrate more on the underlying concepts being studied. Mastropieri and Scruggs (1993) have listed specific recommendations for teaching the various units covered with hands-on science activities.

SOCIAL STUDIES

Social studies involves the study of people and their institutions and encompasses such areas as state and local history, U.S. history, world history, and geography, as well as constitution, government, civics, and political science. Most people consider a basic knowledge and understanding of history, geography, and government essential to public education. This section will consider these three areas in turn.

History

History in secondary schools is usually subdivided into state and local, United States, and world history content areas. If students lack prerequisite skills, such as independent reading and writing, they may not be enrolled in mainstream classes and must, therefore, learn history content in the special class. Special education teachers should consult with regular class teachers and administrators to determine the optimal scope and sequence of objectives for the students. If these objectives have not been clearly specified in the mainstream classes, special education teachers should adapt objectives from existing textbooks and other classroom materials. Students in special classes should pass through content as similar as possible to that used in regular classes in the appropriate grade levels. If students later develop their basic skills for functioning in mainstream settings, they should also have been provided with necessary prior information from their special classes to help them succeed in the mainstream.

Much of what is taught in history classes involves factual learning. Although it is very important to analyze, synthesize, and evaluate historical events and situations, in most cases, historical facts are what is taught and what is tested.

Students with serious reading problems will not be able to learn historical information from age-appropriate textbooks. They can benefit, however, from clear teacher presentation of relevant information, as well as from visual information such as pictures from textbooks, filmstrips, videotapes, and films. After review, introduction, presentation questions, and feedback on historical information, guided and independent practice activities can be implemented. Students can be asked to match names of historical figures with accomplishments or to write brief answers to short written questions. Finally, as in all lessons, formative data can be collected on student progress. A sample table of specifications for a lesson in American history is given in Table 8.3, and excerpts from a sample lesson are in Figure 8.7.

In some school systems, mastery of basic facts about history and government is a requirement necessary for graduation. If this is the case, teachers should place specific emphasis on the mastery of those particular facts.

Geography

Geography deals with the natural features, climate, products, and inhabitants of different regions of the world. Again, special education teachers should attempt to incorporate mainstream objectives into their own scope and sequence of objectives.

TABLE 8.3. Table of Specifications for a U.S. History Unit.

CONTENT	BEHAVIOR				
	Identification	Production			
	A. Acquisition	B. Acquisition	C. Fluency	D. Application	E. Generalization
1. *1763–1787*					
(1) Political events	1(1)A	1(1)B	1(1)C	1(1)D	1(1)E
(2) Economic events	1(2)A	1(2)B	1(2)C	1(2)D	1(2)E
(3) Military events	1(3)A	1(3)B	1(3)C	1(3)D	1(3)E
2. *1787–1816*					
(1) Political events	2(1)A	2(1)B	2(1)C	2(1)D	2(1)E
(2) Economic events	2(2)A	2(2)B	2(2)C	2(2)D	2(2)E
(3) Military events	2(3)A	2(3)B	2(3)C	2(3)D	2(3)E
3. *1816–1850*					
(1) Political events	3(1)A	3(1)B	3(1)C	3(1)D	3(1)E
(2) Economic events	3(2)A	3(2)B	3(2)C	3(2)D	3(2)E
(3) Military events	3(3)A	3(3)B	3(3)C	3(3)D	3(3)E

Sample Objectives:

1(1)A Given a list of 20 events of national importance from the period 1763–1787, student will identify political events with 100% accuracy.

1(3)B Student will answer 10 questions on military events of the period 1763–1787 from age-appropriate U.S. history textbook with 90% accuracy.

2(2)D Student will apply information about economic events of the period 1787–1816 in an essay on the American Revolution.

3(1)E Student will answer questions on political events of the period 1816–1850 on a mainstream history test to 90% accuracy.

Component	Examples
Daily review	"Last week we were talking about the events that led to the War of 1812 between America and England. What were some of these events, Ed? . . ."
State purpose	"Today we are going to learn some more reasons why the War of 1812 was fought. . . ."
Provide information	"After the Revolutionary War, the Americans gained control of land west of the Appalachian Mountains. [Show on map.] However, the many Indian tribes that lived there became resentful of the encroachment of their lands. . . ."
	"Why did the Indians become resentful, Terry? [Answers.] Good. The white settlers were coming into their lands and beginning to destroy some of their hunting grounds. . . ."
	"The English in Canada saw this resentment develop and encouraged the Indians to attack the settlers. . . ."
	"These events led to the Battle of Tippecanoe, where the Indians were defeated by the army of William Henry Harrison. After the battle, many white American settlers felt there would never be peace with the Indians as long as the British were in Canada. Now, let's summarize what I said and write the points on the board. What did I say first, Bill? . . ."
Guided practice	"Now let's all read about these events in the chapter and answer some questions together. . . ."
Independent practice	"Now, finish the questions by yourself. . . ."
Formative evaluation	"When you finish, turn the papers in, and I'll tell you how well you did."

FIGURE 8.7.   Sample history lesson.

Geography instruction involves the frequent use of maps—both to describe physical features of different regions and to show relationships between regions, whether in size or in proximity. For this reason, teachers should be certain that students fully understand the relevance and meaning of maps. To develop such understanding, it might be helpful to start with a map of the classroom, so that students can match exactly the map features with classroom features. Students can be asked to construct their own symbols for chairs, desks, tables, and so on. When students have demonstrated this ability, maps of the school and the local community can be constructed. As the maps become larger and larger, students can begin to study broader areas, such as their state, region, or country.

Geography, of course, involves much more than the study of maps. Geography is also the study of the peoples who inhabit different regions of the earth. Again, the more meaningful the information is made, the more likely it is to be remembered. For example, it may be helpful to describe certain concepts, such as *fall line* (the point on a river near a coast that, although navigable by ships, nonetheless has sufficient current to run manufacturing equipment). When students have learned this, as well as relevant geographical features (e.g., Appalachian piedmont, Atlantic coastal plain, major rivers), they should be able to identify the location of many eastern cities in the United States on a topographical map (e.g., Trenton, Philadelphia, Baltimore, Washington, Richmond, Augusta), rather than simply being told their location. Textbook pictures and instructional media can be very helpful. Additional drill and practice techniques can reinforce these facts and help ensure that they will be remembered.

Government

Constitution and government courses are often required for graduation from secondary schools, so teachers should ensure that students learn the necessary information. Much of this content is factual, so strategies for enhancing factual learning are appropriate. For example, in learning the organizational structure of the United States government, students must learn, among other things, that there are three major branches of government (executive, legislative, judicial), that each branch is associated with specific functions, that the executive branch consists of a president and the president's cabinet, that the legislative branch consists of the two houses of Congress (Senate and House of Representatives, with two senators per state and representatives based on state population), and that the judicial branch consists of the nine-member Supreme Court and the lower federal courts.

Courses in government can seem overwhelming to special education students who exhibit difficulty with memory and study skills. In order to cover the most information possible, teachers should first be certain that all of the information presented is essential to the objectives. Teaching unnecessary facts not only consumes instructional time but also can make the learning of necessary facts more difficult. Second, teachers should provide careful sequencing of information, intensive drill and practice, and overlearning procedures so that information will be retained. Third, efforts should be made to ensure that the information is presented in as meaningful a way as possible. To this end, media presentations that address specific objectives, models of government buildings, and pictures from textbooks can be helpful. Situations in which students act out various governmental roles or life-styles of specific periods or create clothing and prepare foods from time periods and cultures can also be helpful in promoting comprehension. Finally, formative data collection procedures can provide the teacher with information concerning how well the information is being learned.

Generalization tasks in this content area may take the form of production of correct responses on competency tests taken outside the class; thus, preparing students to take such tests is important. Other generalization tasks include applying learned information to discussions about current events or issues, writing letters to specific government officials to acquire a social security number, and completing federal and state income tax forms. Additional generalization examples are provided in the independent living chapter (see Chapter 11).

SPECIAL PROBLEMS

Figure 8.8 indicates many of the problems that are commonly encountered in science and social studies instruction. As seen in the figure, some of these problems may involve lack of attention or poor social behavior. For these problems, some type of self-monitoring procedure may be helpful. If note-taking or test-taking skills are a problem, the student should be given instruction in these skills (see Chapter 9). Chapter 9 also provides suggestions for helping the student prepare research papers, if such skills are thought to be lacking. In a great number of cases, however, students may have difficulty learning and retaining factual information of the type that

Problem	Instructional Procedures
Paying attention	• Reteach preskills. • Teach listening and note-taking skills. • Teach self-monitoring procedures. • Monitor and reinforce attending.
Social behavior	• Be certain academic prerequisites are met. • Teach social skills. • Reinforce social behavior. • Teach self-monitoring procedures.
Factual learning	• Increase time-on-task for learning. • Make information more meaningful. • Teach organizational strategies. • Teach mnemonic strategies.
Study skills	• Teach skills outlined in Chapter 10.
Report writing	• Teach skills outlined in Chapter 10.

FIGURE 8.8. Problems in content area instruction.

frequently appears on tests. Research has identified learning and memory problems as major factors contributing to mainstreaming failures in school. Figure 8.9 lists some techniques to use for improving memory for content area information. In the section that follows, we discuss organizational and mnemonic techniques in more detail.

Organizational Strategies

There are a variety of techniques for organizing content area information to enhance learning and memory. One of the simplest, outlining, should always be used, as it conforms to the "structure" component of the SCREAM

1. *Increase attention.* Students will certainly not remember what they have not attended to in the first place.

2. *Use external memory.* Whenever possible, have the student write things down, write on calendars, use checklists, or use stickers to help remember things.

3. *Enhance meaningfulness.* Relate new information to things the student already knows. Use lots of familiar examples when introducing new concepts.

4. *Use pictures or imagery.* Things are better remembered when they are pictured or imaged. Make sure students study pictures carefully and can describe all relevant details.

5. *Minimize irrelevant or interfering information.* Avoid digressions, and place most emphasis on the most important aspects of a topic.

6. *Promote active manipulation.* Use concrete examples of real things whenever possible, and encourage students to actively manipulate these examples. Have them describe their experiences during and after the activity.

7. *Promote active learning.* Prompt students to think about new facts and concepts for themselves (e.g., "Why do you think vultures have no feathers on their heads? What do you know about vultures that might help you figure this out?"). Encourage them to think of novel instances of new concepts ("Who can think of another example of a first-class lever?").

8. *Increase practice.* Find additional opportunities, even if only for a few minutes, for students to go over the important information again and gain additional engaged time-on-task.

9. *Use organizational strategies.* Material that is clearly presented in a well-organized format is easier to remember than material that is not well organized.

10. *Use mnemonic strategies.* Mnemonic strategies, when appropriate, have been extremely effective for students with mild disabilities.

FIGURE 8.9. Recommendations for improving memory. Adapted from *Guidelines for Effective Mainstreaming in Science* by M. A. Mastropieri and T. E. Scruggs, 1993, West Lafayette, IN: Purdue Research Foundation. Adapted with permission.

teacher-presentation variables. Clear, direct, and simple outlines presented on an overhead projector or on the blackboard can help direct a teacher presentation and keep students informed of the organization and pace of the presentation. Some researchers have promoted the use of advance organizers, in which overall information is organized, at a higher level of abstraction, prior to the presentation of information. This strategy is intended to promote activation of prior knowledge and organized thinking about the concepts to be covered.

More complex organizational techniques involve spatial organization. This can be done in a "relationship" chart in which the things being studied (e.g., plants, minerals, rivers) are listed down the left side of the chart and attributes or characteristics of these things are listed across the top. For content that contains superordinate and subordinate concepts, a "relationship map" or "web" can be used (Bos & Anders, 1990a, 1990b). In this case, superordinate concepts and their descriptors are placed in a central location and enclosed in a circle or rectangle. Related concepts are clustered together and placed in "subordinate" circles or boxes. Sometimes such a spatial arrangement of content information is referred to as a "visual spatial display" (Darch & Carnine, 1986). "Concept diagrams" (Bulgren, Schumaker, & Deshler, 1988) list a new concept at the top of the chart, beneath which are definitions, characteristics, or attributes that are organized into *sometimes, always,* or *never present.* Below this can be instances and noninstances of the concept, organized into separate lists. Some researchers (e.g., Bos & Anders, 1990a, 1990b) have recommended an interactive teaching model in which the teacher and students collaborate in spatially organizing the content.

In general, information that is well organized is better understood and better remembered than information that is not. In some cases, spatial placement of target information (e.g., the meat-eaters are all on the right side) can help facilitate recall. However, while students with mild disabilities can remember the spatial placement of familiar information (e.g., tiger, rhinoceros), they are less likely to remember the spatial placement of unfamiliar information (e.g., rhodochrosite, ornitholestes). Teachers should ensure that information is meaningful and familiar before using spatial organizing strategies, and for this purpose, mnemonic techniques may be helpful.

Mnemonic Strategies

Some mnemonic techniques were discussed previously in the reading, language arts, and mathematics chapters. However, mnemonic strategies can be particularly effective for increasing content area learning and memory. Mnemonic techniques are among the best-researched strategies in special education and have been employed successfully with students with learning disabilities, behavioral disorders, and mild mental disabilities across a variety of content areas and age levels. Three particularly effective mnemonic techniques are the keyword method, the pegword method, and letter strategies.

The Keyword Method

The keyword method was introduced in Chapter 6 in the context of vocabulary learning. However, the keyword method can also be very helpful for making content area information easier to remember. For example, to teach students to remember that the patriot Thomas Paine wrote the pamphlet, *Common Sense*, urging Americans to fight the British, teachers can create a keyword, such as *pain*, that sounds like Paine and can be pictured. A picture is then created (see Figure 8.10) of Thomas Paine having a pain from writing *Common Sense*. A woman in the picture says, "If you had common sense, you'd stop writing," to remind students of the name of the pamphlet.

Likewise, to help students remember that Antonie van Leeuwenhoek was an early microscope scientist, teachers can create the keyword *glue-on-hook* for *Leeuwenhoek* and show a picture of an early microscope being held in place with glue on a hook. To help students remember that George M. Cohan wrote the patriotic World War I song, "Over There," teachers can picture a child with an ice cream cone (keyword for *Cohan*). When asked where he bought it, the child points to an ice cream stand and sings, "Over there," as in Figure 8.11.

FIGURE 8.10. Thomas Paine wrote "Common Sense." From *Teaching Students Ways to Remember: Strategies for Learning Mnemonically* by M. A. Mastropieri and T. E. Scruggs, 1991, Cambridge, MA: Brookline Books. Reprinted with permission.

FIGURE 8.11. George M. Cohan (cone) wrote: "Over There." From *Teaching Students Ways to Remember: Strategies for Learning Mnemonically* by M. A. Mastropieri and T. E. Scruggs, 1991, Cambridge, MA: Brookline Books. Reprinted with permission.

Keywords can also be used for word parts, which can be combined to form scientific terms. For example, to teach that *paleo–* means *old*, show a picture of old people carrying pails (keyword for *paleo–*). To teach that *–ology* means *the study of*, show a picture of an owl (keyword for *–ology*) studying. To teach that *–zo–* means *animals*, show a picture of animals in a zoo (keyword for *–zo–*). Students can learn to apply these word parts to understand larger terms: paleontology = the study of old things; paleozoic era = the age of old animals, before dinosaurs; zoology = the study of animals.

Keywords can also build on one another. To teach that the core of the earth is composed of iron and nickel, show an apple core (keyword for *core*) made with irons (for ironing clothes) and (5-cent) nickels. To teach that the earth's mantle is made of rock, show a man (keyword for *mantle*) made of solid rock. Indicate the earth's crust by drawing crusts of bread on the earth's mountains, plains and ocean floors. These pictures can then be combined in one illustration that shows the relative positions of these parts of the earth, as shown in Figure 8.12.

Keywords can also be used to show multiple attributes. To show that the Cenozoic era was characterized by the growth of mammals, the origin of humans, and ice ages, show a picture of a caveman (humans) with other

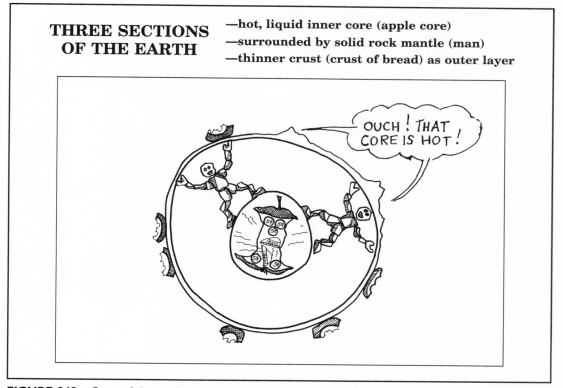

THREE SECTIONS OF THE EARTH

—hot, liquid inner core (apple core)
—surrounded by solid rock mantle (man)
—thinner crust (crust of bread) as outer layer

OUCH! THAT CORE IS HOT!

FIGURE 8.12. Parts of the earth: core (apple core), mantle (man), crust (crust of bread). From *Teaching Students Ways to Remember: Strategies for Learning Mnemonically* by M. A. Mastropieri and T. E. Scruggs, 1991, Cambridge, MA: Brookline Books. Reprinted with permission.

mammals in an ice-age scene. The caveman is shown flipping a cent, keyword for *Cenozoic* (new animals) era.

Keywords have also been shown to help spatial learning, such as recall of map features. For example, a tiger (keyword for *Fort Ticonderoga*) placed correctly on a map may facilitate learning of the location of Fort Ticonderoga more than just providing the name in the appropriate location.

Finally, keywords can be used as both the stimulus (question) and the response (answer) terms. For example, to help students remember that the capital of Arkansas is Little Rock, teachers can show students a picture of Noah's Ark (keyword for *Arkansas*) landing on a little rock (keyword for *Little Rock*). To help students remember that Frankfort is the capital of Kentucky, show a picture of dogs in a kennel (keyword for *Kentucky*) eating frankfurters (keyword for *Frankfort*).

The Pegword Method

The pegword method, first mentioned in Chapter 7, creates rhyming proxies for numbers (e.g., *one* is *bun*, *two* is *shoe*, etc.) and is useful for linking new information to numbers. For instance, to help students remember that a wheelbarrow is an example of a second-class lever, picture a wheelbarrow with the wheel resting against a shoe (pegword for *two*, or *second*). To promote recall of Newton's first law of motion—that an object at rest tends to stay at rest—picture a bun (pegword for *one*) at rest (e.g., lying in bed). To help students remember that the 19th amendment to the U.S. Constitution guaranteed women the right to vote, show a picture of a knight (19 = "knighting") taking women to a voting booth.

Pegwords can also be combined with keywords. For example, to teach that the mineral wolframite is number four on the Mohs hardness scale, show a picture of a wolf (keyword for *wolframite*) looking in a door (pegword for *four*). To promote recall of the multiple facts that wolframite, in addition to being hardness level four, is often black in color and is used as a source of tungsten filaments in light bulbs, show a black wolf looking in a door and turning on a light. Research has shown that students with mild disabilities can remember color cues in mnemonic pictures, either literally (e.g., an orange crocodile = the mineral crocoite is orange in color) or symbolically (e.g., a green broccoli = the dinosaur brachiosaurus is herbivorous [green color]).

Letter Strategies

Letter strategies are very often used by secondary and college students to help them remember lists or categories of information. In one type of letter strategy, the acronym, each letter of the word stands for another word in a list. This strategy has already been introduced in this book in listing teacher presentation elements as the SCREAM variables (structure, clarity, redundancy, etc.). A common example of an acronym is HOMES to describe the names of the Great Lakes (Huron, Ontario, Michigan, etc.). For more examples, ROY G. BIV is often used to help students remember the colors of the spectrum of visible light (red, orange, yellow, etc.), and FARM-B can be used to remember the five classes of vertebrates (fish, amphibians, reptiles, etc.).

Acronyms can also be used in conjunction with keywords or pegwords. For example, to remember the countries associated with the World War I–era Central Powers Alliance, show a picture of children playing tag in Central Park. *Central Park* is the keyword for *Central Powers*, and TAG stands for Turkey, Austria-Hungary, and Germany. Likewise, to remember the freedoms guaranteed by the first amendment to the U.S. Constitution, think of a singer who raps about buns. *Bun* is the pegword for *one*, or first, amendment, and RAPS stands for the freedoms of religion, assembly, press, and speech guaranteed by that amendment.

Acronyms are also used to list steps in cognitive strategies or routines to be executed by students. Some of these strategies are described in Chapter 9. For example, Englert and Mariage (1991) recently described the reading "POSSE." The letters in the acronym POSSE stand for *predicting ideas,* *o*rganizing predicted ideas, *s*earching text structure and *s*ummarizing main ideas, and *e*valuating comprehension.

Some lists of information are difficult to transform into meaningful acronyms. However, other letter strategies can also be helpful. For example, a meaningful acronym can not be constructed from the names of the planets of the solar system, but an *acrostic* is possible: "*M*y *v*ery *e*ducated *m*other *j*ust *s*erved *u*s *n*ine *p*izzas" stands for *M*ercury, *V*enus, *E*arth, etc., in their usual order. Likewise, a similar mnemonic letter strategy, "King Philip's class ordered a family of gentle spaniels," can promote recall of classifications in life science (in order: Kingdom, Phylum, Class, Order, Family, Genus, Species). In this case, each term is represented by more than one letter.

One important consideration to make when using first-letter strategies is that all information in the list to be learned is familiar. It does little good, for example, to teach the acronym HOMES if students are not sufficiently familiar with the names of the Great Lakes that one letter can prompt their recall. Additionally, it may be helpful to link the acronym to the category being remembered, e.g., homes pictured on lakes to help students remember that HOMES is a strategy for remembering the Great Lakes and not some other list.

Limitations

Although the effectiveness of mnemonic strategies is very strongly supported by research evidence, mnemonic instruction should not be considered a panacea for content learning in special education. Some considerations to make when using mnemonic strategies are as follows:

1.   Mnemonic strategies have not been seen to inhibit comprehension; in fact, performance on comprehension tests is usually higher for mnemonically instructed students, generally because they recall more information that they can apply on comprehension questions. However, students can learn (mnemonically or otherwise) factual information without comprehending it, and use of mnemonic techniques does not guarantee that remembered information will be comprehended. Whenever associative-factual information is taught, teachers must require application and generalization levels of learning to ensure that the information is comprehended. Since mnemonics are essentially verbal learning strategies, it is important to ensure that students have had relevant learning experiences to enforce awareness of the concepts represented by the words.

2.   Mnemonics work well because they link unfamiliar or abstract information (e.g., *ranidae, twelve*) to familiar and concrete information (*rain, elf*) and carefully associate these reconstructed terms with meaning (ranidae = rain = frog in the rain = scientific term for common frogs; twelve = elf =

jury of elves = twelve people in a jury). However, there is no guarantee that a particular mnemonic strategy will be helpful. Teachers must test students for recall of associated strategies as well as recall of facts. If a particular strategy does not appear to be working, even if it is a well-constructed mnemonic, discontinue its use.

3. As effective as mnemonic strategies are, they nevertheless will require practice to ensure their effectiveness. Teachers can use drill and practice, tutoring or cooperative group learning, or relevant teacher-constructed worksheets to provide sufficient task engagement. When questioning students, it is also helpful for teachers to ask first for the target information and, second, how the student remembered the information.

4. Many teachers express concern about their ability to draw mnemonic pictures. Some recommended alternatives include: (a) draw simple stick figures, (b) use cut-outs from magazines, (c) employ an artistically talented student to draw pictures, (d) ask students to draw their own pictures, and (e) help students create mental images of the relevant mnemonic pictures. If the latter alternative is chosen, ensure that students have carefully thought out all the relevant details of their image and can describe it to you in detail. Additional practice will probably be necessary if mental images are substituted for pictures.

5. Given all the information students need to learn and remember in school, creation of sufficient mnemonics to cover school content in a variety of subject areas may at first appear to be an impossible task. Collect just a few good mnemonic strategies at first, for information students need to know but easily forget (e.g., states and capitals, order of U.S. presidents). Add to these strategies a little at a time, enlisting the help of students and other teachers. More complete information for constructing and using mnemonics, and more examples, are provided in Mastropieri and Scruggs (1991).

RELEVANT RESEARCH AND RESOURCES

A comprehensive review describing all science education intervention research for students with disabilities is described in Mastropieri and Scruggs (1992), and a forthcoming issue of *Remedial and Special Education* (Cawley, in press) is devoted entirely to science education and students with disabilities. Various approaches to content area instruction are described by Scruggs and Mastropieri (1992b, 1993a, 1993b) and Mastropieri and Scruggs (in press a, in press b). Parmar and Cawley (1993) described science textbook recommendations for teaching students with disabilities. Research in content area instruction has focused on teaching strategies such as: effective teaching variables (Kinder & Bursuck, 1993); text adapta-

(continues)

(Relevant Research and Resources continued)

tions, precision teaching, and framed outlines (Lovitt, Rudsit, Jenkins, Pious, & Benedetti, 1985, 1986); interactive semantic feature analysis (Bos & Anders, 1987, 1990a, 1990b); content area enhancement strategies (Hudson, Lignugaris-Kraft, & Miller, 1993; Lenz, Bulgren, & Hudson, 1990); critical thinking maps (Idol, 1987); MULTIPASS and SOS (Schumaker, Deshler, Alley, Warner, & Denton, 1982; Schumaker, Deshler, Alley, & Warner, 1983); concept routines (Bulgren, Schumaker, & Deshler, 1988); activities-based instruction (Scruggs, Mastropieri, Bakken, & Brigham, 1993); adaptations of activities (Mastropieri & Scruggs, 1993, in press b; Scruggs & Mastropieri, in press a); vocabulary strategies (Mastropieri, Scruggs, & Fulk, 1990); spatial learning (Brigham, 1992a, 1992b; Scruggs, Mastropieri, Brigham, & Sullivan, 1992); and visual spatial strategies (Darch & Carnine, 1986). A model and procedures for content area instruction is provided by Nolet and Tindal (1993).

Mastropieri, Scruggs, and Levin (1983); Scruggs and Mastropieri (1984b, 1985); Mastropieri and Peters (1987); and Scruggs and Mastropieri (1984d) provided information on the use of pictures in facilitating recall of content area information. Support for the use of mnemonic illustrations in enhancing content area information is provided by Mastropieri (1985, 1988); Mastropieri and Scruggs (1984b); Mastropieri, Scruggs, and Levin (1983, 1985a, 1985b, 1986, 1987a, 1987b); Condus, Marshall, and Miller (1986); Scruggs, Mastropieri, Levin, and Gaffney (1985); Mastropieri, Scruggs, McLoone, and Levin (1985); Scruggs, Mastropieri, Levin, McLoone, Gaffney, and Prater (1985); Scruggs, Mastropieri, and Levin (1986, 1987); Veit, Scruggs, and Mastropieri (1986); Scruggs, Mastropieri, McLoone, Levin, and Morrison (1987); Scruggs and Mastropieri (1984c, 1992c); Scruggs and Laufenberg (1986); Laufenberg and Scruggs (1986); McLoone, Scruggs, Mastropieri, and Zucker (1986); Levin, Morrison, McGivern, Mastropieri, and Scruggs (1986); and Levin, Dretzke, McCormick, Scruggs, McGivern, and Mastropieri (1983). Studies involving content area classroom applications of mnemonics instruction are described in King-Sears, Mercer, and Sindelar (1992); Mastropieri, Emerick, and Scruggs (1988); Mastropieri and Scruggs (1988, 1989a, 1989b, 1989c, 1989d); Scruggs and Mastropieri (1989a, 1989b, 1989c, 1992a); Mastropieri, Scruggs, Bakken, and Brigham (1992); and Mastropieri, Scruggs, Whittaker, and Bakken (1994). Descriptions of the model of reconstructive elaborations as applied to content area learning are described by Mastropieri and Scruggs (1989a, 1989b, 1991), while comprehensive syntheses are presented by Scruggs and Mastropieri (1990a, 1990b, 1992a, 1992b). Research investigating the coaching of thinking skills related to content area instruction has been conducted by Sullivan (1993), and similar research on coached elaborations is reported by Scruggs, Mastropieri, Sullivan, and Hesser (1993); and Scruggs, Mastropieri, and Sullivan (in press). Support for the use of advance organizers is provided by Lenz, Alley, and Schumaker (1987), and support for the use of learning strategies is provided by Alley and Deshler (1979) and Ellis, Lenz, and Sabornie (1987). Wong (1985) presented suggestions for facilitating content area learning. Several comprehensive reviews on cognitive strategy instruction that can be applied to content area instruction

(continues)

(Relevant Research and Resources continued)

are written by Pressley and Associates (1990); Gaskins and Elliot (1991); Ciborowski (1992); and Pressley, Scruggs, and Mastropieri (1989). Finally, the integration of thinking skills and strategy training is discussed by Scruggs and Mastropieri (1993b).

Curricular Materials

Commercial materials representing both textbook and activities-oriented (hands-on science) approaches to instruction are available that can be used with students with mild disabilities. Many of the programs integrate science and math activities. Both *SAVI/SELPH* (Lawrence Hall of Science, University of California, Berkeley) and *Me Now* (Hubbard) are activities-based science curricular materials that were originally developed to meet the needs of students with disabilities. Other activities-based programs that might need modifications to meet students' needs include those distributed by Delta Education (*Delta Science Modules, Elementary Science System, Science—A Process Approach, Science Curriculum Improvement Study*), by Brittanica Software (*Full Option Science System*), and by Carolina Biological Supply (*Science and Technology for Children*). Hands-on science kits are available as supplements to many textbook series, including those published by Addison-Wesley, Charles E. Merrill and Harcourt Brace Jovanovich. *AIMS* (AIMS Education Foundation) is an activity-based program that integrates math and science. Creative Publications also distributes manipulative materials and kits in science, such as *Windows on Beginning Science*. Materials intended to facilitate critical thinking in science include *Developing Critical Thinking Through Science: Books One and Two* and *Organizing Thinking Graphic Organizers: Book 2* (Critical Thinking Press & Software) and the *Laboratory Science Series* (SRA). An excellent resource for teachers that lists all science materials is *Science for Children: Resources for Teachers* (National Science Resources Center [NSRC]) and a forthcoming volume from the NSRC listing materials for secondary students.

Social studies materials include *The World We Share* (Curriculum Associates), *HEP: History–Economics–Political Science* (PRO-ED), *World History and You* (Steck-Vaughn), and the *Social Studies Series* (SRA).

Computer Software and Technology

Computer software and technologically advanced materials have become available in science and social studies. Many programs can be used as supplements for practice activities, while some programs can be used as major components of the curriculum. For example, the Bank Street College of Education developed several multimedia curriculum programs that integrate science, social studies, language, and math. The Voyage of the Mimi and The Second Voyage of the Mimi (WINGS for Learning) combine video or videodisc, computer software, and print materials. Videodiscs (e.g., Optical Data's Videodiscovery) can also be

(continues)

(Relevant Research and Resources continued)

helpful as supplements or as entire curricula that do not emphasize reading. MECC also produces computer software programs that can be used as problem-solving activities, including The Oregon Trail and Miner's Cave, for example. Sunburst Communications distributes Science Databases and Social Studies Databases computer programs in a wide variety of topics.

Additional software programs that are available in science include: Senses, Hands-on Math, and The Fetal Pig (Gamco Industries); and Animal Rescue, Ant Farm, Playing with Science Motion, and Playing with Science Temperature (Sunburst Communications). IBM also distributes software, including: Measurement Process, Concept Development, Theory Formation, Ratio Reasoning, Scientific Models, Hydrologic Cycle, Moisture in the Atmosphere, Ground Water, Surface Water, Volcanoes, Landslides, Earthquakes, and Glacial Landforms. Problem-solving software includes the Where in Time is Carmen San Diego series (Brøderbund Software).

Social studies programs that are available include: States and Capitals and Space Commander: A States and Capitals Game (Gamco Industries) and Trading Post and Solve It! American History Mysteries 1492–1865 (Sunburst Communications). Several programs are available in geography and history (U.S. Geography, U.S. Government, U.S. History [American Educational Computer]) that teach information that corresponds with information presented in many textbooks. The Carmen San Diego software mentioned in the previous paragraph includes relevant geography information. See Appendix B for a list of addresses of producers and distributors of software and curricular materials.

CHAPTER 9

✤ ✤ ✤

Study Skills

AS STUDENTS MOVE FROM ELEMENTARY TO SECONDARY EDUCATIONAL settings, the demands for independent learning skills increase. A special education student at the junior high school or high school level frequently attends mainstream content area classes for which a specific set of skills is expected—and required—for success. It is important to emphasize that these study skills are different from the basic skills remediation techniques that have been covered previously. As a separate set of skills, they must be taught separately.

Basically, study skills instruction involves teaching the student how to apply the techniques that teachers have been applying all along. To this extent, much of study skills instruction is procedural in nature and requires the student to (a) *recognize* instances in which the specific procedure (study skill or strategy) is called for, (b) *recall* the steps involved in executing the procedure, and (c) *execute* the procedure. Students who have mastered basic skills and who have learned how to learn independently in mainstream settings are well on their way to "graduating" from special services and re-entering the mainstream on a full-time basis.

Study skills involve a wide range of independent behaviors that cover a variety of school-related situations. In this chapter, study skills are subdivided into the following general areas: (a) listening and note taking, (b) homework, (c) reading for later retrieval, (d) test taking, (e) library skills, (f) report writing, and (g) independent projects. In each section, a description of relevant skills is followed by specific teaching techniques.

LISTENING AND NOTE TAKING

Listening and note-taking skills refer to the behaviors a student should exhibit during mainstream classroom instruction. Research has shown that students on both elementary and secondary levels spend the majority of their time listening. In secondary schools, the ability to listen efficiently may make the difference between passing and failing a particular course.

Although many teachers believe that good listening is a naturally developed ability, research has demonstrated that good listening skills can be taught. In most cases, these skills are critical for special education students.

Although listening itself is composed of several different skills, which will be discussed later, listening skills have common elements that distinguish them from other skills or abilities. First, listening can be distinguished from paying attention, which may involve such skills as good posture and eye contact. Neither can it be said that listening is the same as intelligence in that good listeners are "bright" while poor listeners are "not bright." Good listening involves specific cognitive effort and applies active thinking to classroom lecture information. Active-thinking skills are described in the following sections, and a possible table of specifications for listening and note taking is given in Table 9.1.

Determining the Purpose

The first thing effective listeners must do in a lecture situation is to determine their purpose for listening. If students are certain of their purpose, they are more likely to set and meet relevant goals. For example, the purpose for listening might be (and often is) to obtain the information necessary for an upcoming test. The lecture may be the sole source of such information, or it may serve to highlight important information from a textbook. On the other hand, the purpose for listening might be to learn directions for completing an assignment. In this case, listeners need to understand all of the procedures necessary and relevant for completing the assignment. Effective lecturers, of course, always state the purpose of the presentation. If the purpose is not clearly stated, students must ask the speaker to clarify the purpose of the lecture.

Finally, when the presentation has ended, students should determine whether or not the purpose has been achieved. If, for example, the speaker's purpose was to inform students of specific factual information that will be tested later, students must determine whether or not they have been provided with this information. If they have not or if there is any uncertainty, students should request restatement or clarification. If the speaker's purpose was to provide directions for an assignment, students should determine whether they now have all the information they need to complete the assignment. If they do not, asking for clarification or further information is necessary.

Determine Plan of Organization

Once the purpose of the presentation is clear, students should determine how the information presented should be organized. Teachers who employ effective teaching practices, of course, are explicit about how infor-

TABLE 9.1. Table of Specifications for Listening and Note Taking.

CONTENT	BEHAVIOR				
	Identification	Production			
	A. Acquisition	B. Acquisition	C. Fluency	D. Application	E. Generalization
1. Determines purpose of presentation	1A	1B	1C	1D	1E
2. Determines plan of organization	2A	2B	2C	2D	2E
3. Summarizes and relates main ideas (1) oral (2) written	3(1)A 3(2)A	3(1)B 3(2)B	3(1)C 3(2)C	3(1)D 3(2)D	3(1)E 3(2)E

Sample Objectives:

1A Given teacher statements during a lecture in a role-play situation, student orally identifies purpose statement four of five times.

2B Given teacher statements during a lecture in a role-play situation, student accurately states plan for organization of information in four of five instances.

3(1)C Given a role-play, teacher-lecture situation, student orally summarizes the main idea and relates main ideas of lecture within 2 minutes of the presentation.

3(2)D Student accurately summarizes and relates main idea of class lecture, in writing, in four of five cases.

3(2)E Student accurately summarizes and relates main idea of a mainstream class lecture, in writing, in four of five cases.

mation is to be organized. If the overall organization of the presentation is not explicitly stated, students should attempt to determine the speaker's overall plan of organization. This can be accomplished by (a) recognizing the speaker's main points, (b) noting supporting details or examples of these main points, (c) following sequences of ideas, and (d) attending to transitional words or phrases. To be good listeners, students should acquire skills for identifying the overall organization of the presentation and taking notes that emphasize this organization. However, when the overall organization is not apparent to students, the speaker should be asked to clarify the organization.

Student note taking should strongly reflect the purpose and organization of the presentation. Notes should be clear and legible and provide room for later elaboration. Notes should indicate the main points of the presentation, and supporting points or examples should be clearly related to the main points. Points that appear to be of particular importance from the speaker's presentation (i.e., possible test questions) should be highlighted in the notes. Note takers should also be able to discriminate between information that is important and relevant to the main ideas being discussed and information that is not. Excluding less relevant or irrelevant information from notes can be as important as including relevant information.

It is important to remember that it is possible to take too many notes as well as to take too few notes. Notes should be succinct and to the point and should not take time away from active listening. Finally, notes should be read as soon as possible after class so that ambiguous or carelessly written sections can be rewritten.

Summarizing and Relating Main Ideas

Throughout the presentation, students should summarize the main points being covered and relate these main ideas to their own experiences. Summarizing and relating should be done both mentally and on paper. Summarizing provides additional rehearsal of the speaker's main points and organizational plan, while relating main ideas to the student's experience makes information more meaningful and ties it to information already in the student's long-term memory, which facilitates later retrieval.

Finally, the entire presentation should be summarized. A teacher using effective teaching variables will be certain to do this, but students should, nevertheless, make sure that all of the important points have been summarized. Students' notes should reflect this overall summary of the information presented.

HOMEWORK

In special education settings, assigned homework may best be considered an extended form of an independent practice activity. That is, students have had guided practice on the task and may also have had some independent practice. The homework assignment is intended to help in fluency building in cases in which responses are mostly correct and it seems unlikely that students will be inappropriately practicing error responses. If students are given worksheet-type activities as homework, teachers should ensure that directions are clearly understood and that students can complete the first few examples independently and accurately. Of course, homework assignments should reflect specific instructional objectives.

Sometimes homework assignments represent application or generalization tasks that cannot easily be completed in class, or assignments are given in mainstream classes in which a higher level of independent learning is expected. In these cases, the homework-completion skills are procedural in nature and involve the student executing a specific routine to fulfill task requirements. In such cases, it may be beneficial to have the student complete a self-monitoring checklist in which all subtasks and subroutines are listed in order. As with any independent assignment, the teacher should review the product as soon as possible after completion and deliver feedback. If the task has not been completed satisfactorily, it may be necessary to review the self-monitoring sheet in order to determine the reason. Some students with mild disabilities may be less likely to complete tasks independently, so teachers in these cases should enlist parent or guardian assistance and reinforce task completion.

READING FOR LATER RETRIEVAL

Teachers frequently make a reading assignment by simply saying, "Read Chapter 12 for Monday," without providing additional information concerning the manner in which the chapter is to be read or the purpose for the reading exercise. When this occurs, the student must determine the purpose of the reading assignment, either by questioning the teacher, questioning other students, or thinking back to similar assignments. (Although it may seem appropriate to question the teacher, some teachers may resent being asked too many questions by the same student. It is important for students to determine how much questioning a specific teacher is willing to accept.) Once the purpose of the reading assignment is determined, the best method of studying for the test can be determined.

Several strategies have been suggested to facilitate comprehension and memory of text. These methods commonly involve procedures in which mnemonic first-letter cues are provided. All of the methods require proceeding through the reading assignment several times, typically skimming, reading in depth, and reviewing. One of the most commonly proposed methods is referred to as SQ3R (for survey, question, read, recite, review). Other similar strategies have been proposed, including PQRST (preview, question, read, state, test), Triple S (scan, search, and summarize), and OARWET (overview, achieve, reading, write, evaluate, test), or the POSSE strategy discussed in Chapter 8. Use of any of these acronyms may be helpful to students. In general, however, all of these strategies suggest that students preview, read, think about, and review text material. In addition, most include self-questioning and answering to enforce major points of the reading assignment. These procedures are described below.

Prereading

The purpose of prereading activities is to develop a general idea of the content to be studied and to develop an *advance organizer* that will allow students to organize information more efficiently when it is studied. During prereading activities, students look over the entire passage and activity and consider how it is organized and what the main points are. Students

Lesson Component	Examples
Daily review	"We have been reading textbook information for meaning. What are the rules we discussed, George? . . ."
State purpose	"Today I am going to tell you what to do before you start to read carefully . . . ."
Deliver information	"Before you read carefully, look over the whole passage. First, look at the title, subheadings, graphs, pictures, or other illustrations. Second, read the introduction and summary. Third, ask yourself: What is this passage about? What is the main idea and how is it organized? When you can answer these questions, you are ready to read the whole passage carefully. Now, let's go over the steps again . . . ."
Guided practice	"Now, let's practice on Chapter 4 of your history book. Let's pre-read the chapter together. What do you do first, Bill? . . ."
Independent practice	"I think you all have the idea now. I want everybody to pre-read Chapter 5 of your textbook. It should take you no longer than 5 minutes . . . ."
Formative evaluation	"OK, close your book and answer this self-questioning sheet about the chapter. When you're done, we'll check them . . . ."

FIGURE 9.1. A pre-reading lesson.

should look at the title, subheadings, graphs, charts and other illustrative materials, headings, and introductory and summary sections. All of these sections should give the reader an idea of what is being covered in the text. During prereading, students should question themselves on the general points covered in the material. At this stage, questions such as "What is this chapter about? How is it organized? What specific points are being emphasized?" are appropriate for students to ask themselves. An excerpt from a lesson on prereading is given in Figure 9.1.

Reading

During this stage, students should carefully and deliberately read through the entire assignment. Introduction and summary sections should be read most carefully; less important points should be read more quickly. As the student reads, he or she should take notes on the main points. Important parts can also be highlighted in the book. If the teacher has identified any points of the assignment as particularly important (e.g., "Pay particular attention to the section on the Missouri Compromise"), these should also be highlighted. If written responses to questions about the reading assignment are required, these should be considered while the passage is being read, rather than after it has been read. A major threat to comprehension is the use of new or unfamiliar vocabulary. As students read, they should note any words with which they are unfamiliar. If they are unable to determine the meaning of these words through the use of context cues or knowledge of root words, a dictionary or glossary should be consulted. Students should realize that, without an understanding of key vocabulary words, comprehension of the passage will be difficult if not impossible.

Throughout the reading stage, students should continue to monitor their comprehension (e.g., "Do I understand what I am reading?"), should not allow their minds to wander during the reading (radio and TV are nearly *always* distracting influences), and should continue to question themselves regarding the author's main purpose throughout the assignment.

Many textbooks contain illustrations that are intended to facilitate learning. Students should be taught to study these illustrations carefully. While studying each illustration, they should ask themselves questions such as "What section of the text does the illustration describe? What is the relevance/purpose of the illustration? Can I describe the important parts of the illustration without looking at it?" Such questions can ensure that students will benefit from text illustrations.

Review

After the reading stage, students should briefly skim the entire assignment again, including their own notes, and ask themselves questions concerning the passage. Appropriate questions include: "What was the main purpose of the assignment? What was the overall organization? What were the main points? What is likely to appear on the next test?" It is generally best to review the assignment immediately after completion and then review again a day or so later to evaluate typed comprehension.

Attribution

Once students have learned a particular strategy for reading comprehension or recall, they must effectively apply it and generalize its use to appropriate contexts. In order to facilitate generalization, attribution training is often recommended. Attribution was first discussed in Chapter 4 in the context of behavior management. Teachers who emphasize strategy attribution help students attribute their academic successes to effort and to appropriate and effective strategy execution. Likewise, when students fail, teachers help the students attribute the failure to inadequate or inappropriate strategy use, when appropriate. In general, attribution training attempts to help students make statements such as "I succeeded because I tried hard and used the correct strategy" and to avoid statements such as "I failed because I am stupid." Helping students attribute success or failure to things that are in their control helps empower students and helps them assume more responsibility for themselves.

Study for Tests

Once information from the text has been thoroughly read and comprehended, it can often be committed to memory for later recall on tests. Before beginning to memorize information, students should have demonstrated (at least to themselves) that they thoroughly understand and comprehend the relevant information. Next, it is important for students to know what type of information is likely to be tested as well as how it will be tested. For example, if factual recall is expected and multiple-choice formats are to be employed, as is often the case, this information should tell students to focus on facts with the intention of *identifying* rather than *producing* correct answers. If, on the other hand, more conceptual information will be asked on an essay-type test, students should focus their studying on general themes, elaborating these themes, and relating them to other concepts.

As stated previously, information is more easily remembered if it is meaningful to the learner. Therefore, any type of elaboration the student can provide that serves to make the information more meaningful is likely to improve the recall of this information. In many cases, students can make information more meaningful by relating it to events in their own lives. Analogies of this type are helpful in promoting understanding of school-related concepts. Additionally, self-questioning procedures of the type described in Chapter 5 are helpful.

Using strategies for organizing information from notes and text can also be very helpful in preparing for tests. Some of these organizational strategies were discussed in Chapter 8. Students who have been involved in "interactive teaching" models, in which organizational charts and maps are created in collaboration with students and the teacher, will be more likely to be able to create such charts and maps independently.

Overlearning and drill are also likely to improve recall. Important information can be recited again and again until a high level of fluency is attained and then overlearned to improve long-term retention. One disadvantage of self-instructional drill and practice routines is that they can seem dull and repetitive to the learner. This can be ameliorated somewhat by employing short (10- to 15-minute), intensive drill and practice routines over a longer period of time and recording progress on a chart or graph to improve motivation.

Finally, memory for many kinds of factual information can be improved by means of the mnemonic strategies discussed in previous chapters. The keyword method can be particularly helpful in learning terminology and new vocabulary, as well as lists of information. The pegword method can be useful in learning numbered or ordered information or facts that come in a specified series. In some cases, first-letter clues can be helpful in learning serial lists or information that can be clustered.

Researchers have described several strategies for promoting independent generation of mnemonic strategies. Essentially, students must first identify the important information that they think they may have difficulty remembering. Once they have identified unfamiliar terms, names, places, dates, etc., they must determine what type of strategy is most appropriate. They must then reconstruct the unfamiliar information using the relevant mnemonic (keyword, pegword, or letter strategy). Then they must depict it in a meaningful way with the associated information, practice the strategy, and monitor their recall. King-Sears, Mercer, and Sindelar (1992) described the "IT FITS" strategy for using the keyword method: *i*dentify the term; *t*ell the definition of the term; *f*ind a keyword; *i*magine the definition interacting with the keyword; *t*hink about the definition interacting with the keyword; *s*tudy the mnemonic strategy.

Students will probably have the most difficulty independently creating keywords, as this is a production task that requires insight and analysis of speech sounds. It may be helpful for students to say the syllables separately to themselves and determine whether any of these syllables remind them of familiar words. They also may find a rhyming dictionary to be helpful. Scruggs and Mastropieri (1992a) used classroom brainstorming strategies to create class-generated keywords. It seems likely that such classroom strategy creation could be a valuable step toward independent strategy creation.

Test-Taking Skills

Research has shown that students with mild disabilities, particularly those characterized as learning disabled or behaviorally disordered, can be taught strategies for improving their performance on tests. These strategies represent application skills for previously learned information. In other words, students not only need to learn and remember important content area information but also must be able to apply this knowledge in appropriate test-taking situations. A thorough description of test-taking skills in a wide variety of areas is provided by Millman and Pauk (1969) and Scruggs and Mastropieri (1992d). Some of this information is summarized below.

Test-taking skills that can be employed in nearly every test-taking situation include (a) using time wisely, (b) reading all directions and questions carefully, (c) attempting to answer every question, and (d) actively reasoning through each test item. Students should also be taught to ask for clarification whenever any aspect of the test process is not fully understood. In addition to these general test-taking strategies, there are specific strategies that can be employed with different types of tests. These can be divided into test-taking strategies appropriate for *objective* tests (multiple choice,

Lesson Component	Examples
Daily review	"Last week we talked about answering multiple-choice questions on a test. What was one important rule for answering multiple-choice questions, Bill? . . . ."
State purpose	"Today I am going to teach you the SNOW strategy to answer essay questions . . . ."
Provide information and guided practice	"The first thing you do is *s*tudy the question carefully and be sure you understand what it means. Let's take some examples from your history class . . . ."
	"The second thing you do is *n*ote down everything you can think of about the question. Let's practice on the example question on the Bill of Rights . . . ."
	"Now the third thing you do is *o*rganize what you have written into an outline. How can we organize the Bill of Rights ideas, Mary? . . . ."
	"When you have your outline, the last step is to *w*rite the answer. What are all the steps, Richard? . . . ."
Independent practice	"Now I'm going to give you two practice essay questions. These are questions just like you might get on your history test next week. What I want you to do is the first three steps: (1) *study* the question carefully, (2) *note* down everything you can think of about the question, and (3) *organize* your thoughts into an outline . . . ."
Formative evaluation	"When you finish, we'll look at your outlines and see how well you did . . . ."

FIGURE 9.2. Test-taking skills lesson.

true/false, matching) and strategies appropriate for *written* tests (short answer and essay). An example of a lesson on test-taking skills is given in Figure 9.2.

Objective Tests

The following section discusses strategies that can be employed in answering objective test questions. The purpose of these strategies is to maximize use of the knowledge that students have, rather than to help students guess the correct answer when they clearly do not know the answer. The following strategies can be used to maximize complete or partial knowledge of the content being tested.

1. *Be familiar with test formats.*   Sometimes students perform poorly on tests not because they do not know the information asked, but because they are unfamiliar with the format demands of the particular test. For

example, group-administered reading decoding tests may require students to choose one of four options that sounds most like a letter combination indicated in the stem. Although students may have learned how to read these letter sounds in context (the real purpose of the test), they may not be able to apply word-attack knowledge to this particular format. When test formats are known in advance, provide students opportunities to practice applying their knowledge on these formats (using, of course, different items from those that will appear on the test). Test publishers often publish "practice tests" to help familiarize students with test formats. In addition, teachers can create their own worksheets using specific test formats.

2. *Respond to the intention of the test makers.* Answers to objective test items should reflect the level of instruction and learning addressed in the course. For example, in the question:

> During the occupation of Boston, the British received their most severe losses at Bunker Hill.
> (True or False)

some students may answer "False," arguing that the Battle of Bunker Hill was fought on Breed's Hill. The wise test taker, however, would choose an answer based on the level of information addressed in the class. If, after reflection, the answer still appears ambiguous, the ambiguity should be addressed directly (e.g., by questioning the teacher or explaining the issue in a written comment on the test).

3. *Anticipate the answer, then look for it.* A careful evaluation of the meaning of the question can help avoid error in choosing an answer. Although students may not anticipate exactly the answer called for, logical characteristics can be anticipated. Such anticipation can prevent students from being misled by an incorrect item choice.

4. *Consider all alternatives.* Because students (particularly students with mild disabilities) frequently jump at the first plausible option, test makers may place an attractive decoy prior to the correct answer. This will not be a problem if the student examines all items individually.

5. *Use logical reasoning.* If the exact answer is not known for certain, use of partial knowledge to eliminate unlikely alternatives can increase the probability of a correct response. For example, in the question:

> The Whisky Rebellion occurred as a direct result of:
> (a) objection to Jefferson's embargo
> (b) British occupation of distilleries
> (c) Washington's tax policies
> (d) westward expansion into Indian territory

If the student knows that the Whiskey Rebellion took place during Washington's administration, he or she can choose between (c) and (d), improving the probability of a correct response from 25% to 50%.

6. *Look for specific determiners.*   Statements that contain the words *always* and *never* (rather than, for example, *usually* or *rarely*) should be taken literally. Most of the time these questions are false, since few statements allow for no exceptions. However, they are not *necessarily* false. Students should carefully consider the content as well as the intent of the test maker.

In addition to the above-mentioned strategies, there are a number of other strategies that should *not* be directly taught. These strategies rely entirely upon flaws in test construction. Poorly constructed tests often contain cues in test items that can be used to the test taker's advantage, even with no accompanying knowledge of the content. For example, on poorly constructed tests, items with the following characteristics provide cues to the correct answer:

1. The *longest* answer is usually correct.

2. The correct answer will not be the *first* or *last* option.

3. The correct answer will not contain extreme words such as "stupid" or "nonsense."

4. The correct answer will not be a flippant remark or an absurd idea.

5. The correct answer will be the most carefully qualified option.

6. The correct answer will be a sentence bearing familiar phraseology or technical language.

There are three arguments against the use of such cues in test taking. First, time is most profitably used in active examination of the content of test items; second, guessing on the basis of *any* partial knowledge is better than presupposing a test flaw. Finally, developing reliance on such strategies could prove detrimental when taking standardized objective tests, which contain few, if any, flaws. The overall purpose of teaching test-taking skills is to maximize the validity of students' test performances by providing strategies that maximize the application of partial and complete knowledge. Teaching students to use tricks for correctly guessing the answers is not a purpose of these strategies. In fact, if consistent flaws in test items are found, the teacher should be alerted to these flaws.

Written Tests

Sentence-completion tests

Short-answer tests generally involve sentence-completion items or answers in which one to three sentences are expected. Strategies for one- to three-sentence answers are included in those described for essay questions in the next section. Selected strategies for sentence-completion items include:

1. If otherwise unsure, *guess.*   Sentence-completion items rarely involve a penalty for incorrect answers. In addition, students may be closer to the correct answer than they think they are.

2. Use *partial knowledge.*   Students should respond to a sentence-completion question with information they do have. An example is the following item:

Constantinople fell to the Turks in _____.
(Answer: 1453)

If the exact date is not known, the answer "the 15th century" may earn partial credit. On the other hand, if the student knows that the instructor requires precise answers, he or she should attempt a "best guess" answer.

3. Make the sentence sound *logical* and *consistent.*   The part of the sentence that is presented contains cues that restrict possible answers. For example, the item:

An important use of magnesium is _____.

restricts the answer possibilities to those considered (by the test maker) to be important. Such a cue should restrict possible answers.

Other strategies that are useful for evaluating sentence-completion items include the use of grammatical cues and consideration of the length of the answer blank. These cues should be taught only as they interact with partial knowledge of the content of the test item.

Short-answer and essay tests

In general, short-answer and essay questions are the most difficult to answer; and as with any other type of test question, there is no substitute for knowledge of the content. However, students are rarely presented with a test question about which they have absolutely *no* information. The strategies to be taught, then, will involve developing a careful understanding of the question and organizing and presenting known information in a manner that maximizes the resulting test score. The first four steps presented here correspond to the SNOW strategy in Figure 9.2.

1. *Read the question carefully.* The best written answer to a test question is useless unless the major purpose of the question is carefully considered and addressed. If there are different parts or subquestions in a question, they must be addressed directly. Underlining or circling important words or terms in the question can help students to think clearly about the answer. Questions also often provide cues on the expected length of the answer. A longer-than-expected answer is not only unnecessary, it takes time away from answering other questions.

2. As students read the essay question, they should *immediately write down the points that first occur to them.* Often, the first few minutes of the test provide the best opportunities for recall of factual information. Later in the test period, as students begin to tire, time is better spent organizing and elaborating than attempting to retrieve new factual information.

3. *Organize information before writing.* Once the facts about each question have been noted, the test taker should organize them prior to writing. A good way to do this is to note major points and then decide the order in which they should be presented. Secondary points should be included under appropriate major points.

4. *Write directly to the point of the question.* If the answer is well known to the test takers, they should directly answer the major stated purpose of the question in the first sentence. The remainder of the answer should be devoted to providing evidence that directly supports the answer, written in a clear, concise, and well-organized form.

5. *Answer every question.* Often, questions for which the test taker has only partial understanding are given. Since examiners nearly always give partial credit for partial information, test takers should provide the information they do have that is directly related to the content being asked. Long-winded answers that provide irrelevant factual information are usually not helpful.

6. *Use time wisely.* Students should schedule enough time to answer each question. If time begins to run out, however, students should answer remaining essay questions using outline form. Since many graders evaluate the number of important points covered, such answers may still earn many points.

Finally, considerations such as neatness and legibility of handwriting can be of critical importance in maximizing a test score.

LIBRARY SKILLS

Any student enrolled in mainstream classes will frequently be called upon to use the school library or to consult other reference materials. Although many students are able to learn these skills by themselves and know how and when to ask for help, students receiving special education services often exhibit difficulty using the library unless they are explicitly taught the specific procedures involved in library use. Generally speaking, the optimal setting for such instruction is the library itself, where appropriate skills can be practiced using real library materials. In this section, specific library skills will be described separately, followed by appropriate instructional procedures. These skills include: (a) use of reference books, (b) use of periodical indexes, and (c) use of the card catalog. Finally, techniques for teaching students how to prepare research papers will be described. A table of specifications for library skills is given in Table 9.2.

Reference Books

Reference books commonly found in libraries include dictionaries, encyclopedias, biographical sources, and almanacs. Students should understand the different purposes served by each type of reference book and should be able to describe when each type of book is employed. Students should be taught the purpose of each type of reference book as *factual* information; that is, dictionaries are typically used for looking up the pronunciation,

TABLE 9.2. Table of Specifications for Library Skills.

CONTENT	BEHAVIOR				
	Identification	Production			
	A. Acquisition	B. Acquisition	C. Fluency	D. Application	E. Generalization
I. *Reference books* (1) encyclopedia (2) dictionary	IA I(I)A I(2)A	IB I(I)B I(2)B	IC I(I)C I(2)C	ID I(I)D I(2)D	IE I(I)E I(2)E
2. *Periodical index*	2A	2B	2C	2D	2E
3. *Card catalog*	3A	3B	3C	3D	3E
4. *Dewey Decimal System*	4A	4B	4C	4D	4E

Sample Objectives:

IA Student correctly identifies reference books in the school library (e.g., encyclopedias and dictionaries).

2B Student accurately describes uses of the periodical index.

3C Student accurately describes the uses and location of the card catalog with less than 5 seconds hesitation.

3D Student finds five books on a given subject in the card catalog.

4E Student correctly uses the Dewey Decimal System to find books for a mainstream class assignment.

meanings, spellings, or histories (etymology) of specific words, while encyclopedias are commonly used to gain factual information on topics. Biographical sources, such as *Who's Who* references, are used to gain information on people from a specific, recent year. This can be taught by examples, modeling, and drill. Students should then be able to identify which type of reference book should be used to answer different types of questions. For example, if a teacher asks, "Where would you go to find out how to pronounce a word?", students should be able to answer "dictionary." Students should then be able to *use* reference books to find answers to specific questions, such as, "Who discovered New Zealand?" or "How is chthonian pronounced?" Before this can be done, however, students must know how to look up information that is organized alphabetically.

Finding Alphabetically Organized Information

Looking up items that have been organized in alphabetical order is a common source of frustration and discouragement for many special education students. However, if approached systematically, these skills can be mastered. A necessary prerequisite skill, of course, is learning the alphabet. Teachers should be certain that students are fluent and automatic in this skill and do not simply produce the letters of the alphabet in correct serial order. They must also be able to start at any given place in the alphabet and produce all letters that follow. If students need to know whether *l* comes before *q*, they should not need to start at the beginning of the alphabet but should be able to start with the letter *l* or *q* and recite forward to determine the answer. If these preskills are mastered, looking up words or topics is much less difficult.

When students know the word to be investigated and know the appropriate reference material, it is important that they know the correct spelling of the word. (An exception is when students use a dictionary for determining the spelling of a particular word. In this case the student determines the *most likely* spelling of several possibilities.) Once the correct spelling is determined, looking up the word is a matter of comparing the word to the reference order, one letter at a time. For instance, in looking up the word *bird* in an encyclopedia, students first find the volume that contains all words starting with the letter *b*. They then find the section of the volume that contains words starting with *bi*. To do this, they open the volume and compare the first two letters of those words (usually printed at the top of the page) with *bi*. For instance, if the book is opened to a word starting with *bl*, the student should determine that *i* comes before *l* and proceed backward to the *bi* words. Once these have been found, the student should examine the third letter of the words until *bir* words are found. After this, finding the one word spelled *bird* should not be difficult. This skill will seem less frustrating if students are encouraged to concentrate, at least at first, on accuracy of task completion rather than speed (fluency). It is also helpful to start on simple words (like *bird*) and move to more complicated words as the task becomes easier for students.

Periodical Index

Periodical indexes, such as the *Readers' Guide to Periodical Literature* (Wilson, 1987), contain magazine references arranged by topic, title, or author. Like reference books, entries are arranged in alphabetical order. Students should be taught that magazine references can be more informative, more current, and more interesting than information gained from other sources. One additional skill students will need in using a periodical index is determining the important words to be referenced. For example, if a student needs information on former Soviet espionage activities in the United Nations, it may be necessary to look up *Soviet* (or *U.S.S.R.* or *Russia*), *espionage* (or *spying* or *intelligence*), and *United Nations*. Each of these areas could be surveyed to find relevant information. Once relevant articles are found, students should be sure to write down (a) the name of the periodical, (b) the date published, (c) the title of the article, and (d) the page numbers. Once these have been noted, the student should know the procedures for locating the periodical. Students should not only be familiarized with the exact procedure for locating magazines in the school library, they should also be taught how to ask for needed information so that they would be able to use *any* library. When students have demonstrated ability to employ skills necessary for using periodical indexes, they should be taught additional library skills.

Card Catalogs

Generally, three types of card catalogs are used in school libraries: author, subject, and title. Sometimes two of these, such as author and title, or all three are combined. Students need to know (a) how to determine the topic words (or titles or authors) to be referenced, (b) how to locate the appropriate card catalog, (c) how to find the entry in the card catalog, (d) how to find the correct call number for the book, and (e) given the correct call number, how to find the book. Finding a book from the card catalog, then, requires a number of different procedures, and it is unlikely that all of them can be taught in one lesson. However, students who have mastered procedures for using reference books and periodical indexes will already know how to find an alphabetized entry and how to identify topic words. Additionally, students should be taught how to identify the correct card catalog and locate the needed entry. They must then be shown where to look for the call number and how to become familiar with the system used in the school library for locating books. Finally, if they have a question or if they are unable to find what they are looking for, they should be aware of the procedure for soliciting information.

More recently, computers have been used to assist library searches. Students will probably need specific guided practice in employing this technology.

Some of the card catalog skills, such as locating and recording a call number, can be taught in class prior to entering the library. Most, however, must be modeled and exhibited using the library itself. For these activities, students should be prefamiliarized with the assignment and how it is to be accomplished. Once all of the above procedures have been learned completely, students can learn skills necessary for preparing a research paper.

REPORT WRITING

Choosing a Topic

One problem common to many students is selecting a topic for a research paper. If students have difficulty selecting a topic, they lose valuable time necessary for writing a paper. They also lose time if their initial choice of a topic is not well thought out and they must choose a more appropriate topic. Finding an appropriate topic usually involves three main considerations: (a) personal interest, (b) the student's own ability and experience level, and (c) time limits necessary for completion. If these three criteria are met, students should have little difficulty preparing for the paper.

To find an appropriate topic, students should be taught to "brainstorm" different ideas and then find the one that seems to meet the above considerations the best. To develop this skill, direct teaching of topic finding is appropriate. Teachers can present a general topic area to students (e.g., trees) and direct them to prepare a list of possible topics that are interesting, within the student's ability, and appropriate to a specified time limit. Students should prepare a list, consider all possibilities, and decide on one topic. Activities such as this can make it easier for students to choose topics for mainstream assignments.

Finding Information

Once the topic is selected, students should prepare a list of information needed from the library. If students know very little about a particular topic, they will need to obtain further information before they can prepare the list. Usually, general information on a particular topic can be obtained in an encyclopedia or book.

Before going to the library, students should prepare a list of information that will be needed to write the paper. In addition to the information needed, this list should contain the sources where such information can be found (see Figure 9.3). Students can then enter the library with knowledge

Topic: Human Exploration of Space

| **Information Needed** | | **Library Sources** |

I. *Mercury Missions*

1. *Encyclopedia: Mercury, Space Exploration*
2. *Reader's Guide: Mercury Mission, Alan Shepard, Virgil Grissom, John Glenn*
3. *Card Catalog: Space, Mercury Missions, Astronaut*

II. *Gemini Missions*

1. *Encyclopedia: Gemini Missions, Space Exploration*
2. *Reader's Guide: Gemini Missions, Grissom, Armstrong*
3. *Card Catalog: Space, Gemini, Astronaut*

III. *Apollo Missions*

1. *Encyclopedia: Apollo Missions, Space Exploration, Moon*
2. *Reader's Guide: Apollo Mission, Armstrong, Gene Cernan*
3. *Card Catalog: Space Exploration, Moon, Astronaut, Armstrong, Apollo Missions*

IV. *Skylab*

1. *Encyclopedia: Skylab, Space Exploration*
2. *Reader's Guide: Skylab, Space Exploration*
3. *Card Catalog: Skylab, Astronaut, Space Exploration*

V. *Space Shuttle*

1. *Encyclopedia: Space Shuttle, Challenger, Columbia, Space Exploration*
2. *Reader's Guide: Space Shuttle, Challenger, Columbia, Sally Ride*
3. *Card Catalog: Space Shuttle, Space Exploration*

FIGURE 9.3. Student checklist for library skills.

of (a) the purpose of the library visit, (b) the procedures necessary for fulfilling the purpose, and (c) criteria for which the purpose will be said to have been met.

Writing the Paper

Students should begin by writing an outline for the paper, once enough information has been gathered for such an outline. In the outline, students can insert what further information will be required and how it can be obtained. Further trips to the library can then be made to acquire specific pieces of information. All information should be collected neatly on note cards that include the source of the information.

If library skills are used systematically and purposefully and students have mastered necessary subskills (e.g., reading for meaning, writing, note taking), writing the research paper should not be a difficult task. In writing the paper, students should first make sure that the topic is carefully outlined and that necessary information is neatly organized within the outline. Writing the paper should then be approached as a series of small tasks, each referring to a part of the outline, rather than one enormous project. Students can monitor their own progress by checking each section off a list when it is completed. Overall, written reports should follow a clear central purpose and a well-defined, consistent outline. Table 9.3 provides a possible table of specifications for preparing a research paper. Additional information on writing is given in Chapter 6.

TABLE 9.3. Table of Specifications for Writing a Research Paper.

CONTENT	BEHAVIOR				
	Identification	Production			
	A. Acquisition	B. Acquisition	C. Fluency	D. Application	E. Generalization
I. *Choose topic*	IA	IB	IC	ID	IE
2. *Find information*	2A	2B	2C	2D	2E
3. *Organize paper*	3A	3B	3C	3D	3E
4. *Write paper*	4A	4B	4C	4D	4E

Sample Objectives:

IA Given a subject and five possible paper topics, student identifies the two topics most suitable for a paper (interest, appropriate scope, etc.).

2B Given five topics for a research paper, student accurately describes appropriate methods for finding information.

3D Student organizes information collected from the library for a class paper assignment.

4E Student writes a term paper for mainstream class assignment and receives a grade of C or better.

Special Problems

Students who have been referred for special services may exhibit great difficulty preparing written reports or research papers. In a sense, preparing an independent written product requires the highest levels of school functioning. To this extent, some students may be well into school before necessary prerequisite skills have been learned. On the other hand, it is not unusual for third and fourth graders to be assigned a written report that is several pages long. In some cases, tasks can be simplified by having students report on magazine, encyclopedia articles, or a field trip experience.

In the case of students with mild disabilities, students may at first need a great deal of attention (similar to guided practice) on every step of the process before they are able to proceed independently on later projects. After a few papers have been completed with teacher involvement, it should be easier for students to write independently, particularly if the student has become familiar with all of the important procedural steps.

Students who have become accustomed to structured special education environments may exhibit problems generalizing social behavior appropriate to the library setting. This may be particularly true of students characterized as behaviorally disordered. Compared with special education classrooms, libraries can be seen as highly distracting and unstructured and requiring a high degree of self-control skills. In order to minimize potential problems in library settings, teachers should make all students aware of the purpose of the library visit beforehand. Students should also know the procedures they are to employ in the library and the consequences for breaking library rules. Many times problems that occur in the library visits can be attributed to a lack of clear purpose in the visit. Finally, if problems are anticipated, it may be helpful to bring students to the library in small numbers when other students are not present. On the other hand, students can sometimes benefit from the appropriate modeling of library-related behaviors provided by regular class students.

A final concern for any low-achieving student is an understanding of *plagiarism*. Students who are discouraged and frustrated at the prospect of writing a research paper are more likely to be tempted to copy whole sections from other authors' works. Students must be familiarized with the ethical and legal implications of plagiarism; and perhaps even more importantly, students must be provided with the skills needed to paraphrase or cite the work of others without copying it and to derive satisfaction in a truly independent effort well done.

INDEPENDENT PROJECTS

Sometimes students are assigned projects to complete independently. Such projects are most common in science and are executed somewhat differently than a written report, although a written report or presentation may be a component of the project. Figure 9.4 provides a checklist for completing science projects.

1. Identify general area of interest (e.g., plants, goldfish) through discussion, reading, and brainstorming.

2. Identify the specific question to be investigated (e.g., the effects of salt on plant growth) through discussion, reading, and brainstorming.

3. Identify specific methods for addressing the question (e.g., adding different amounts of salt to the water of different plants), and confirm the methods with the teacher.

4. Obtain necessary equipment and/or supplies.

5. Conduct the experiment, and keep records of procedures and progress.

6. Observe and record findings (e.g., plant growth).

7. Summarize steps 1–6 above.

8. Organize summaries for class presentation. Decide on exhibits, charts, or diagrams to be displayed. Practice the presentation and get feedback.

9. Present the entire project and its findings to the class.

FIGURE 9.4. Checklist for preparing science projects. Adapted from *Guidelines for Effective Mainstreaming in Science* by M. A. Mastropieri and T. E. Scruggs, 1993, West Lafayette, IN: Purdue Research Foundation. Adapted with permission.

RELEVANT RESEARCH AND RESOURCES

Much of the research available on study skills training with learning-disabled adolescents has been conducted by Deshler, Schumaker and their colleagues at the Institute for Research on Learning Disabilities at Kansas University and is described in Alley and Deshler (1979) and Schumaker, Deshler, Alley, and Warner (1983). Deshler and Schumaker (1990) described their learning strategies model and developed numerous training packages in the strands of acquisition, storage, and expression of knowledge. Additional procedures on study skills are provided in Carman and Adams (1977), Alverman (1983), and Devine (1981). Generalization skills are discussed by Scruggs and Mastropieri (1984b) and Mastropieri and Scruggs (1984a).

An overview on test-taking skills is provided by Millman and Pauk (1969). Specific research applications of test-taking skills training with mildly disabled students is provided by Lee and Alley (1981); Scruggs, Bennion, and Lifson (1985a, 1985b); Scruggs and Jenkins (1985); Scruggs and Lifson (1986); Lifson, Scruggs, and Bennion (1984); Scruggs and Lifson (1985); Scruggs and Mastropieri (1986); Scruggs, Mastropieri, and Veit (1986); Scruggs, Mastropieri, Tolfa, and Jenkins (1985); Osguthorpe and Scruggs (1986); Scruggs (1985a, 1985b); and Scruggs and

(continues)

(Relevant Research and Resources continued)

Tolfa (1985). A meta-analysis of test-taking skills training is provided by Scruggs, White, and Bennion (1986).

Transfer of learning and self-instruction research are provided by Borkowski and Varnhagen (1984); Wong (1982, 1985); Wong and Wong (1986); and Brown, Campione, and Barclay (1979). Research cited in the science and social studies chapter can also be cited as evidence supporting the efficacy of various learning and study strategies. Test-taking strategies are described in detail by Scruggs and Mastropieri (1988, 1992d), while comprehensive procedures to use in teaching mnemonic strategies are presented in Mastropieri and Scruggs (1991). Polloway, Foley, and Epstein (1992) provided a discussion on the issues of homework between nondisabled students and students with disabilities. Texts by Pressley and Associates (1990), Gaskins and Elliot (1991), and Ciborowski (1992) provide useful information on the implementation of strategy-based instruction, while Mastropieri and Scruggs (1993) provided detailed guidelines for facilitating school success. Strategies for training generalized use of the keyword method are validated by Fulk, Mastropieri, and Scruggs (1992); McLoone, Scruggs, Mastropieri, and Zucker (1986); Scruggs and Mastropieri (1992a); and King-Sears, Mercer, and Sindelar (1992).

Curricular Materials

The Institute for Research in Learning Disabilities at the University of Kansas has produced numerous learning strategies packages. Some of the specific training modules include the *Word Identification Strategy*, the *Paraphrasing Strategy*, the *FIRST-Letter Mnemonic Strategy*, and the *Sentence Writing Strategy* (contact the Institute for Research in Learning Disabilities at the University of Kansas for procedures for participating in their training sessions and obtaining training materials). Curriculum Associates produces *Classification and Organization Skills*, a booklet aimed at teaching outlining skills, and *Advanced Skills for School Success*, a program emphasizing organizational skills. *Study Skills Series* (Media Materials) provides materials for teaching a variety of study and test-taking skills. The *Bad Speller's Dictionary* (Random House) and the *Misspeller's Dictionary* (Simon & Schuster) are available for checking written products for spelling errors when the correct spelling is unknown.

Computer Software and Technology

Software programs have also become available in the area of test-taking skills and study skills. Test Taking Made Easy is available from MECC, and the Essential Study Skills Series is available from Media Materials. Many of the word-processing programs and word prediction programs mentioned in Chapter 6 would also be beneficial for students in preparing written reports and projects. Scholastic distributes Multiscribe I and IIGS, Bank Street Writer III, Story Tree, Success With Writing, and Story Maker, which are all listed as composing and postcomposing software programs. See Appendix B for a list of addresses of producers and distributors of software and curricular materials.

✛ ✛ ✛

CHAPTER 10

Social Skills

RESEARCHERS HAVE DOCUMENTED THAT MANY SPECIAL EDUCATION STU-dents, including those categorized as behaviorally disordered, learning disabled, and mentally handicapped, exhibit deficits in age-appropriate social skills. Some educators have suggested that many of the current mainstreaming efforts fail because special education students lack appropriate and acceptable social behavior. Other educators have indicated that appropriate social skills are necessary for success in all aspects of life. For example, research results indicate that many former special education students who are now young adults lose their jobs not due to their competence at executing the required job-related skills, but due to their poor social skills. Many are fired for neglecting to follow directions or not asking for clarification of directions, as well as forgetting to call in sick and being unable to receive and execute suggestions for improvement. Social skills can, therefore, be considered critical for success in school, at home, and at work.

Researchers have addressed ways to increase positive social behaviors. This chapter is intended to present the major issues surrounding social skills instruction. First, social skills are clearly defined; second, specific procedures for assessing social skills are presented; and third, instructional procedures that fit within the teacher-effectiveness model are described, with a special emphasis on training generalization of social skills.

DEFINITION OF SOCIAL SKILLS

The area of social skills has resisted precise definition simply because so many educators and researchers have adopted specific definitions to meet their particular needs during specific situations. Most definitions emphasize that social skills are those *behaviors necessary for successful interactions* at home, school, and in the community. Some educators refer to social skills as social competence and refer to the *socially competent individual* as one who can function adequately in his or her environment by meeting goals without disrupting others. Social skills can, therefore, be considered a collection of behaviors in a learner's repertoire of skills that enables him or her to interact successfully in the environment. So defined, many specific skills have been identified as social skills (see Figure 10.1).

The degree to which individuals execute the social skills presented in Figure 10.1 influences how well they interact with, get along with, and are accepted by their peers and others in the environment. The list is, obviously, not exhaustive; it does, however, provide a general listing of the skills that are most commonly reported as social skills and those that appear in many published social skills programs.

A major problem in the social skills area is the lack of a definite scope and sequence or a hierarchy of social skills. It is much easier for a special educator to conduct a curriculum-based assessment, identify specific skill deficits, and instruct students in reading, language, or mathematics than it is in social skills. The next section presents procedures recommended for assessing and prioritizing social skills.

SOCIAL SKILLS ASSESSMENT

The purpose of social skills assessment is similar to that in the academic areas; that is, assessment first identifies students with particular social skills deficits. Second, assessment identifies where along a continuum of objectives instruction needs to begin. Finally, ongoing formative evaluation provides information on student performance and progress along that continuum of objectives.

Typical social skills assessment procedures include the following methods: (a) sociometric measures, (b) teacher ratings, (c) role-play tests, and (d) naturalistic or direct observation. In the following sections, each procedure is briefly described, followed by a task-analytical model of assessment that is linked to a specific social skills curriculum area.

Sociometric Measures

Sociometric measures are intended to assess interpersonal attraction or degree of social acceptance among the sampled populations. Three of the most common sociometric techniques include (a) the peer-nomination method, (b) the rating scale, and (c) the paired comparison method. The peer-nomination method requires students to name specific classmates who meet a particular social criterion. For example, all of the students in Ms. Hunt's classroom could be asked to write down the names of (a) the three classmates they like the most and (b) the three classmates they like the least. A student's score is the total number of "nominations," based on either the positive or the negative criteria. The resulting totals can be viewed as an indication of social acceptance (positive nominations) or social rejection

Content Area	Component Skills
Conversation skills	Joining a conversation
	Interrupting a conversation
	Starting a conversation
	Maintaining a conversation
	Ending a conversation
	Use of appropriate tone of voice
	Use of appropriate distance and eye contact
Assertiveness skills	Asking for clarifications
	Making requests
	Denying requests
	Negotiating requests
	Exhibiting politeness
"Play" interaction skills (e.g., making friends)	Sharing with others
	Inviting others to play
	Encouraging others
	Praising others
Problem-solving and coping skills	Staying calm and relaxed
	Listing possible solutions
	Choosing the best solution
	Taking responsibility for self
	Handling name calling and teasing
	Staying out of trouble
Self-help skills	Good grooming (clean, neat)
	Good dressing (wearing clothes that fit)
	Good table manners
	Good eating behaviors
Classroom task-related behaviors	On-task behavior
	Attending to tasks
	Completing tasks
	Following directions
	Trying your best
Self-related behaviors	Giving positive feedback to self
	Expressing feelings
	Accepting negative feedback
	Accepting consequences
Job interview skills	Being prepared (dress, attitude, etc.)
	Being attentive
	Listening skills
	Asking for clarification
	Thinking prior to speaking

FIGURE 10.1. Specific social skills.

(negative nominations). Some researchers have suggested that the nomination method actually provides a measure of "best friendship," which can be viewed as similar to social acceptance.

The rating scale method requires students to rank all of their classmates on a numerical scale according to a social criterion. In the above example, students would be provided with a listing of all their classmates and a Likert-type rating scale. The rating scale could range from 1 to 5, with 1 equal to "don't like to play with" and 5 equal to "like to play with a lot." Students would be required to circle the number that best represents their feelings toward each classmate. A student's measure of social acceptance or rejection is the average rating from all their classmates.

The paired comparison method is a variation of the rating scale technique. Students are presented with one classmate and all possible pairings with other classmates. Each time students must select the "most liked" or "least liked" peer. Measures of social acceptance or rejection are derived by totaling the number of times each student is selected for all pairings.

The advantages of sociometric measures include (a) administration ease and (b) quick identification or screening of a student's acceptance or rejection by peers. The disadvantages, however, include (a) lack of identification of specific social skill deficits; (b) lack of use as a continuous monitoring evaluation measure (since the measure does not identify specific social skill deficits and since it is not necessarily sensitive to students' social skill changes); and (c) lack of identification of students who are neither intensely liked or disliked, but simply tolerated, and yet lack appropriate social skills.

Teacher Ratings

Teacher ratings are intended to provide information relevant to students' particular strengths and weaknesses in social skills. The most common type of teacher rating scale lists social behaviors and requires teachers to identify "how well" or "how frequently" students exhibit those behaviors appropriately. Many social skills packages have begun to include teacher checklists as accompanying screening devices.

The advantages of teacher ratings include (a) administration ease, (b) reliance on teachers' expertise and daily experience with students, and (c) fair utility as a screening device. Typically, however, such devices lack necessary reliability and validity data. If the teacher rating scale is linked directly to a social skills curriculum, it can be used as a formative evaluation device to monitor students' progress. Unfortunately, many widely promoted teacher rating scales are *not* linked to specific curricular materials.

Role-Play Tests

Role-play tests, or analogue observations, are intended to assess a student's ability to execute appropriate social behaviors in contrived settings. Various scenarios are presented to the student, and the student's responses are evaluated for the appropriateness of specific social behaviors. Many researchers have developed their own role-play tests because certain social behaviors are difficult to observe in natural settings. For example, it is virtually impossible to assess whether or not a student possesses appropriate conversation skills when observing the student during a history lecture. In order to provide the student with opportunities to execute specific social skills, various role-play scenarios have been designed and used.

The advantages of role-play tests include (a) the ability to assess specific social skills in controlled settings and (b) the ability to determine whether or not the student has acquired the social skill, is fluent at performing the skill, has generalized the skill, or is at the acquisition level of learning. The disadvantages, however, include (a) lack of normative data, including reliability and validity, and (b) lack of direct correspondence between contrived scenarios and naturalistic settings with respect to demonstrated competencies.

Naturalistic or Direct Observation

Direct observation procedures can be employed in natural settings to determine which social behaviors are appropriate. As described in Chapter 3, various observation techniques can be employed to determine the frequency of appropriate and inappropriate social behaviors and the quality of such behaviors. Additionally, continuous records can be used to analyze the antecedents and consequences of social interactions.

To be successful, direct observation procedures must meet several prerequisites. First, the specific social skills must be operationally defined (see Chapter 3). Second, observers must be trained to a criterion performance. Third, reliability of observations should be assessed frequently; and, finally, the behaviors targeted must be high-frequency behaviors or contrived settings must be constructed in order to evaluate low-frequency behaviors. Additionally, if direct observation procedures are tailored to correspond to specific social skills instructional objectives, then these observation procedures can be used to monitor progress continuously throughout instruction.

All of the social skills assessment procedures discussed have limitations, some of which are more serious than others. Major limitations include (a) lack of reliability and validity data, (b) lack of social norms, and (c) lack of a direct correspondence with curriculum materials. Teachers should select a simple, reliable screening device and use a task-analytical, curriculum-based assessment procedure similar to the one described in the next section.

Task-Analytical/Curriculum-Based Assessment

Procedures for specifying skill sequences, levels of learning and behaviors, and performance criteria can be identified in the social skills area, just as they can be specified in academic skill areas such as reading and mathematics. Once these sequences are delineated, teachers will find it easy to implement systematic instruction using the teacher-effectiveness variables. The instructional sequences will assist teachers in ensuring mastery and generalization of social skills.

The most difficult tasks that teachers face are selecting a specific social skills curriculum and specifying performance criteria. The latter is difficult since the acceptable standards for social behaviors tend to be based on subjective rather than objective criteria. For example, what one teacher considers appropriate classroom behavior may be considered inappropriate by another teacher. However, special educators can begin to develop such standards for their students based on a composite of the performance criteria enforced by the regular classroom educators in their particular schools. Special educators can distribute questionnaires to regular educators that contain items such as (a) What are your classroom rules and regulations? (b) What are the materials students need to bring to class in order to be considered prepared for class? (c) What are the standards for acceptable behavior in terms of entering and exiting the classroom, requesting permission to use the restrooms, sharpening pencils, requesting assistance on assignments, and leaving their seat/desks? Responses to these and other relevant items can assist special educators in developing standards for performance criteria for social behaviors.

The issue of selecting a social skills curriculum is equally confusing. Many social skills training packages have been published, some of which appear well organized and some of which lack sufficient instructional procedures, guided and independent practice activities, and formative evaluation procedures. Additionally, many social skills programs are targeted for a particular population (e.g., preschool, elementary, or secondary levels). A checklist for evaluating published social skills materials is provided in Figure 10.2. Examples of social skills materials are the *Getting Along with Others* series and the *Skillstreaming* series, both published by Research Press. It is recommended, however, that teachers use task-analysis skills to subdivide the content along particular social skills domains of behavior and combine that subdivision with the levels of learning, behavior, conditions, and performance criteria to form a table of specifications. This table of specifications can be used to generate assessment objectives and instruction objectives. For example, assume that one major goal in social skills training is to improve conversation skills. A task analysis on conversation skills might reveal the following subskills:

1. Appropriate eye contact
2. Appropriate distance
3. Appropriate tone of voice
4. Starting a conversation

5. Maintaining a conversation
6. Interrupting a conversation
7. Joining a conversation
8. Ending a conversation

Title:	*Getting Along With Others*
Author(s):	Jackson, N. F., Jackson, D. A., and Monroe, C. (1983). Research Press
Target Population: *(Age and Severity Levels)*	Elementary-age children, but authors contend materials can be adapted for mildly disabled students.
Cost:	Moderate
Brief Description of Material: *(textbook, video, audio, etc.)*	1. Program Guide Workbook 2. Skill Lessons and Activities
Scope and Sequence of Skills Available: Yes ☑ No ☐ *If yes, describe briefly.*	Seventeen skills are presented throughout the materials. The skills range from introduction, following directions, and saying no to staying out of trouble.
Pre- and Post-Assessment Measures Available: Yes ☑ No ☐	A consumer satisfaction pretest/posttest is included, and a training check sheet is incorporated. However, no specific pretest/posttest for the curriculum is included.
Amount and Types of Practice Activities in Program: *(e.g., modeling, role-playing, directed rehearsal, homework)*	Positive feedback, discrimination training, role-playing, homework activities.
Generalization Training Incorporated: Yes ☑ No ☐ *If yes, how?*	Homework activities are included, during which time students are expected to practice the skills in new situations.
Criteria for Acceptable Performance of Objectives/Skills Specified: Yes ☐ No ☑	It is suggested that teachers determine the necessary standards for acceptable performance.
Formative Evaluation Data on Program's Effectiveness Specified: Yes ☐ No ☑ *If yes, how many subjects used the program, for how long, how were results assessed, etc.*	Authors described an initial project that implemented this program; however, no efficacy data were presented.
Behavior Management Plan Included: Yes ☑ No ☐ *If yes, describe briefly.*	Specified on page 4.
Adaptability of Materials: *(Would it be easy to modify the materials? How?)*	Fairly easy to adapt to middle school-age or junior high school-age students.
In 100 words or less, write your impression of the package:	The 17 skills presented have some good ideas associated with them. I think my elementary-age resource students could benefit from instruction in some of the skill areas.

FIGURE I0.2. Evaluation of a commercial social skills package.

The subskills on page 306 can be combined with the following levels of behavior, learning, and conditions:

1. Identification of appropriate behavior

2. Production of appropriate behavior in a role-play situation (first at the acquisition level, followed by the fluency level)

3. Production of appropriate behavior spontaneously in special education setting (first at the acquisition level, followed by a fluent production)

4. Generalization/production of appropriate behavior in regular class setting

5. Generalization/production of appropriate behavior at lunch, recess, and at home

6. Execution of appropriate behavior at all times

By combining the content subdivisions listed along the left vertical axis and the levels of learning, behavior, and conditions listed across the top horizontal axis, a table of specifications that has as its overall goal improving conversation skills is formed. Each cell within the table can be used to generate individual behavioral objectives for assessment and instructional purposes. Teachers will have designated specific standards for each objective. Typically, a trials-to-criterion approach has been used to demonstrate mastery of social behavioral objectives.

Another instructional goal in social skills or table of specifications that could be widely used with special education students, especially behaviorally disordered students, is improvement of classroom task-related behaviors. Task analysis of the general goal could yield the following subskills:

1. Attending to tasks

2. Following directions

3. Asking for clarifications

4. Completing tasks

5. Staying on task

6. Putting forth best effort

The breakdown of levels of learning, behavior, and conditions may be identical to those in Table 10.1. Again, this analysis provides the special educator with a more ecologically valid assessment and instructional plan.

TABLE 10.1. Table of Specifications for Conversation Skills.

CONTENT	BEHAVIOR				
	Identification	Production			
	A. Acquisition	B. Acquisition	C. Fluency	D. Application	E. Generalization
1. eye contact	1A	1B	1C	1D	1E
2. tone of voice	2A	2B	2C	2D	2E
3. appropriate distance	3A	3B	3C	3D	3E
4. starting a conversation	4A	4B	4C	4D	4E
5. maintaining conversation	5A	5B	5C	5D	5E
6. interrupting conversation	6A	6B	6C	6D	6E
7. joining a conversation	7A	7B	7C	7D	7E
8. ending a conversation	8A	8B	8C	8D	8E

Sample Objectives:

1A Students will identify appropriate eye contact from inappropriate eye contact 10 out of 10 times after viewing role-plays on a videotape.

4B Students will start a conversation appropriately 10 out of 10 times during role-play situations.

5C Students will maintain a conversation appropriately 10 out of 10 times in the special education setting.

6D Students will interrupt conversations appropriately during recess.

7E Students will join conversations appropriately at home.

It is important to note that all subskill areas need to be operationally defined. An excellent method to use with students is the provision of several relevant, concrete examples and several irrelevant examples.

In summary, it is recommended that this task analytical approach toward summary skills be combined with levels of learning, behavior, and conditions to form curriculum-based social skill assessment devices. In the assessment of any social skills, it must first be determined whether or not the student *recognizes* that certain social behaviors are called for. For example, prior to exhibiting appropriate conversational skills, the student must be able to identify the fact that this is a situation that calls for appropriate conversational skills. Finally, when planning social skills assessment and instruction teachers should ensure that considerations are given to cultural and ethnic diversity. The next section describes how these devices can be used for planning and delivery of social skills instruction.

DESIGN AND DELIVERY OF SOCIAL SKILLS INSTRUCTION

Social skills instruction involves teaching the student to *apply* all of the skills being directly taught. To this extent, much of social skills instruction is procedural in nature and requires the student to *recognize* instances in which specific social skills are called for from noninstances. Students must then *recall* the steps necessary to execute the skill and, finally, *execute* the procedure effectively and efficiently in a variety of settings and situations.

Design and delivery of social skills instruction includes all of the teacher-effectiveness variables emphasized throughout this text, including (a) daily review, (b) presentation of material to be learned, (c) guided practice, (d) independent practice, (e) weekly and monthly reviews, and (f) formative evaluation. These teaching functions are presented below as used with social skills content. A sample lesson is excerpted in Figure 10.3.

Daily Review

Each social skills lesson should begin with a review of the content previously covered. It is also appropriate to review the homework assignment at this time. If the previous lesson emphasized the identification of appropriate eye contact and tone of voice in conversations, the next lesson should begin with a review that includes discrimination practice of instances and noninstances of appropriate eye contact and tone of voice. If these subtasks cannot be accurately identified, additional practice emphasizing examples and nonexamples of each subtask should be introduced. These review procedures provide teachers with opportunities to assess students' performance and provide students with opportunities for overlearning previously acquired information.

Presentation of New Content

Teachers first need to clarify the goals and main objectives to be covered. If the lesson's major objectives include producing appropriate eye contact during conversations and producing the appropriate tone of voice during conversations in role-play situations, teachers could explicitly state to the students: "Yesterday, you practiced identifying when appropriate eye contact and tone of voice were used in conversations. Recall that when you watched people during conversations you were able to *recognize* appropriate eye contact from inappropriate eye contact, as well as appropriate tone of voice from inappropriate tone of voice. Today, we are going to practice *using* appropriate eye contact and tone of voice during conversations."

Review	"Last week we practiced the appropriate way to have eye contact with someone during a conversation. Can you all turn to your neighbor on your left and show me appropriate eye contact? [Signal.] Good, everyone seems to remember that appropriate eye contact means holding your head up and looking at your partner directly in the eyes."
Goal statement and teacher presentation	"Today we are going to practice identifying the appropriate tone to use during conversations. Watch the video monitor while I play some examples for you. [Video presents several examples of "This is an appropriate tone of voice" and several nonexamples (i.e., "This is *not* an appropriate tone of voice.")] Remember, an appropriate tone of voice is not too loud or too soft, and it is interpreted as one in which you are interested in speaking with your partner." [Show several additional examples and nonexamples.]
Guided practice	"Now, we are going to select the examples that show us an appropriate tone of voice. [Turn on video for additional examples and nonexamples.] Is this appropriate? [Signal.]" [Provide corrective feedback as necessary throughout the presentation of several instances and noninstances.]
Independent practice	[Student continues with similar activity that requires individual responding on paper.]
Formative evaluation	[Teacher uses a similar practice activity but collects examples to grade and score later.]

FIGURE 10.3. Sample lesson for teaching social skills.

Next, teachers should provide a step-by-step presentation of the new material. Teachers can model and demonstrate several examples of appropriate eye contact and tone of voice during a role-play conversation. Re-explanations of *why* the examples are appropriate should be supplied, and a couple of nonexamples should be interspersed among the examples to verify students' understanding of the concepts. After several minutes of this modeling, demonstration, and questioning, teachers should require students to practice these two behaviors in role-play scenarios. Two students could be selected to model the appropriate eye contact and tone of voice for the rest of the students. With most students teachers should supply scripted scenarios in which students play the roles of various characters. Supplying scripts allows students to concentrate on producing the correct responses (i.e., appropriate eye contact and tone of voice), rather than wasting time and effort thinking of topics for conversation.

Guided Practice

After students have modeled several examples for the class and teachers have monitored their performances and provided immediate corrective feedback, all students should be paired off and provided with scripted scenarios for practice exercises.

The major goal during guided practice is to allow all of the students as many opportunities as possible to practice accurately executing the new skill. This can be accomplished in several ways. For example, teachers can tell everyone to begin executing Scenario A and simultaneously wander around to specific pairs and provide immediate corrective feedback. Teachers could also have pairs practice different scenarios and then randomly call on pairs to demonstrate the appropriate skills for the class. Observers from the class could be required to critique the demonstrations and, if they were inappropriate, explain how the models could be altered to be appropriate. Teachers can involve all of the observers by asking the group to respond by signaling with hands or thumbs up or down the correctness of the demonstration. All accurate responses should be reinforced with praise.

In general, activities that are directly relevant to the objective and that require active participation by all of the students are most likely to maximize the learning. During guided practice, errors are expected, and it is mandatory for teachers to provide immediate corrective feedback. Usually, a model–lead test approach is an acceptable procedure to use in correcting students' errors. Teachers must be sure students have mastered the objective to the required level of proficiency before allowing them to practice independently.

Independent Practice

Independent practice activities need to be directly relevant to instructional objectives. Independent practice is usually not monitored as closely as guided practice by teachers, who may frequently be reading to another instructional group while students complete independent practice activities. It is a challenge to design independent practice activities for many of the social skills objectives. Since the production of the appropriate behavior is the desired response (e.g., the production of appropriate eye contact and tone of voice), traditional paper–pencil activities are often inappropriate. However, scripted scenarios can be presented on worksheets, and students can be required to execute the scenarios appropriately with a peer. Similar scenarios should be sent home as independent practice activities. Additionally, teachers can begin to emphasize the importance of these behaviors throughout the day (e.g., during all interpersonal interactions). Although this objective will be emphasized more in the progression of skill development, it is appropriate for teachers to explain to students that these skills will be used in all conversations.

The most successful social skills training interventions have employed a great many practice activities, including homework assignments. When practice activities are designed to be executed in different scenarios, different settings, and with different people, teachers provide practice that should help students to generalize and apply the desired behaviors to other settings. During such practice activities, accurate responses should be reinforced.

Weekly and Monthly Reviews

As in all content areas, special educators need to provide for weekly and monthly reviews of all social skills objectives covered. This type of formal review demonstrates to students the amount of progress they have made, while simultaneously providing opportunities for practice in applying previously learned skills to new situations. This overlearning and generalization practice appears to be necessary in order for special education students to achieve success in mainstream settings. Teachers can present these review periods as challenges for the students. Many students appear quite surprised by the amount of ground that they have covered.

Formative Evaluation

As with all lessons, teachers should include a short assessment at the end of each session to determine whether students have or have not mastered the lesson's objectives. In social skills training, a short scenario or two that require all students to produce the responses can be given at the end of the lesson. Teachers record whether or not students respond correctly. These student performance data are then used to make an instructional decision regarding the next session. Based on student performance, the following variables can be altered for the next lesson:

1. Increase or decrease engaged time-on-task

2. Increase or decrease teacher presentation

3. Increase or decrease number and type of examples and nonexamples

4. Increase or decrease guided practice activities

5. Increase or decrease corrective feedback

6. Increase or decrease independent practice activities

7. Increase or decrease cumulative review

8. Alter one or more of 1 through 7 above

9. Alter the formative evaluation

Any of the variables listed above can be manipulated in making an instructional decision based on actual performance data. Teachers can also decide that only two or three students need additional engaged time-on-task and, therefore, can insert another practice activity for those particular students. In any event, it is necessary to administer a formative evaluation measure and to use that information to guide future instructional sessions.

On-the-Spot Social Skills Instruction

Since social skills are exhibited in all situations, teachers may find it especially beneficial to incorporate "on-the-spot" instructional sessions in addition to the regularly scheduled sessions. In other words, as inappropriate and appropriate social behaviors occur throughout the day, it is good practice to emphasize newly practiced social skills to students. For instance, teachers can positively reinforce students who exhibit the appropriate social skills. Concomitantly, teachers can provide additional instruction and require students to practice social skills that are considered appropriate. A teacher might provide the on-the-spot instruction after observing a student exhibit a skill inappropriately by stating, "Remember how we learned the correct way of obtaining someone's attention? Let's try doing it that way now."

This section has provided an example that illustrates how the teacher-effectiveness variables can be used in the design, delivery, and evaluation of social skills instruction. Important features in designing social skills instruction include (a) instructional objectives be clearly specified; (b) teachers present relevant information through models of examples and nonexamples of skills; (c) relevant guided practice activities involve all of the students; (d) teachers monitor and adjust instruction based on student performance; (e) relevant independent practice activities, including homework, be assigned; (f) daily, weekly, and monthly reviews be included; and (g) formative evaluation procedures be implemented to assess ongoing performance.

RELEVANT RESEARCH AND RESOURCES

Recent reviews of social competence and skills are provided by Sullivan and Mastropieri (1994); Vaughn, McIntosh, and Hogan (1990); and Zaragoza, Vaughn, and McIntosh (1991). Reviews related to social competence and social skills include those on cognitive behavioral interventions and self-management (Ager & Cole, 1991; Nelson, Smith, Young, & Dodd, 1991).

Social skills training and influences on social competence have been among the most active applied-research areas in special education (Gresham, 1981, 1982, 1984; Gresham & Lemanek, 1983; Keogh, 1981). Interest in the area of social skills training can be attributed to the failures of mainstreaming efforts (Gresham, 1981) and to the fact that special educators have historically spent more time instruct-

(continues)

(Relevant Research and Resources continued)

ing students in basic skill areas, such as reading, and assumed that social skills did not need explicit instruction. Additionally, recent research results have revealed that most students with disabling conditions exhibit deficiencies in social competence when compared to their nondisabled peers (Bryan & Bryan, 1981; Cartledge & Milburn, 1978; Zigmond & Sainato, 1981). Consequently, in the past decade, numerous investigations using students with disabilities have been conducted to determine the optimal type of social skills training to ameliorate these deficiencies in social skills. Many variables have been examined in studies on social skills training, including:

1. *instructional procedures* employed, including:
   a. use of *multiple intervention strategies* such as direct instruction, modeling, and role-rehearsal (Vaughn, Ridley, & Cox, 1983); direct instruction, modeling, role-rehearsal, prompting, and feedback (LeGreca & Mesibov, 1981; Matson et al., 1980); direct instruction, modeling, role-playing, role-rehearsal, feedback, and self-monitoring (Thorkildsen, 1984); games and self-reporting (Amerikaner & Summerline, 1982); reinforcement of some type in combination with other intervention strategies (Schloss, Schloss, & Harris, 1984; Thorkildsen, 1984; Walker et al., 1983); and use of homework activities in combination with other strategies (Thorkildsen, 1984); and
   b. use of *single intervention strategies* such as modeling (Donahue & Bryan, 1983) and contracting (Lanunziata, Hill, & Krause, 1981).

2. *behaviors targeted* for improvement, including:
   a. greeting and joining a conversation (LeGreca & Mesibov, 1981);
   b. peer interaction, such as helping others, playing with others, and assertiveness (Evers & Schwartz, 1973);
   c. facial expressions and verbalizations for positive and negative situations (Kazdin, Esveldt-Dawson, & Matson, 1983);
   d. providing positive and negative feedback, solving problems, resisting peer pressure, negotiating, and following instructions (Hazel, Schumaker, Sherman, & Sheldon, 1982; Schumaker & Ellis, 1982);
   e. providing compliments, appropriate requests, tone of voice, eye contact, and body posture (Matson et al., 1980);
   f. appropriate social play (Strain & Wiegerink, 1976);
   g. appropriate response to instruction (Warrenfeltz et al., 1981); and
   h. positive social behavior (Ragland, Kerr, & Strain, 1981).

(continues)

(Relevant Research and Resources continued)

3. *instructional settings* in which social skills training typically occurs:
   a. public schools (Amerikaner & Summerline, 1982; Donahue & Bryan, 1983; Evers & Schwartz, 1973; Thorkildsen, 1984; Walker et al., 1983);
   b. residential treatment centers (Ford, Evans, & Dworkin, 1982; Kazdin et al., 1983; Matson et al., 1980);
   c. clinical settings (Cooke & Apolloni, 1976); and
   d. multiple settings (Ragland et al., 1981; Hazel et al., 1982).

4. type of *trainers employed*, including:
   a. trained experimenters or therapists (Hazel et al., 1982; Schloss et al., 1984);
   b. classroom teacher (Schumaker & Ellis, 1982; Strain and Wiegerink, 1976); and
   c. peer tutors (Lancioni, 1982; Ragland et al., 1981).

5. *instructional format*, including:
   a. small group instructional sessions (Amerikaner & Summerline, 1982; Evers & Schwartz, 1973; Cooke & Apolloni, 1976);
   b. individual instructional sessions (Donahue & Bryan, 1983; Hazel et al., 1982; Thorkildsen, 1984); and
   c. combinations of small group and individual sessions (Matson et al., 1980).

6. *duration of social skills training programs*, ranging from:
   a. shorter numbers of training sessions (1 to 5) (Donahue & Bryan, 1983);
   b. medium number of training sessions (6 to 15 sessions) (Amerikaner & Summerline, 1982; Ford et al., 1982); and
   c. larger number of training sessions (more than 15) (Thorkildsen, 1984; Strain & Wiegerink, 1976).

7. *type of disabled students*, including:
   a. learning disabled (Schumaker & Ellis, 1982);
   b. mentally retarded (Lancioni, 1982); and
   c. behaviorally disordered (Kiburz, Miller, & Morrow, 1984).

8. *age of the disabled students*, including:
   a. preschoolers (Mastropieri & Scruggs, 1985–1986; Strain & Wiegerink, 1976);
   b. elementary-age students (Amerikaner & Summerline, 1982);
   c. preadolescent students (Bierman & Furman, 1984); and
   d. adolescent students (Schumaker & Ellis, 1982).

(continues)

(Relevant Research and Resources continued)

Curricular Materials

Social skills curricular materials have become widely available. It is recommended that teachers carefully evaluate the programs to ensure they will meet the needs of their students. The *Walker Social Skills Curriculum*, including the *ACCEPTS Program* (A Curriculum for Children's Effective Peer and Teacher Skills) and the *ACCESS Program* (Adolescent Curriculum for Communication and Effective Social Skills), *Personal Power: Student Effectiveness Training, Developing Appropriate Teacher Interaction Skills, Gaining Self-Control,* and *Peer Interaction Skills* are available from PRO-ED. *Getting Along with Others: Teaching Social Effectiveness to Children, Skillstreaming the Elementary School Child, Skillstreaming the Adolescent,* and *ASSET: A Social Skills Program for Adolescents* are available from Research Press. *The Solution Book* is available from Science Research Associates, and American Guidance Service distributes *Social Skills for Daily Living, Toward Affective Development,* and *Developing Understanding of Self and Others.*

Computer Software and Technology

Several of the programs listed as curricular materials have optional video and/or audio components (e.g., *The Walker Social Skills Curriculum*). Additionally, some researchers have developed videodisc programs for social skills training (e.g., Thorkildsen, 1984). See Appendix B for a list of addresses of producers and distributors of software and curricular materials.

❖   ❖   ❖

CHAPTER II

Teaching for Transition: Life Skills, Career, and Vocational Education

REMEDIATION OF ACADEMIC AND SOCIAL FUNCTIONING IS A PRIMARY responsibility of special education teachers. The overall goal of special education is successful functioning in mainstream environments. Ultimately, this means successful functioning in post-school environments, the domain of adult living. Although academic and social skills remediation is extremely important to success in life, it is by no means sufficient for many of the students enrolled in special education. Recently, a great deal of attention has been paid to the importance of preparing students for the transition from school to occupational and independent living environments.

Such instruction should not be put off until a year or two before the student is expected to graduate. Orientation of the student to the world of work and adult living should begin early in the elementary school years and should be integrated into all aspects of the school curriculum at all grade levels.

One important feature of transitional education to which all teachers should attend is the relevance of existing curricular materials to independent living skills. This relevance should be made explicitly clear to students. For example, it is important to teach students the basic skills and operations in mathematics so that they will ultimately be able to use these skills in solving word problems. However, it should also be remembered that the purpose of learning to solve word problems in school is to be able to solve practical math problems in home or occupational environments. If this final generalization step is not learned, the preceding steps will prove to be of little value outside of a school setting. Likewise, many other content or curricular areas have direct relevance to adult functioning, and this relevance should be made explicit to learners.

In this chapter, several different aspects of life skills, career, and vocational education will be considered. Although everything taught in school should be relevant to everyday living, the following sections will focus on content of obvious and immediate importance to adult living. These sections will describe life skills, career, and vocational education, respectively.

Life Skills

Life skills instruction typically refers to those skills that are relevant to independent, day-to-day living. Instruction includes personal finance, health and fitness, and leisure activities, which are considered separately.

Personal Finance

Personal finance is often included within mathematics curricula and includes all aspects of saving, spending, and budgeting money. Students who have been taught effective skills for personal finance stand a far greater chance of success in life than those who have not been taught these skills. Aspects of personal finance appropriate for instruction in special education settings are described in the following sections.

Budget balancing

Lessons on personal finance can be started with instruction in developing a personal budget. Students can be taught the distinction between "gross salary" and "take home pay." Simulated paychecks can be used to illustrate income tax withholding, as well as social security, insurance, and other deductions.

When students have learned to compute monthly take-home pay, they should be shown how to budget their resources so that they can live most efficiently. Many consumer specialists suggest that an expenditure of 25% to 33% of monthly take-home income on housing is desirable. Students should estimate their future incomes based on salaries or wages advertised in the help wanted section of the newspaper, from library research, or from information obtained from the guidance counselor's office. Once they have computed their approximate take-home pay, students should check the newspaper listings for available housing and determine where they could live given a rent of approximately one-third of their income.

If they plan to live alone, of course, the cost for housing would likely be much higher than if they arranged to share a house or apartment. Also, students may consider living with parents until a specific amount of money is saved, which could be put toward a car, for example. Regardless, students should be taught to consider the specific economic consequences of various forms of living arrangements (see Figure 11.1).

Similar considerations can be made for budgeting food. Local TV news stations frequently report on the cost of groceries to the average shopper. These costs can be compared with the cost of eating out in restaurants, and estimates can be made of the proportion of monthly income spent on food. Finally, students should consider the amount of monthly income remaining after expenditures for housing and food for other expenses such as clothing, transportation (including car payments, bus fares, parking charges, and car maintenance), home furnishings, medical expenses, entertainment and recreational costs, and savings. Expenses can be estimated by asking students what type and level of goods and services they desire and determining the costs of these goods and services from newspapers, television, and library sources.

Students can also be introduced to various forms, including computer software, that can be used to budget income. As with other instructional activities in special education, it is not sufficient to simply "introduce" students to practices for managing personal finance. Budgeting should be practiced on a regular basis until students' responses are automatic and likely to be carried on into the transitional environment.

Income	
Gross monthly wages	$ 820.00
Less deductions and withholding	−220.00
Net income	$ 600.00
Expenses	
Rent	$ 220.00
Utilities	70.00
Food	90.00
Transportation (bus)	20.00
Clothing	50.00
Personal (toothpaste, etc.)	15.00
Medical	35.00
Entertainment	40.00
Subtotal	$ 540.00
Savings	+ 60.00
Total	$ 600.00

FIGURE 11.1. Monthly budget.

Using a checkbook

A critical skill for independent living is managing checking accounts. Typically, students characterized as mildly disabled have acquired math skills appropriate for such computation by the time they reach high school, but they may need practice on the specific aspects of check writing and correctly subtracting the amount of the check from the checking account balance. These procedures can best be taught by acquiring facsimiles of checkbooks and providing instruction and guided and independent practice on aspects of check writing. Figure 11.2 provides some excerpts from a lesson on check writing.

Credit

Any student who is preparing to enter the world of independent living should be aware of the possible consequences of using various forms of credit. It is important for students to learn how to compute additional expenses incurred by finance charges and to consider such additional charges when making purchases on credit. Students can become efficient at such computation through provision of problems in math classes that use real-

Component	Examples
Daily review	"Last week we learned the names of the parts of a check. Look at this example. What is the name of this part of the check? . . ."
State objective and teacher presentation	"Today we are going to practice writing checks. [Show overhead transparency of a blank check.] Everyone look up at this example with me. We are going to write out a check to Dr. Sydney for $35.63. First, I write in today's date in the date spot. [Write in date.] Then, I find the part of the check that says *Pay to the order of,* and I write in Dr. Sydney. Next, I find the enclosed box with the dollar sign, and I write in the amount of the check, in this case, $35.63. Then . . . . Let's practice several additional examples together . . . ."
Guided practice	"Now, I want each of you to practice writing the following checks to your neighbor. [Distribute checks worksheets and circulate around room.] Let's check the first example together . . . ."
Independent practice	[Worksheets similar to the ones just completed are distributed]. "This activity is exactly like the one we just finished. This time I want you to work independently. If you have any questions, raise your hand and I will come to your desk . . . ."
Formative evaluation	"You have three minutes to complete this activity. You are expected to fill in the appropriate information on these two checks. Ready, begin. . . ."

FIGURE II.2. Sample lesson on check writing.

world examples (e.g., computing the total cost of an automobile purchased on credit and comparing it with the price of purchasing the same vehicle without finance charges). Finally, students should be informed of the consequences of obligating too much monthly income to installment payments, as well as the consequences of failing to meet such obligations.

Purchasing goods and services

Since many students enrolled in special education settings are not likely to earn large salaries upon graduation from high school, it is important for them to learn how to obtain the greatest value for the income they do have. For this reason, students should learn how to make sensible purchases, how to shop for values, how to find and use coupons, and how to comparison shop. Lessons that could be taught in this area include the relative merit of generic "store" brands versus established brand names, as well as how to interpret misleading advertising (e.g., that a particular brand of toothpaste will make one more popular among peers).

Health and Fitness

Health and physical fitness are arguably among the most important concerns in any life skills curriculum. Instruction in health and fitness has three major components: an information component that communicates facts about health and fitness; an attitude component that strives to impress upon students the importance of health concerns so that the informational component will be implemented; and finally, development of habits of good health and fitness.

The most important information about good health is not difficult to learn; basic facts concerning regular checkups, proper diet, avoidance of alcohol and drugs, weight regulation, and regular exercise can be communicated in a few short lessons. Developing optimal attitudes about health and fitness can take much longer, however, and developing appropriate health habits is most difficult of all.

Appropriate attitudes toward fitness and health should be modeled by the teacher. Teachers who are themselves overweight, out of shape, or otherwise unhealthy due to personal negligence have little to say to their students concerning health habits. Teachers should practice good health habits and actively communicate the importance of doing so to their students. Information concerning the harmful effects of drugs, alcohol, and tobacco can be acquired from organizations such as the American Cancer Society and is best communicated by adult models who do not themselves abuse these substances. Finally, appropriate habits can be promoted by encouragement from physical education teachers and by support of exercise programs in the classroom settings. Teachers can help students conduct formative evaluation of their physical progress (e.g., number of chin-ups or times for running 400 meters) and encourage them to set personal goals and take personal satisfaction in meeting these goals. Encouragement and support of physical fitness helps to promote a positive attitude in the independent living environment.

Leisure Activities

Many students with mild disabilities are less able to enumerate options available to them than are their more average peers. This relative shortcoming applies as much to leisure activities as it does to employment options or living alternatives. Even though a basic function of school is to provide training relevant to the world of work, effective use of leisure time is also important in the development of the whole person. Some relevant information on leisure activities can be provided in academic classes (for example, promotion of reading for enjoyment provided in reading or English classes). Other options for leisure-time activities can be taught separately. Students should be taught about the various social, service, or athletic organizations that exist in a community and how to become a member of these organizations. Likewise, it may be profitable to acquaint students with community recreational facilities, such as public parks, lakes and swimming pools, and athletic facilities. Community organizations can alert the teacher to the variety of public facilities that are available for leisure activities. As is true of health and fitness, it is important to encourage the appropriate attitudes toward constructive leisure activities so that individuals actively pursue these activities as adults and do not resign themselves to television watching as their major leisure activity.

Some of the major concerns in life skills instruction have been outlined. Many additional related areas can be incorporated into a life skills curriculum. Related areas include personal identity and values clarification, dealing with conflict and disappointment, dating and marriage, home repairs, buying and using medicines, voting and political activity, and finding new friends. Which topics should be included in a life skills curriculum can be determined by interaction with guidance and administrative personnel, parent and teacher organizations, and community service personnel. Decisions concerning life skills curricula should be a function of the total school and community orientation toward such training (for example, some communities have very specific views concerning sex education in the schools). It is also important to determine what life skills are currently being taught in the existing regular education curriculum. As with content area and other types of instruction, care should be taken to ensure that (a) regular class instruction is not a preferable alternative and (b) the scope and sequence of life skills instruction parallels as closely as possible the special education objectives addressed in the regular classroom.

CAREER EDUCATION

A distinction is often made between *vocational* education, which is concerned with specific job-related training, and *career* education, which is concerned with a more general orientation to the world of work that can begin in elementary school. Although many different components could conceivably be included in a career-education curriculum, the following four major components will be considered here: (a) developing appropriate attitudes and habits related to work, (b) developing appropriate work-related social skills, (c) developing awareness of occupational alternatives, and (d) developing awareness of individual career preferences through career counseling and vocational assessment. Each component will be considered separately in the following sections.

Attitudes and Habits

It is important for every person to develop a positive attitude toward work in general and effective, goal-oriented work habits. Students in school should learn to work hard and take pride in their accomplishments. If their achievement or ability is below average in some areas, as is often the case in special education, students should nonetheless take pride in what they do achieve, as well as the amount of progress they are able to make. If these attitudes are thoroughly internalized with respect to school tasks during the school years, they are more likely to generalize to work-related tasks in the outside world.

It is difficult to influence attitudes and habits through direct instruction in individual lessons. Although students may be taught to recite the types of habits and attitudes that are desirable and linked to success, it is another matter altogether to adopt these attitudes and habits as their own, as reflected in classroom behavior. This process, which can take years, can be promoted through the establishment of a classroom atmosphere that, although warm and friendly, is nonetheless businesslike and achievement oriented. Students should be continually encouraged to put forth their best efforts and be rewarded for doing so. In many cases, student *performance* may not meet expectations, but students should be aware that their *level of effort* can *always* meet expectations. To this end, teacher praise for effort (e.g., "You should be proud of yourself for all the hard work you put into that assignment. Not everyone would have stuck with it the way you did") can be helpful. Such statements deliver a message to students that hard work and persistent efforts are valuable in and of themselves. On the other hand, it is equally important to recognize when students are not working up to their potential and to deliver appropriate feedback. In such cases, lower-than-expected effort should be acknowledged, and specific behaviors that the student can improve should be pointed out with statements such as "I am sorry to see that you didn't try very hard on that assignment. I noted you spent a lot of time looking out the window and going up to the pencil sharpener. I know you can do better work than this and that you can work much harder than you worked last period." It is important to end these statements on an encouraging note regarding higher expectations for the child. It is also important to note when the student is not working hard because the assignment is too difficult or is not clearly understood.

As students progress in school, they should be made as responsible as possible for their own work, since independent work will be expected of them on most jobs. Students who are used to teachers watching their every move will be poorly prepared for occupations in which the level of supervision is considerably less. If appropriate work habits and positive attitudes are encouraged throughout school, students are far more likely to be successful outside of school.

Social Skills

Research has indicated that individuals are much less likely to lose their jobs because of lack of ability or intelligence than they are to lose them because of a lack of appropriate job-related social skills. Employees who have good attitudes, good work habits, and good social skills are likely to be well liked by their employers. When they do exhibit performance deficits, they are likely to receive additional feedback or training. On the other hand, employees who exhibit poor work habits, bad attitudes, and poor social skills are not likely to be well liked by their employers. When such workers exhibit performance deficits, they are more likely to be fired, as often as not because these performance deficits can be used as an excuse to get rid of an unpopular employee.

There are several areas of appropriate job-related social skills instruction. Students should be encouraged to exhibit good interpersonal skills with their teachers as a prerequisite to exhibiting good social skills with their future employers. To this end, students should be encouraged to exhibit many of the same skills that effective teachers exhibit toward students; that is, students should learn to interact with teachers as individual human beings as well as teachers. Polite social conversation that acknowledges the teacher-student relationship can be helpful in promoting good interpersonal relations. Likewise, conversation and behavior that suggests that the student is considerate of the teacher's needs can help to develop an atmosphere in which teachers and students alike are more comfortable. Students who practice such behaviors have an advantage over students who do not; the same is true of employer–employee relationships. Although excessively attentive or obsequious behavior is generally not appreciated by employers or teachers, and peers do not respect a teacher's pet, students in special education classes often have the opposite problem. Some students are slow to realize that teacher–student relationships have as much to do with the student as they do with the teacher. The same will be true of employer–employee relations, so teachers are wise to point out and reinforce student behavior that facilitates teacher–student relations.

Another situation that is appropriate for job-related instruction is during the course of social skills training (see Chapter 10). As students approach the age at which they are likely to enter the job market, the relevance of social skills training to employment should be made explicit. Students can be taught to ask questions and show an interest in performing competently on their jobs. Additionally, students need to learn to ask for clarification when they do not understand directions. Many performance difficulties on the job site can be attributed to unclear or poorly understood directions. Jobs that are not well understood cannot be competently executed, so clarity in directions should be assured before the task is begun. Likewise, interpersonal skills with peers are also important, particularly since many jobs require cooperative effort. Asking for help, doing one's share, and acknowledging assistance (e.g., "thank you") are all important aspects of good peer relations on the job. Students should also be encouraged to use what they have learned about teasing, name-calling, and gossiping when they arrive on the job site. These behaviors are even less likely to be tolerated at work than they were at school. A possible table of specifications for job-related social skills is presented in Table 11.1.

Finally, job-related social skills can be promoted during any vocational instruction students receive in school. Employer–employee relations can be modeled through execution of assigned projects, and good peer relation can be stressed on projects that require cooperative effort. Again, appropriate social behaviors in classes can be stressed as being of at least equal importance as appropriate vocational skills.

Occupational Alternatives

Most of us, at one time or another, have been asked, "What do you want to do for a living?" or "What would you like to do when you grow up?" Children often answer with the occupations of a favorite adult or an occupation that appears glamorous on television. A mature and practical vocational decision, however, depends on careful consideration of occupational alternatives.

Students are unlikely to acquire this information on their own. Good career education includes systematic instruction in the many different types of employment available. Students should also be informed of which occupations are most widely represented in their immediate geographical area. As students grow older and learn more about their own interests and abilities, they are more likely to make informed career choices for themselves, based upon a thorough knowledge of career alternatives.

The school guidance counselor or staff development office should be able to supply information on occupational alternatives that can be transmitted to the class as factual information using instructional procedures

TABLE 11.1. Table of Specifications for Job-Related Social Skills.

CONTENT	BEHAVIOR				
	Identification	Production			
	A. Acquisition	B. Acquisition	C. Fluency	D. Application	E. Generalization
1. *Conversation* *skills* (1) with employer (2) with coworker (3) with customers	1(1)A 1(2)A 1(3)A	1(1)B 1(2)B 1(3)B	1(1)C 1(2)C 1(3)C	1(1)D 1(2)D 1(3)D	1(1)E 1(2)E 1(3)E
2. *Task-related* *skills* (1) asking for clarification (2) asking for assistance (3) volunteering to assist	2(1)A 2(2)A 2(3)A	2(1)B 2(2)B 2(3)B	2(1)C 2(2)C 2(3)C	2(1)D 2(2)D 2(3)D	2(1)E 2(2)E 2(3)E
3. *Personal* *appearance* (1) appropriate grooming (2) appropriate dress	3(1)A 3(2)A	3(1)B 3(2)B	3(1)C 3(2)C	3(1)D 3(2)D	3(1)E 3(2)E

Sample Objectives:

1(1)A Students will identify the scenarios that exhibit an employee having appropriate conversation skills with an employer 10 out of 10 times.

2(2)C Students will ask for assistance in completing job-related tasks as often as appropriate during all of the role-play scenarios.

3(1)E Students will come to work after they have showered and neatly combed their hair.

similar to those described earlier. In addition, adults from the community can be asked to come to class and describe their occupations to the students. As with any "community speaker" activity, it is important for the speaker, the teacher, and the students to understand the objectives of the activity and how those objectives will be evaluated. Asking the speaker to submit a brief outline of his or her presentation can give students some advance information on the topic.

Another source of information on occupations is through media presentations such as slide presentations, filmstrips, films, and videotapes. These may be available from the guidance counselor, school district office, or local library. Again, when these materials are used, it is important to specify the objectives beforehand.

A final consideration in teaching about career alternatives is that information should be cumulative; that is, student awareness of career alternatives should increase over time and not be forgotten. To facilitate cumulative recall, students can be required to compile a permanent record of career information (e.g., a career notebook in which information relevant to specific careers, students' notes, and information cut out from magazines or scrapbooks can be included). Such a notebook could be used for periodic review regarding career options. In addition, any new information that the student receives on a particular occupation can be inserted into the appropriate space on an ongoing basis.

Making Specific Career Choices

Aspects of career education covered to this point include development of appropriate work habits and attitudes, development of job-related social skills, and development of knowledge of career alternatives. This section discusses developing awareness of individual career preferences. Two important considerations in making career decisions are that such choices be *informed* and that they be realistic. Informed choice means that the individual is well aware not only of career alternatives but also of the specific demands of those particular careers. In addition to personal interest level, other aspects of particular career choices to be considered include level of salary, regularity, length of hours, working conditions including social as well as physical environment, and amount of training necessary. Students should be well-informed on all these aspects of specific careers before they are seriously considered.

Realistic choices refer to career choices for which the student shows potential ability and one for which sufficient employment demand exists. For example, many high school-age students may express a desire to be a professional athlete or musician. These choices may provide information regarding the student's perceived need for attention or popularity but in most cases reflect neither informed nor realistic choices. In order to make a realistic career choice, students must understand their own level of ability with respect to the choice as well as the general likelihood of obtaining employment in that particular field. Students can easily underestimate as well as overestimate their own level of ability, so some type of objective feedback can be helpful. Records of previous student performance in vocationally relevant courses, as well as performance on vocational aptitude tests, can be useful materials for providing this kind of feedback. Finally, published interest inventories can be used to clarify where students' general interests lie. As with any other tests, however, vocational aptitude and interest tests are only as useful as their reliability and validity data; that is, an interest inventory is reliable when a high correlation (at least .70 or .80) is found over time. This means that if a student expresses interest in animal husbandry, this interest should also be apparent 2 weeks later (reliability). Likewise, if a vocational aptitude test discriminates between people with high versus low aptitude for automobile mechanics, the test maker should supply data that indicates that persons scoring high on this test become better automobile mechanics than persons scoring low on this test (validity).

Most schools employ counselors whose job, in part, is to help students make informed and reasonable career choices. It is important for special education teachers to work closely with these personnel to ensure that each student makes informed and reasonable career choices. One possible avenue to career decisions is encouraging students to find related employment on either a part-time basis after school hours or as part of a work–study program incorporated into the school day. Although it is unlikely that students will be able to find exactly the type of employment they are interested in, they may find employment that shares some common characteristics. For example, if a career they are considering involves a good deal of contact with the public, students may find part-time employment that involves contact with the public and then evaluate their reactions to this aspect of their career alternative.

VOCATIONAL EDUCATION

Vocational education is usually taken to mean direct training in career-related skills. Students are taught the skills they will use in their chosen field. Typical vocational areas include carpentry and construction, automotive repair, metalwork, electricity, and drafting. These areas of instruction require well-equipped instructional settings and trained instructors who are proficient in the vocational skills being taught.

Vocational instruction is often an area of difficulty for special education. Although many special education students can benefit from vocational instruction, relatively few special education teachers have extensive knowledge of vocational education. Likewise, few vocational education teachers have extensive knowledge of special education procedures. Nevertheless, special education teachers can do much to ensure that students receive high-quality, relevant vocational training. The section that follows focuses on issues of curriculum planning, instructional techniques, and placement and follow-up.

Curriculum Planning

One important consideration in planning vocational curricula is which vocational training area specific students should be placed in. As stated above, several techniques can be employed to help students identify vocational preferences. Special education teachers, however, should attempt to determine which skill areas are most likely to result in employment. This requires an evaluation of several factors. Are sufficient job opportunities available in the community? Many legitimate vocational skill areas are unlikely to result in employment unless the potential employee is prepared to move to another part of the country. For students who intend to continue to reside in the same geographical area after graduation, this is an important consideration. Information on the potential job market can be gathered by examining the classified section of the local newspaper, by contacting the local chamber of commerce, and by contacting potential employers.

Another consideration to be made in determining areas for vocational instruction is the level of competition for particular jobs. If employment exists but is highly competitive, students characterized as disabled may have difficulty obtaining employment even when adequately trained. It may be more practical to counsel students to enroll in training in areas that are less competitive. A final consideration involves evaluating the attitudes of potential employers toward individuals with mild disabilities. In many cases, employers are more than willing to make certain allowances (e.g., low reading ability or a slower rate of initial learning) in return for good work habits, positive attitudes, and good social skills. Other employers may be reluctant to make special allowances of any kind and may, in fact, be somewhat hostile to the idea of hiring workers with mild disabilities. In some cases, these attitudes can be changed, either through education or through provision of positive examples. In other cases, it may be wiser to look elsewhere for positive employment opportunities. It may be helpful to compile a notebook or other record of possible employment alternatives and add to it over time as more information is gained. In addition, previous successes can help with future placements. If employers have had successful experiences with mildly disabled individuals in the past, they are more likely to hire individuals from such programs in the future.

When potential employers and relevant vocational areas are identified, it is wise to consult with employers regarding the skills they value most and to ensure that these skills are included in the vocational curriculum. Specific training in these skills can increase the probability of later employment.

Vocational Instruction

If the special education teacher is qualified to provide instruction in one or more vocational areas, he or she may be the primary vocational skills instructor of special education students. However, it should first be determined that students cannot be taught effectively in a mainstream environment. In most cases, however, special education students are taught vocational skills by the vocational education teacher, and the special education teacher acts as a consultant. In this capacity, special education teachers should learn as much as possible about the areas being taught so that they can provide helpful feedback based on knowledge of special education as well as knowledge of particular students. If time permits, the special education teacher can work as an assistant in vocational skills classes to ensure success of their students. As a consultant, special education teachers can provide valuable information regarding instructional features such as careful task analysis, positive practice, behavioral contingencies, feedback and reinforcement, and formative evaluation, many of which may not be included as regular components of mainstream vocational instruction. In order to communicate effectively with the vocational education teacher, however, it is important for special education teachers to learn as much as possible about the vocational skills being taught.

If students exhibit persistent difficulties with particular vocational areas, additional teacher attention may be required. As with any other content area, teachers should carefully task-analyze the content, isolate the particular areas of difficulty, and provide additional instruction in those particular areas.

Many vocational texts and manuals are written beyond the reading levels of many students enrolled in special education. In these cases, materials can be supplemented with teacher-directed instruction and help with chapter outlines. Rewriting some sections in order to make them more readable and comprehensible to students may also help.

Often, students exhibit difficulty because they have failed to master important technical vocabulary. Almost any vocational area has its own unique terminology, and students who do not master this terminology will be unable to learn any new information that follows. Special education teachers can acquire a list of relevant vocabulary words from the vocational teacher and ensure that these words have been mastered. Additional teacher- or tutor-led drill and practice is likely to be beneficial. In some cases, use of the keyword mnemonic technique described earlier may prove helpful. In any case, teachers should ensure that students not only can define relevant vocabulary but also have made it part of their working vocabulary (e.g., in communicating with the vocational teacher).

Additionally, knowledge of specific facts is necessary for success in vocational areas. If such knowledge is not acquired efficiently, additional practice provided by teachers or tutors or the use of mnemonic techniques may be helpful.

Much of vocational learning is procedural in nature. If difficulty is noticed in mastering procedural aspects of vocational skills training, teachers can employ relevant teaching strategies: modeling, prompting, and evaluating student performance on each step in the task. If tasks involve a particularly long sequence of operations, teachers should introduce the task a few steps at a time and, as previously learned steps are mastered, gradually add additional steps. It should also be remembered that *application* of procedural information is necessary. For example, it is not sufficient for students to simply be able to recite the steps necessary to complete a particular assembly task. Ultimately, it will be necessary for students to actually execute these steps in the appropriate setting. To meet this objective, additional hands-on training may be necessary.

Placement and Follow-up

After students have learned specific vocational skills, appropriate job placement is necessary. In some cases, the training provided is really *prevocational* in that placement is into a vocational or technical school. Students will have been taught skills appropriate for this type of placement (for example, independent behaviors at work stations, appropriate social skills, and adequate levels of basic skills).

Regardless of the exact nature of the placement, the teachers need to determine that a specific placement is appropriate to the ability and skill level of the individual and that potential support services are available if problems arise. If time permits, teachers can include themselves as a potential resource. Openness and an honest appraisal of students' abilities can ensure that placement will be successful.

Once students graduate from school and obtain employment, they are no longer directly the responsibility of the school. However, periodic follow-up, either through mail, telephone, or personal visits, can ensure that placements are successful. Although teachers do not have the time or resources to make a major impact on outside placements, they can nonetheless evaluate sources of failure in placements and take steps to ensure that similar failures do not occur again. For example, if students are found to be lacking in specific skills, instruction on these skills can be included or intensified in the school curriculum in the future.

Finally, a notebook or other permanent record is helpful in documenting, over time, which placements have been most successful, along with probable reasons for success. Likewise, placements that were less successful can also provide useful information for future training and programming. Although special education teachers should not feel personally responsible for every failure, or success, of each student after he or she leaves the school, they should take some satisfaction in knowing that they did everything reasonably possible to promote success in their students' transition to adult life.

RELEVANT RESEARCH AND RESOURCES

Research and discussion in the area of transition have recently increased. In 1992, *Learning Disability Quarterly* devoted a special issue [15(4)] on employment of individuals with learning disabilities. Brown and Gerber (1992), Reiff and deFur (1992), and Mellard and Hazel (1992) discussed issues surrounding social competence and developing independence. Jacobs and Hendricks (1992) and Grossman (1992) addressed job opportunities. Zigmond (1990) presented issues surrounding a reconceptualization of secondary programs for students with learning disabilities, Okolo (1988) addressed environmental issues in vocational settings

(continues)

(Relevant Research and Resources continued)

for adolescents with mild disabilities, and Trapani (1990) discussed transition goals for adolescents with learning disabilities, including social competence, social skills, and secondary curriculum. Several researchers have addressed vocational assessment issues, including reliability and validity (Greenan & Browning, 1989; Rojewski & Greenan, 1992) and curriculum-based assessment for vocational education (Schloss, Smith, & Schloss, 1990). Grossman (1992) addressed legal issues surrounding employment for individuals with disabilities.

Knowles (1978) provided specific important information on potential life problems of the adult learner. Further information on career education in special education is found in Brolin (1978, 1982), Clark (1979), and Phelps and Lutz (1977). Many of these sources also provide information on vocational education. Bender, Brannan, and Verhoven (1984) wrote an informative text on leisure education. Additional information on several aspects of life skills instruction, career education, and vocational education, including assessment and evaluation, particularly as these areas apply to mildly mentally retarded students, can be found in Polloway, Payne, Patton, and Payne (1985) and Beirne-Smith, Coleman, and Payne (1986). Finally, Miller and Schloss (1983) provided a comprehensive text on career and vocational education for students with disabilities. Issue 6, Volume 9 (November/December, 1986) of *Remedial and Special Education* is devoted to employment issues.

A historical overview of transition and federally sponsored initiatives is described by Rusch and Phelps (1987). A statewide study of transition services for mildly disabled students is described by Benz and Halpern (1987). Interagency collaboration models for transition are provided by Johnson, Bruininks, and Thurlow (1987). Issues on transition are described by Edgar (1987) and Knowlton and Clark (1987).

Curricular Materials

Various curricular materials have been published in the area of daily living skills and transition. It is critical that teachers evaluate these materials, as materials range dramatically focusing on skills and levels for students with severe disabilities to those with mild disabilities. Bender and Valletutti (1982) published a curriculum guide for transition for adolescents. *How to Write for Everyday Living* and *Math for Everyday Living* are distributed by Educational Activities. *Vocational Entry-Skills for Secondary Students* is distributed by Academic Therapy, and *Get Set for Work!* is distributed by Marfex Associates. Opportunities for Learning distributes *Me and Jobs* and *Exploring Careers*, and the *Life Skills Workshop* is distributed by LinguiSystems. Finally, Cronin and Patton (1993) authored a guide for integrating life skills instruction into the curriculum for students with special needs.

Computer Software and Technology

Some of the technology mentioned in the social skills chapter (see Chapter 10) is suitable for teaching transition skills. Word-processing programs are avail-

(continues)

(Relevant Research and Resources continued)

able (see Chapter 6) and would also be helpful for teaching students transition skills. Finally, Microcomputer Educational Programs distributes software programs called <u>Filling Out Job Applications</u> and <u>Resumes Made Easy</u>. See Appendix B for a list of addresses of producers and distributors of software and curricular materials.

❖ ❖ ❖

CHAPTER 12

The Special Educator as a Consultant

THE PRECEDING CHAPTERS EMPHASIZED THE IMPLEMENTATION OF THE teacher-effectiveness variables in skill and content areas ranging from reading to social skills instruction. Research has demonstrated that teachers can make a great difference in student achievement when these instructional variables are consciously manipulated. Improving academic progress facilitates mainstreaming opportunities for special education students. There is, however, another equally important role that special educators must play, the role of the *consultant teacher*. Special educators need to develop exceptional interpersonal skills to effectively communicate with (a) parents, (b) regular educators, (c) building administrators, (d) school special services personnel (e.g., psychologist), and (e) community support personnel (e.g., probation officers, mental health workers). Additionally, many school districts have recently adopted service delivery models that require special educators not only to directly teach students with mild and moderate disabilities several hours a day, but also to consult and work with regular educators for the remainder of the school day. Both teaching and consulting skills are necessary for effective performance. Since these skills are essential for special educators to develop, this chapter is intended to present an overview of the special educator as a consultant. First, effective communication is discussed. Then, strategies for effective communication are presented, followed by current models of consultation.

EFFECTIVE COMMUNICATION

Any situation that requires interpersonal interactions necessitates the use of communication skills. The quality of the communication skills used determines whether or not the interactions are successful. Effective communication skills can be learned and practiced. Communication techniques can be subdivided into several areas, which are described in the next section.

Communication Techniques

Active listening

Whenever a teacher is communicating with another professional or parent, active listening is important. *Active listening* means sending messages that relay to the speaker that the listener is interested and concerned with trying to understand the message being conveyed. Active listening involves listener interaction with the speaker and provides the speaker with feedback of the listener's understanding. In order to do this, the listener must first understand the major message and demonstrate to the speaker that he or she is concerned by paying attention to the speaker. Maintaining eye contact with the speaker conveys that the listener is devoting attention and importance to the speaker and the topic of conversation. The type of body posture displayed by the listener is another nonverbal means of communicating active listening. A listener who leans toward the speaker would be interpreted as someone who is actively listening, while a listener who leans back and looks away from the speaker would be interpreted as someone not so concerned. Additionally, an active listener devotes all of his or her present attention to the speaker, rather than allowing distractions to interrupt the conversation. Finally, an active listener is able to summarize and restate the other person's major concerns.

Depersonalizing situations

Whenever a conversation occurs, it is critical to *depersonalize the situation* and orient conversation toward specific goals or possible solutions. In any conversation it is optimal to address the situation and not an individual's personality or character. For example, if a student arrives late to class, it is preferable to state, "It is better to arrive to class on time" than to say, "You are so lazy, you don't care about class. That's why you are late again." In a conversation with a parent of a child who has been delinquent in completing class and homework assignments, it is better to simply state the facts than to insult the child to the parent, to say, for example, "A number of class homework assignments have not been turned in this semester" rather than "Your child doesn't care about succeeding in my class or he would turn in his work on time." Depersonalization can change the focus of the conversation from negative comments toward an individual's personality to positive goal-oriented statements that may help solve the problem.

Identifying common goals

Another major purpose of special educators' conversations with parents, students, and regular educators is to identify common goals or objectives. A special educator can restate problems so that common objectives are seen. For example, during the parent conference mentioned above regarding a student who is obviously not succeeding, the teacher might identify the common goal as "*We both want* the best for your child. *We both* would like to see him succeed in school by passing all of his classes." Assume a similar scenario in which a special educator is at a meeting with the mainstreamed regular educator. The topic of conversation is a special education student, Ed, who has performed poorly on his regular classroom tests, and the regular educator is questioning the appropriateness of his mainstream placement. The special educator might summarize their common goal by saying, "We both would like to see Ed perform up to his potential." Summarizing the major goals is necessary prior to identifying solutions.

Devising systematic procedures for obtaining goals

Once common goals have been identified and mutually agreed upon, systematic steps for realizing those goals must be identified. At first, it is generally a good idea to brainstorm solutions; in this way, no value judgment is placed on the ideas. The special educator should attempt to elicit ideas by initiating statements such as, "What are some possible ways of doing this?" All possible options should be listed. For example, refer back to Ed's problem above and assume that the special educator said the following to the regular educator: "How do you think we should assist Ed in achieving his potential in your class?" The regular educator would need to identify positive possible solutions, such as "Perhaps if Ed completed some extra assignments or if he had one of the better students in my class tutor him . . . ." The special educator should also identify any other possible solutions. If all of the parties involved elicit ideas, the problem solving is shared, and several potential alternative solutions are defined.

Selecting the optimal solution

The next stage in effective communication is selection of the optimal solution. After all possible solutions to a problem have been identified, it is necessary to prioritize them by considering (a) the most likely to succeed and (b) ease of implementation. Some solutions can be rejected easily; others may need to be re-examined to determine their ultimate feasibility. In fact, it may be decided to try solution A first, since it requires the least amount of extra effort on everyone's part. However, if solution A does not yield the desired results within a specified time period, then solution B will be implemented. Finally, if solution B fails, solution C will be put into action. At this time it is also desirable to identify the individuals who will be responsible for specified components during each phase of implementation. Each solution can be briefly described and each individual's responsibilities listed. Additionally, potential initiation dates can be assigned to each potential option.

Summarizing the conversation

Finally, it is important to summarize the major points covered during the conversation. It is generally a good idea to (a) restate the major issues, (b) list the agreed-upon solutions, (c) reiterate the persons responsible for implementing the agreed-upon solutions, (d) restate what needs to be done, and (e) arrange a tentative follow-up time.

Generally, if the procedures described above are employed during meetings, effective communication will occur. These procedures can be effectively implemented during meetings with parents, students, regular educators, building administrators, or community service personnel. Figure 12.1 summarizes the major components of effective communication, and Figure 12.2 presents a sample scenario in which a special educator implements the principles of listening. Special educators are often confronted with problems similar to those described above and in Figure 12.2. If such issues are handled inappropriately, severe conflicts can arise that can result in breakdowns of effective communication. Ineffective communication can be extremely detrimental for special education and can greatly hinder efforts at facilitating mainstreaming. The next section presents some suggestions for ensuring effective communication with parents, regular educators, building administrators, and community personnel.

Body language	Direct eye contact.
	Upright posture, leaning forward slightly when seated.
	Maintaining attention.
Identify common goals	Direct conversation toward aspirations for the present and future, not frustration about the past.
	Define the ways in which teacher's goals are similar.
	Provide objective evidence when goals do not match.
Resolve disagreements	In objective terms, identify the exact source of the disagreement.
	Determine that both parties have access to the same information. If differences exist in the relative importance of information, provide additional objective information. If information is not credible to one party, search for additional verification.
	If all avenues have been attempted without agreement, "agree to disagree" on that particular issue and search for other points of agreement.
Set objectives and determine follow-up	Summarize the meeting with respect to stated objectives of the meeting.
	Identify tasks that must be completed for common goals and objectives to be met.
	Determine who will complete each task and set a date for completion.
	Set a time for follow-up meeting.

FIGURE 12.1. Strategies for effective communication.

Jeff, a high school special education student, has recently been main-streamed into Mr. Easton's regular education math class. Jeff storms into Mr. Halleran's (the special education teacher) room after school and the following discussion evolves:

> **Jeff:** I hate Mr. Easton, and I hate his math class. I am never going back there.
>
> **Mr. Halleran:** Now, Jeff, you sound upset. What happened to make you so upset?
>
> **Jeff:** Mr. Easton hates me, and he is unfair to me.
>
> **Mr. Halleran:** But what happened to make you feel this way?
>
> **Jeff:** Well, I did my homework and handed it in on time, but Mr. Easton failed me on it.
>
> **Mr. Halleran:** Why do you think you received a failing grade?
>
> **Jeff:** He said I didn't follow directions.
>
> **Mr. Halleran:** And did you follow his directions?
>
> **Jeff:** Yes, but he doesn't tell me what to do.
>
> **Mr. Halleran:** How could you find out what to do on your homework assignments?
>
> **Jeff:** I don't know. He hates me.
>
> **Mr. Halleran:** What do the other students do to find out homework directions?
>
> **Jeff:** I don't know; they ask, I guess.
>
> **Mr. Halleran:** I'll tell you what. Next time, you and I will talk to Mr. Easton together about his assignment, and we'll both make sure you know what you have to do.
>
> **Jeff:** OK.
>
> **Mr. Halleran:** And later, you will be able to ask him yourself.
>
> **Jeff:** OK.

FIGURE 12.2. An active listening scenario.

STRATEGIES FOR EFFECTIVE COMMUNICATION

Special educators play many roles throughout their work days. From the parents' viewpoint, the special educator is the expert and may even seem intimidating. In the regular educators' eyes, the special educator is viewed as a colleague who has equal status and position. Building administrators, on the other hand, see the special educator as one of their teachers who implements and abides by the school's policies and procedures. Special service administrators, such as school psychologists, tend to view the special educator as the one who implements IEPs. Community service personnel, such as local mental health center workers and probation officers, tend to see the special educator as a support service delivery person. Given the necessity of dealing with such a wide range of people and backgrounds, special educators must be able to adapt their communication styles to deal effectively with all of the above personnel. Communication strategies appropriate for use with each subgroup are presented in the following sections.

Communicating with Parents

Parents should be viewed as the special educator's primary source of support. Special educators must maintain regular contact with parents, and this open line of communication should be used primarily to disseminate news of students' positive progress. It is good practice to send home "happy grams" and "good day notes" on a regular basis to inform parents of their child's positive growth. It is bad practice to contact parents only when problems arise. Most parents will tend to be more supportive of the school's program if regular positive contact is maintained. Figure 12.3 displays an example of a positive note to a parent.

Many special educators have successfully established monthly parent support meetings. Regular meetings are used to inform parents of the program's goals and objectives, to enlist parental support of those goals and objectives, and to allow parents to meet one another. Some programs also feature different speakers at their monthly meetings. For example, one month the program might feature special techniques for implementing behavior-management plans at home; another session might focus on how

---

Dear Mr. and Mrs. Atwood:

Billy has had an especially good week in school. He has completed all his assignments on time, and he has had a very good attitude toward school.

Sincerely,

Ms. Westwater
Resource Teacher

FIGURE 12.3. Positive note to parents.

to implement appropriate teaching techniques at home; and the next session might feature a presentation on drugs and their effects. In most instances, parent groups have been very successful and have increased the special educator's communication with parents. Figure 12.4 presents a listing of possible topics to be discussed in parent group meetings.

It is valuable for special educators to establish cooperative work efforts with parents. Many times special educators want parents to do things at home to support the efforts undertaken at school. It is very likely that parents will be asked to do at least one of the following at home: (a) check assignment notebooks, (b) check to ensure homework completion, (c) provide additional guided drill and practice, (d) monitor regular class performance, (e) employ behavior-management contracts, and (f) reinforce positive school performance. When any or all of the above are desired, it is necessary to have effective and open communication with parents. When appropriate communication techniques are adhered to and common goals are established, parents will usually follow through and reinforce teaching activities.

Occasionally special problems arise in dealing with parents. If handled properly, these problems can usually be resolved. For example, assume that a parent has said that the special educator has been unfair to his or her child in assigning class grades. In this case, a meeting should be scheduled as soon as possible to show the parent that his or her concern is taken

Month	Topic	Speakers
September	Description of Granby's Resource Programs	Ms. M (High School Program) Ms. C (Junior High Program) Mr. S (Elementary Program)
October	Home tutoring in basic skill areas	Ms. M
November	Drug awareness	Dr. P
December	Behavior management	Ms. C
January	Interpreting test scores	Ms. M
February	Study skill strategies	Mr. S
March	Community support services	Mr. K
April	Vocational awareness	Ms. C
May	Summer placement options	Staff

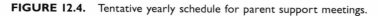

FIGURE 12.4. Tentative yearly schedule for parent support meetings.

seriously. At the meeting, the special educator should employ the active-listening techniques described earlier. Once the problem has been clearly identified, the special educator can refer to the formative evaluation data documenting the student's performance and progress to determine whether the expectations and grade assignments have been fair. Formative data can be shared with the parent to provide the necessary documentation of the student's grades, progress, or lack of progress. Usually, once such data are shared with parents, they have a better understanding of the attempts that are being made in school to assist their child.

Another problem that can occur in special education is lack of communication with parents. Some parents do not or cannot seem to make the time to attend parent conferences. Other parents have special concerns themselves, including financial difficulties, several other children, or being single parents. Whatever the reason, some parents seem unable to assist teachers by following through with behavior-management plans and/or tutoring activities at home or even by attending parent conferences. Special efforts should be made to maintain contact with these parents, even though they seem unable to reciprocate. Although the teacher may decide not to ask these parents to implement extra work at home, positive notes and phone calls should continue to inform them of their child's progress.

In summary, open lines of communication should be maintained with parents. Conversations with parents should be professional and directly relevant to special education activities. If additional social services are called for, teachers can recommend the services of professional organizations in the community, such as the local mental health center. It should be remembered that *special educators are trained as teachers* and not anything else.

Communicating with Regular Educators

Effective communication with regular educators is a necessary prerequisite for special education. With the recent emphasis on mainstreaming efforts it is mandatory for special and regular educators to maintain open lines of communication. Special and regular educators should be viewed as parents sharing equal goals—those that will assist students in maximizing their potentials. The regular educator may have made the initial special education referral. By making that referral, the teacher said very clearly that the student did not seem able to maintain the level of performance necessary to succeed in his or her classroom. It is, therefore, critical to determine what prerequisite skills the regular educator considers necessary for success in that regular education classroom. Typically, necessary skills can be subdivided into several areas, including (a) social behavior standards, (b) academic survival and study skill standards, and (c) academic performance standards.

Determining Social Behavior Standards

Special educators need to determine the precise standards of social behavior that each regular educator uses to evaluate students. Although every school has guidelines for student behavior, individual teachers may interpret and implement those guidelines differently. For example, Ms. Walker, one fourth-grade teacher, might be exceptionally strict and consistent in implementing the school's rules. She might require students to be seated and prepared for first period prior to the actual ringing of the bell. Additionally, she might not allow any out-of-seat behavior or talking unless students first raise their hands for permission. Conversely, Mr. Levi, the other fourth-grade teacher, might not enforce the school's rules as strictly or as consistently. He may allow students to linger in the doorway and hall until the bell rings. He might also allow students to get up to sharpen pencils throughout his class. During class discussions, his students might be encouraged to speak out without raising their hands to be called upon. As can be seen from these two illustrations, the standards for acceptable social behavior can and do vary dramatically from teacher to teacher. Although regular education students may be able to discern these differences on their own, special education students may need explicit instruction in what standards of behavior are expected in each class. This problem is exacerbated at the secondary level when students may have as many as five to seven different teachers.

Special educators can, however, deal effectively with these differences in social behavior standards by communicating with regular educators. For instance, special educators can compile a listing of social behavior standards that are enforced by each regular educator. They might, for example, ask regular educators to complete a questionnaire on class rules similar to the one presented in Figure 12.5. This information allows special and regular educators to decide whether or not special education students can be successfully mainstreamed into those particular classes. If special education students can consistently meet the social behavior standards of a particular mainstream class, they will probably succeed in that class. If, however, students cannot meet those standards, they probably require further remediation and practice prior to being mainstreamed. In summary, special educators must determine the standards of social behavior for each regular classroom. Once these standards have been determined, both teachers can more effectively discuss realistic placement options for students.

Determining Academic Survival and Study Skills Standards

Special educators must also determine the acceptable standards for academic survival and study skills in each regular classroom—in other words, what academically related behaviors students need in order to be successful in each regular classroom. For instance, Mr. Juarez might expect

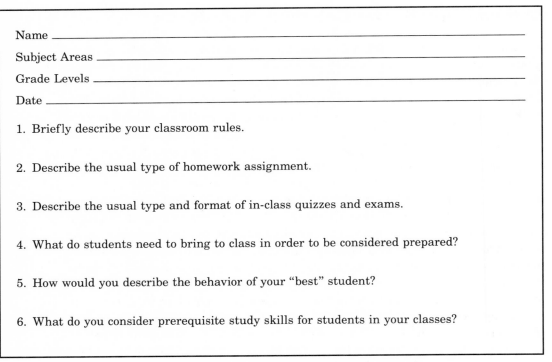

Name _____

Subject Areas _____

Grade Levels _____

Date _____

1. Briefly describe your classroom rules.

2. Describe the usual type of homework assignment.

3. Describe the usual type and format of in-class quizzes and exams.

4. What do students need to bring to class in order to be considered prepared?

5. How would you describe the behavior of your "best" student?

6. What do you consider prerequisite study skills for students in your classes?

FIGURE 12.5. Survey of regular educators to determine class rules and expectations.

students to (a) be prepared for class by bringing writing materials including a pen and pencil, (b) bring a three-ring notebook with dividers and folders for organizing all handouts and assignments, (c) hand in all assignments on time, (d) participate in class discussions by volunteering answers and asking relevant questions, and (e) appear interested in the topics by maintaining eye contact, sitting up straight, and paying attention in class. Ms. Hanson, on the other hand, has extra pencils available for students, accepts late assignments, never asks to see students' notebooks, and does not have a class-participation component to her grading system. These two examples illustrate the wide variance in the degree of organization and survival skills in different classrooms. Again, it is necessary for special educators to determine what the particular standards are in each teacher's classroom. Once the standards and expectations are clearly understood, both teachers will be better able to communicate effectively. Special educators can compile a list of these standards using methods similar to those described for standards of social behavior.

Determining Academic Performance Standards

It is also critical for special educators to determine the standards used to evaluate academic performance in regular classrooms. These standards can also vary dramatically from teacher to teacher and subject area to subject area. Some teachers may use textbooks that have an especially difficult reading level; others may use texts that are written on lower levels. Some teachers may require additional outside reading and research reports, while others require only successful performance on in-class examinations. More importantly, the types of examinations administered by different teachers can require very different types of studying behavior. Some teachers may administer only identification-format tests that require students to select answers from multiple-choice formats. Other teachers may require sentence-completion and essay items that force students to produce the answers in writing. The type of questions typically asked by some teachers may be factual recall items that require students to use associative-learning strategies, or the type of questions used might require students to apply learned information to novel instances.

Determining particular standards and requirements for each academic area enables special educators to have more effective, open communication with regular educators. Again, this information could be gathered from survey questionnaires or through individual meetings and conferences with teachers.

In summary, once special educators have clearly identified each regular educator's standards in social behavior, academic survival skills, and academic performance areas, they will be better able to carry on effective communication.

Special Problems

Special educators have reported some common problems that tend to cause breakdowns in communication with regular educators. Since these problems usually can be circumvented, they are presented in this section to demonstrate that, if special educators use the effective communication skills described earlier, they may be able to avoid some of the following problems that, if not avoided, will make communication difficult.

1. *Generalization problems.* Special educators feel that their students are ready to be mainstreamed when they appear to have mastered all of their instructional objectives. Many times, however, when these students are returned to the mainstream settings, they fail again. This failure can be attributed to the student's failure to *generalize* learned skills and behaviors to new settings and situations. If this occurs, two problems arise. First, the regular education teacher becomes frustrated since he or she was told the student was ready for the class. Second, the student becomes frustrated with the situation. In order to circumvent these problems, special educators need to teach using the table of specifications model presented throughout this text. Recall that the last two cells along the behavioral axis are *application* and *generalization* instructional objectives. When application and generalization objectives have been instructed and mastered, special education students are more likely to succeed.

2. *Curriculum discrepancy problems.* Many times special educators begin instructing students with materials not used by regular educators. Using different materials can be very beneficial. Recall that Chapter 5 emphasized the use of code-emphasis reading series with many special education students. However, prior to mainstreaming the students back into the regular classroom, special educators should begin to use the same materials that are used in the regular classrooms. Otherwise, students will not have had the opportunity to be taught the material covered in the regular education curriculum. Consequently, students may fail due to the discrepancy in the curriculum materials used rather than due to their skills and abilities. If, for example, the regular classroom teacher is using a "whole language" approach to language and literacy development, the special education teacher must ensure that students have sufficient independent skills to function in such a class and have been provided with successful practice using the same type of activities used in the regular classroom.

3. *Inappropriate placement.* Occasionally, the special education student is mainstreamed into an inappropriate placement. If this occurs, communication between the regular and special educators will be strained. Inappropriate placements may be due to one of many things, including (a) class level, (b) class size, (c) student capabilities, or (d) inappropriate instructional materials or procedures. Placement decisions are often difficult to make. Sometimes, the exceptionally good regular educator is "rewarded" by being the recipient of *all* of the special education students being mainstreamed. This situation can be very detrimental to teacher morale. Therefore, some placement decisions made by building administrators may address teacher needs rather than student needs. At times, these placement decisions seem inappropriate for particular students. However, if this occurs, special educators should still attempt to maintain open lines of communication with regular educators.

4. *Inadequate independent skills.* Regular education teachers typically expect very high levels of independence from students, and many times the recently mainstreamed students do not possess adequate independence. When this occurs, effective communication is threatened. However, if special educators meet with these teachers and use the active-listening principles, realistic goals and objectives that will ultimately assist the student in the mainstreaming efforts can be established.

5. *Inadequate knowledge about regular classroom standards.* As mentioned previously, lack of knowledge about standards in regular education can be especially problematic for special educators. Communication efforts will be threatened if both regular and special educators do not have a clear understanding of the standards required for success in the classroom. Special educators should try to keep track of those standards using some of the ideas presented earlier.

This section has presented some of the more commonly encountered problems that can interfere with effective communication between regular and special educators. Many of these problems can be avoided. It is recom-

Strategy	Appropriate Use
Regular communication	With regular educators
	With student
	With parents
Teaching generalization	Across settings
	Across skills
	Across situations
Using gradual mainstreaming	One period a day at first
	Slowly increase amount of time spent in regular classroom
Formative evaluation	Maintenance of progress data
	Clear instructional decision making
Teacher-effectiveness variables	Maximizing time-on-task
	Teaching to objectives
	Using relevant activities

FIGURE 12.6. Circumventing mainstreaming difficulties.

mended that special educators learn as much as possible about the standards for success in education programs, as well as the specific scope and sequence and curriculum materials used. Once they know this information, special educators are better equipped to facilitate mainstreaming efforts with their students. Figure 12.6 presents a summary of suggestions to circumvent potential communication breakdowns between special and regular classroom educators.

Effective Communication With Other Personnel

The special educator must use the principles described earlier in dealing with all other relevant personnel, ranging from building administrators to community support personnel. Building administrators can often greatly facilitate communication efforts for special education teachers. In-service programs can be established to explain the entire continuum of special education services to all educators, allowing regular educators to learn about the processes involved in special education and the shared team-effort approach required to educate these students. After participation in such programs, regular educators have a better understanding of what special educators do. This understanding usually helps communication efforts later on.

Communication With Students

Finally, it is of utmost importance for special educators to use effective communication with special education students. All of the principles described in this chapter can be applied to communication efforts with the students. This is especially true at the secondary level. Students at this level typically participate in their IEP meetings and in their meetings with related service personnel such as psychologists and counselors. The special educators who are most successful tend to apply the same communication skills with their special education students.

For instance, if a student seems to have a problem, the successful educator will use active-listening principles to determine the nature of the problem and to show concern for the student. It is also important to specify objectives for meeting the student's goals and to determine how they will be met. Finally, the student and teacher must agree on what is to be done and who will do it, and a follow-up meeting should be scheduled to determine whether the objectives have been met.

In another instance, a particular student may be having problems with a mainstream class teacher because of tardiness. The special education teacher should employ active listening to determine the student's point of view and to communicate concern. The teacher should show the student that both teacher and student want that student to do well and not get into trouble in school. Next, meeting objectives should be discussed—in this case, procedures for arriving to class on time. Perhaps the teacher can help identify the source of the problem (transportation, distance between classes, social exchanges with other students, avoidance, etc.) and suggest means for overcoming the problem. Finally, the necessary steps for solving the problem should be specified, and a follow-up meeting should be scheduled to ensure that objectives have been met. Although it is important to listen to students' problems, it is also necessary for teachers to adopt a strict problem-solving attitude in such situations. Simply venting anxieties or frustrations is not likely to be helpful unless problems are identified and solutions are attempted. To this end, keeping a written record of problems expressed, solutions proposed, and follow-up evaluations can be valuable, whether the problem is tardiness, homework completion, fighting, or personal animosity with specific teachers.

CONSULTATION TEACHER MODELS

This section presents several consultation models currently being implemented by school districts and universities. The first is a prereferral model, which operates on the assumption that a consulting teacher can assist regular educators in designing interventions so that students may not even need to be referred for special education services. The second and third models are presently being implemented in teacher training programs. The final model relies on the sharing of the teacher-effectiveness variables that have been emphasized throughout this text.

Prereferral Consultation Models

Some researchers have proposed alternatives to the system of service delivery currently used in special education classrooms. For example, Graden, Casey, and Christenson (1985) proposed that a prereferral intervention model be used as an alternative to traditional service delivery systems. This particular model uses six stages, the first four of which rely on consultation implemented prior to a formal referral step. Stage one is the request for consultation and consists of an informal process whereby the referring teacher requests problem-solving assistance from a consultant. This consultant is typically the building special education teacher. Stage two is the phase during which the initial consultation occurs. The goals of the consultation are (a) to identify the problem in objective and measurable terms, (b) to analyze the problem in terms of current performance and desired performance, (c) to design and implement an intervention plan, and (d) to evaluate the intervention. Both the referring teacher and consultant work collaboratively on each of the above steps.

Stage three is implemented if stage two is unsuccessful. The purpose of stage three is to collect extensive observational data on the student and characteristics of his or her classroom and peers. Based on the accumulated data, the observer and teacher meet again to design more extensive interventions. Following this, a meeting is scheduled with the student, parents, and teacher to discuss the new intervention, and, finally, the intervention is implemented.

Stage four is put into action if stage three is unsuccessful. During stage four, a child-study team convenes to share information on all of the behaviors and interventions implemented to date. Based on these data, the child-study team can make one of the following decisions: (a) continue the recently implemented intervention, (b) alter the current intervention, or (c) refer the child for assessment and possible special education services.

The fifth and final stage is the implementation of the formal referral process. At this time, all of the previously obtained data is used to assist in selecting assessment devices. Graden, Casey, and Bonstrom (1985) provided some initial data to support this model. Their results indicated that, in four of six schools, many teachers did use the consultation stage, and formal referrals for special education services decreased. It is thought that using this type of consultation model opens lines of communication between regular and special educators.

More recently, Fuchs, Fuchs, and Bahr (1990) used multidisciplinary "mainstream assistance teams" to create and implement prereferral intervention strategies.

University-Based Consultation Models

Several universities have implemented teacher training programs designed to prepare consulting teachers. Most of the models share similar components and rely on a behavioral orientation. For example, a preparation program for consulting teachers that specifically trained teachers in the process and content of consultation was developed at the University of Illinois. Problem-solving and communication skills were emphasized as process skills, while empirically based interventions, such as direct instruction and generalization training, were emphasized as components of the content. (See Idol-Maestas [1983] for a more complete description of the program.) The University of Vermont offered a similar consulting teacher training program. Their model emphasized the interaction of the consultant, the regular educator, and the targeted student. Consultants were trained to facilitate problem solving with regular educators and to assist regular educators in identifying optimal intervention strategies. (See Paolucci-Whitcomb & Nevin [1985] for a complete description of the program.) Many consulting teacher programs are being implemented at other universities as well, and many school districts have included some consultation time in job descriptions for prospective resource teachers. The most essential skills for these consultants are those identified from the research on teacher effectiveness that was described in Chapter 1. A brief summary of some of the variables that influence teacher effectiveness is presented in the next section.

Effective Teaching Skills

The effective skills for teaching and consulting can be subdivided into three broad categories: (a) classroom management, (b) organization of instruction, and (c) teacher presentation skills. Recall that good classroom management is a necessary prerequisite of effective teaching. Consulting teachers may be able to assist regular educators in identifying procedures to deal more effectively with classroom management. Regular educators can also benefit from ideas on maximizing the amount of engaged time on academic tasks, as well as the teacher presentation variables such as (a) daily review; (b) clear presentation of goals and objectives; (c) models, demonstrations, and corrective feedback; (d) guided and independent practice; (e) formative evaluation; and (f) weekly and monthly reviews.

INCLUSION MODELS

Recently, some professionals and advocates have proposed *inclusion* models of service delivery for students with disabilities. Although there are many different descriptions of exactly what is meant by inclusion, the general notion is that students with disabilities are served completely within the regular classroom and special education teachers serve as consultants and support personnel. Inclusion models recently have been implemented in specific locations throughout the country.

The present authors have maintained throughout this book that successful functioning in mainstream environments is the ultimate goal of special education. Nevertheless, we are supportive of the variety of educational services made possible by federal law in the Individuals with Disabilities Education Act (Public Law 101–476) (U.S. Department of Education, 1992), and we are concerned to see that in some schools, different educational settings for service delivery are not considered service options. It seems certain that the regular classroom is not the best service alternative in *every* instance; in fact, when direct comparisons have been made based on specific performance data, students with mild disabilities have generally learned better in special education settings (Fuchs, Fuchs, & Fernstrom, 1993; Marston, 1987–1988; Rudenga, 1992). Further, surveys of special and regular education teachers (e.g., Semmel, Abernathy, Butera, & Lesar, 1991), surveys of students with mild disabilities (Jenkins & Heinen, 1989), and observational studies of students with mild disabilities (Rudenga, 1992) have indicated that students and school personnel alike prefer having the resource room or special education classroom as a placement option. Parents of students with mild disabilities also have expressed satisfaction with current placement and service delivery options (Singer & Butler, 1987) and have expressed concerns about inclusive schools (Carr, 1993). Finally, analyses of existing regular education classrooms (Baker & Zigmond, 1990) and of the ability and willingness of regular education teachers to modify and adapt curriculum and teaching methods (Jenkins & Leicester, 1992) suggest that many of these environments are not optimal for students with mild disabilities. It is also true that several states do not require any special education coursework for "regular" teacher certification, and this lack of professional preparation may be an important consideration.

It is also important to note that virtually all professional organizations concerned with students with mild disabilities have issued statements expressing support for resource rooms and special education classrooms as placement options, even while emphasizing the desirability of regular class placements when warranted (Learning Disabilities Association of America, 1993; Council for Learning Disabilities, 1993; Division for Learning Disabilities, 1993; National Joint Committee on Learning Disabilities, 1993; and Council for Children with Behavior Disorders, 1993). It is important and necessary to continue to examine service delivery alternatives in special education. Nevertheless, in most cases, students were referred initially for special education services because adequate learning did not occur in the regular classroom. When inclusion models are employed, school personnel must collect evidence that individual students are meeting important IEP objectives optimally in the regular class setting. Inclusion is a positive option only if it can be demonstrated that students with disabilities are learning critical academic, social, and life skills optimally in these environments.

RELEVANT RESEARCH AND RESOURCES

Some suggestions for active-listening techniques are provided by Ginott (1972). Information about influencing generalization between classrooms is given by Mastropieri and Scruggs (1984a); Scruggs and Mastropieri (1984a); and Ellis, Lenz, and Sabornie (1987). Developing consultation models in special education is described by Reisberg and Wolf (1986), Idol-Maestas (1983), Paolucci-Whitcomb and Nevin (1985), Friend (1984, 1985), Cook and Friend (1991) and Friend and Cook (1992). Issue 6, Volume 9 (1988) of *Remedial and Special Education (RASE)* is devoted to school consultation practice. Alternative delivery models are described in *RASE* Volume 10, Issue 6 (November/December 1989) and Volume 11, Issue 1 (January/February 1990). In addition to the references cited within this chapter, Volume 11, Issue 3 (May/June 1990) of *RASE* is devoted to inclusion issues. Debate concerning these issues is ongoing. Detailed recommendations for adapting instruction in mainstream settings are offered in Mastropieri and Scruggs (1993); Graden, Casey, and Christenson (1985); and Graden, Casey, and Bonstrom (1985). Information on dealing with parents is discussed by Turnbull and Turnbull (1978). The need for interdisciplinary cooperation is emphasized by results of meta-analysis on medication presented by Kavale and Nye (1983) and by intervention models presented by Hewett and Forness (1984). Information on working with parents is in Gordon (1974a, 1974b, 1978).

Forness and his colleagues presented procedures for bridging the gap between school psychologists and special educators (Forness & Kavale, 1987; Forness, 1970, 1981, 1982; Sinclair, Forness, & Alexson, 1985). Johnson and Johnson (1975, 1983, 1984) and Johnson, Johnson and Holubec (1991) presented suggestions on arranging cooperative learning situations.

Curricular Materials, Computer Software and Technology

Recently, curricular materials and supporting videotapes have been published in the area of consultation and collaboration. Most of these materials are intended for teachers and teacher trainers. PRO-ED distributes *Effective Instruction of Difficult-to-Teach Students: An Inservice and Preservice Professional Development Program for Classroom, Remedial, and Special Education Teachers, Collaboration in the Schools: An Inservice and Preservice Curriculum for Teachers, Support Staff, and Administrators* (includes video component), *Teaching: A Venture in Problem Solving* (a videotape program), *What I Need to Know About Special Education: Answers for Parents and Professionals, Special Educator's Consultation Handbook, The Educational Consultant: Helping Professionals, Parents, and Mainstreamed Students*, and *Conferencing Parents of Exceptional Children*. Fuchs, Fuchs, Reeder et al. (1989) wrote *Mainstream Assistance Teams: A Handbook on Prereferral Intervention*. Longman publishes *Interactions: Collaboration Skills for School Professionals*. Finally, it is recommended that teachers use data base software programs and word-processing software programs to document their consultation activities. See Appendix B for a list of addresses of producers and distributors of software and curricular materials.

CHAPTER 13

❖ ❖ ❖

Epilogue

IN THIS BOOK, WE HAVE ATTEMPTED TO DESCRIBE THE BEST PRACTICES IN special education as supported by recent research. Research suggests that teachers can and do make a great difference in the degree to which their students are able to succeed. Some overall suggestions that will, we hope, be implemented by teachers, regardless of the type of instructional setting, include the following.

1. *Teach directly to relevant objectives.* These objectives should be derived from IEPs and should reflect skills students need to reenter the mainstream or a less restrictive environment.

2. *Maximize engaged time-on-task.* Teachers should use all means at their disposal to provide as much engaged, teacher-directed interaction as possible with students in areas that are directly relevant to instructional objectives.

3. *Include the "PASS" variables.* Remember to prioritize objectives; to adapt instructional procedures, curriculum materials, and the environment; to use the "SCREAM" variables; and to systematically monitor progress.

4. *Provide relevant guided and independent practice activities.* When giving students practice activities, teachers should avoid assigning busy work and ensure that students work only on material that is directly relevant to educational objectives.

5. *Use formative evaluation techniques to monitor student progress toward prespecified goals and objectives.* Teachers should make frequent, ongoing assessment of learner progress toward meeting IEP objectives throughout the year and not wait for the end of the school year to determine whether or not instruction was effective.

6. *Modify instruction in response to outcomes of formative data.* Avoid an overly rigid approach to teaching. Do not be afraid to make changes in instructional procedures or materials if instructional objectives are not being met.

7. *Monitor transfer and generalization of learned skills.* Do not assume that students will automatically apply learned skills in new situations (very often they will not). Teach in such a way that students are able to benefit maximally from new skills they have learned.

8. *Make the classroom a positive and pleasant place to be.* Although research on teacher effectiveness has de-emphasized personality as an alterable variable, remember that enthusiasm, warmth, positive expectations, and display of sincere caring about the students are necessary to maximize success in the classroom. Teachers who are enthusiastic about teaching and concerned for the welfare of their students should make sure their students are aware of this. Teachers who are neither enthusiastic nor concerned should consider another profession.

9. *Make school work as meaningful and concrete as possible and encourage students to actively reason through all tasks.* Meaningfulness, concreteness, and active thinking are keys to success.

10. *Remember that acceptable performance in the mainstream is the final goal of special education.* Special education teachers should familiarize themselves with the expectations of the regular classroom and direct their teaching activities to helping their students meet these expectations. The degree to which students are able to return to mainstream settings is an important measure of the effectiveness of the special education teacher.

We also have presented a number of specific recommendations for effective teaching practices. However, it is difficult to include in one text anything approaching the total amount of information a teacher needs in order to deal with every situation that may arise. If teachers carefully attend to the 10 major recommendations we have listed above, we do feel that chances for overall success in the classroom will be very high.

Finally, we would like to stress the need for attention to further developments in the field of special education. Given the progress that has been made in recent years, our knowledge of optimal instructional practices is likely to increase in the future. In order to keep up with future trends and developments in the field, we encourage all practicing special education teachers to join a professional organization in their particular field of interest. Most of these organizations issue professional journals, which keep members informed on recent developments in their field, and sponsor conferences, which provide means for professionals to get together to exchange ideas. Such activities, we feel, are essential components of overall professional development and can help to ensure the continued application of effective instruction in special education.

❖ ❖ ❖

Individualized Education Program

Individualized Education Program

IEP MEETING DATE _____ September 24, 1993 _____

IEP FROM _____ September 24, 1993 _____ TO _____ June 3, 1994 _____

(1) Student	(2) Committee

NAME: Andrew Smith
SCHOOL: Brookfield Elementary
  Brookfield, Indiana
GRADE: Second
CURRENT PLACEMENT: Regular Class
DATE OF BIRTH: July 12, 1984
AGE: 9
	NAME POSITION SIGNATURE
	Rebecca Eash *Teacher* *Rebecca Eash*
	Dr. L. Victor *Psychologist* *L. Vior*
	Mr. R. Halleran *Special Ed.* *R. Halleran*
	  Teacher
	
	Mrs. Louise Smith *Parent* *Louise Smith*

(3) Present Level of Educational Functioning

Reading

1. *Letter/Sound Correspondence*
   When presented with 26 flash cards containing consonant and vowel letters, Andrew correctly said 10 consonant sounds and 2 vowel sounds (46% accuracy).

   > Letters correct: Consonant = b, c, f, h, k, m, r, s, t, w
   > Vowel = a, o

2. *"At" Words*
   When presented with 9 flash cards containing words that rhyme with "at," Andrew correctly read 5 of them without assistance (56% accuracy).

   > Words correct: bat, fat, hat, mat, sat
   > Words missed: at, cat, pat, rat

3. *Dolch Sight Words*
   When presented with 9 Dolch Sight Words, Andrew correctly read 4 of them without assistance (44% accuracy).

   > Words correct: is, I, a, it
   > Words missed: look, the, my, you, and

Math

1. *Numbers*
   When presented with a blank piece of paper and asked to write the numbers 1–21, Andrew correctly wrote 18 of them in 2 minutes 51 seconds (86% accuracy).

   > Numbers missed: 12, 17, 21

2. *Addition*
   When presented with a worksheet containing 10 addition facts $(1 - 5) + (1 - 7)$, Andrew correctly wrote answers to 3 of them in 1 minute 45 seconds (30% accuracy).

   > Problems correct: 0 + 1, 1 + 1, 2 + 2

(continues)

Individualized Education Program (continued)

(4) Annual Goal Statement	(5) Instructional Objectives	(6) Evaluation Procedures	Date Started	Date Completed
A. When given a short story from the second-grade basal (containing 500 words), Andrew will be able to orally read the story with 95% accuracy in 10 minutes.	1. When given 26 flash cards containing the letters of the alphabet, Andrew will say the name of the letter and the sound that letter makes, with 100% accuracy.	Responses recorded on a chart after each session.	9/24/93	10/20/93
	2. Andrew will be able to read CV and CVC words with 100% accuracy, e.g., at, bat, cat, fat, hat, mat, rat, sat, pat, pan, can, pot	Based on Andrew's ability to blend letter sounds together to form a word. Progress charted on a graph after each tutoring session.	10/8/93	11/12/93
	3. When given flash cards containing the following sight words, Andrew will read the word on each card with 100% accuracy. look, the, is, my, I, you, and, a, it, will, had, on, to, saw, have	Based on Andrew's ability to recall words by sight. Responses recorded on a chart.	Set 1 10/8/93 Set 2 11/5/93	11/19/93
	4. Andrew will be able to read CVCe words with 100% accuracy.	Based on same criteria as the CV and CVC words.	11/12/93	
	5. When given a list of 15 sentences containing sight words and phonetically regular VC, CVC, and CVCe words, Andrew will be able to read the sentences in 5 minutes with 5 or less errors.	Check ability to read and pronounce words correctly when in sentences.	11/12/93	

(continues)

Individualized Education Program (continued)

(4) Annual Goal Statement	(5) Instructional Objectives	(6) Evaluation Procedures	Date Started	Date Completed
A. *(continued)*	6. When given stories from the second-grade basal, Andrew will be able to orally read the stories, summarize the stories, and answer questions on what he read.	Check Andrew's ability to comprehend by asking reading comprehension and summary questions.	11/12/93	
B. Andrew will be able to compute 25 basic single math addition and story problems, using digits from 0–9, in 5 minutes.	1. Andrew will count the number of tokens placed on the table in front of him, with 100% accuracy.	Based on accuracy in counting.	10/8/93	11/19/93
	2. When given numbers between 0–9, Andrew will "count on" to 18 with 100% accuracy.	Based on accuracy of responding.	10/15/93	10/29/93
	3. When presented with 25 simple addition problems, Andrew will add each problem and write his answer down, in 4 minutes with 100% accuracy.	Based on accuracy and fluency.	10/15/93	12/3/93
	4. Andrew will demonstrate knowledge of the following math concepts: numeration, one-to-one correspondence, equivalence, and addition by manipulating relevant materials (e.g., blocks) with 100% accuracy.	Based on application tasks with manipulative materials.	10/8/93	12/3/93

(continues)

Individualized Education Program (continued)

(7) Educational Services To Be Provided

Services Required	Date Initiated	Duration of Service	Individual Responsible for the Service
Resource Room	September 24, 1993	June 3, 1994	Roy Halleran

Extent of Time in the Regular Education Program:
Andrew is capable of being placed in a regular class 80% of the time.

Justification of the Educational Placement:
Andrew will have the opportunity to improve his reading and math skills.

(8) I Have Had the Opportunity To Participate in the Development of the Individualized Education Program.

I AGREE WITH THE INDIVIDUALIZED EDUCATION PROGRAM   ☐

I DISAGREE WITH THE INDIVIDUALIZED EDUCATION PROGRAM   ☐

Parent's Signature

Publishers of Books, Tests, Curricular Materials, and Software

Academic Software
1415 Queen Anne Road
Teaneck, NJ 07666

Academic Therapy Publications
20 Commercial Boulevard
Novato, CA 94947

Adapt Press
808 Waven
Sioux Falls, SD 57104

Addison-Wesley Publishing
   Company
2725 Sand Hill Road
Menlo Park, CA 94025

AIMS Education Foundation
P.O. Box 7766
Fresno, CA 93747

Allied Education Council
P.O. Box 78
Galien, MI 49113

Allyn & Bacon
160 Gould Street
Needham, MA 02194

Alpha Resources Center
P.O. Box 70647
Washington, DC 20024

American Book Company
450 West 33rd Street
New York, NY 10001

American Educational Computer,
   Inc.
525 University Avenue
Palo Alto, CA 94303

American Guidance Service
4202 Woodland Road
P.O. Box 99
Circle Pines, MN 55014-1796

American Micro Media, Inc.
19 North Broadway
Red Hook, NY 12571

American Speech-Language-
   Hearing Association
9030 Old Georgetown Road
Washington, DC 20014

Ann Arbor Publishers
P.O. Box 338
Worthington, OH 43085

Apple Century Crofts
440 Park Avenue South
New York, NY 10016

Apple Computer, Inc.
10260 Bandley Drive
Cupertino, CA 95014

Argus Communications
P.O. Box 4000
One DLM Park
Allen, TX 75002

Aspen Publishers
7201 McKinney Circle
P.O. Box 990
Frederick, MD 21701

Association for Supervision and
   Curriculum Development
1250 North Pitt Street
Alexandria, VA 22314

Avant Garde Creations
P.O. Box 30160
Eugene, OR 97403

Barnell Loft
958 Church Street
Baldwin, NY 11510

Behavioral Research Laboratories
P.O. Box 577
Palo Alto, CA 94302

Bell and Howell
7100 McCormick Road
Chicago, IL 60645

Benefic Press
10300 West Roosevelt Road
Westchester, IL 60153

Biological Science Curriculum
Study
P.O. Box 930
Boulder, CO 80306

Bobbs-Merrill Company
4300 West 62nd Street
Indianapolis, IN 46206

Book Lab Inc.
1449 37th Street
Brooklyn, NY 11218

Borg-Warner Educational System
600 West University Drive
Arlington, VA 60004

Britannica Software
345 Fourth Street
San Francisco, CA 94107

Brøderbund Software, Inc.
17 Paul Drive
San Rafael, CA 94903-2101

Brookline Books
P.O. Box 1046
Cambridge, MA 02238

Brooks/Cole Publishing Co.
511 Forest Lodge Road
Pacific Grove, CA 93950

Brown Bag Software
2155 South Bascom
Suite 114
Campbell, CA 95008

C & C Software
5713 Kentford Circle
Wichita, KS 67220

Cambridge Development
Laboratory, Inc.
86 West Street
Waltham, MA 02154

Carolina Biological Supply
Company
2700 York Road
Burlington, NC 27215

Center for Multisensory Learning
Lawrence Hall of Science
University of California
Berkeley, CA 94720

Childcraft Education Corporation
20 Kilmer Road
Edison, NH 08817

Children's Press
5440 North Cumberland Avenue
Chicago, IL 60656

Claris
440 Clyde Avenue
Mountain View, CA 94043

Communication Skill Builders
3130 North Dodge Boulevard
Tucson, AZ 85733

Compu-Teach
78 Olive Street
New Haven, CT 06511

Computer Education
6438 West Glendale Avenue
Phoenix, AZ 85069

Continental Press
520 East Bainbridge Street
Elizabethtown, PA 17022

Council for Exceptional Children
1920 Association Drive
Reston, VA 22091

Creative Publications
5040 West 111th Street
Oak Lawn, IL 60453

Critical Thinking Press & Software
P.O. Box 448
Pacific Grove, CA 93950

Cross Educational Software
1802 North Trenton
P.O. Box 1536
Ruston, LA 71270

Cuisenaire Company of America
12 Church Street
New Rochelle, NY 10805

Curriculum Associates
5 Esquire Road
North Billerica, MA 01862-2589

Dale Seymour Publications
P.O. Box 10888
Palo Alto, CA 94303

Delta Education, Inc.
P.O. Box 915
Hudson, NH 03051-0915

Developmental Learning Materials
P.O. Box 4000
One DLM Park
Allen, TX 75002

Devereux Foundation Press
19 South Waterloo Road
Devon, PA 19333

Don Johnston Development
   Equipment
1000 Rand Road
Building 115
P.O. Box 639
Wauconda, IL 60084

Dormac
P.O. Box 752
Beavertown, OR 97075

EBSCO Curriculum Materials
Div. of EBSCO Industries, Inc.
Birmingham, AL 35201

Economy Company
1901 North Walnut Street
P.O. Box 25308
Oklahoma City, OK 73152

Edge Enterprises
P.O. Box 1304
Lawrence, KS 66045

Edmark Corporation
P.O. Box 3903
Bellevue, WA 98009

Education Development Center,
   Inc.
55 Chapel Street
Newton, MA 02160

Educational Achievement Systems
P.O. Box 7449
Delray Beach, FL 33484

Educational Activities
P.O. Box 392
Freeport, NY 11520

Educational Publishing Services
75 Moulton Street
Cambridge, MA 02138

Educational Resources
1550 Executive Drive
Elgin, IL 60123

Educational Teaching Aids
159 West Kinzie Street
Chicago, IL 60610

Edusoft
P.O. Box 2560, Dept. 50
Berkeley, CA 94702

Edu-Ware Services
28035 Dorothy Avenue
Agouna, CA 91301

Encyclopedia Britannica
   Educational Corporation
310 South Michigan Avenue
Chicago, IL 60604

Fearon Janus Quercus
500 Harbor Boulevard
Belmont, CA 94002

Fisher-Price Toys
East Aurora, NY 14052

Follett Publishing Company
1010 West Washington Boulevard
Chicago, IL 60607

Gamco Industries, Inc.
P.O. Box 310R8
Big Spring, TX 79721-1911

Ginn and Company
191 Spring Street
Lexington, MA 02173

Grune and Stratton
111 Fifth Avenue
New York, NY 10003

H & H Enterprises
946 Tennessee
Lawrence, KS 66044

Harcourt Brace Jovanovich
6277 Sea Harbor Drive
Orlando, FL 32821

Harper & Row
10 East 53rd Street
New York, NY 10022

Hawthorne Educational Services
P.O. Box 7570
Columbia, MO 65205

D.C. Heath and Company
125 Spring Street
Lexington, MA 02173

Heinemann
70 Court Street
Portsmouth, NH 03801

Holt, Rinehart, and Winston
301 Commerce Street
Fort Worth, TX 76102

Houghton Mifflin
13400 Midway Road
Dallas, TX 75244

Hubbard
P.O. Box 104
Northbrook, IL 60062

Humanities Software
P.O. Box 950
408 Columbia
Hood River, OR 97031

Huntington Computing
P.O. Box 1297
Corcoran, CA 93212

Idea Factory
10710 Dixon Drive
Riverview, FL 33569

Ideal School Supply Company
11000 South Lavergne Avenue
Oak Lawn, IL 60453

Incentive Publications
6 East 43rd Street
Nashville, TN 37212

Initial Teaching Alphabet
    Publications
6 East 43rd Street
New York, NY 10017

Innovative Learning Concepts, Inc.
6760 Corporate Drive
Colorado Springs, CO 80919-1999

International Business Machines
    (IBM) Corporation
1133 Westchester Avenue
White Plains, NY 10601

Institute for Research in Learning
    Disabilities
P.O. Box 972
Lawrence, KS 66045

International Reading Association
800 Barksdale Road
Newark, DE 19711

Janus Books
2501 Industrial Parkway West
Hayward, CA 94545

Jastak Associates
1526 Gilpin Avenue
Wilmington, DE 19806

Lakeshore Lifeskills
2695 East Dominguez Street
P.O. Box 6261
Carson, CA 90749

Lawrence Hall of Science
University of California
Berkeley, CA 94720

The Learning Company
4370 Alpine Road
Portola Valley, CA 94025

Learning Concepts
2501 North Lamar Boulevard
Austin, TX 78705

Learning Resources
151 South Pfingsten Road
Unit M
Deerfield, IL 66015

Learning Systems
P.O. Box 9046
Fort Collins, CO 80525

Learning Well
200 South Service Road
Roslyn Heights, NY 11577

LEGO Systems, Inc.
555 Taylor Road
Enfield, CT 06082

LinguiSystems
3100 4th Avenue
P.O. Box 747
East Moline, IL 61244

J.B. Lippincott Company
East Washington Square
Philadelphia, PA 19105

Little Bee Educational Programs
P.O. Box 262
Massilon, OH 44648

Little Brown and Company
34 Beacon Street
Boston, MA 02108

Longman
95 Church Street
White Plains, NY 10601

Love Publishing Company
177 South Bellaire Street
Denver, CO 80222

Macmillan Publishing Company
866 Third Avenue
New York, NY 10022

Marfex Associates
90 Cherry Street
P.O. Box 519
Johnston, PA 15907

McGraw-Hill Book Company
1221 Avenue of Americas
New York, NY 10020

MECC
6160 Summit Drive North
Minneapolis, MN 55430-4003

Media Materials
1821 Portal Street
Baltimore, MD 21224

Charles E. Merrill Publishing
1300 Alum Creek Drive
Columbus, OH 43216

Microcomputer Educational
  Programs
157 South Kalamazoo Mall
Suite 250
Kalamazoo, MI 49007

Microsystems Software
600 Worcester Road
Framingham, MA 01701

Milton Bradley Company
74 Park Street
Springfield, MA 01101

MindPlay
82 Montvale Avenue
Stoneham, MA 02180

Mindscape
3444 Dundee Road
Northbrook, IL 60062

Modern Curriculum Press
13900 Prospect Road
Cleveland, OH 44136

National Education Association
  Publications
1201 16th Street
Washington, DC 20036

National Gardening Association
180 Flynn Avenue
Burlington, VT 05401

National Geographic Society
17th and M Street NW
Washington, DC 20036

National Science Resources Center
Smithsonian Institution
Arts and Industries Building
Room 1201
Washington, DC 20560

National Science Teachers
  Association
1742 Connecticut Avenue
Washington, DC 20009

National Wildlife Federation
1412 16th Street NW
Washington, DC 20036

Open Court Publishing Company
1039 Eighth Street
P.O. Box 599
LaSalle, IL 61301

Opportunities for Learning, Inc.
20417 Nordhoff Street
Chatsworth, CA 91311

Optical Data Corporation
30 Technology Drive
Warren, NJ 07059

Orton Dyslexia Society
8415 Bellona Lane
Towson, MD 21204

Prentice-Hall
Englewood Cliffs, NJ 07632

PRO-ED
8700 Shoal Creek Boulevard
Austin, TX 78757-6897

Project Wild
1416 9th Street
Sacramento, CA 95814

Psychological Corporation
555 Academic Court
San Antonio, TX 78204

Putnam Publishers
200 Madison Avenue
New York, NY 10016

Random House
201 East 50th Street
New York, NY 10022

Reader's Digest Services
Educational Division
Pleasantville, NY 10570

Research Press
P.O. Box 9177
Champaign, IL 61826

Scholastic
2931 East McCarty Street
P.O. Box 7502
Jefferson City, MO 65102

Science and Technology for
  Children
National Science Resources Center
Smithsonian Institution
Arts and Industries Building
Room 1201
Washington, DC 20560

Science Research Associates (SRA)
Macmillan/McGraw-Hill
P.O. Box 543
Blacklick, OH 43004-0543

Scott, Foresman and Company
1900 East Lake Avenue
Glenview, IL 60025

Simon & Schuster
P.O. Box 2987
New York, NY 10185

Software Publishing Corporation
1901 Landings Drive
Mountain View, CA 94039-7210

Spinnaker
One Kendall Square
Cambridge, MA 02139

Steck-Vaughn Co.
8701 North MoPac Expressway
Austin, TX 78759

Summit Learning
P.O. Box 493F
Fort Collins, CO 80522

Sunburst Communications
101 Castleton Street
Pleasantville, NY 10570-3498

Teachers College Press
1234 Amsterdam Avenue
New York, NY 10027

The Teacher's Laboratory, Inc.
214 Main Street
P.O. Box 6480
Brattleboro, VT 05301-6480

Video Discovery, Inc.
1700 Westlake Avenue North
Suite 600
Seattle, WA 98109-3012

Western Psychological Services
Publishers and Distributors
12031 Wilshire Boulevard
Los Angeles, CA 90025

WINGS for Learning/Sunburst
 Communications
1600 Green Hills Road
P.O. Box 660002
Scotts Valley, CA 95067-0002

Words + Inc.
P.O. Box 1229
Lancaster, CA 93534

WordPerfect Corporation
1555 North Technology Way
Orem, UT 84057

References

Adams, M. J. (1990). Beginning to read: Thinking and learning about print. Cambridge, MA: M.I.T. Press.

Ager, C. L., & Cole, C. L. (1991). A review of cognitive-behavioral interventions for children and adolescents with behavioral disorders. *Behavioral Disorders, 16,* 276–287.

Algozzine, B., & Meheady, L. (Eds.). (1986). In search of excellence: Instruction that works in special education classrooms [Special issue]. *Exceptional Children, 52*(6), 484–590.

Alley, G., & Deshler, D. (1979). *Teaching the learning disabled adolescent: Strategies and methods.* Denver: Love Publishing.

Alverman, D. E. (1983). Putting the textbook in its place—your students' hands. *Academic Therapy, 18*(3), 345–351.

Amerikaner, M., & Summerline, M. L. (1982). Group counseling with learning disabled children: Effects of social skills and relaxation training on self-control and classroom behavior. *Journal of Learning Disabilities, 15,* 340–346.

Anderson, L. M., Evertson, C. M., & Brophy, J. E. (1979). An experimental study of effective teaching in first-grade reading groups. *Elementary School Journal, 79,* 193–223.

Anderson, L. M., Evertson, C. M., & Emmer, E. T. (1980). Dimensions in classroom management derived from recent research. *Journal of Curriculum Studies, 12,* 343–346.

Anderson, M. G. (1992). The use of selected theatre rehearsal technique activities with African-American adolescents labeled "behavior disordered." *Exceptional Children, 59,* 132–140.

Arter, J. A., & Jenkins, J. R. (1977). Examining the benefits and prevalence of modality considerations in special education. *The Journal of Special Education, 11,* 281–298.

Atkinson, B. (1983). Arithmetic remediation and the learning disabled adolescent: Fractions and interest level. *Journal of Learning Disabilities, 16,* 403–407.

Bacon, E. H., & Carpenter, D. (1989). Learning disabled and nondisabled college students' use of structure in recall of stories and text. *Learning Disability Quarterly, 12,* 108–118.

Baker, J. G., Stanish, B., & Frazer, B. (1972). Comparative effects of a token economy in a nursery school. *Mental Retardation, 10,* 16–19.

Baker, J. M., & Zigmond, N. (1990). Are regular education classes equipped to accommodate students with learning disabilities? *Exceptional Children, 56,* 515–526.

Baker, T., Dixon, N. P., Englebert, B., Kahn, M., Siegel, B. L., & Wood, J. L. (1982). Mainstreaming minimanual: Ten steps to success. *Instructor, 91,* 63–66.

Barbe, W. B., Lucas, V. H., Hackney, C. S., Braun, L., & Wasylyk, T. M. (1984). *Zaner-Bloser handwriting: Basic skills and applications.* Columbus, OH: Merrill Publishing.

Baroody, A. J. (1989). *A guide to teaching mathematics in the primary grades.* Boston: Allyn & Bacon.

Baroody, A. J., & Hume, J. (1991). Meaningful mathematics instruction: The case for fractions. *Remedial and Special Education, 12,* 54–68.

Baumann, J. F. (1986). The direct instruction of main idea comprehension ability. In J. F. Baumann (Ed.), *Teaching main idea comprehension ability* (pp. 133–178). Newark, DE: IRA.

Beck, S., Matson, J. L., & Kazdin, A. E. (1983). An instructional package to enhance spelling performance in emotionally disturbed children. *Child and Family Behavior Therapy, 4,* 69–77.

Becker, W. C., Madsen, C. H., & Arnold, C. R. (1967). The contingent use of teacher praise in reducing behavior problems. *The Journal of Special Education, 1,* 287–307.

Beirne-Smith, M. (1991). Peer tutoring in arithmetic for children with learning disabilities. *Exceptional Children, 57,* 330–337.

Beirne-Smith, M., Coleman, L. J., & Payne, J. P. (1986). Career and vocational planning. In J. R. Patton, J. S. Payne, & M. Beirne-Smith (Eds.), *Mental retardation* (2nd ed., pp. 384–407). Columbus, OH: Merrill Publishing.

Bender, M., Brannan, S., & Verhoven, P. (1984). *Leisure education for the handicapped.* San Diego: College-Hill Press.

Bender, M., & Valletutti, P. J. (1982). *Teaching functional academics: A curriculum guide for adolescents and adults with learning problems.* Baltimore: University Park Press.

Benz, M. R., & Halpern, A. S. (1987). Transition services for secondary students with mild disabilities: A statewide perspective. *Exceptional Children, 53,* 507–513.

Berliner, D. C., & Rosenshine, B. V. (1977). The acquisition of knowledge in the classroom. In R. C. Anderson, E. J. Spiro, & W. E. Montague (Eds.), *Schooling and the acquisition of knowledge* (pp. 375–396). Hillsdale, NJ: Lawrence Erlbaum Associates.

Bickel, W. E., & Bickel, D. D. (1986). Effective schools, classrooms and instruction: Implications for special education. *Exceptional Children, 52*(6), 489–500.

Biddle, B. J., & Anderson, D. S. (1986). Theory, methods, knowledge and research on teaching. In M. C. Wittrock (Ed.), *Handbook of research on teaching* (3rd ed., pp. 230–252). New York: Macmillan Publishing.

Bierman, K. L., & Furman, W. (1984). The effects of social skills training and peer involvement on the social adjustments of preadolescents. *Child Development, 55,* 151–162.

Blackman, L. S., Burger, L. A., Tan, N., & Weiner, S. (1982). Strategy training and the acquisition of decoding skills in EMR children. *Education and Training of the Mentally Retarded, 17*(2), 83–87.

Blankenship, C. S. (1978). Remediating systematic inversion errors: Subtraction through use of demonstration and feedback. *Learning Disability Quarterly, 1,* 12–22.

Blankenship, C. S. (1986). Using curriculum-based assessment data to make instructional decisions. *Exceptional Children, 52,* 233–238.

Blankenship, C. S., & Baumgartner, M. D. (1982). Programming generalization of computational skills. *Learning Disability Quarterly, 5,* 152–162.

Bloom, B. S., Hastings, J. T., & Madaus, G. F. (1971). *Handbook on formative and summative evaluation of student learning.* New York: McGraw-Hill.

Bording, C., McLaughlin, T. F., & Williams, R. L. (1984). Effects of free time on grammar skills of adolescent handicapped students. *Journal of Educational Research, 77,* 312–318.

Borkowski, J. G., & Varnhagen, C. K. (1984). Transfer of learning strategies: Contrast of self-instructional and traditional training formats with EMR children. *American Journal of Mental Deficiency, 88*(4), 369–379.

Borkowski, J. G., Weyhing, R. S., & Carr, M. (1988). Effects of attributional retraining on strategy-based reading comprehension in learning disabled students. *Journal of Educational Psychology, 80*, 46–53.

Bos, C. S. (1982). Getting past decoding: Assisted and repeated readings as remedial methods for learning disabled students. *Topics in Learning and Learning Disabilities, 1*, 517–555.

Bos, C. S., & Anders, P. L. (1987). Semantic feature analysis: An interactive teaching strategy for facilitating learning from text. *Learning Disabilities Focus, 3*, 55–59.

Bos, C. S., & Anders, P. L. (1990a). Effects of interactive vocabulary instruction on the vocabulary learning and reading comprehension of junior-high learning disabled students. *Learning Disability Quarterly, 13*, 31–42.

Bos, C. S., & Anders, P. L. (1990b). Interactive teaching and learning: Instructional practices for teaching content and strategic knowledge. In T. E. Scruggs & B. Y. L. Wong (Eds.), *Intervention research in learning disabilities* (pp. 116–185). New York: Springer-Verlag.

Bottge, B. A., & Hasselbring, T. S. (1993). A comparison of two approaches for teaching complex, authentic mathematics problems to adolescents in remedial math classes. *Exceptional Children, 59*, 556–566.

Bower, G. H., & Hilgard, E. R. (1981). *Theories of learning* (5th ed.). Englewood Cliffs, NJ: Prentice-Hall.

Bridge, C. A., & Hiebert, E. H. (1985). A comparison of classroom writing practices, teacher's perception of their writing instruction, and textbook recommendations on writing practices. *The Elementary School Teacher, 86*, 155–172.

Brigham, F. J. (1992a). *Enhancing recall of information presented in maps by students with learning disabilities.* Unpublished doctoral dissertation, Purdue University, West Lafayette, IN.

Brigham, F. J. (1992b). Spatial learning and instruction of students with learning disabilities. In T. E. Scruggs & M. A. Mastropieri (Eds.), *Advances in learning and behavioral disabilities* (Vol. 7, pp. 57–85). Greenwich, CT: JAI Press.

Brigham, F. J., Bakken, J. P., Scruggs, T. E., & Mastropieri, M. A. (1992). Cooperative behavior management: Strategies for promoting a positive classroom environment. *Education and Training of the Mentally Retarded, 27*, 3–12.

Brigham, F. J., Scruggs, T. E., & Mastropieri, M. A. (1992). Teacher enthusiasm in learning disabilities classrooms: Effects on learning and behavior. *Learning Disabilities Research & Practice, 7*, 68–73.

Broden, M., Bruce, C., & Mitchell, M. A. (1970). Effects of teacher attention on attending behavior of two boys at adjacent desks. *Journal of Applied Behavior Analysis, 3*, 199–203.

Broden, M., Hall, R. V., & Mitts, B. (1971). The effect of self-recording on the classroom behavior of two eighth grade students. *Journal of Applied Behavior Analysis, 4*, 191–199.

Brolin, D. E. (Ed.). (1978). *Life-centered career education: A competency-based approach.* Reston, VA: Council for Exceptional Children.

Brolin, D. E. (1982). *Life-centered career education for exceptional children.* Reston, VA: Council for Exceptional Children.

Brophy, J. E. (1979). Teacher behavior and its effects. *Journal of Educational Psychology, 71*, 733–750.

Brophy, J. E. (1981). Teacher praise: A functional analysis. *Review of Educational Research, 51*, 5–32.

Brophy, J. E., & Good, T. L. (1986). Teacher behavior and student achievement. In M. C. Wittrock (Ed.), *Handbook of research on teaching* (3rd ed., pp. 328–375). New York: Macmillan Publishing.

Brown, A. L., Campione, J. C., & Barclay, C. R. (1979). Training self-checking routines for estimating test readiness: Generalization from list learning to prose recall. *Child Development, 50*, 501–512.

Brown, D. S., & Gerber, P. J. (1992). Introduction to special issue on employment. *Learning Disability Quarterly, 15*, 235–236.

Bruce, H. B., & Chan, L. K. S. (1991). Reciprocal teaching and transenvironmental programming: A program to facilitate the reading comprehension of students with reading difficulties. *Remedial and Special Education, 12*(5), 44–55.

Bryan, T. H., & Bryan, J. H. (1981). Some personal and social experiences of learning disabled children. In B. K. Keogh (Ed.), *Advances in special education: Socialization and influences on exceptionality* (pp. 146–186). Greenwich, CT: JAI Press.

Bulgren, J., Schumaker, J. B., & Deshler, D. D. (1988). Effectiveness of a concept teaching routine in enhancing the performance of LD students in secondary-level mainstream classes. *Learning Disability Quarterly, 11*, 3–17.

Bullock, J., Pierce, S., & McClelland, L. (1987). *Touch math: Teacher's manual.* Colorado Springs, CO: Touch Learning Concepts.

Bullock, J., Pierce, S., & McClelland, L. (1989). *Touch Math.* Colorado Springs, CO: Innovative Learning Concepts, Inc.

Calfee, R., & Drum, P. (1986). Research on teaching reading. In M. C. Wittrock (Ed.), *Handbook of research on teaching* (3rd ed., pp. 804–849). New York: MacMillan Publishing.

Canter, L. (1979). *Assertive discipline workshop leader's manual.* Los Angeles: Author.

Carlisle, J. F. (1993). Selecting approaches to vocabulary instruction for the reading disabled. *Learning Disabilities Research & Practice, 8*, 97–105.

Carman, R. A., & Adams, W. R. (1977). *Study skills: A student's guide for survival.* New York: John Wiley & Sons.

Carpenter, R. L. (1985). Mathematics instruction in resource rooms: Instruction time and teacher competence. *Learning Disability Quarterly, 8*, 95–100.

Carr, M. N. (1993). A mother's thoughts on inclusion. *Journal of Learning Disabilities, 26*, 590–592.

Cartledge, G., & Milburn, J. F. (1978). The cause of teaching social skills in the classroom: A review. *Review of Educational Research, 14*, 295–309.

Case, L. P., Harris, K. R., & Graham, S. (1992). Improving the mathematical problem solving skills of students with learning disabilities: Self-regulated strategy development. *Journal of Special Education, 26*, 1–19.

Cawley, J. (Guest ed.). (In press). Science education [Special issue]. *Remedial and Special Education.*

Cawley, J. F. (1984). *Developmental teaching of mathematics for the learning disabled.* Rockville, MD: Aspen.

Cawley, J. F., Fitzmaurice-Hayes, A. M., & Shaw, R. A. (1988). *Mathematics for the mildly handicapped.* Boston: Allyn & Bacon.

Chall, J. S., & Stahl, S. A. (1982). Reading. In H. E. Mitzel (Ed.), *Encyclopedia of educational research* (5th ed.). New York: Free Press.

Chan, L. K. S., Cole, P. G., & Morris, J. N. (1990). Effects of instruction in the use of a visual-imagery strategy on the reading comprehension competence of disabled and average readers. *Learning Disability Quarterly, 13*, 2–11.

Church, G., & Bender, M. (1989). *Teaching with computers! A curriculum for special educators.* Boston: Little Brown and Company.

Ciborowski, J. (1992). *Textbooks and the students who can't read them: A guide to teaching content.* Cambridge, MA: Brookline Books.

Clark, F. L., Deshler, D. D., Schumaker, J. B., Alley, G. R., & Warner, M. M. (1984). Visual imagery and self-questioning: Strategies to improve comprehension of written material. *Journal of Learning Disabilities, 17*, 145–149.

Clark, G. M. (1979). *Career education for the handicapped child in the elementary classroom*. Denver: Love Publishing.

Clay, M. M., & Watson, B. (1987). *Reading recovery book list*. Auckland, New Zealand: University of Auckland.

Coble, A. (1982). Improving math fact recall: Beating your own score. *Academic Therapy, 17*(5), 547–556.

Cohen, A. L., Torgesen, J. K., & Torgesen, J. L. (1988). Improving speed and accuracy of word recognition in reading disabled children: An evaluation of two computer variations. *Learning Disability Quarterly, 11*, 333–341.

Condus, M. N., Marshall, K. J., & Miller, S. R. (1986). Effects of the keyword mnemonic strategy on vocabulary acquisition and maintenance by learning disabled children. *Journal of Learning Disabilities, 19*, 609–613.

Connell, D. (1983). Handwriting: Taking a look at the alternatives. *Academic Theory, 18*, 413–420.

Cook, L., & Friend, M. (1991). Collaboration in school services for students with disabilities. *Preventing School Failure, 35*(4), 24–27.

Cook, S., Scruggs, T. E., Mastropieri, M. A., & Casto, G. C. (1985–86). Handicapped students as tutors: A meta-analysis. *The Journal of Special Education, 19*, 483–492.

Cooke, T. E., & Apolloni, T. (1976). Developing positive socio-emotional behavior: A study of training and generalization effects. *Journal of Applied Behavior Analysis, 9*, 65–78.

Cooper, J. D. (1981). *Measuring behavior* (2nd ed.). Columbus, OH: Merrill Publishing.

Council for Children with Behavior Disorders. (1993). *CCBD Newsletter November 1993*. Reston, VA: Author.

Council for Learning Disabilities. (1993). Concerns about the full inclusion of all students with learning disabilities in regular education classrooms. *Journal of Learning Disabilities, 26*, 594.

Cronin, M. E., & Patton, J. R. (1993). *Life skills instruction for all students with special needs: A practical guide for integrating real-life content into the curriculum*. Austin, TX: PRO-ED.

Cullinan, D., Lloyd, J., & Epstein, M. H. (1981). Strategy training: A structured approach to arithmetic instruction. *Exceptional Education Quarterly, 2*(1), 41–49.

Cummins, J. (1989). A theoretical framework for bilingual special education. *Exceptional Children, 56*, 111–119.

Darch, C., & Carnine, D. (1986). Teaching content area material to learning disabled students. *Exceptional Children, 53*, 240–246.

Deno, S. D. (1986). Curriculum-based assessment: The emerging alternative. *Exceptional Children, 52*, 219–232.

Deno, S. L., Marston, D., & Mirkin, P. (1982). Valid measurement procedures for continuous evaluation of written expression. *Exceptional Children, 48*, 368–371.

Deno, S. L., Mirkin, P. K., & Chiang, B. (1982). Identifying valid measures of reading. *Exceptional Children, 49*, 36–45.

Deshler, D. D., Alley, G. R., Warner, M. W., & Schumaker, J. B. (1981). Instructional practices for promoting skill acquisition and generalization in severe learning disabled adolescents. *Learning Disability Quarterly, 4*, 415–422.

Deshler, D. D., & Schumaker, J. B. (1990). *Learning strategies model* (training package). Lawrence: University of Kansas, Institute for Research in Learning Disabilities.

Devine, T. G. (1981). *Teaching study skills: A guide for teachers*. Boston: Allyn & Bacon.

DiGangi, S. A., & Maag, J. W. (1992). A component analysis of self-management training with behaviorally disordered youth. *Behavioral Disorders, 17*, 181–290.

DiGangi, S. A., Maag, J. W., & Rutherford, R. B., Jr. (1991). Self-graphing of on-task behavior: Enhancing the relative effects of self-monitoring on-task behavior and academic performance. *Learning Disability Quarterly, 14*, 221–230.

Division for Learning Disabilities. (1993). *Inclusion: What does it mean for students with learning disabilities?* Reston, VA: Author.

Donahue, M., & Bryan, T. (1983). Conversational skills and modeling in learning disabled boys. *Applied Psycholinguistics, 4*, 251–278.

Dowis, C. L., & Schloss, P. (1992). The impact of mini-lessons on writing skills. *Remedial and Special Education, 13*, 34–42.

Doyle, W. (1986). Classroom organization and management. In M. C. Wittrock (Ed.), *Handbook of research on teaching* (3rd ed., pp. 392–431). New York: Macmillan Publishing.

EBSCO Curriculum Materials. (1990). *IEP Generator*. Birmingham, AL: Author.

Edgar, E. (1987). Secondary programs in special education: Are many of them justifiable? *Exceptional Children, 53*, 555–561.

Ellis, E. S., Lenz, B. K., & Sabornie, E. J. (1987). Generalization and adaptation of learning strategies to natural environments: Part I, critical agents. *Remedial and Special Education, 8*, 6–20.

Engelmann, S., & Osborne, J. (1976). *DISTAR language: An instructional system*. Chicago: Science Research Associates.

Englert, C. S. (1983). Measuring special education teacher effectiveness. *Exceptional Children, 50*, 247–254.

Englert, C. S. (1984). Effective direct instruction practices in special education settings. *Remedial and Special Education, 5*, 38–47.

Englert, C. S. (1990). Unraveling the mysteries of writing through strategy instruction. In T. E. Scruggs & B. Y. L. Wong (Eds.), *Intervention research in learning disabilities* (pp. 186–223). New York: Springer-Verlag.

Englert, C. S., Culatta, B. E., & Hein, D. G. (1987). Influence of irrelevant information in addition word problems on problem solving. *Learning Disability Quarterly, 10*, 29–36.

Englert, C. S., Hiebert, E. H., & Stewart, S. R. (1985). Spelling unfamiliar words by an analogy strategy. *The Journal of Special Education, 19*, 291–306.

Englert, C. S., & Mariage, T. V. (1991). Making students partners in the comprehension process: Organizing the reading POSSE. *Learning Disability Quarterly, 14*, 123–138.

Englert, C. S., Raphael, T. E., Anderson, L. M., Anthony, H. M., & Stevens, D. D. (1991). Making strategies and self-talk visible: Writing instruction in regular and special education classrooms. *American Educational Research Journal, 28*, 337–372.

Etscheidt, S. (1991). Reducing aggressive behavior and improving self-control: A cognitive behavioral training program for behaviorally disordered adolescents. *Behavioral Disorders, 16*, 107–115.

Evers, W. L., & Schwartz, J. C. (1973). Modifying social withdrawal in preschoolers: The effects of filmed modeling and teacher praise. *Journal of Abnormal Child Psychology, 1*, 248–256.

Ferro, S. C., & Pressley, M. G. (1991). Imagery generation by learning disabled and average achieving 11- to 13-year-olds. *Learning Disability Quarterly, 14*, 231–239.

Ferster, C. B., & Skinner, B. F. (1957). *Schedules of reinforcement*. New York: Appleton-Century-Crofts.

Figueroa, R. A., Fradd, S. H., & Correa, V. I. (Guest Eds.). (1989). Meeting the multicultural needs of the Hispanic students in special education [Special issue]. *Exceptional Children, 56*(2).

Fisher, E. L., White, J. M., & Fisher, J. H. (1984). Teaching figurative speech. *Academic Therapy, 19*, 403–407.

Five, C. L. (1992). *Special voices*. Portsmouth, NH: Heinemann Educational Books.

Fleischner, J. E., Nuzum, M. B., & Marzola, E. S. (1987). Devising an instructional program to teach arithmetic problem-solving skills to students with learning disabilities. *Journal of Learning Disabilities, 20*, 214–217.

Ford, D., Evans, H. J., & Dworkin, L. K. (1982). Teaching interaction procedures: Effects upon the learning of social skills by an emotionally disturbed child. *Education and Treatment of Children, 5*, 1–11.

Forness, S. R. (1970). Educational prescription for the school psychologist. *Journal of School Psychology, 8*, 96–98.

Forness, S. R. (1981). Concepts of school learning and behavior disorders: Implications for research and practice. *Exceptional Child, 48*, 56–64.

Forness, S. R. (1982). Diagnosing dyslexia: A note on the need for ecologic assessment. *American Journal of Diseases of Children, 136*, 794–799.

Forness, S. R., & Kavale, K. A. (1987). De-psychologizing special education. In R. B. Rutherford, Jr., C. M. Nelson, & S. R. Forness (Eds.), *Severe behavior disorders of children and youth* (pp. 2–14). Boston: Little Brown and Company.

Forness, S. R., & MacMillan, D. L. (1972). Reinforcement overkill: Implications for the education of the retarded. *The Journal of Special Education, 6*, 221–230.

Franklin, M. E. (1992). Culturally sensitive instructional practices for African-American learners with disabilities. *Exceptional Children, 59*, 115–122.

Friend, M. (1984). Consulting skills for resource teachers. *Learning Disability Quarterly, 7*, 246–250.

Friend, M. (1985). Training special educators to be consultants: Considerations for developing programs. *Teacher Education and Special Education, 8*, 115–120.

Friend, M., & Cook, L. (1992). *Interactions: Collaboration skills for school professionals.* New York: Longman.

Fuchs, D., Fuchs, L. S., & Bahr, M. W. (1990). Mainstream assistance teams: A scientific basis for the art of consultation. *Exceptional Children, 57*, 128–139.

Fuchs, D., Fuchs, L. S., & Fernstrom, P. (1993). A conservative approach to special education reform: Mainstreaming through transenvironmental programming and curriculum-based measurement. *American Educational Research Journal, 30*, 149–177.

Fuchs, D., Fuchs, L. S., Reeder, P., Gilman, S., Fernstrom, P., Bahr, M., & Moore, P. (1989). *Mainstream assistance teams: A handbook on prereferral intervention.* Nashville, TN: Peabody College of Vanderbilt University, Department of Special Education.

Fuchs, L., Fuchs, D., Hamlett, C. L., & Ferguson, C. (1992). Effects of expert system consultation within curriculum-based measurement, using a reading maze task. *Exceptional Children, 58*, 436–450.

Fuchs, L. S. (1986). Monitoring among mildly handicapped pupils: Review of current practice and research. *Remedial and Special Education, 7*, 5–12.

Fuchs, L. S. (1987). Curriculum-based measurement or instructional program development. *Teaching Exceptional Children, 20*, 42–44.

Fuchs, L. S., Deno, S. L., & Marston, D. (1983). Improving the reliability of curriculum-based measures of academic skills for psychoeducational decision making. *Diagnostique, 8*, 135–149.

Fuchs, L. S., Deno, S. L., & Mirkin, P. K. (1984). The effects of frequent curriculum-based measurement and evaluation on pedagogy, student achievement, and student awareness learning. *American Educational Research Journal, 21*, 449–460.

Fuchs, L. S., & Fuchs, D. (1986a). Curriculum-based assessment of progress toward long- and short-term goals. *The Journal of Special Education, 20*, 69–82.

Fuchs, L. S., & Fuchs, D. (1986b). Effects of systematic formative evaluation: A meta-analysis. *Exceptional Children, 53*, 199–208.

Fuchs, L. S., Fuchs, D., Allinder, R. M., & Hamlett, C. L. (1992). Diagnostic spelling analysis within curriculum-based measurement: Implications for students with learning and behavioral disabilities. In T. E. Scruggs & M. A. Mastropieri (Eds.), *Advances in learning and behavioral disabilities* (Vol. 7, pp. 35–56). Greenwich, CT: JAI.

Fuchs, L. S., Fuchs, D., Hamlett, C. L., & Whinnery, K. (1991). Effects of goal line feedback on level, slope, and stability of performance within curriculum-based measurement. *Learning Disabilities Research & Practice, 6*, 65–74.

Fulk, B. J. M., & Mastropieri, M. A. (1990). Training positive attitudes: "I tried hard and did well!" *Intervention in School and Clinic, 26*(2), 79–83.

Fulk, B. J. M., Mastropieri, M. A., & Scruggs, T. E. (1992). Mnemonic generalization training for students with learning disabled adolescents. *Learning Disabilities Research & Practice, 7*, 2–10.

Gaffney, J. S. (1984). *LD children's prose recall as a function of prior knowledge, instruction, and context relatedness*. Unpublished doctoral dissertation, Arizona State University, Tempe.

Gagne, R. M. (1965). *The conditions of learning*. New York: Holt, Rinehart & Winston.

Gagne, R. M. (1970). *The conditions of learning* (2nd ed.). New York: Holt, Rinehart & Winston.

Gagne, R. M., & Briggs, L. J. (1974). *Principles of instructional design*. New York: Holt, Rinehart & Winston.

Gajria, M., & Salvia, J. (1992). The effects of summarization instruction on text comprehension of students with learning disabilities. *Exceptional Children, 58*, 508–516.

Galagan, J. E. (1986). Psychoeducational testing: Turn out the lights, the party's over. *Exceptional Children, 52*, 288–298.

Ganschow, L. (1984). Analyze error patterns to remediate severe spelling difficulties. *The Reading Teacher, 37*, 288–293.

Garnett, K. (1992). Developing fluency with basic number facts: Intervention for students with learning disabilities. *Learning Disabilities Research & Practice, 7*, 210–216.

Gaskins, I. W., Downer, M. A., Anderson, R. C., Cunningham, P. M., Gaskins, R. W., Schommer, M., & the teachers of the Benchmark School. (1988). A metacognitive approach to phonics: Using what you know to decode what you don't know. *Remedial and Special Education, 9*(1), 36–41.

Gaskins, I., & Elliot, T. (1991). *Implementing cognitive strategy training across the school: The Benchmark manual for teachers*. Cambridge, MA: Brookline Books.

Gerber, M. M. (1984). Techniques to teach generalizable spelling skills. *Academic Therapy, 20*, 49–58.

Gerber, P. J. (1992). Personal perspective—At first glance: Employment for people with learning disabilities at the beginning of the Americans-with-Disabilities-Act era. *Learning Disability Quarterly, 15*, 330–332.

Germann, G., & Tindal, G. (1986). An application of curriculum-based assessment: The use of direct and repeated measurement. *Exceptional Children, 52*, 244–265.

Gersten, R., & Dimino, J. (1993). Visions and revisions: A special education perspective on the whole language controversy. *Remedial and Special Education, 14*(4), 5–13.

Gersten, R., Woodward, J., & Darch, C. (1986). Direct instruction: A research-based approach to curriculum design and teaching. *Exceptional Children, 53*, 17–31.

Gettinger, M. (1984). Applying learning principles to remedial spelling instruction. *Academic Therapy, 20*, 41–47.

Gettinger, M., Bryant, N. D., & Fayne, H. R. (1982). Designing spelling instruction for learning-disabled children: An emphasis on unit size, distributed practice, and training for transfer. *The Journal of Special Education, 16*(4), 439–448.

Gickling, E. E., & Thompson, V. P. (1986). A personal view of curriculum-based assessment. *Exceptional Children, 2*, 205–218.

Ginott, H. G. (1972). *Teacher and child*. New York: MacMillan Publishing.

Giordano, G. (1984). Analyzing and remediating writing disabilities. *Journal of Learning Disabilities, 17*, 78–83.

Gleason, M., Carnine, D., & Vala, N. (1991). Cumulative versus rapid introduction of new information. *Exceptional Children, 57*, 353–358.

Glynn, E. L., Thomas, J. D., & Shee, S. M. (1973). Behavioral self-control of on-task behavior in an elementary classroom. *Journal of Applied Behavior Analysis, 6*, 105–113.

Goin, M. T., Peters, E. E., & Levin, J. R. (1986). *Effects of pictorial mnemonic strategies on LD students.* Paper presented at the International Council for Exceptional Children meeting, New Orleans.

Good, T. L., & Grouws, D. A. (1979). The Missouri mathematics effectiveness program. *Journal of Educational Psychology, 71*, 355–362.

Good, T. L., Grouws, D. A., & Ebmeier, H. (1983). *Active mathematics teaching.* New York: Longman Scientific & Technical.

Gordon, J., Vaughn, S., & Schumm, J. S. (1993). Spelling interventions: A review of the literature and implications for instruction for students with learning disabilities. *Learning Disabilities Research & Practice, 8*, 175–181.

Gordon, T. (1974a). *P.E.T.: Parent effectiveness training: The tested new way to raise responsible children.* New York: P.H. Wyden.

Gordon, T. (1974b). *Teacher effectiveness training.* New York: P.H. Wyden.

Gordon, T. (1978). *P.E.T. in action.* New York: Bantam Books.

Graden, J. L., Casey, A., & Bonstrom, O. (1985). Implementing a prereferral intervention system: Part II. The data. *Exceptional Children, 51*, 487–496.

Graden, J. L., Casey, A., & Christenson, S. L. (1985). Implementing a prereferral intervention system: Part I. The model. *Exceptional Children, 51*, 377–384.

Graham, S. (1982). Composition research and practice: A unified approach. *Focus on Exceptional Children, 14*, 1–16.

Graham, S. (1983). The effect of self-instructional procedures on LD students' handwriting performance. *Learning Disability Quarterly, 6*, 231–234.

Graham, S., & Harris, K. R. (1987). Improving compositional skills with self-instructional strategy training. *Topics in Language Disorders, 7*(4), 66–77.

Graham, S., Harris, K. R., MacArthur, C. A., & Schwartz, S. (1991). Writing and writing instruction with students with learning disabilities: A review of a program of research. *Learning Disability Quarterly, 14*, 89–114.

Graham, S., & MacArthur, C. A. (1991). Introduction: Research and practice in writing. *Learning Disabilities Research & Practice, 6,* 200.

Graham, S., MacArthur, C. A., Schwartz, S., & Page-Voth, V. (1992). Improving the composition of students with learning disabilities using a strategy involving product and process goal setting. *Exceptional Children, 58*, 322–334.

Graham, S., & Miller, L. (1979). Spelling research and practice: A unified approach. *Focus on Exceptional Children, 12*, 1–16.

Graham, S., & Miller, L. (1980). Handwriting research and practice: A unified approach. *Focus on Exceptional Children, 13*, 1–16.

Graves, A. W. (1986). Effects of direct instruction and meta-comprehension training on finding main ideas. *Learning Disabilities Research, 1*, 90–100.

Greenan, J. P., & Browning, D. A. (1989). Generalizable interpersonal relations skills for students with handicapping conditions: Are assessment strategies and procedures valid? *Journal for Vocational Special Needs Education, 11*(2), 23–28.

Greenwood, C. R., Hops, H., & Delquadri, J. (1974). Group contingencies for group consequences in classroom management: A further analysis. *Journal of Applied Behavior Analysis, 7*, 413–425.

Gresham, F. M. (1981). Social skills training with handicapped children: A review. *Review of Educational Research, 51*, 139–176.

Gresham, F. M. (1982). Misguided mainstreaming: The case for social skills training with handicapped children. *Exceptional Children, 48*, 422–433.

Gresham, F. M. (1984). Social skills and self efficacy for exceptional children. *Exceptional Children, 51*, 253–261.

Gresham, F. M., & Lemanek, K. L. (1983). Social skills: A review of cognitive-behavioral training procedures with children. *Journal of Applied Developmental Psychology, 4,* 239–261.

Griffey, Q. L., Zigmond, N., & Leinhardt, G. (1988). The effects of self-questioning and story structure on the reading comprehension of poor readers. *Learning Disabilities Research, 4*(1), 45–51.

Grimm, J. A., Bijou, S. W., & Parsons, J. A. (1973). A problem solving model for teaching remedial arithmetic to handicapped young children. *Journal of Abnormal Child Psychology, 1,* 26–39.

Grossman, P. D. (1992). Employment discrimination law for the learning disabled community. *Learning Disability Quarterly, 15,* 287–329.

Gurney, D., Gersten, R., Dimino, J., & Carnine, D. (1990). Story grammar: Effective literature instruction for high school students with learning disabilities. *Journal of Learning Disabilities, 23*(6), 335–342, 348.

Hachett, R. (1975). In praise of praise. *American Education, 11,* 11–15.

Hagen, R. A. (1983). Write right—or left: A practical approach in handwriting. *Journal of Learning Disabilities, 16,* 266–271.

Hallahan, D. P., Marshall, K. J., & Lloyd, J. W. (1981). Self-recording during group instruction: Effects on attention to task. *Learning Disability Quarterly, 4,* 407–413.

Hammill, D. D., & Larsen, S. (1978). *The test of written language.* Austin, TX: PRO-ED.

Hanover, S. (1983). Handwriting comes naturally? *Academic Therapy, 18,* 407–412.

Haring, N., Lovitt, T., Hansen, C., & Eaton, J. (1978). *The fourth R: Research in the classroom.* Columbus, OH: Merrill Publishing.

Harris, K. R., & Graham, S. (1992). *Helping young writers master the craft: Strategy instruction and self-regulation in the writing process.* Cambridge, MA: Brookline Books.

Haynes, M. C., & Jenkins, J. R. (1986). Reading instruction in special education resource rooms. *American Educational Research Journal, 23,* 161–190.

Hazel, J. S., Schumaker, J. B., Sherman, J. A., & Sheldon, J. (1982). Application of a group training program in social skills and problem solving to learning disabled and nonlearning disabled youth. *Learning Disability Quarterly, 5,* 398–408.

Heinisch, B., & Hecht, J. (1993). A comparison of six programs: Word prediction software. *TAM Newsletter, 8*(3), 4–9.

Hendrickson, J., Roberts, M., & Shores, R. E. (1978). Antecedent and contingent modeling to teach basic sight vocabulary to learning disabled children. *Journal of Learning Disabilities, 11,* 524–528.

Hewett, F. (1968). *The emotionally disturbed child in the classroom.* Boston: Allyn & Bacon.

Hewett, F., & Forness, S. R. (1984). *Education of exceptional children* (3rd ed.). Boston: Allyn & Bacon.

Higgins, T. S., Jr. (1982). A comparison of two methods of practice on the spelling performance of learning disabled adolescents (Doctoral dissertation, Georgia State University, Atlanta). *Dissertation Abstracts International, 43*(06), 4021B.

Hillocks, G., Jr. (1984). What works in teaching composition: A meta-analysis of experimental treatment studies. *American Journal of Education, 93,* 133–170.

Hine, M. S., Goldman, S. R., & Cosden, M. A. (1990). Error monitoring by learning handicapped students engaged in collaborative microcomputer-based writing. *Journal of Special Education, 23,* 407–422.

Houghton Mifflin. *Houghton Mifflin reading series.* (1976). Boston: Author.

Howell, K. W., & Kaplan, J. S. (1980). *Diagnosing basic skills: A handbook for deciding what to teach.* Columbus, OH: Merrill Publishing.

Howell, K. W., & Morehead, M. K. (1987). *Curriculum-based measurement for special and remedial education.* Columbus, OH: Merrill Publishing.

Hudson, P., Lignugaris-Kraft, B., & Miller, T. (1993). Using content enhancements to improve the performance of adolescents with learning disabilities in content classes. *Learning Disabilities Research & Practice, 8*, 106–126.

Hughes, C. A., Ruhl, K. L., & Misra, A. (1989). Self-management with behaviorally disordered students in school settings: A promise unfulfilled? *Behavioral Disorders, 14*, 250–262.

Hutchinson, N. (1993). Effects of cognitive strategy instruction on algebra problem solving of adolescents with learning disabilities. *Learning Disability Quarterly, 16*, 34–63.

Idol, L. (1987). A critical thinking map to improve content area comprehension of poor readers. *Remedial and Special Education, 8*, 28–40.

Idol-Maestas, L. (1983). *Special educator's consultation handbook.* Rockville, MD: Aspen.

Isaacson, S. L. (1984). Evaluating written expression: Issues of reliability, validity, and instructional utility. *Diagnostique, 9*, 96–116.

Isaacson, S. L. (1985a). *Assessing the potential syntax development of third and fourth grade writers.* Unpublished doctoral dissertation. Arizona State University, Tempe.

Isaacson, S. L. (1985b). Assessing written language skills. In S. Simon (Ed.), *Communication skills and classroom success: Assessment methodologies for language-learning disabled students* (pp. 403–424). San Diego: College-Hill Press.

Isaacson, S. L. (1987). Effective instruction in written language. *Focus on Exceptional Children, 19*(6), 1–12.

Jacobs, A. E., & Hendricks, D. J. (1992). Job accommodations for adults with learning disabilities: Brilliantly disguised opportunities. *Learning Disability Quarterly, 15*, 274–285.

Jenkins, J. R., & Gorrafa, S. (1974). Academic performance of mentally handicapped children as a function of token economics and contingency contracts. *Education and Training of the Mentally Retarded, 9*, 183–186.

Jenkins, J. R., & Heinen, A. (1989). Students' preferences for service delivery: Pull-out, in-class, or integrated models. *Exceptional Children, 55*, 516–523.

Jenkins, J. R., Heliotis, J. D., Stein, M. L., & Haynes, M. C. (1987). Improving reading comprehension by using paragraph restatements. *Exceptional Children, 54*, 54–59.

Jenkins, J. R., & Jewell, M. (1993). Examining the validity of two measures of formative teaching: Reading aloud and maze. *Exceptional Children, 59*, 421–432.

Jenkins, J. R., & Leicester, N. (1992). Specialized instruction within general education: A case study of one elementary school. *Exceptional Children, 58*, 555–563.

Jenkins, J. R., Stein, M. L., & Osborne, J. R. (1981). What next after decoding? Instruction and research in reading comprehension. *Exceptional Education Quarterly, 2*, 27–39.

Johnson, D. R., Bruininks, R. H., & Thurlow, M. L. (1987). Meeting the challenge of transition service planning through improved interagency cooperation. *Exceptional Children, 53*, 522–530.

Johnson, D. W., & Johnson, R. T. (1975). *Learning together alone: Cooperation, competition, and individualization.* Englewood Cliffs, NJ: Prentice-Hall.

Johnson, D. W., & Johnson, R. T. (1984). Building acceptance of differences between handicapped and nonhandicapped students: The effects of cooperative and individualistic instruction. *The Journal of Social Psychology, 122*, 257–267.

Johnson, D. W., Johnson, R. T., & Holubec, E. J. (1991). *Cooperation in the classroom* (rev. ed.). Edina, MN: Interaction Book Company.

Johnson, R. T., & Johnson, D. W. (1983). Effects of cooperative, competitive, and individualistic learning experiences on social development. *Exceptional Children, 49*, 323–329.

Kavale, K., & Nye, C. (1983). The effectiveness of drug treatment for severe behavioral disorders: A meta-analysis. *Behavioral Disorders, 9*, 117–130.

Kavale, K. A., & Forness, S. R. (1985). *The science of learning disabilities*. San Diego: College-Hill Press.

Kavale, K. A., & Forness, S. R. (1987). The far side of heterogeneity: A critical analysis of empirical subtyping research in learning disabilities. *Journal of Learning Disabilities, 20,* 374–382.

Kazdin, A. E., Esveldt-Dawson, K., & Matson, J. L. (1983). The effects of instructional set on social skills performance among psychiatric inpatient children. *Behavioral Therapy, 14,* 413–423.

Kendall, P. C., & Braswell, L. (1985). *Cognitive behavior therapy for impulsive children*. New York: Guilford Press.

Keogh, B. K. (Ed.). (1981). *Advances in special education: Socialization influences on exceptionality*. Greenwich, CT: JAI Press.

Kerr, M. M., & Nelson, C. M. (1983). *Strategies for managing behavior problems in the classroom*. Columbus, OH: Merrill Publishing.

Kiburz, C. S., Miller, S. R., & Morrow, L. W. (1984). Structured learning using self-monitoring to promote maintenance and generalization of social skills across settings for a behaviorally disordered adolescent. *Behavior Disorders, 10,* 47–55.

Kinder, D., & Bursuck, W. (1993). History strategy instruction: Problem-solution-effect analysis, timeline, and vocabulary instruction. *Exceptional Children, 59,* 324–335.

King-Sears, M. E., Mercer, C. D., & Sindelar, P. T. (1992). Toward independence with keyword mnemonics: A strategy for science vocabulary instruction. *Remedial and Special Education, 13,* 22–33.

Knowles, M. (1978). *The adult learner: A neglected species* (2nd ed.). Houston: Gulf Publishing.

Knowlton, H. E., & Clark, G. M. (1987). Transition issues for the 1990s. *Exceptional Children, 53,* 562–563.

Kosiewicz, M. M., Hallahan, D. P., Lloyd, J., & Graves, A. W. (1982). Effects of self-instruction and self-correction procedures on handwriting performance. *Learning Disability Quarterly, 5,* 71–78.

Lancioni, G. E. (1982). Normal children as tutors to teach social responses to withdrawn mentally retarded schoolmates: Training, maintenance, and generalization. *Journal of Applied Behavioral Analysis, 15,* 17–40.

Lanunziata, L. J., Jr., Hill, D. S., & Krause, L. A. (1981). Teaching social skills in classrooms for behaviorally disordered students. *Behavioral Disorders, 6,* 238–246.

Laufenberg, R., & Scruggs, T. E. (1986). Effects of a transformational mnemonic strategy to facilitate digit span recall of mildly handicapped students. *Psychological Reports, 58,* 811–820.

Learning Disabilities Association of America. (1993). Position paper on full inclusion of students with learning disabilities in regular education classes. *Journal of Learning Disabilities, 26,* 595.

Lee, P., & Alley, G. (1981). *Training junior high LD students to use a test-taking strategy* (Research Rep. No. 38). Lawrence: University of Kansas, Institute for Research in Learning Disabilities.

LeGreca, A. M., & Mesibov, G. B. (1981). Facilitating interpersonal functioning with peers and learning disabled children. *Journal of Learning Disabilities, 14,* 197–299.

Leinhardt, G., Zigmond, N., & Cooley, W. W. (1981). Reading instruction and its effect. *American Educational Research Journal, 18,* 343–361.

Lenz, B. K., Alley, G. R., & Schumaker, J. B. (1987). Activating the inactive learner: Advance organizers in the secondary content classroom. *Learning Disability Quarterly, 10,* 53–68.

Lenz, B. K., Bulgren, J., & Hudson, P. (1990). Content enhancement: A model for promoting the acquisition of content by individuals with learning disabilities. In T. E. Scruggs & B. Y. L. Wong (Eds.), *Intervention research in learning disabilities* (pp. 122–165). New York: Springer-Verlag.

Lenz, B. K., & Hughes, C. A. (1990). A word identification strategy for adolescents with learning disabilities. *Journal of Learning Disabilities, 23*(3), 149–158, 163.

Leon, J. A., & Pepe, H. J. (1983). Self-instructional training: Cognitive behavior modification for remediating arithmetic deficits. *Exceptional Children, 50,* 54–60.

Levin, J. R., Dretzke, B. J., McCormick, C. B., Scruggs, T. E., McGivern, J. E., & Mastropieri, M. A. (1983). Learning via mnemonic pictures: Analysis of the presidential process. *Educational Communication and Technology Journal, 3,* 161–173.

Levin, J. R., Morrison, C. R., McGivern, J. E., Mastropieri, M. A., & Scruggs, T. E. (1986). Mnemonic facilitation of text-embedded science facts. *American Educational Research Journal, 23,* 489–506.

Lewis, R. B. (1983). Learning disabilities and reading: Instructional recommendations from current research. *Exceptional Children, 50,* 230–240.

Lifson, S., Scruggs, T. E., & Bennion, K. (1984). Passage independence in reading achievement tests: A follow-up. *Perceptual and Motor Skills, 58,* 945–946.

Liton, L., & Pumroy, D. K. (1975). A brief review of classroom group-oriented contingencies. *Behavior Research and Therapy, 8,* 341–347.

Lloyd, J., Cullinan, D., Heins, E. D., & Epstein, M. H. (1980). Direct instruction: Effects on oral and written language comprehension. *Learning Disability Quarterly, 3,* 70–76.

Lloyd, J., Saltzman, N. J., & Kauffman, J. M. (1981). Predictable generalization in academic learning as a result of preskills and strategy training. *Learning Disability Quarterly, 4,* 203–216.

Lloyd, J. W., & Landrum, T. (1990). Self-recording of attending to task: Treatment components and generalization of effects. In T. E. Scruggs & B. Y. L. Wong (Eds.), *Intervention research in learning disabilities* (pp. 235–262). New York: Springer-Verlag.

Loomes, B. M. (1982). *The most commonly asked questions about spelling . . . and what the research says.* North Billerica, MA: Curriculum Associates.

Lovitt, T., Rudsit, J., Jenkins, J., Pious, C., & Benedetti, D. (1985). Two methods of adapting science materials for regular and learning disabled seventh graders. *Learning Disability Quarterly, 8,* 275–285.

Lovitt, T., Rudsit, J., Jenkins, J., Pious, C., & Benedetti, D. (1986). Adapting science materials for regular and learning disabled seventh graders. *Remedial and Special Education, 7*(1), 31–39.

MacArthur, C. A., Graham, S., & Schwartz, S. (1991). Knowledge of revision and revising behavior among students with learning disabilities. *Learning Disability Quarterly, 14,* 61–73.

MacArthur, C. A., Schwartz, S., & Graham, S. (1991). Effects of a reciprocal peer revision strategy in a special education classroom. *Learning Disabilities Research & Practice, 6,* 201–210.

MacMillan, D. L., Forness, S. R., & Trumball, B. M. (1973). The role of punishment in the classroom. *Exceptional Children, 40,* 85–96.

Madsen, C. H., Becker, W. C., & Thomas, D. R. (1968). Rules, praise, and ignoring: Elements of elementary classroom control. *Journal of Applied Behavior Analysis, 1,* 139–150.

Mager, R. F. (1962). *Preparing instructional objectives.* Belmont, CA: Fearon.

Majsterek, D. J., Wilson, R., & Mandlebaum, L. (1990). Computerized IEPs: Guidelines for product evaluation. *Journal of Special Education Technology, 10,* 207–219.

Malone, L. D., & Mastropieri, M. A. (1992). Reading comprehension instruction: Summarization and self-monitoring training for students with learning disabilities. *Exceptional Children, 58,* 270–279.

Malouf, D. B., Wizer, D. R., Pilato, V. H., & Grogan, M. M. (1990). Computer assisted instruction with small groups of mildly handicapped students. *Journal of Special Education, 24,* 51–68.

Marik, R. (1982). *Special education students write: Classroom activities and assignments. Writing teachers at work.* Berkeley: University of California, National Writing Project. (ERIC Document Reproduction Service No. ED 251 837)

Marston, D. (1987–1988). The effectiveness of special education: A time series analysis of reading performance in regular and special education settings. *Journal of Special Education, 21,* 13–26.

Marston, D., & Magnusson, D. (1986). Implementing curriculum-based measurement in special and regular education settings. *Exceptional Children, 52,* 266–276.

Martin, G., & Pear, J. (1978). *Behavior modification: What it is and how to do it.* Englewood Cliffs, NJ: Prentice-Hall.

Mastropieri, M. A. (1985). *Increasing learning and memory skills of learning disabled students.* Logan: Utah State University, Developmental Center for Handicapped Persons. (ERIC Document Reproduction Service No. ED 275 278)

Mastropieri, M. A. (1988). Increasing vocabulary acquisition and recall with the keyword method. *Teaching Exceptional Children, 20*(2), 4–8.

Mastropieri, M. A. (1989). Using general education teacher effectiveness literature in the preparation of special education personnel. *Teacher Education and Special Education, 12,* 170–172.

Mastropieri, M. A., Bakken, J. P., & Scruggs, T. E. (1991). Mathematics instruction for individuals with mental retardation: A perspective and research synthesis. *Education and Training in Mental Retardation, 26,* 115–129.

Mastropieri, M. A., Emerick, K., & Scruggs, T. E. (1988). Mnemonic instruction of science concepts. *Behavioral Disorders, 14,* 48–56.

Mastropieri, M. A., Jenne, T., & Scruggs, T. E. (1988). A level system for managing problem behaviors in a high school resource program. *Behavioral Disorders, 13,* 202–208.

Mastropieri, M. A., & Peters, E. E. (1987). Increasing prose recall of learning disabled and reading disabled students via spatial organizers. *The Journal of Educational Research, 80,* 272–276.

Mastropieri, M. A., & Scruggs, T. E. (1984a). Generalization of academic and social behaviors: Five effective strategies. *Academic Therapy, 19,* 427–432.

Mastropieri, M. A., & Scruggs, T. E. (1984b). *Memory strategies for learning disabled students.* Logan, UT: Utah State University, Exceptional Child Center. (ERIC Document Reproduction Service No. ED 246-620)

Mastropieri, M. A., & Scruggs, T. E. (1985–1986). Early intervention for socially withdrawn children. *Journal of Special Education, 19,* 429–442.

Mastropieri, M. A., & Scruggs, T. E. (1988). Increasing the content area learning of learning disabled students: Research implementation. *Learning Disabilities Research, 4*(1), 17–25.

Mastropieri, M. A., & Scruggs, T. E. (1989a). Constructing more meaningful relationships: Mnemonic instruction for special populations. *Educational Psychology Review, 1,* 83–111.

Mastropieri, M. A., & Scruggs, T. E. (1989b). Mnemonic social studies instruction: Classroom applications. *Remedial and Special Education, 10*(3), 40–46.

Mastropieri, M. A., & Scruggs, T. E. (1989c). Reconstructive elaborations: Strategies for adapting content area information. *Academic Therapy, 24*(4), 391–406.

Mastropieri, M. A., & Scruggs, T. E. (1989d). Reconstructive elaboration: Strategies that facilitate content learning. *Learning Disabilities Focus, 4*(2), 73–77.

Mastropieri, M. A., & Scruggs, T. E. (1991). *Teaching students ways to remember: Strategies for learning mnemonically.* Cambridge, MA: Brookline Books.

Mastropieri, M. A., & Scruggs, T. E. (1992). Science and students with disabilities. *Review of Educational Research, 62,* 377–411.

Mastropieri, M. A., & Scruggs, T. E. (1993). *Guidelines for effective mainstreaming in science.* West Lafayette, IN: Purdue Research Foundation.

Mastropieri, M. A., & Scruggs, T. E. (in press a). An analysis of science curriculum in four school districts: Implications for students with disabilities. *Remedial and Special Education.*

Mastropieri, M. A., & Scruggs, T. E. (in press b). Trends in science education: Implications for special education. In C. Warger & M. Pugach (Eds.), *What's worth knowing: How curriculum trends will affect special education.* New York: Teachers College Press.

Mastropieri, M. A., Scruggs, T. E., Bakken, J., & Brigham, F. J. (1992). A complex mnemonic strategy for teaching states and capitals: Comparing forward and backward associations. *Learning Disabilities Research & Practice, 7,* 96–103.

Mastropieri, M. A., Scruggs, T. E., & Bohs, K. (1994). Mainstreaming an emotionally handicapped student in science: A qualitative investigation. In T. E. Scruggs & M. A. Mastropieri (Eds.), *Advances in learning and behavioral disabilities* (Vol. 8, pp. 131–146). Greenwich, CT: JAI Press.

Mastropieri, M. A., Scruggs, T. E., & Fulk, B. J. M. (1990). Teaching abstract vocabulary to LD students with the keyword method: Effects on comprehension and recall. *Journal of Learning Disabilities, 23,* 92–107.

Mastropieri, M. A., Scruggs, T. E., & Levin, J. R. (1983). Pictorial mnemonic strategies for special education. *Journal of Special Education Technology, 6,* 24–33.

Mastropieri, M. A., Scruggs, T. E., & Levin, J. R. (1985a). Maximizing what exceptional children can learn: A review of keyword and other mnemonic strategy research. *Remedial and Special Education, 6*(2), 39–45.

Mastropieri, M. A., Scruggs, T. E., & Levin, J. R. (1985b). Memory strategy instruction with learning disabled adolescents. *Journal of Learning Disabilities, 18,* 94–100.

Mastropieri, M. A., Scruggs, T. E., & Levin, J. R. (1986). Direct vs. mnemonic instruction: Relative benefits for exceptional learners. *The Journal of Special Education, 20,* 299–308.

Mastropieri, M. A., Scruggs, T. E., & Levin, J. R. (1987a). Transformational mnemonic strategies in special education. In M. McDaniel & M. Pressley (Eds.), *Imagery and related mnemonic processes: Theories, individual differences, and applications* (pp. 358–376). New York: Springer-Verlag.

Mastropieri, M. A., Scruggs, T. E., & Levin, J. R. (1987b). Mnemonic facilitation of learning-disabled students' memory for expository prose. *American Educational Research Journal, 24,* 505–519.

Mastropieri, M. A., Scruggs, T. E., Levin, J. R., Gaffney, J., & McLoone, B. (1985). Mnemonic vocabulary instruction for learning disabled students. *Learning Disability Quarterly, 8,* 57–63.

Mastropieri, M. A., Scruggs, T. E., McLoone, B., & Levin, J. R. (1985). Facilitating the acquisition of science classification in LD students. *Learning Disability Quarterly, 8,* 299–309.

Mastropieri, M. A., Scruggs, T. E., & Shiah, S. (1991). Mathematics instruction with learning disabled students: A review of research. *Learning Disabilities Research & Practice, 6,* 89–98.

Mastropieri, M. A., Scruggs, T. E., Whittaker, M. E. S., & Bakken, J. P. (1994). Applications of mnemonic strategies with students with mental disabilities. *Remedial and Special Education, 15*(1), 34–43.

Mather, N. (1992). Whole language reading instruction for students with learning disabilities: Caught in the cross fire. *Learning Disabilities Research & Practice, 7,* 87–95.

Matson, J. L., Esveldt-Dawson, K., Andrasid, F., Ollendick, T. H., Petti, T., & Hersen, M. (1980). Direct, observational, and generalization effects of social skills training with emotionally disturbed children. *Behavior Therapy, 11,* 522–531.

Mayer, R. (1993). Understanding individual differences in mathematical problem solving. *Learning Disability Quarterly, 16,* 2–5.

McLeod, T. M., & Armstrong, S. W. (1982). Learning disabilities in mathematics skills deficits and remedial approaches at the intermediate and secondary levels. *Learning Disability Quarterly, 5,* 305–311.

McLoone, B. B., Scruggs, T. E., Mastropieri, M. A., & Zucker, S. H. (1986). Memory strategy instruction and training with LD adolescents. *Learning Disabilities Research, 2,* 45–53.

Mellard, D. F., & Hazel, J. S. (1992). Social competencies as a pathway to successful life transitions. *Learning Disability Quarterly, 15,* 251–271.

Mercer, C. D., & Miller, S. P. (1992). Teaching students with learning problems in math to acquire, understand, and apply basic math facts. *Remedial and Special Education, 13*(3), 19–35, 61.

Meyer, L. A. (1982). The relative effects of word-analysis and word-supply correct procedures with poor readers during word-attack training. *Reading Research Quarterly, 17*(4), 544–555.

Miller, S., & Schloss, P. (1983). *Career-vocational education for handicapped youth.* Rockville, MD: Aspen Publishers.

Millman, J., & Pauk, W. (1969). *How to take tests.* New York: McGraw-Hill.

Minskoff, E. H. (1982). Sharpening language skills in secondary LD students. *Academic Therapy, 18,* 53–60.

Mitchell, D. W., & Crowell, P. J. (1973). Modifying inappropriate behavior in an elementary art class. *Elementary School Guidance and Counseling, 8,* 34–42.

Montague, M., & Applegate, B. (1993). Middle school students' mathematical problem solving: An analysis of think aloud protocols. *Learning Disability Quarterly, 16,* 19–33.

Montague, M., Bos, C., & Doucette, M. (1991). Affective, cognitive, and metacognitive attributes of eighth-grade mathematical problem solvers. *Learning Disabilities Research & Practice, 6,* 145–151.

Moran, M. R. (1983). Learning disabled adolescents' responses to a paragraph-organization strategy. *Pointer, 27,* 28–31.

Morsink, C. V., Soar, R. S., Soar, R. M., & Thomas, R. (1986). Research on teaching: Opening door to special education classrooms. *Exceptional Children, 52*(6), 32–40.

National Joint Committee on Learning Disabilities. (1993). A reaction to full inclusion: A reaffirmation of the right of students with learning disabilities to a continuum of services. *Journal of Learning Disabilities, 26,* 596.

Neef, N. A., Iwata, B. A., & Page, T. J. (1980). The effects of interpersonal training versus high-density reinforcement of spelling acquisition and retention. *Journal of Applied Behavior Analysis, 13,* 153–158.

Negin, G. A. (1978). Mnemonics and demonic words. *Reading Improvement, 15,* 180–182.

Nelson, J. R., Smith, D. J., Young, R. K., & Dodd, J. M. (1991). A review of self-management outcome research conducted with students who exhibit behavioral disorders. *Behavioral Disorders, 16,* 169–179.

Noble, J. K. (1966). *Better handwriting for you.* New York: Noble & Noble.

Nolet, V., & Tindal, G. (1993). Special education in content area classes: Development of a model and practical procedures. *Remedial and Special Education, 14,* 36–48.

Nutter, N., & Safran, J. (1984). Improving writing with sentence combining exercises. *Academic Therapy, 19,* 449–455.

Obiakor, F. E., Patton, J. M., & Ford, B. A. (Guest Eds.). (1992). Issues in the education of African-American youth in special education settings [Special issue]. *Exceptional Children, 59*(2).

O'Conner, R. E., Jenkins, J. R., Cole, K. N., & Mills, P. E. (1993). Two approaches to reading instruction with children with disabilities: Does program design make a difference? *Exceptional Children, 59,* 312–323.

O'Conner, R. E., Jenkins, J. R., Leicester, N., & Slocum, T. A. (1993). Teaching phonological awareness to young children with learning disabilities. *Exceptional Children, 59,* 532–546.

Okolo, C. M. (1988). Instructional environments in secondary vocational education programs: Implications for LD adolescents. *Learning Disability Quarterly, 11,* 136–148.

Okolo, C. M., Bahr, C. M., & Reith, H. J. (1993). A retrospective view of computer-based instruction. *Journal of Special Education Technology, 12,* 1–27.

O'Leary, R. D., Kaufman, K. F., Kass, R. E., & Drabman, R. S. (1970). Effects of loud and soft reprimands on the behavior of disruptive students. *Exceptional Children, 37,* 145–155.

Osguthorpe, R. T., & Scruggs, T. E. (1986). Special education students as tutors: A review and analysis. *Remedial and Special Education, 7*(4), 15–25.

O'Shea, L. J., Sindelar, P. T., & O'Shea, D. J. (1987). The effects of repeated readings and attentional cues on the reading fluency and comprehension of learning disabled readers. *Learning Disabilities Research, 2*(2), 103–109.

Palincsar, A. S., & Brown, A. L. (1984). Reciprocal teaching of comprehension-fostering monitoring activities. *Cognition and Instruction, 1,* 117–175.

Pany, D., & Jenkins, J. R. (1978). Learning word meanings: A comparison of instructional procedures. *Learning Disability Quarterly, 1,* 21–32.

Pany, D., Jenkins, J. R., & Schreck, J. (1982). Vocabulary instruction: Effects on word knowledge and reading comprehension. *Learning Disability Quarterly, 5,* 202–215.

Paolucci-Whitcomb, P., & Nevin, A. (1985). Preparing consulting teachers through a collaborative approach between university faculty and field-based consulting teachers. *Teacher Education and Special Education, 8,* 132–143.

Paris, S., & Oka, E. R. (1989). Strategies for comprehending text and coping with reading difficulties. *Learning Disabilities Research, 12,* 32–41.

Parker, R. I., Tindal, G., & Hasbrouck, J. (1991). Progress monitoring with objective measures of writing performance for students with mild disabilities. *Exceptional Children, 58,* 61–73.

Parmer, R. S., & Cawley, J. F. (1993). Analysis of science textbook recommendations provided for students with disabilities. *Exceptional Children, 59,* 518–531.

Peterson, J., Heistad, D., Peterson, D., & Reynolds, M. (1986). Montevideo individualized prescriptive instructional management system. *Exceptional Children, 52,* 239–243.

Pflaum, S. W., & Bryan, T. H. (1982). Oral reading research and learning disabled children. *Topics in Learning and Learning Disabilities, 1,* 33–42.

Phelps, L. A., & Lutz, R. J. (1977). *Career exploration and preparation for the special needs learner.* Boston: Allyn & Bacon.

Pickering, E., Pickering, A., & Buchanan, M. (1988). LD and nonhandicapped boys' comprehension of cartoon humor. *Learning Disability Quarterly, 10,* 45–51.

Polloway, E. A., Foley, R. M., & Epstein, M. (1992). A comparison of the homework problems of students with learning disabilities and nondisabled students. *Learning Disabilities Research & Practice, 7,* 203–209.

Polloway, E. A., Payne, J. S., Patton, J. R., & Payne, R. A. (1985). *Strategies for teaching retarded and special needs learners* (3rd ed.). Columbus, OH: Merrill Publishing.

Popham, W. J., & Husek, T. R. (1969). Implications of criterion-referenced measurement. *Journal of Educational Measurement, 6,* 1–9.

Prater, M. A., Joy, R., Chilman, B., Temple, J., & Miller, S. R. (1991). Self-monitoring of on-task behavior by adolescents with learning disabilities. *Learning Disability Quarterly, 14,* 164–177.

Pressley, M., & Associates (1990). *Cognitive strategy instruction that really improves children's academic performance.* Cambridge, MA: Brookline Books.

Pressley, M., Scruggs, T. E., & Mastropieri, M. A. (1989). Memory strategy instruction for learning disabilities: Present and future directions for researchers. *Learning Disabilities Research, 4,* 68–77.

Ragland, E., Kerr, M. M., & Strain, P. S. (1981). Social play for withdrawn children. *Behavior Modification, 5,* 347–359.

Reid, E. R. (1986). Practicing effective instruction: The Exemplary Center for Reading Instruction. *Exceptional Children, 52*(6), 510–521.

Reiff, H. B., & deFur, S. (1992). Transition for youths with learning disabilities: A focus on developing independence. *Learning Disability Quarterly, 15*, 237–249.

Reisberg, L., & Wolf, R. (1986). Developing a consulting program in special education: Implementation and interventions. *Focus on Exceptional Children, 19*(1), 1–14.

Reith, H. J., Polsgrove, L., & Eckert, R. (1984). A computer-based spelling program. *Academic Therapy, 20*, 49–56.

Resnick, L. M., & Ford, W. W. (1981). *The psychology of mathematics for instruction.* Hillsdale, NM: Erlbaum.

Rivera, D. M., & Smith, D. D. (1987). Influence of modeling on acquisition and generalization computational skills: A summary of research findings from three sites. *Learning Disability Quarterly, 10*, 69–80.

Robbins, P. (1986). The Napa-Vacaville follow-through project: Qualitative outcomes, related procedures, and implications for practice. *The Elementary School Journal, 87*, 139–157.

Roberts, M., & Deutsch-Smith, D. (1980). The relationship among correct and error oral reading rates and comprehension. *Learning Disability Quarterly, 3*, 54–65.

Robin, A., Armel, S., & O'Leary, K. (1975). The effects of self-instruction on writing deficiency. *Behavior Therapy, 6*, 178–187.

Rojewski, J. W., & Greenan, J. P. (1992). Teacher certification policies and practices for vocational special education personnel: A national study. *Teacher Education and Special Education, 15*, 194–201.

Romberg, T. A., & Carpenter, T. P. (1986). Research on teaching and learning mathematics: Two disciplines of scientific inquiry. In M. C. Wittrock (Ed.), *Handbook of research on teaching* (3rd ed., pp. 850–873). New York: Macmillan Publishing.

Rose, M. C., Cundick, B. P., & Higbee, K. L. (1983). Verbal rehearsal and verbal imagery: Mnemonic aids for learning disabled children. *Journal of Learning Disabilities, 16*, 352–354.

Rosenshine, B. (1983). Teaching functions in instructional programs. *Elementary School Journal, 83*, 335–352.

Rosenshine, B., & Stevens, R. (1986). Teaching functions. In M. C. Wittrock (Ed.), *Handbook of research on teaching* (3rd ed., pp. 376–391). New York: MacMillan Publishing.

Rottman, T. R., & Cross, D. R. (1990). Using informed strategies for learning to enhance the reading and thinking skills of children with learning disabilities. *Journal of Learning Disabilities, 23*(5), 270–278.

Rudenga, E. V. A. (1992). *Incompatibility? Ethnographic case studies of learning disabled students in a whole language classroom.* Unpublished doctoral dissertation, Purdue University, West Lafayette, IN.

Ruedy, L. R. (1983). Handwriting instruction: It *can* be part of the high school curriculum. *Academic Therapy, 18*, 421–429.

Rusch, F. R., & Phelps, L. A. (1987). Secondary special education and transition from school to work: A national priority. *Exceptional Children, 53*, 487–492.

Rutherford, R. B., & Nelson, C. M. (1982). Analysis of the response-contingent time-out literature with behaviorally disordered students in classroom settings. *Behavior Disorders, 5*, 79–105.

Salend, S. L., & Nowak, M. R. (1988). Effects of peer-previewing on LD students' oral reading skills. *Learning Disability Quarterly, 11*, 47–53.

Salvia, J., & Hughes, C. (1990). *Curriculum-based assessment: Testing what is taught.* New York: MacMillan Publishing.

Salvia, J., & Ysseldyke, J. E. (1981). *Assessment in remedial and special education* (2nd ed.). Boston: Houghton Mifflin.

Schloss, P. J., Schloss, C. N., & Harris, L. (1984). A multiple baseline analysis of an interpersonal skills training program for depressed youth. *Behavioral Disorders, 9,* 182–188.

Schloss, P. J., Smith, M. A., & Schloss, C. N. (1990). *Instructional methods for adolescents with learning and behavior problems.* Boston: Allyn & Bacon.

Schumaker, J. B., Deshler, D. D., Alley, G. R., & Warner, M. M. (1983). Toward the development of an intervention model for learning disabled students: The University of Kansas Institute. *Exceptional Children Quarterly, 4,* 45–74.

Schumaker, J. B., Deshler, D. D., Alley, G. R., Warner, M. M., & Denton, P. H. (1982). Multipass: A learning strategy for improving reading comprehension. *Learning Disability Quarterly, 5,* 295–304.

Schumaker, J. B., & Ellis, E. S. (1982). Social skills training of LD adolescents: A generalization study. *Learning Disability Quarterly, 5,* 388–397.

Schunk, D. H., & Rice, M. J. (1992). Influence of reading comprehension strategy information on children's achievement outcomes. *Learning Disability Quarterly, 15,* 51–64.

Schworm, R. W. (1979). The effects of selective attention on the decoding skills of children with learning disabilities. *Journal of Learning Disabilities, 12,* 639–644.

Scott, K. S. (1993). Multisensory mathematics for children with mild disabilities. *Exceptionality, 4,* 97–111.

Scruggs, T. E. (1985a). *Administration and interpretation of standardized achievement tests with learning disabled and behaviorally disordered elementary school children: Final report.* Logan: Utah State University, Developmental Center for Handicapped Persons. (ERIC Document Reproduction Service No. ED 256-082)

Scruggs, T. E. (1985b). *The administration and interpretation of standardized achievement tests with learning disabled and behaviorally disordered elementary school children: Year 2 final report.* Logan: Utah State University, Developmental Center for Handicapped Persons. (ERIC Document Reproduction Service No. 260 560)

Scruggs, T. E. (1988). The nature of learning disabilities. In K. A. Kavale (Ed.), Learning disabilities: State of the art and practice (pp. 22–43). Boston: Little Brown/College-Hill.

Scruggs, T. E. (1992). Single subject research methodology in the study of learning and behavior disorders: Design, analysis, and synthesis. In T. E. Scruggs & M. A. Mastropieri (Eds.), *Advances in learning and behavioral disabilities* (Vol. 7, pp. 223–247). Greenwich, CT: JAI Press.

Scruggs, T. E., Bennion, K., & Lifson, S. (1985a). An analysis of children's strategy use on reading achievement tests. *Elementary School Journal, 85,* 479–484.

Scruggs, T. E., Bennion, K., & Lifson, S. (1985b). Learning disabled students' spontaneous use of test-taking skills on reading achievement tests. *Learning Disability Quarterly, 8,* 205–210.

Scruggs, T. E., & Jenkins, V. (1985). *Improving the test-taking skills of learning disabled students.* Logan: Utah State University, Developmental Center for Handicapped Persons. (ERIC Document Reproduction Service No. ED 172 049)

Scruggs, T. E., & Laufenberg, R. (1986). Transformational mnemonic strategies for retarded learners. *Education and Training of the Mentally Retarded, 21,* 165–173.

Scruggs, T. E., & Lifson, S. A. (1985). Current conceptions of test-wiseness: Myths and realities. *School Psychology Review, 14,* 339–350.

Scruggs, T. E., & Lifson, S. A. (1986). Are LD students 'testwise'? An inquiry into reading comprehension test items. *Educational and Psychological Measurement, 46,* 1075–1082.

Scruggs, T. E., & Mastropieri, M. A. (1984a). How gifted students learn: Implications from recent research. *Roeper Review, 5,* 183–185.

Scruggs, T. E., & Mastropieri, M. A. (1984b). Issues in generalization: Implications for special education. *Psychology in the Schools, 21,* 397–403.

Scruggs, T. E., & Mastropieri, M. A. (1984c). Use of content maps to increase children's comprehension and recall. *The Reading Teacher, 37,* 807.

Scruggs, T. E., & Mastropieri, M. A. (1984d). Improving memory for facts with the 'keyword' method. *Academic Therapy, 20,* 159–166.

Scruggs, T. E., & Mastropieri, M. A. (1985). Illustrative aids improve reading comprehension. *Reading Horizons, 25,* 107–110.

Scruggs, T. E., & Mastropieri, M. A. (1986). Improving test-taking skills of behaviorally disordered and learning disabled students. *Exceptional Children, 52,* 63–68.

Scruggs, T. E., & Mastropieri, M. A. (1988). Are learning disabled students 'test-wise'? A review of recent research. *Learning Disabilities Focus, 3*(2), 87–97.

Scruggs, T. E., & Mastropieri, M. A. (1989a). Mnemonic instruction of LD students: A field-based evaluation. *Learning Disability Quarterly, 12,* 119–125.

Scruggs, T. E., & Mastropieri, M. A. (1989b). Reconstructive elaborations: A model for content area learning. *American Educational Research Journal, 26,* 311–327.

Scruggs, T. E., & Mastropieri, M. A. (1990a). The case for mnemonic instruction: From laboratory investigations to classroom applications. *Journal of Special Education, 24,* 7–29.

Scruggs, T. E., & Mastropieri, M. A. (1990b). Mnemonic instruction for students with learning disabilities: What it is and what it does. *Learning Disability Quarterly, 13,* 7–32.

Scruggs, T. E., & Mastropieri, M. A. (1992a). Classroom applications of mnemonic instruction: Acquisition, maintenance, and generalization. *Exceptional Children, 58,* 219–229.

Scruggs, T. E., & Mastropieri, M. A. (1992b). Effective mainstreaming for mildly handicapped students. *Elementary School Journal, 92,* 389–409.

Scruggs, T. E., & Mastropieri, M. A. (1992c). Remembering the forgotten art of memory. *American Educator, 16*(4), 31–37.

Scruggs, T. E., & Mastropieri, M. A. (1992d). *Teaching test-taking skills: Helping students show what they know.* Cambridge, MA: Brookline Books.

Scruggs, T. E., & Mastropieri, M. A. (1993a). Current approaches to science education: Implications for mainstream instruction of students with disabilities. *Remedial and Special Education, 14*(1), 15–24.

Scruggs, T. E., & Mastropieri, M. A. (1993b). Special education for the 21st century: Integrating learning strategies and thinking skills. *Journal of Learning Disabilities, 26,* 392–398.

Scruggs, T. E., & Mastropieri, M. A. (1994). The effectiveness of generalization training: A quantitative synthesis of single-subject research. In T. E. Scruggs & M. A. Mastropieri (Eds.), *Advances in learning and behavioral disabilities* (Vol. 8, pp. 259–280). Greenwich, CT: JAI Press.

Scruggs, T. E., & Mastropieri, M. A. (in press a). Adapting microscope activities for students with disabilities. *Science Scope.*

Scruggs, T. E., & Mastropieri, M. A. (in press b). The effects of prior field experience on student teacher competence. *Teacher Education and Special Education.*

Scruggs, T. E., Mastropieri, M. A., Bakken, J. P., & Brigham, F. J. (1993). Reading vs. doing: The relative effectiveness of textbook-based and inquiry-oriented approaches to science education. *Journal of Special Education, 27,* 1–15.

Scruggs, T. E., Mastropieri, M. A., Brigham, F. J., & Sullivan, G. S. (1992). The effectiveness of mnemonic reconstructions on the spatial learning of students with learning disabilities. *Learning Disability Quarterly, 15,* 154–162.

Scruggs, T. E., Mastropieri, M. A., Cook, S., & Escobar, C. (1986). Early intervention for children with conduct disorders: A quantitative synthesis of single-subject research. *Behavioral Disorders, 11,* 260–271.

Scruggs, T. E., Mastropieri, M. A., & Levin, J. R. (1985). Vocabulary acquisition of retarded students under direct and mnemonic instruction. *American Journal of Mental Deficiency, 89,* 546–551.

Scruggs, T. E., Mastropieri, M. A., & Levin, J. R. (1986). Can children effectively re-use the same mnemonic pegwords? *Educational Communication and Technology Journal, 34*, 83–88.

Scruggs, T. E., Mastropieri, M. A., & Levin, J. R. (1987). Contributions of mnemonic strategy research to a theory of learning disabilities. In H. L. Swanson & K. Gadow (Eds.), *Advances in learning and behavioral disabilities: Memory and learning disabilities* (pp. 225–244). Greenwich, CT: JAI Press.

Scruggs, T. E., Mastropieri, M. A., Levin, J. R., & Gaffney, J. S. (1985). Facilitating the acquisition of science facts in learning disabled students. *American Educational Research Journal, 22*, 575–586.

Scruggs, T. E., Mastropieri, M. A., Levin, J. R., McLoone, B. B., Gaffney, J. S., & Prater, M. (1985). Increasing content area learning: A comparison of mnemonic and visual-spatial direct instruction. *Learning Disabilities Research, 1*, 18–31.

Scruggs, T. E., Mastropieri, M. A., McLoone, B. B., Levin, J. R., & Morrison, C. (1987). Mnemonic facilitation of text-embedded science facts with LD students. *Journal of Educational Psychology, 79*, 27–34.

Scruggs, T. E., Mastropieri, M. A., & Richter, L. L. (1985). Peer tutoring with behaviorally disordered students: Social and academic benefits. *Behavioral Disorders, 10*, 283–294.

Scruggs, T. E., Mastropieri, M. A., & Sullivan, G. S. (in press). Promoting relational thinking skills: Elaborative interrogation for mildly handicapped students. *Exceptional Children*.

Scruggs, T. E., Mastropieri, M. A., Sullivan, G. S., & Hesser, L. S. (1993). Improving reasoning and recall: The relative effects of elaborative interrogation and mnemonic elaboration. *Learning Disability Quarterly, 16*, 233–240.

Scruggs, T. E., Mastropieri, M. A., Tolfa, D., & Jenkins, V. (1985). Attitudes of behaviorally disordered students toward tests. *Perceptual and Motor Skills, 60*, 467–470.

Scruggs, T. E., Mastropieri, M. A., Tolfa, D., & Osguthorpe, R. T. (1986). Behaviorally disordered students as tutors: Effects on social behaviors. *Behavioral Disorders, 12*, 36–44.

Scruggs, T. E., Mastropieri, M. A., & Veit, D. (1986). The effects of coaching on standardized test performances of learning disabled and behaviorally disordered students. *Remedial and Special Education, 7*(5), 37–41.

Scruggs, T. E., & Osguthorpe, R. T. (1986). Tutoring interventions within special education settings: A comparison of cross-age and peer tutoring. *Psychology in the Schools, 22*, 187–193.

Scruggs, T. E., & Richter, L. L. (1985). Tutoring learning disabled students: A critical review. *Learning Disability Quarterly, 8*, 286–298.

Scruggs, T. E., & Tolfa, D. (1985). Improving the test-taking skills of learning disabled students. *Perceptual and Motor Skills, 60*, 847–850.

Scruggs, T. E., White, K. R., & Bennion, K. (1986). Improving achievement test scores in the elementary grades by coaching: A meta-analysis. *Elementary School Journal, 87*, 69–82.

Semmel, M. I., Abernathy, T. V., Butera, G., & Lesar, S. (1991). Teacher perceptions of the regular education initiative. *Exceptional Children, 58*, 9–23.

Shefter, H. (1976). *Six minutes a day to perfect spelling*. New York: Pocket Books.

Shiah, R. L. (1993). *The effects of computer-assisted instruction on the mathematical problem-solving of students with learning disabilities*. Dissertation in progress, Purdue University, West Lafayette, IN.

Shores, R. E., Gunter, P. L., & Jack, S. L. (1993). Classroom management strategies: Are they setting events for coercion? *Behavioral Disorders, 18*, 92–109.

Silbert, J., Carnine, D., & Stein, M. (1981). *Direct instruction mathematics*. Columbus, OH: Merrill Publishing.

Simmonds, E. P. M. (1992). The effects of teacher training and implementation of two methods for improving the comprehension skills of students with learning disabilities. *Learning Disabilities Research & Practice, 7*, 194–198.

Simmons, D. C., Kameenui, E. J., & Darch, C. (1988). The effect of textual proximity on fourth- and fifth-grade LD students' metacognitive awareness and strategic comprehension behavior. *Learning Disability Quarterly, 11*, 380–395.

Sinclair, J., Forness, S., & Alexson, J. (1985). Psychiatric diagnosis: A study of its relationship to school needs. *The Journal of Special Education, 19*, 333–344.

Sindelar, P. T., Smith, M. A., Harriman, N. E., Hale, R. L., & Wilson, R. J. (1986). Teacher effectiveness in special education programs. *Journal of Special Education, 20*, 195–207.

Singer, J. D., & Butler, J. A. (1987). The Education for All Handicapped Children Act: Schools as agents of social reform. *Harvard Educational Review, 57*, 125–152.

Skinner, C. H., Bamberg, H. W., Smith, E. S., & Powell, S. S. (1993). Cognitive cover, copy and compare: Subvocal responding to increase rates of accurate division responding. *Remedial and Special Education, 14*, 49–56.

Slavin, R. E., Madden, N. A., & Leavey, M. (1984a). Effects of cooperative learning individualized instruction on mainstreamed students. *Exceptional Children, 50*, 434–443.

Slavin, R. E., Madden, N. A., & Leavey, M. (1984b). Effects of team assisted individualization on the mathematics achievement of academically handicapped and nonhandicapped students. *Journal of Educational Psychology, 76*, 813–819.

Smith, S. W. (1990a). Individualized education programs (IEPs) in special education—from intent to acquiescence. *Exceptional Children, 57*, 6–15.

Smith, S. W. (1990b). Comparison of individualized education programs (IEPs) of students with behavioral disorders and learning disabilities. *Journal of Special Education, 24*, 85–100.

Snider, V. E. (1989). Reading comprehension performance of adolescents with learning disabilities. *Learning Disability Quarterly, 12*, 86–97.

Spencer, R. J., & Gray, D. F. (1973). A time-out procedure for classroom behavioral change within the public school setting. *Child Study Journal, 3*, 29–38.

Stahl, S. (1992). Saying the "p" word: Nine guidelines for exemplary phonics instruction. *The Reading Teacher, 45*, 618–625.

Stahl, S. A., & Miller, P. D. (1989). Whole language and language experience approaches for beginning reading: A quantitative research synthesis. *Review of Educational Research, 59*, 87–116.

Stallings, J., & Krasavage, E. M. (1986). Program implementation and student achievement in four-year Madeline Hunter follow through project. *The Elementary School Journal, 87*, 117–138.

Stein, C. L., & Goldman, J. (1980). Beginning reading instruction for children with minimal brain dysfunction. *Journal of Learning Disabilities, 13*, 52–55.

Stevens, K. B., & Schuster, J. W. (1987). Effects of a constant time delay procedure on the written spelling performance of a learning disabled student. *Learning Disability Quarterly, 10*, 9–16.

Stokes, T. F., & Baer, D. M. (1977). An implicit technology of generalization. *Journal of Applied Behavior Analysis, 10*, 349–367.

Strain, P. S., & Wiegerink, R. (1976). Effects of socio-dramatic activities on social interaction among behaviorally disordered preschool children. *Journal of Special Education, 10*, 71–75.

Suid, M. (1990). *Demonic mnemonics*. New York: Dell.

Sullivan, G. S. (1993). *Coached elaborations: Helping students with learning disabilities use reasoning to remember*. Unpublished doctoral dissertation, Purdue University, West Lafayette, IN.

Sullivan, G. S., & Mastropieri, M. A. (1994). Social competence of individuals with learning disabilities. In T. E. Scruggs & M. A. Mastropieri (Eds.), *Advances in learning and behavioral disabilities* (Vol. 8, pp. 177–214). Greenwich, CT: JAI Press.

Sulzer-Azaroff, B., & Mayer, G. P. (1977). *Applying behavior-analysis procedures with children and youth.* New York: Holt, Rinehart & Winston.

Swanson, H. L., & Trahan, M. F. (1992). Learning disabled readers' comprehension of computer-mediated text: The influence of working memory, metacognition, and attribution. *Learning Disabilities Research & Practice, 7,* 74–86.

Tateyama-Sniezek, K. M. (1990). Cooperative learning: Does it improve the academic achievement of students with handicaps? *Exceptional Children, 56,* 426–437.

Tawney, J. W., & Gast, D. L. (1984). *Single-subject research in special education.* Columbus, OH: Merrill Publishing.

Thomas, C. C., Englert, C. S., & Gregg, S. (1987). An analysis of errors and strategies in the expository writing of learning disabled students. *Remedial and Special Education, 8,* 21–30.

Thorkildsen, R. J. (1984). *An experimental test of a microcomputer/videodisk program to develop the social skills of mildly handicapped elementary students.* Unpublished doctoral dissertation, University of Oregon, Eugene.

Thornton, C. A., & Toohey, M. A. (1985). Basic math facts: Guidelines for teaching and learning. *Learning Disabilities Focus, 1,* 44–57.

Thurber, D. N., & Jordan, D. R. (1981). *D'Nealian handwriting.* Glenview, IL: Scott, Foresman.

Tindal, G., & Parker, R. (1989). Assessment of written expression for students in compensatory and special education programs. *Journal of Special Education, 23,* 169–184.

Torgesen, J. K., Waters, M. D., Cohen, A. L., & Torgesen, J. L. (1988). Improving sight word recognition in LD children: An evaluation of three computer program variations. *Learning Disability Quarterly, 11,* 125–132.

Trapani, C. (1990). *Transition goals for adolescents with learning disabilities.* Boston: Little Brown and Company.

Treiman, R. (1985). Onsets and rimes as units of spoken syllables: Evidence from children. *Journal of Experimental Child Psychology, 39,* 161–181.

Trifiletti, J. J., Frith, G. H., & Armstrong, S. (1984). Microcomputer versus resource rooms for LD students: A preliminary investigation of the effects on math skills. *Learning Disability Quarterly, 7,* 69–76.

Tucker, J. A. (Ed.). (1985). Curriculum-based assessment [Special issue]. *Exceptional Children, 52*(3), 196–299.

Turnbull, A. P., & Turnbull, H. R. (1978). *Parents speak out.* Columbus, OH: Merrill Publishing.

U.S. Department of Education (1992). *Fourteenth annual report to Congress on implementation of the Individuals with Disabilities Education Act.* Washington, DC: Author.

Vaughn, S., McIntosh, R., & Hogan, A. (1990). Why social skills training doesn't work: An alternative model. In T. E. Scruggs & B. Y. L. Wong (Eds.), *Intervention in learning disabilities* (pp. 279–303). New York: Springer-Verlag.

Vaughn, S. R., Ridley, C. A., & Cox, J. (1983). Evaluating the efficacy of an interpersonal skills training program with children who are mentally retarded. *Education and Training of the Mentally Retarded, 18,* 191–196.

Veit, D. T., Scruggs, T. E., & Mastropieri, M. A. (1986). Extended mnemonic instruction with learning disabled students. *Journal of Educational Psychology, 78*(4), 300–308.

Vellutino, F. R. (1979). *Dyslexia: Theory and research.* Cambridge, MA: The MIT Press.

Walberg, H. J. (1986). Syntheses of research on teaching. In M. C. Wittrock (Ed.), *Handbook of research on teaching* (3rd ed., pp. 214–229). New York: MacMillan Publishing.

Walker, H. M., McConnell, S., Walker, J. L., Clarke, J. Y., Todis, B., Cohen, G., & Rankin, R. (1983). Initial analysis of the ACCEPTS curriculum: Efficacy of instructional and behavior management procedures for improving the social adjustment of handicapped children. *Analysis and Intervention in Developmental Disabilities, 3,* 105–127.

Walmsley, S. A. (1984). Helping the learning disabled child overcome writing disabilities in the classroom. *Topics in Learning and Learning Disabilities, 3,* 81–90.

Warrenfeltz, R. B., Kelly, W. J., Salzberg, C. L., Beegle, C. P., Levy, T. A., & Crouse, T. R. (1981). Social skills training of behavior disordered adolescents with self-monitoring to promote generalization to a vocational setting. *Behavioral Disorders, 7,* 18–27.

Weaver, R. L. (1984). *The effects of training strategic behaviors on the spelling performance of learning disabled children.* Unpublished doctoral dissertation, George Peabody College for Teachers, Vanderbilt University, Nashville, TN.

Weinstein, G., & Cooke, N. L. (1992). The effects of two repeated reading interventions on generalization of fluency. *Learning Disability Quarterly, 15,* 21–28.

Weisberg, R. (1988). 1980s: A change in focus of reading comprehension research based upon an interactive model of reading. *Learning Disability Quarterly, 11,* 149–159.

Western Psychological Services. (1988). *WPS automated IEP system.* Los Angeles, CA: Author.

Weygant, A. D. (1981). *The effects of specific instructions and a lesson on the written language expression of learning disabled elementary children.* Unpublished doctoral dissertation, University of Virginia, Charlottesville.

Williams, J. (1979). Reading instruction today. *American Psychologist, 34,* 917–922.

Wilson, C. L., & Sindelar, P. T. (1991). Direct instruction in math word problems: Students with learning disabilities. *Exceptional Children, 57,* 512–519.

Wilson, H. W. (1987). *Readers' guide to periodical literature.* New York: H. W. Wilson.

Wilson, R., & Wesson, C. (1986). Making every minute count: Academic learning time in LD classrooms. *Learning Disabilities Focus, 2*(1), 13–19.

Wittrock, M. C. (Ed.). (1986). *Handbook of research on teaching* (3rd ed.). New York: MacMillan Publishing.

Wolf, M. M., Hanley, E. L., & King, L. A. (1970). The timer game: A variable interval contingency for the management of out-of-seat behavior. *Exceptional Children, 37,* 113–118.

Wong, B. Y. L. (1979). Increasing retention of main ideas through questioning strategies. *Learning Disability Quarterly, 2,* 42–48.

Wong, B. Y. L. (1980). Activating the inactive learner: Use of questions/prompts to enhance comprehension and retention of implied information in learning disabled children. *Learning Disability Quarterly, 3,* 29–37.

Wong, B. Y. L. (1985). Potential means of enhancing content skills acquisition in learning disabled adolescents. *Focus on Exceptional Children, 17*(5), 1–8.

Wong, B. Y. L. (1986a). A cognitive approach to teaching spelling. *Exceptional Children, 53,* 169–173.

Wong, B. Y. L. (1986b). Metacognition and special education: A review of a view. *The Journal of Special Education, 20,* 9–29.

Wong, B. Y. L., & Jones, W. (1982). Increasing metacomprehension in learning disabled and normally achieving students through self-questioning training. *Learning Disability Quarterly, 5,* 228–238.

Wong, B. Y. L., & Wong, R. (1986). Study behavior as a function of metacognitive knowledge about critical task variables: An investigation of above average, average, and learning disabled readers. *Learning Disabilities Research, 1,* 101–111.

Wong, B. Y. L., Wong, R., & Blenkinsop, J. (1989). Cognitive and metacognitive aspects of learning disabled adolescents' composing problems. *Learning Disability Quarterly, 12,* 300–322.

Wong, B. Y. L., Wong, R., Darlington, D., & Jones, W. (1991). Interactive teaching: An effective way to teach revision skills to adolescents with learning disabilities. *Learning Disabilities Research & Practice, 6,* 117–127.

Zaragoza, N., & Vaughn, S. (1992). The effects of process writing instruction on three 2nd-grade students with different academic profiles. *Learning Disabilities Research & Practice, 7,* 184–193.

Zaragoza, N., Vaughn, S., & McIntosh, R. (1991). Social skills interventions and children with behavior disorders: A review. *Behavioral Disorders, 16,* 260–275.

Zawaiza, T. R. W., & Gerber, M. M. (1993). Effects of explicit instruction on math word-problem solving by community college students with learning disabilities. *Learning Disability Quarterly, 16,* 64–79.

Zaner-Bloser. (1986). *Zaner-Bloser Evaluation scale.* Columbus, OH: Author.

Zigmond, N. (1990). Rethinking secondary school programs for students with learning disabilities. *Focus on Exceptional Children, 23*(1), 1–24.

Zigmond, N., & Sainato, D. (1981). Socialization influences on educationally handicapped adolescents. In B. K. Keogh (Ed.), *Advances in special education: Socialization influences on exceptionality* (pp. 187–208). Greenwich, CT: JAI Press.

Zigmond, N., Vallecorsa, A., & Leinhardt, G. A. (1980). Reading instruction for students with learning disabilities. *Topics in Language Disorders, 1,* 89–98.

Author Index

Subject Index

Applied behavior analysis, 82
Assertive discipline, 107, 109
Attribution, 100–101

Behavior disorders, 87–114, 170

Career education, 325–330
Class contingencies, 104–105
Classroom management, 87–114
Computer software and technology, 58,
    86, 125, 191, 241, 274–275, 299,
    317, 334–335, 354
Consultation, 337–354
    communications skills, 337–350
    models of, 350–353
Content covered, 9–12
Cooperative learning, 227
Criterion-referenced tests, 62–68
Curriculum-based measurement, 63–67,
    119–120, 305–306, 308–309
Curriculum materials, 86, 155–156, 190,
    240–241, 274, 299, 317, 334, 354

Daily review, 24, 121, 123, 182, 199, 253,
    257, 262, 286, 310
Delivery of information, 12–14

Earth and physical science, 254–257
Evaluating materials, 116–119, 194–196,
    305–307
Evaluation, 59–86

Feedback, 15–18, 27–28
Formative evaluation, 18, 20–21, 30, 68–
    69, 125–127, 182–183, 202, 253,
    257, 262, 286, 313–314, 355

Graphic display of data, 76–84

Handwriting, 163–170
    assessment, 164–168
    special problems in, 170

Identification vs. production, 33, 36–37,
    157, 284, 308, 346–347
IEP, 33–36, 58, 355, 357–361
Inclusion, 352–353
Instructional design, 47–58
Instructional grouping, 120–121

Language arts, 157–191
Learning disabilities, preface, 170
Learning, levels of, 36–40, 51
    acquisition and fluency, 37–38, 167–
        168
    application and generalization, 38–39,
        170, 224, 226, 285, 308, 310,
        347, 356
Learning, types of, 40–47, 51
    conceptual learning, 45–46, 171–172,
        203, 207–211, 214–216, 218–219,
        229–231, 248, 252–253, 256,
        271
    discrimination learning, 40–41, 131,
        176, 214, 217, 246–248, 252–
        253, 256
    factual learning, 41–42, 128, 157, 132,
        171, 203, 205, 208–210, 212–
        214, 220–222, 253, 260–261,
        263, 271, 284–285, 291–292,
        347
    problem solving and thinking skills,
        46–47
    procedural learning, 44–45, 216–219,
        222–225, 229–230, 232–234,
        277, 310